STORY

One day, people began manifesting special abilities that came to be known as “Quirks,” and before long, the world was full of superpowered humans. But with the advent of these exceptional individuals came an increase in crime, and governments alone were unable to deal with the situation. At the same time, others emerged to oppose the spread of evil! As if straight from the comic books, these heroes keep the peace and are even officially authorized to fight crime. Our story begins when a certain Quirkless boy and lifelong hero fan meets the world’s number one hero, starting him on his path to becoming the greatest hero ever!

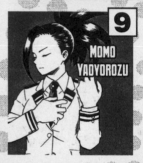

7
SHOTO TODOROKI
8
FUMIKAGE TOKOYAMI
9
MOMO YAOYOROZU
10
EIJIRO KIRISHIMA
11
DENKI KAMINARI
12
KYOKA JIRO
13
MINA ASHIDO
14
YUGA AOYAMA
15
MIRIO TOGATA

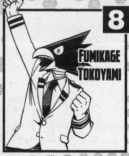

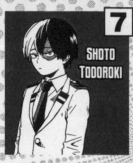

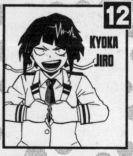

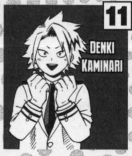

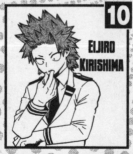

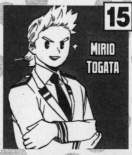

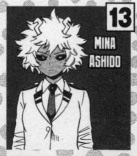

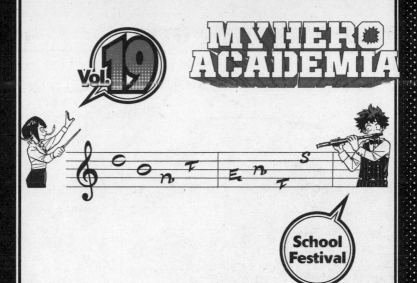

MY HERO ACADEMIA

Vol. 19

CONTENTS

School Festival

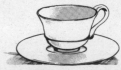

No. 168 - The Strange Tale of Aoyama

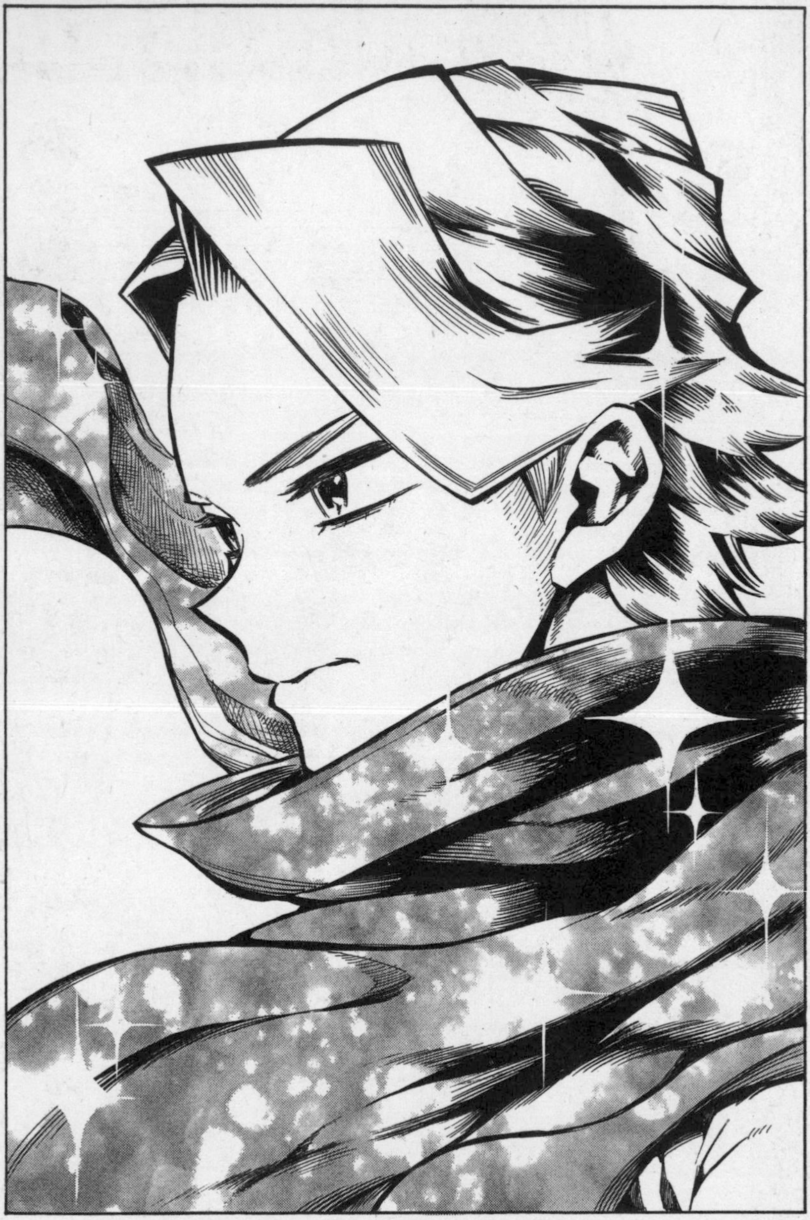

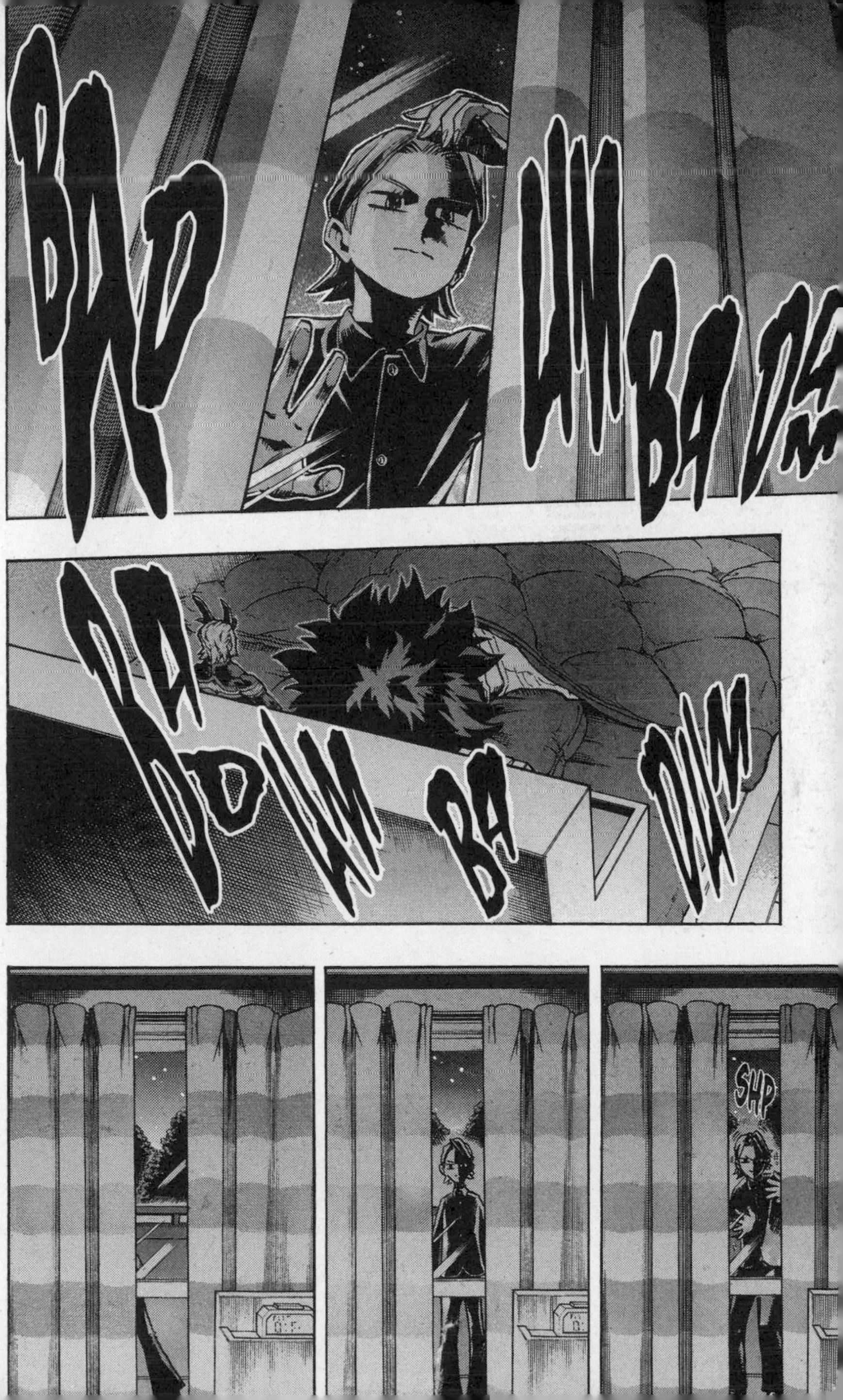
BA DUM BA DUM...
BA DUM BA DUM
SHP

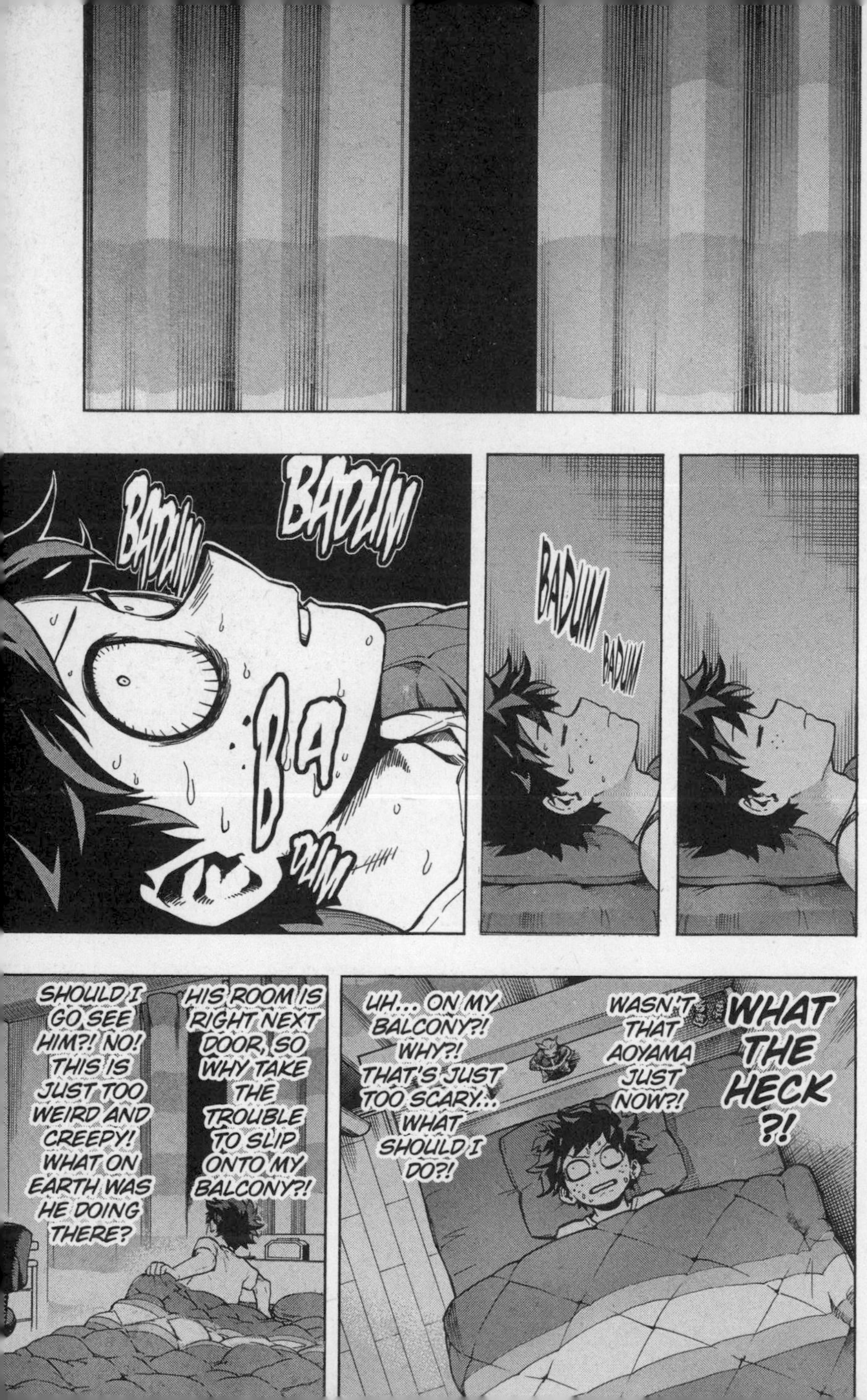
BADUM
BADUM
BADUM
BADUM
BA DUM
WHAT THE HECK?!
WASN'T THAT AOYAMA JUST NOW?!
UH... ON MY BALCONY?! WHY?! THAT'S JUST TOO SCARY... WHAT SHOULD I DO?!
HIS ROOM IS RIGHT NEXT DOOR, SO WHY TAKE THE TROUBLE TO SLIP ONTO MY BALCONY?!
SHOULD I GO SEE HIM?! NO! THIS IS JUST TOO WEIRD AND CREEPY! WHAT ON EARTH WAS HE DOING THERE?

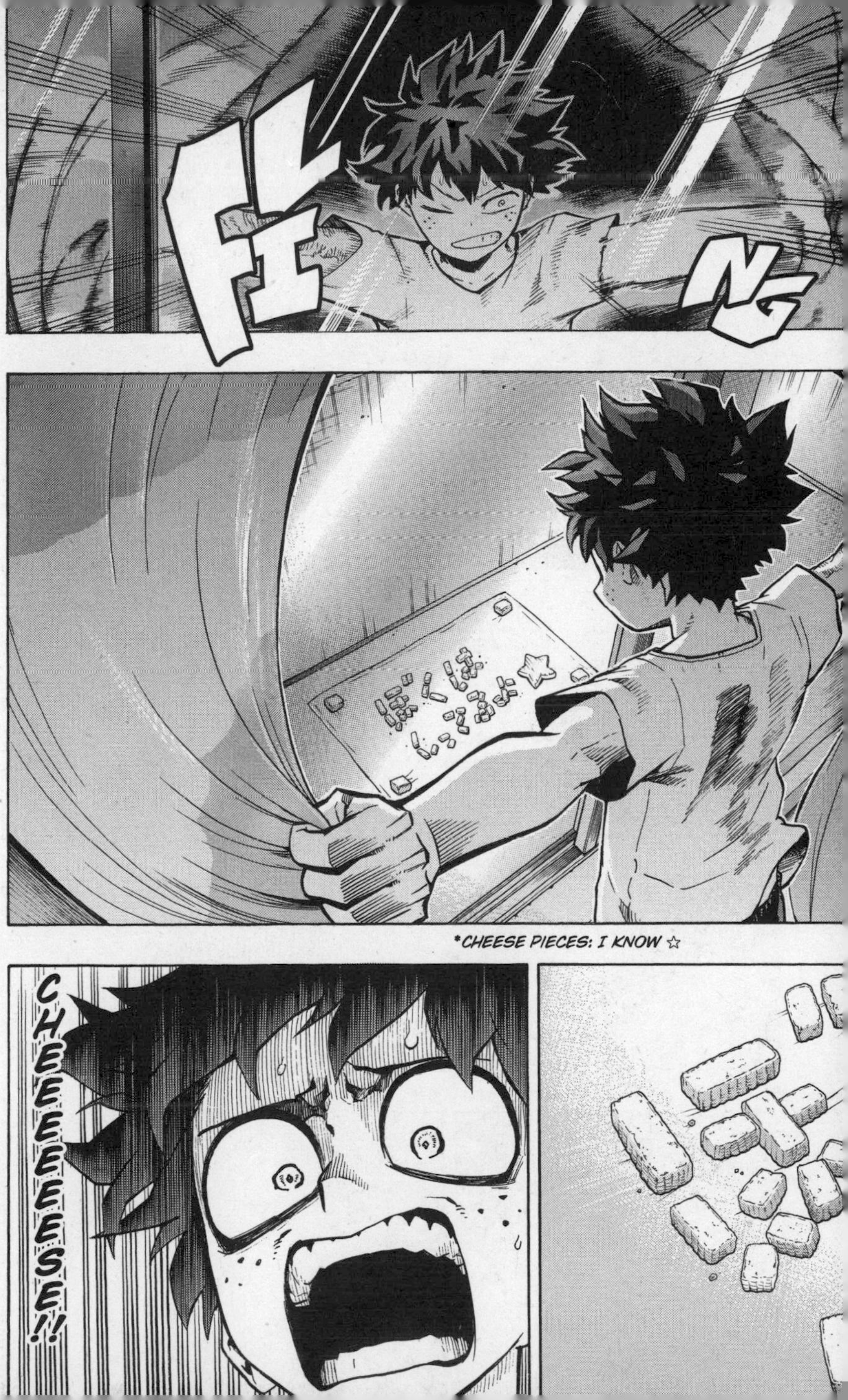
FLING
CHEEEEEEEESE!!
*CHEESE PIECES: I KNOW ☆

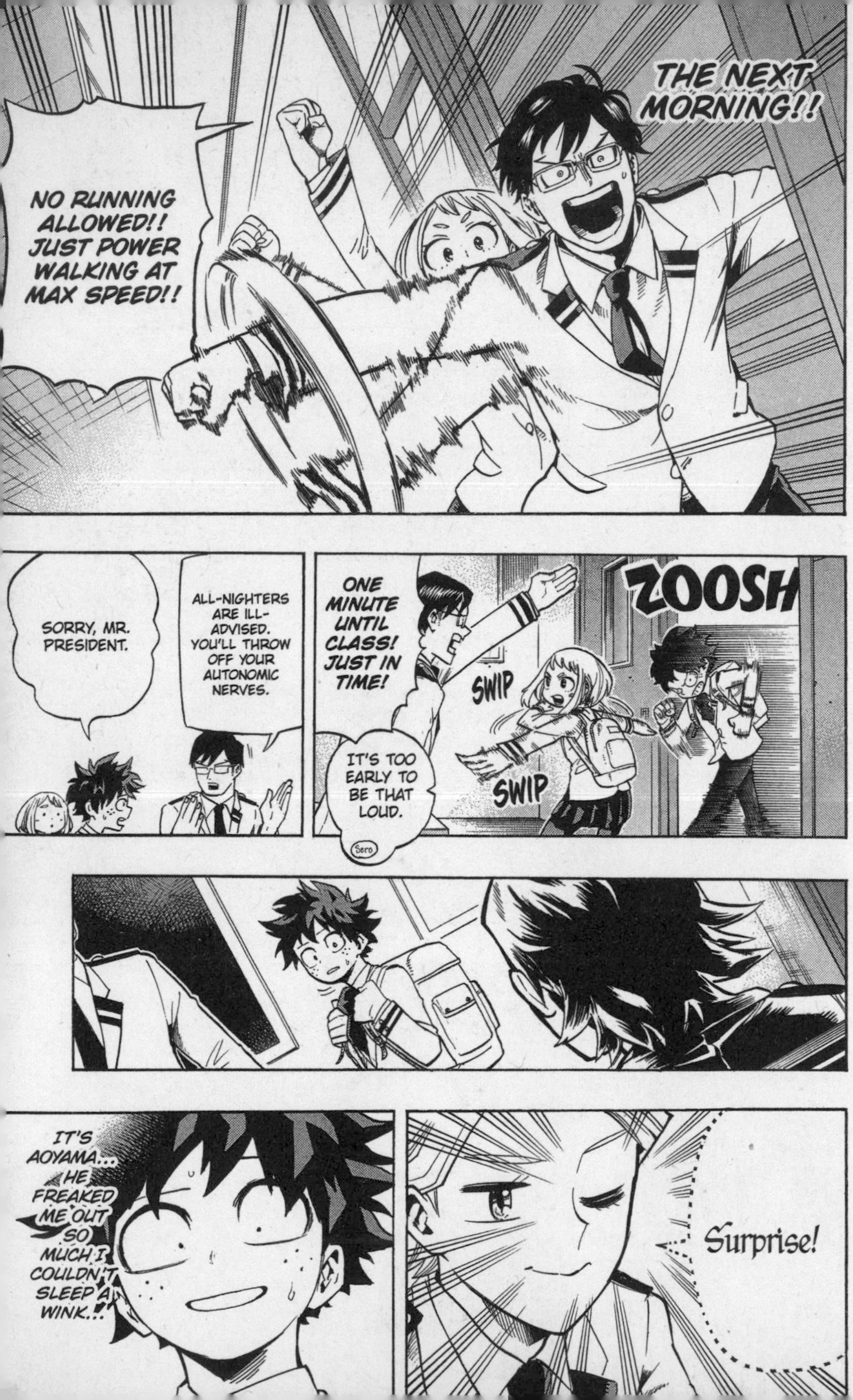
THE NEXT MORNING!!
NO RUNNING ALLOWED!! JUST POWER WALKING AT MAX SPEED!!
ZOOSH
ONE MINUTE UNTIL CLASS! JUST IN TIME!
SWIP
SWIP
IT'S TOO EARLY TO BE THAT LOUD.
Sero
ALL-NIGHTERS ARE ILL-ADVISED. YOU'LL THROW OFF YOUR AUTONOMIC NERVES.
SORRY, MR. PRESIDENT.
Surprise!
IT'S AOYAMA... HE FREAKED ME OUT SO MUCH I COULDN'T SLEEP A WINK...

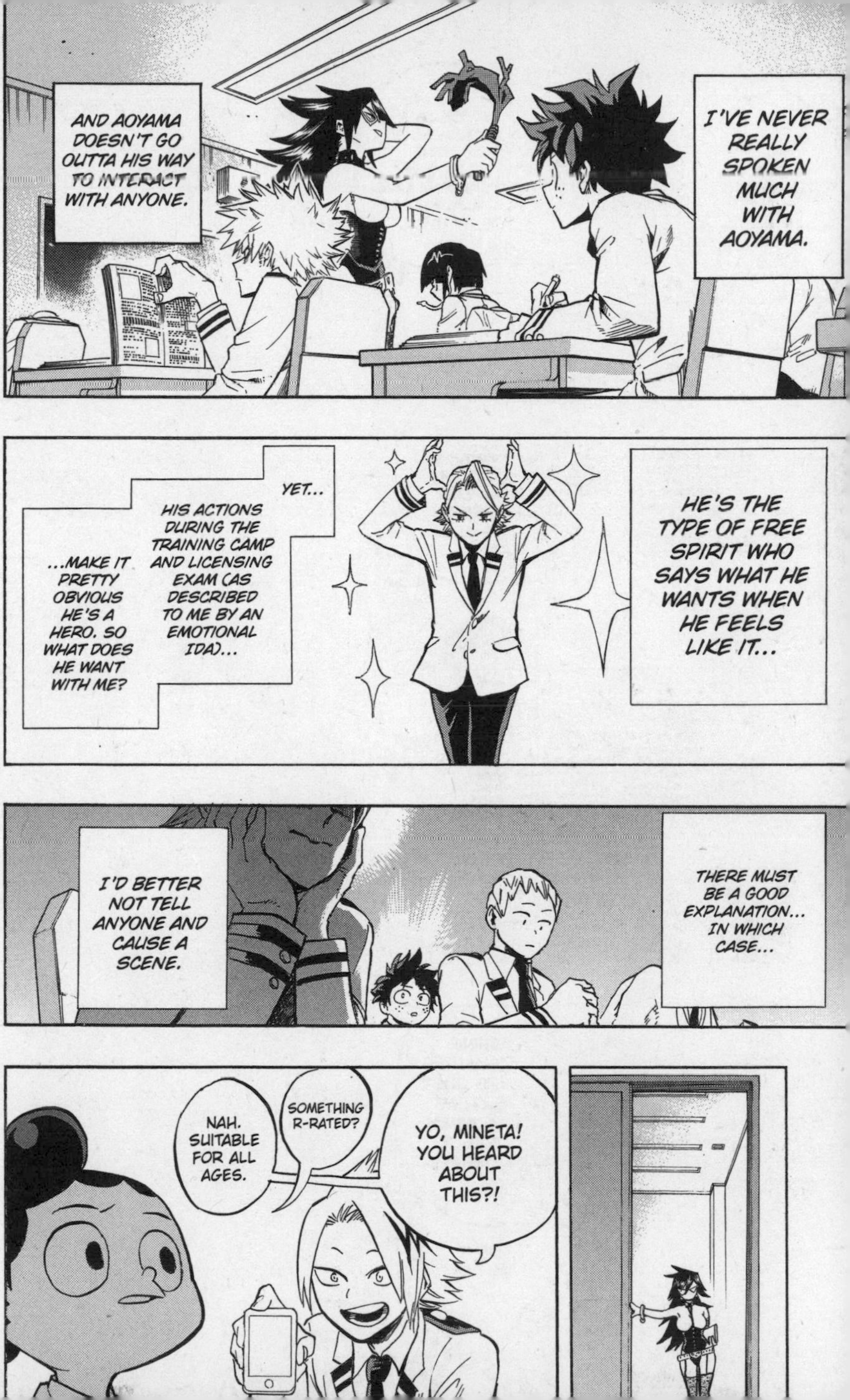
I'VE NEVER REALLY SPOKEN MUCH WITH AOYAMA.
AND AOYAMA DOESN'T GO OUTTA HIS WAY TO INTERACT WITH ANYONE.
HE'S THE TYPE OF FREE SPIRIT WHO SAYS WHAT HE WANTS WHEN HE FEELS LIKE IT...
YET...
HIS ACTIONS DURING THE TRAINING CAMP AND LICENSING EXAM (AS DESCRIBED TO ME BY AN EMOTIONAL IDA)...
...MAKE IT PRETTY OBVIOUS HE'S A HERO. SO WHAT DOES HE WANT WITH ME?
THERE MUST BE A GOOD EXPLANATION... IN WHICH CASE...
I'D BETTER NOT TELL ANYONE AND CAUSE A SCENE.
YO, MINETA! YOU HEARD ABOUT THIS?!
SOMETHING R-RATED?
NAH. SUITABLE FOR ALL AGES.

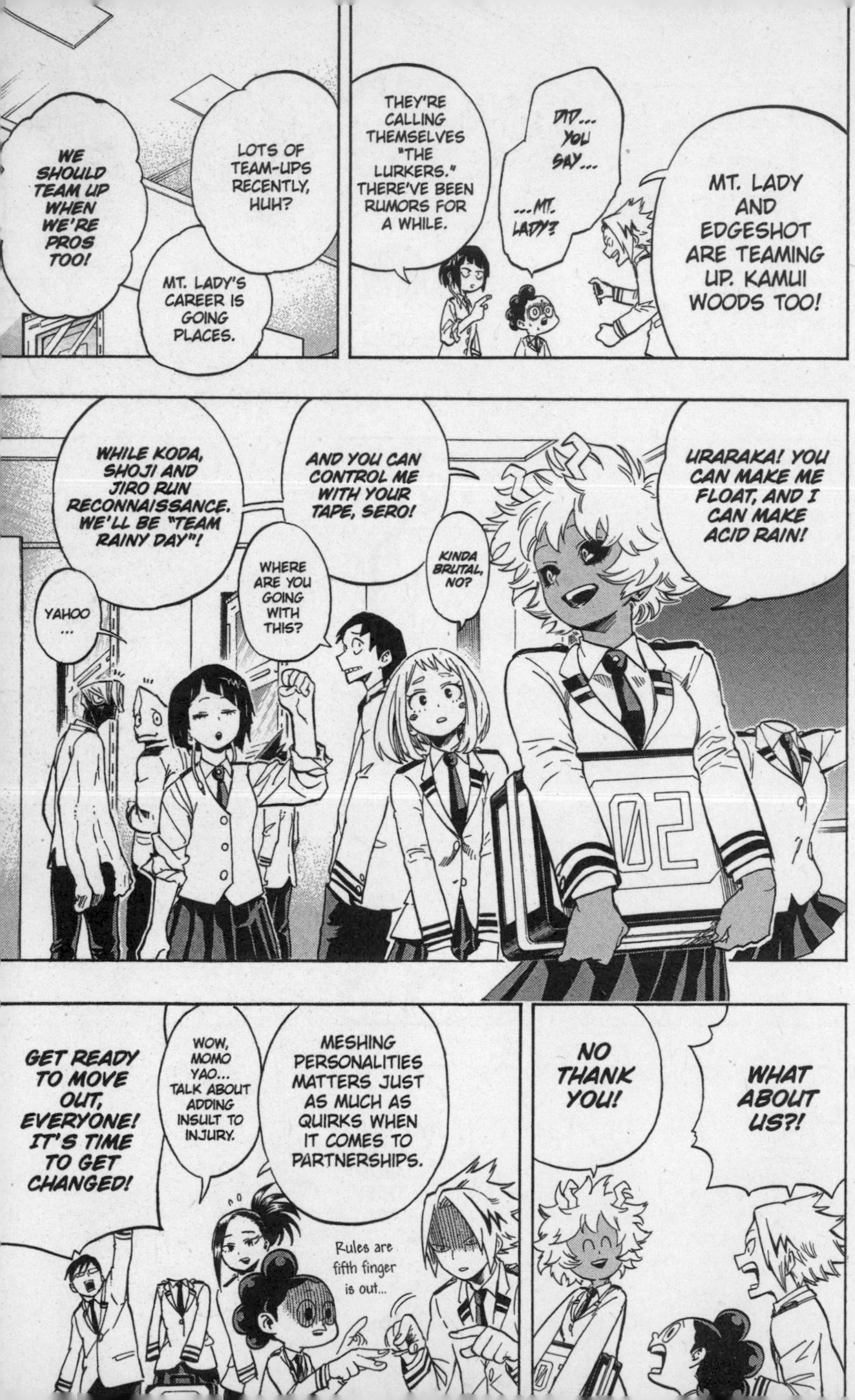
MT. LADY AND EDGESHOT ARE TEAMING UP. KAMUI WOODS TOO!
DID... YOU SAY... ...MT. LADY?
THEY'RE CALLING THEMSELVES "THE LURKERS." THERE'VE BEEN RUMORS FOR A WHILE.
LOTS OF TEAM-UPS RECENTLY, HUH?
MT. LADY'S CAREER IS GOING PLACES.
WE SHOULD TEAM UP WHEN WE'RE PROS TOO!
URARAKA! YOU CAN MAKE ME FLOAT, AND I CAN MAKE ACID RAIN!
KINDA BRUTAL, NO?
AND YOU CAN CONTROL ME WITH YOUR TAPE, SERO!
WHERE ARE YOU GOING WITH THIS?
WHILE KODA, SHOJI AND JIRO RUN RECONNAISSANCE. WE'LL BE "TEAM RAINY DAY"!
YAHOO ...
WHAT ABOUT US?!
NO THANK YOU!
MESHING PERSONALITIES MATTERS JUST AS MUCH AS QUIRKS WHEN IT COMES TO PARTNERSHIPS.
Rules are fifth finger is out...
WOW, MOMO YAO... TALK ABOUT ADDING INSULT TO INJURY.
GET READY TO MOVE OUT, EVERYONE! IT'S TIME TO GET CHANGED!

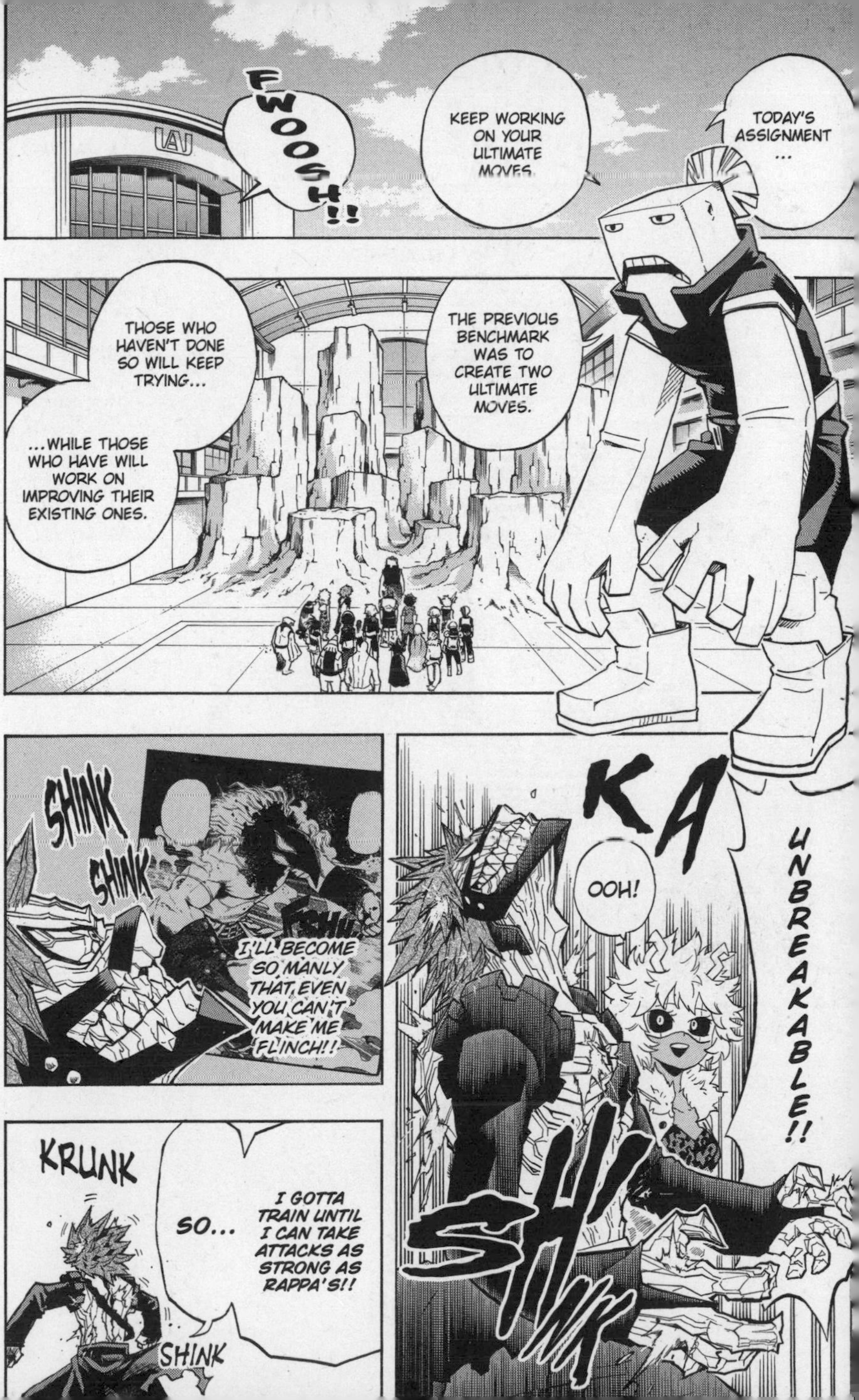
TODAY'S ASSIGNMENT ...
KEEP WORKING ON YOUR ULTIMATE MOVES.
FWOOSH!!
THE PREVIOUS BENCHMARK WAS TO CREATE TWO ULTIMATE MOVES.
THOSE WHO HAVEN'T DONE SO WILL KEEP TRYING...
...WHILE THOSE WHO HAVE WILL WORK ON IMPROVING THEIR EXISTING ONES.
KA
UNBREAKABLE!!
OOH!
SHINK
SHINK
I'LL BECOME SO MANLY THAT EVEN YOU CAN'T MAKE ME FLINCH!!
KRUNK
I GOTTA TRAIN UNTIL I CAN TAKE ATTACKS AS STRONG AS RAPPA'S!!
SO...
SHINK

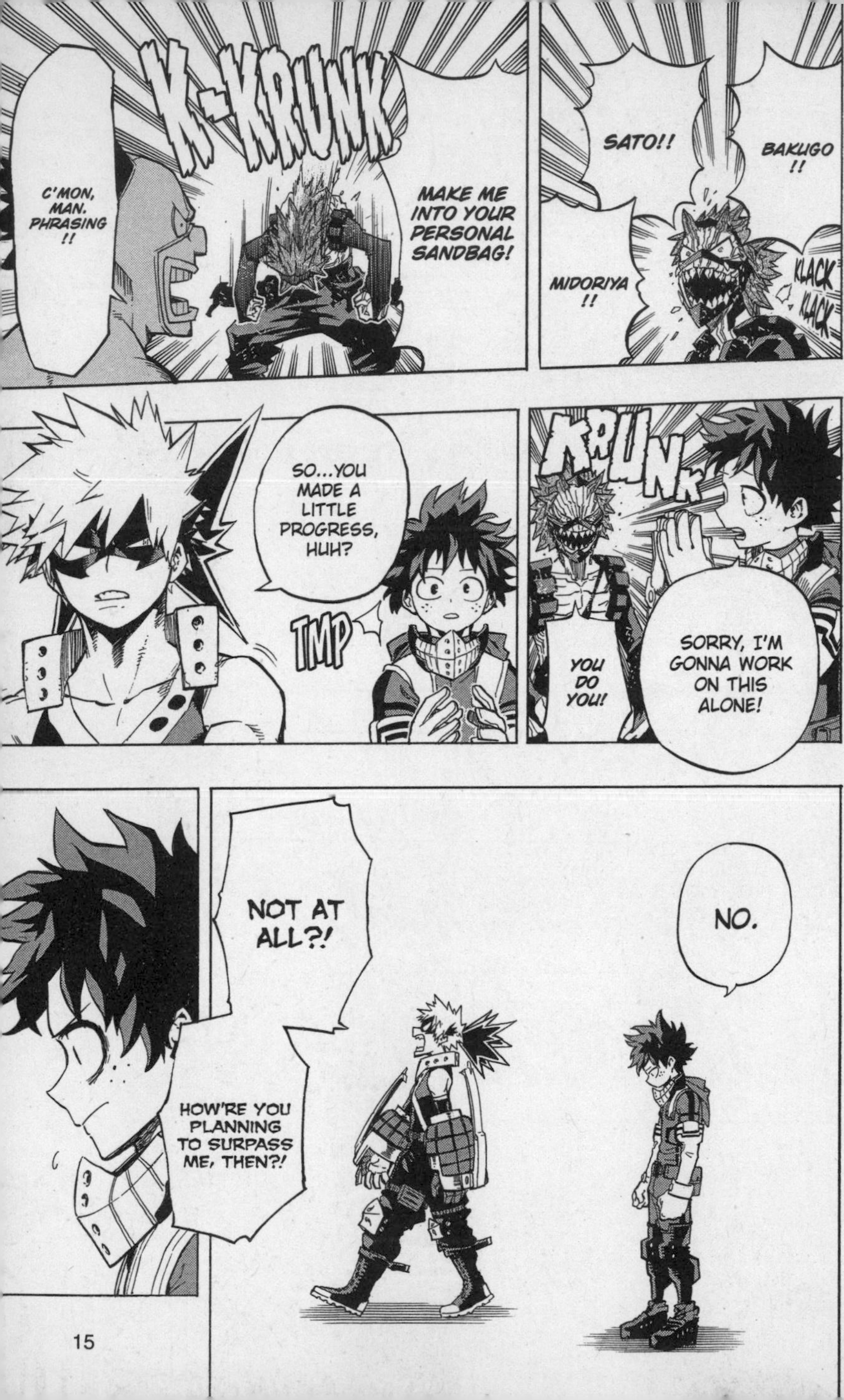
BAKUGO !!
SATO!!
KLACK KLACK
MIDORIYA !!
MAKE ME INTO YOUR PERSONAL SANDBAG!
K-KRUNK
C'MON, MAN. PHRASING !!
KRUNK
SORRY, I'M GONNA WORK ON THIS ALONE!
YOU DO YOU!
SO...YOU MADE A LITTLE PROGRESS, HUH?
TMP
NO.
NOT AT ALL?!
HOW'RE YOU PLANNING TO SURPASS ME, THEN?!

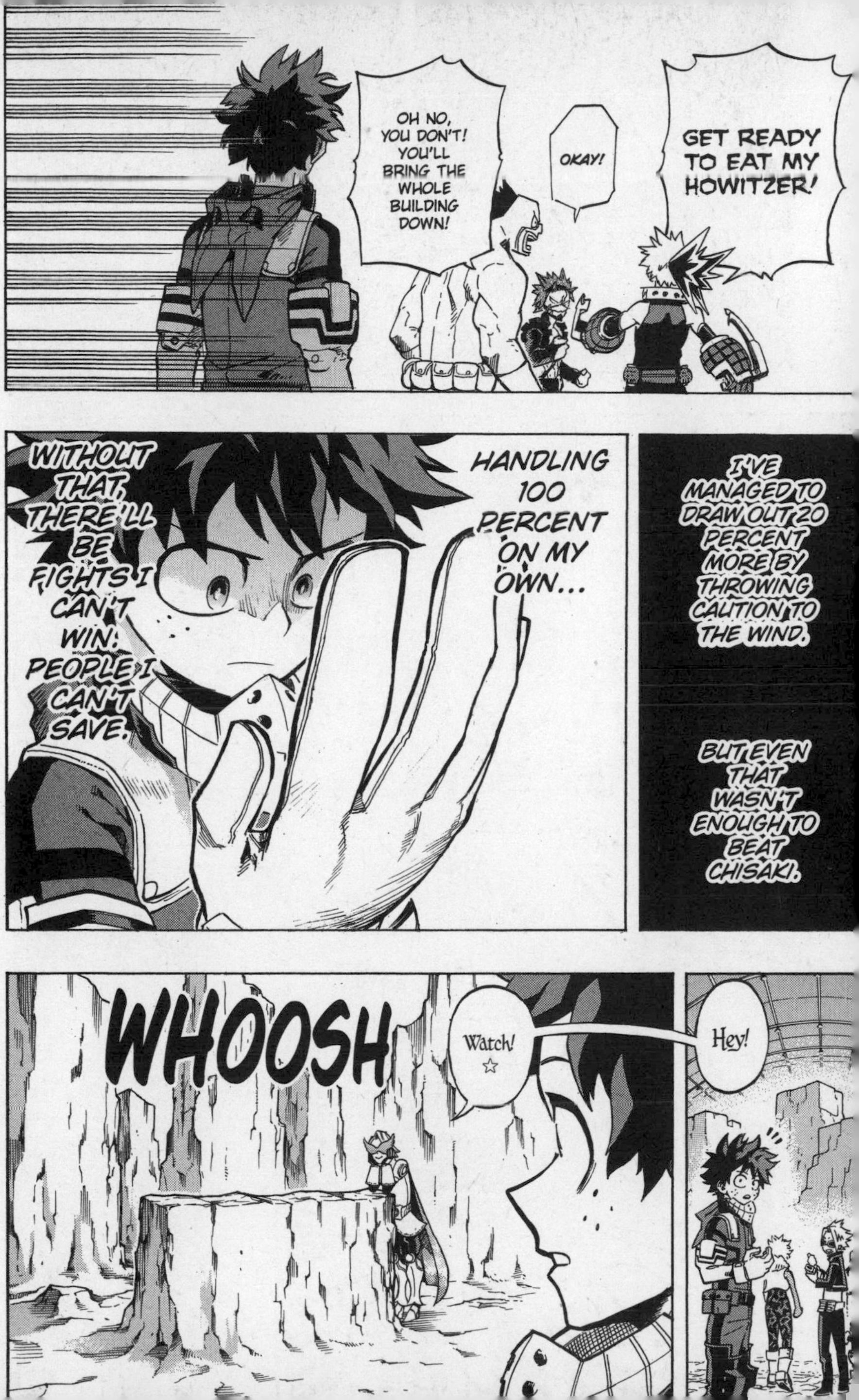
GET READY TO EAT MY HOWITZER!
OKAY!
OH NO, YOU DON'T! YOU'LL BRING THE WHOLE BUILDING DOWN!
I'VE MANAGED TO DRAW OUT 20 PERCENT MORE BY THROWING CAUTION TO THE WIND.
BUT EVEN THAT WASN'T ENOUGH TO BEAT CHISAKI.
HANDLING 100 PERCENT ON MY OWN...
WITHOUT THAT, THERE'LL BE FIGHTS I CAN'T WIN. PEOPLE I CAN'T SAVE.
Hey!
Watch! ☆
WHOOSH

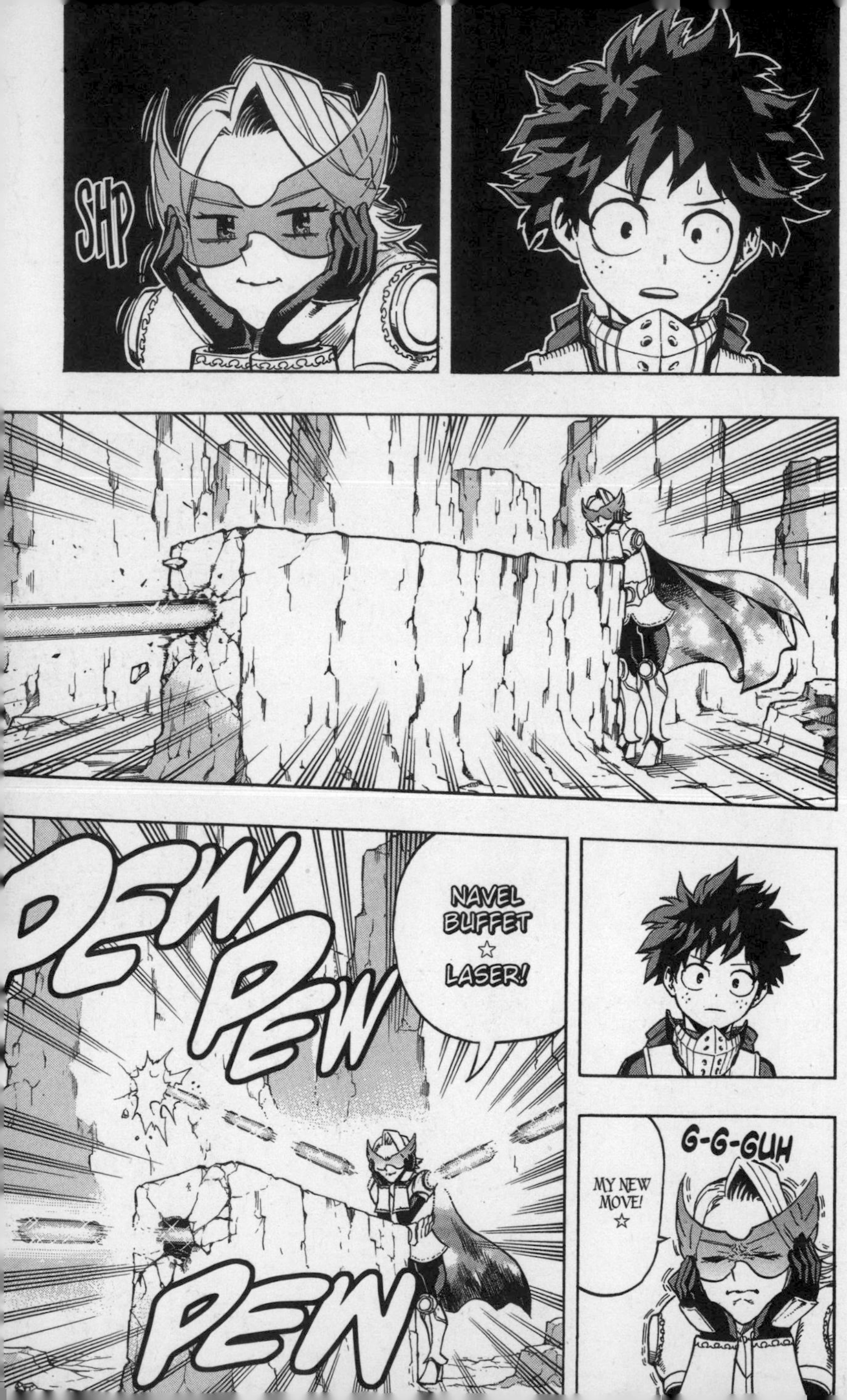
SHP
G-G-GUH
MY NEW MOVE! ☆
NAVEL BUFFET ☆ LASER!
PEW
PEW
PEW

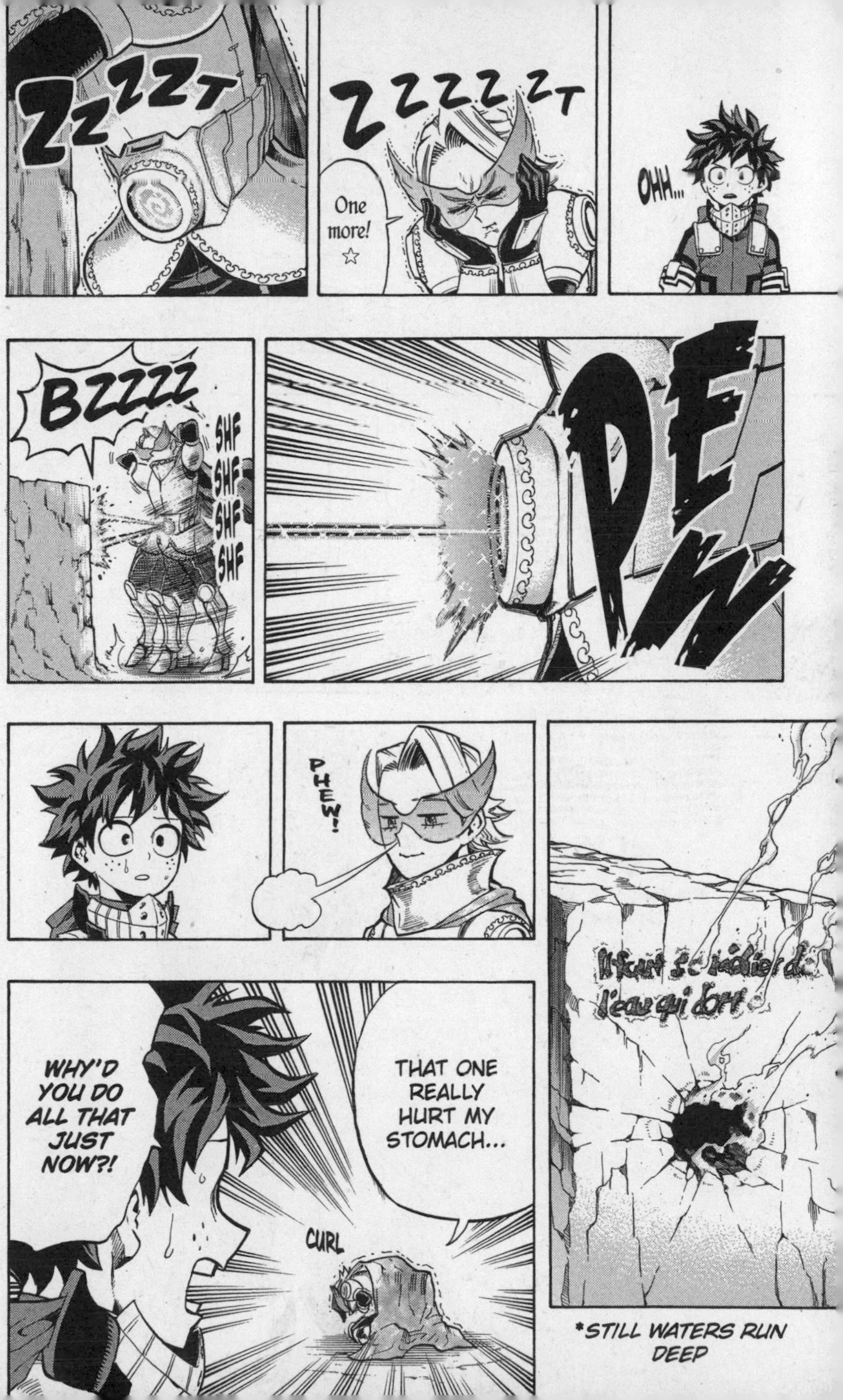
OHH...
ZZZZZZT
One more! ☆
ZZZZZT
PEW
BZZZZZ
SHF SHF SHF SHF
Il faut se méfier de l'eau qui dort*
PHEW!
THAT ONE REALLY HURT MY STOMACH...
CURL
WHY'D YOU DO ALL THAT JUST NOW?!
*STILL WATERS RUN DEEP

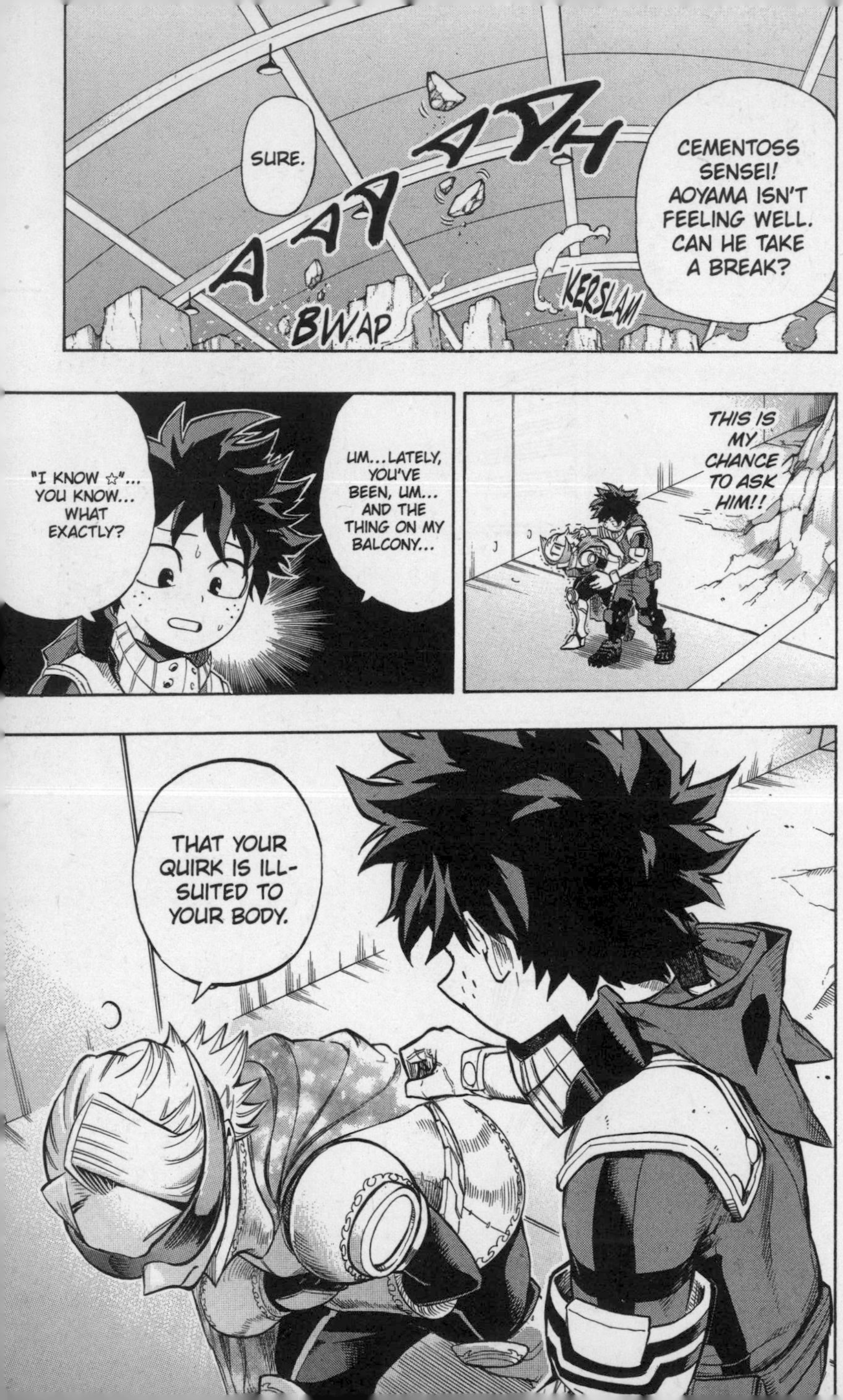
CEMENTOSS SENSEI! AOYAMA ISN'T FEELING WELL. CAN HE TAKE A BREAK?
KERSLAM
AAAAH
SURE.
BWAP
THIS IS MY CHANCE TO ASK HIM!!
UM...LATELY, YOU'VE BEEN, UM... AND THE THING ON MY BALCONY...
"I KNOW ☆"... YOU KNOW... WHAT EXACTLY?
THAT YOUR QUIRK IS ILL-SUITED TO YOUR BODY.

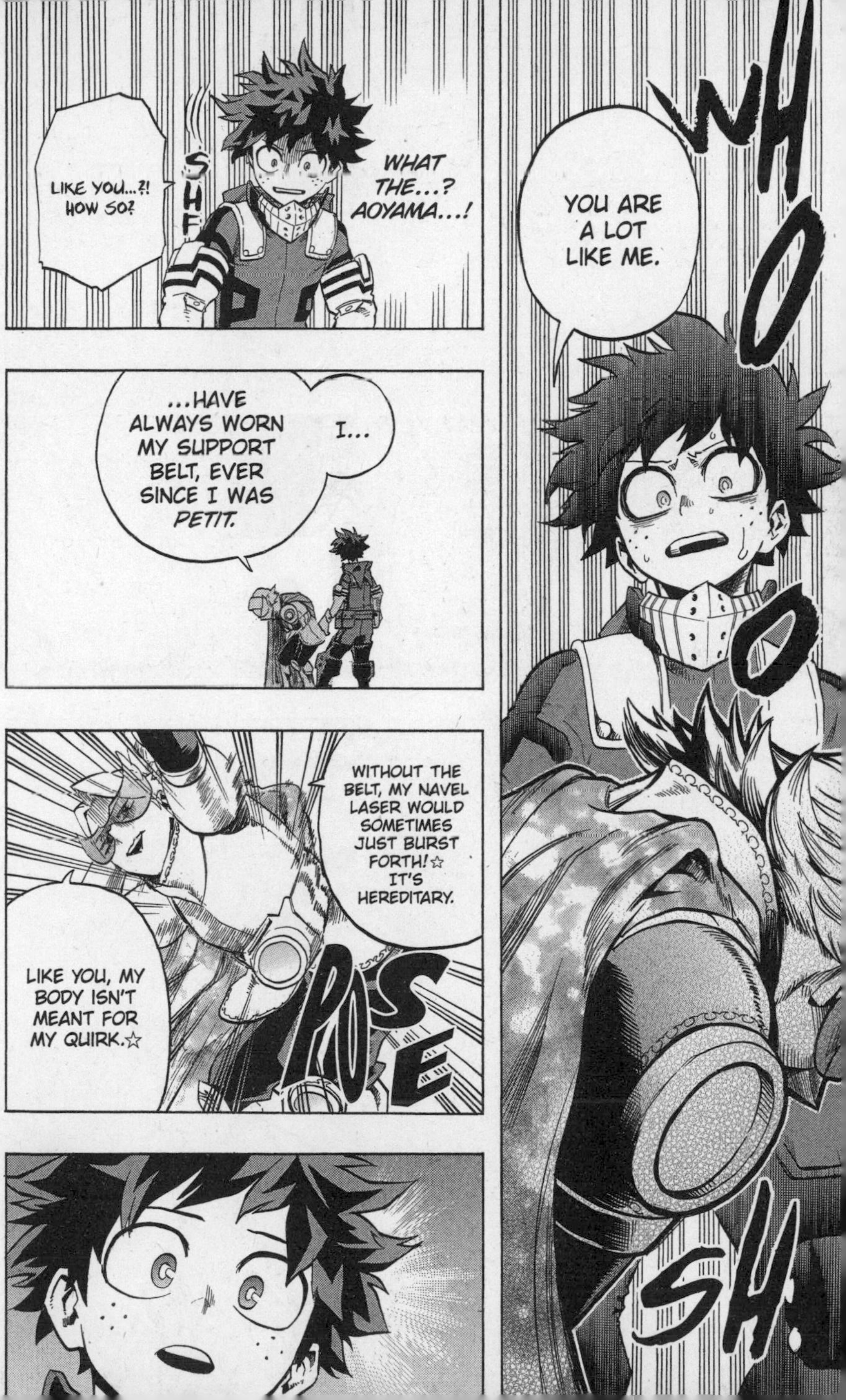
WHOOSH
YOU ARE A LOT LIKE ME.
WHAT THE...? AOYAMA...!
SHF
LIKE YOU...?! HOW SO?
I...
...HAVE ALWAYS WORN MY SUPPORT BELT, EVER SINCE I WAS *PETIT.*
WITHOUT THE BELT, MY NAVEL LASER WOULD SOMETIMES JUST BURST FORTH!☆ IT'S HEREDITARY.
POSE
LIKE YOU, MY BODY ISN'T MEANT FOR MY QUIRK.☆

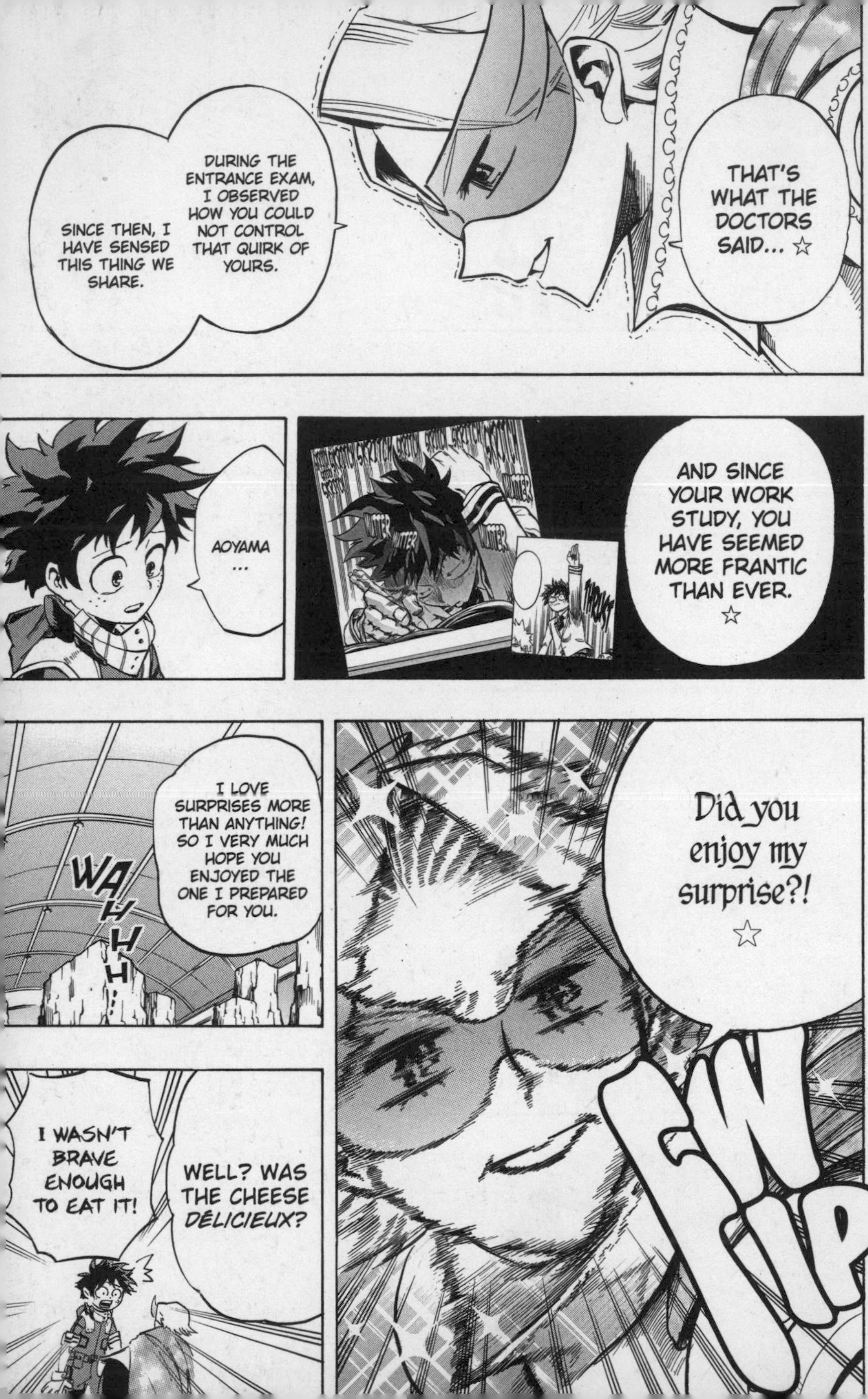
THAT'S WHAT THE DOCTORS SAID... ☆
DURING THE ENTRANCE EXAM, I OBSERVED HOW YOU COULD NOT CONTROL THAT QUIRK OF YOURS.
SINCE THEN, I HAVE SENSED THIS THING WE SHARE.
AND SINCE YOUR WORK STUDY, YOU HAVE SEEMED MORE FRANTIC THAN EVER. ☆
AOYAMA ...
Did you enjoy my surprise?! ☆
I LOVE SURPRISES MORE THAN ANYTHING! SO I VERY MUCH HOPE YOU ENJOYED THE ONE I PREPARED FOR YOU.
WAHHH...
WELL? WAS THE CHEESE DÉLICIEUX?
I WASN'T BRAVE ENOUGH TO EAT IT!

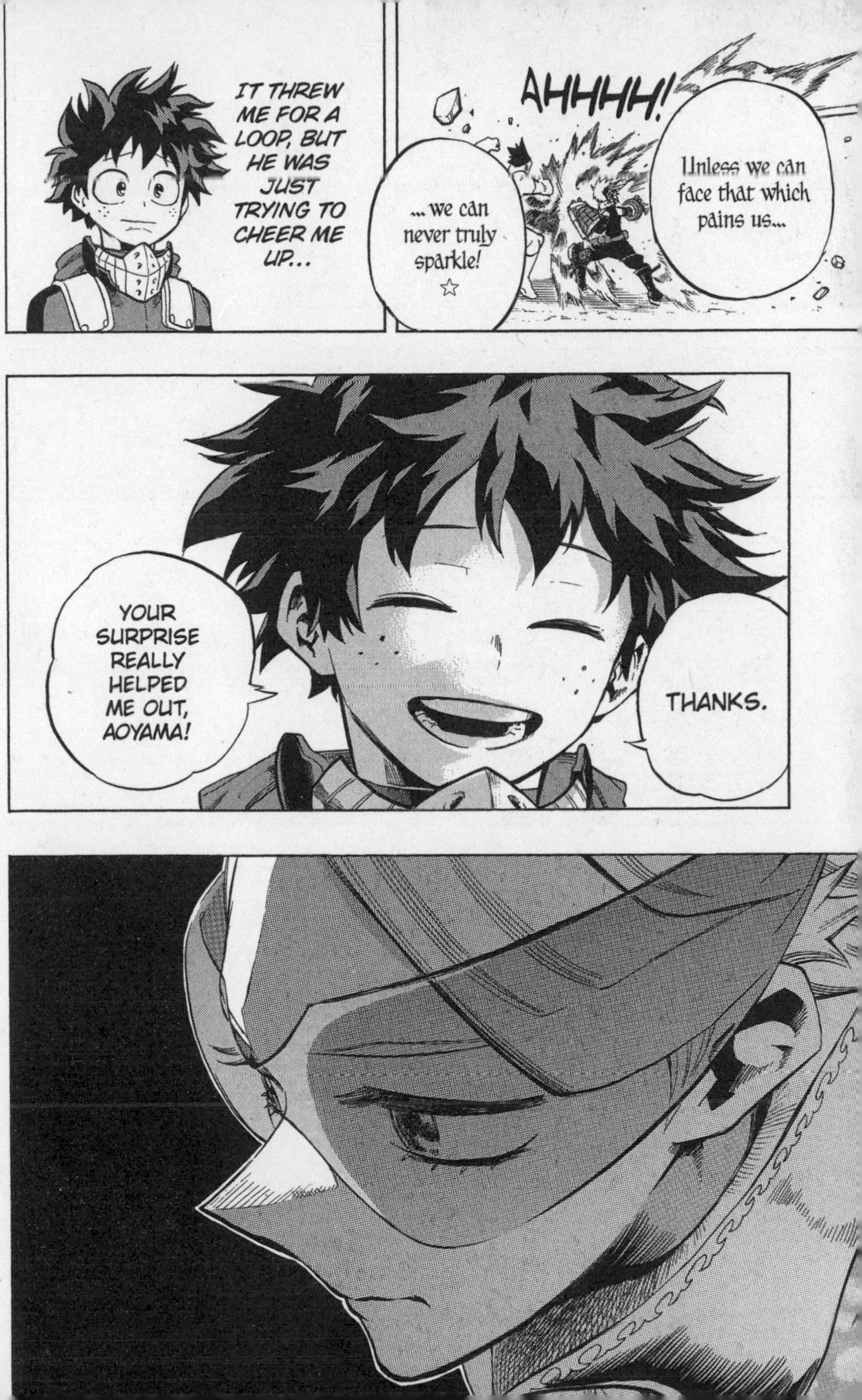
Unless we can face that which pains us...
...we can never truly sparkle! ☆
AHHHH!
IT THREW ME FOR A LOOP, BUT HE WAS JUST TRYING TO CHEER ME UP...
YOUR SURPRISE REALLY HELPED ME OUT, AOYAMA!
THANKS.

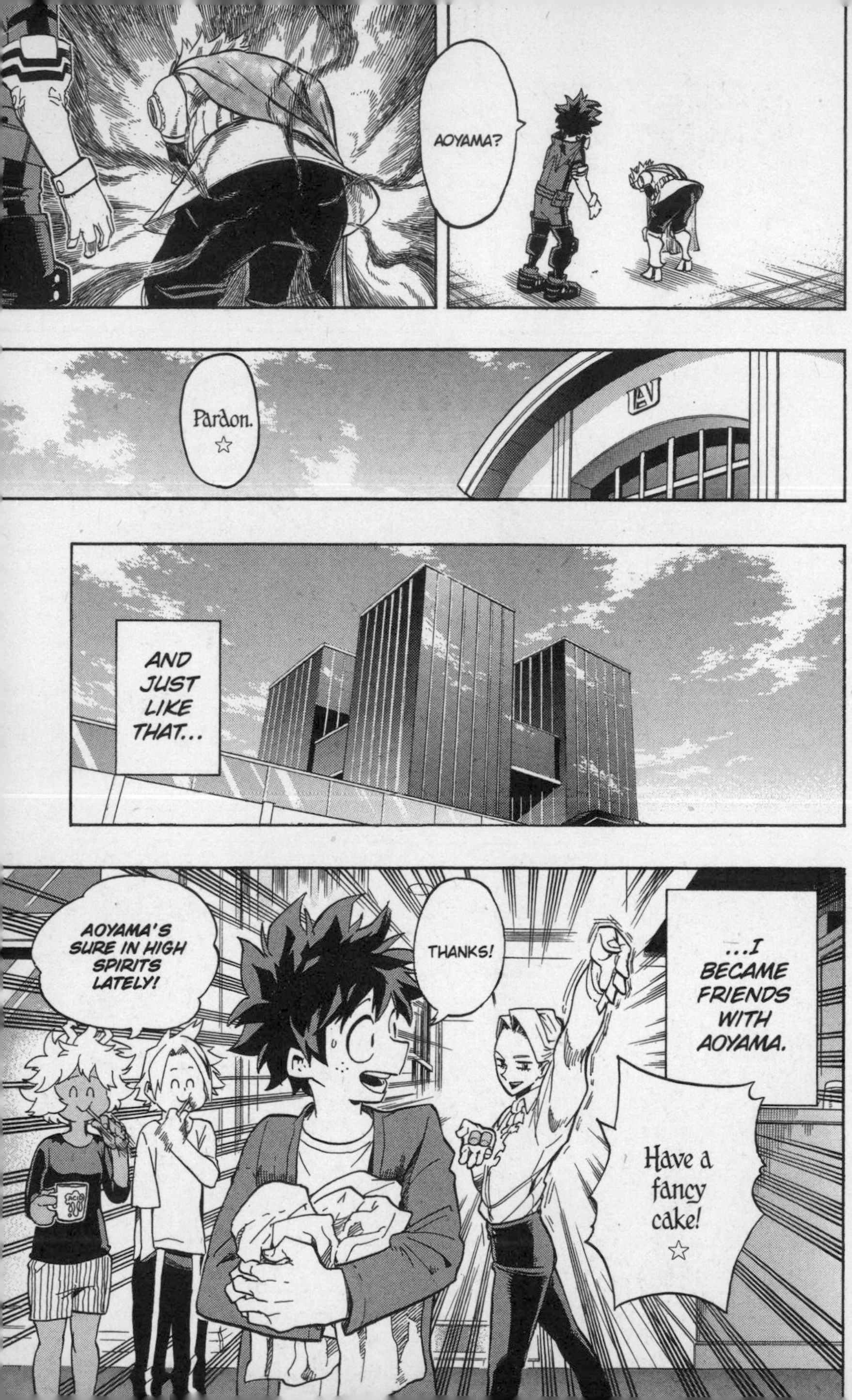
AOYAMA?
Pardon. ☆
AND JUST LIKE THAT...
...I BECAME FRIENDS WITH AOYAMA.
Have a fancy cake! ☆
THANKS!
AOYAMA'S SURE IN HIGH SPIRITS LATELY!

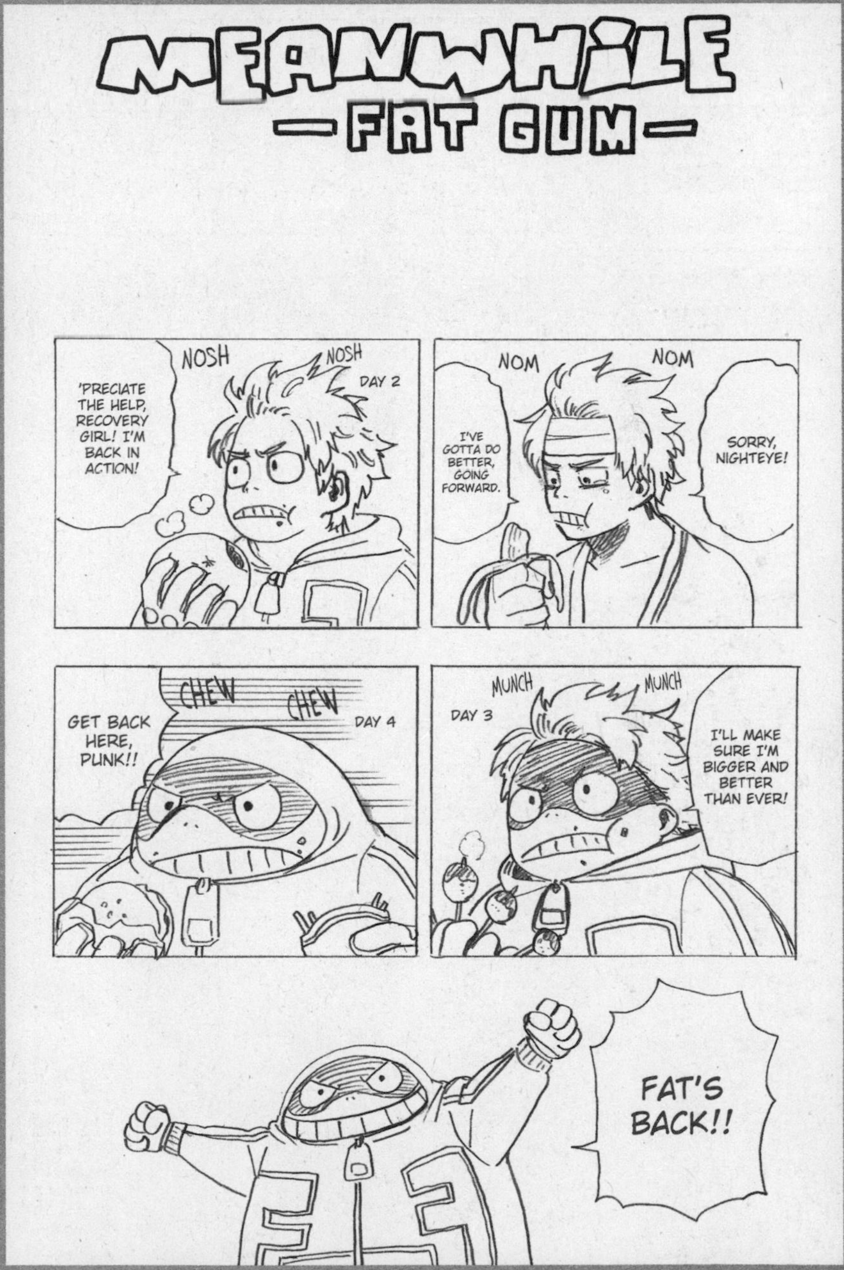
MEANWHILE
-FAT GUM-
NOM
NOM
SORRY, NIGHTEYE!
I'VE GOTTA DO BETTER, GOING FORWARD.
NOSH
DAY 2
NOSH
'PRECIATE THE HELP, RECOVERY GIRL! I'M BACK IN ACTION!
MUNCH
I'LL MAKE SURE I'M BIGGER AND BETTER THAN EVER!
MUNCH
DAY 3
DAY 4
CHEW
CHEW
GET BACK HERE, PUNK!!
FAT'S BACK!!

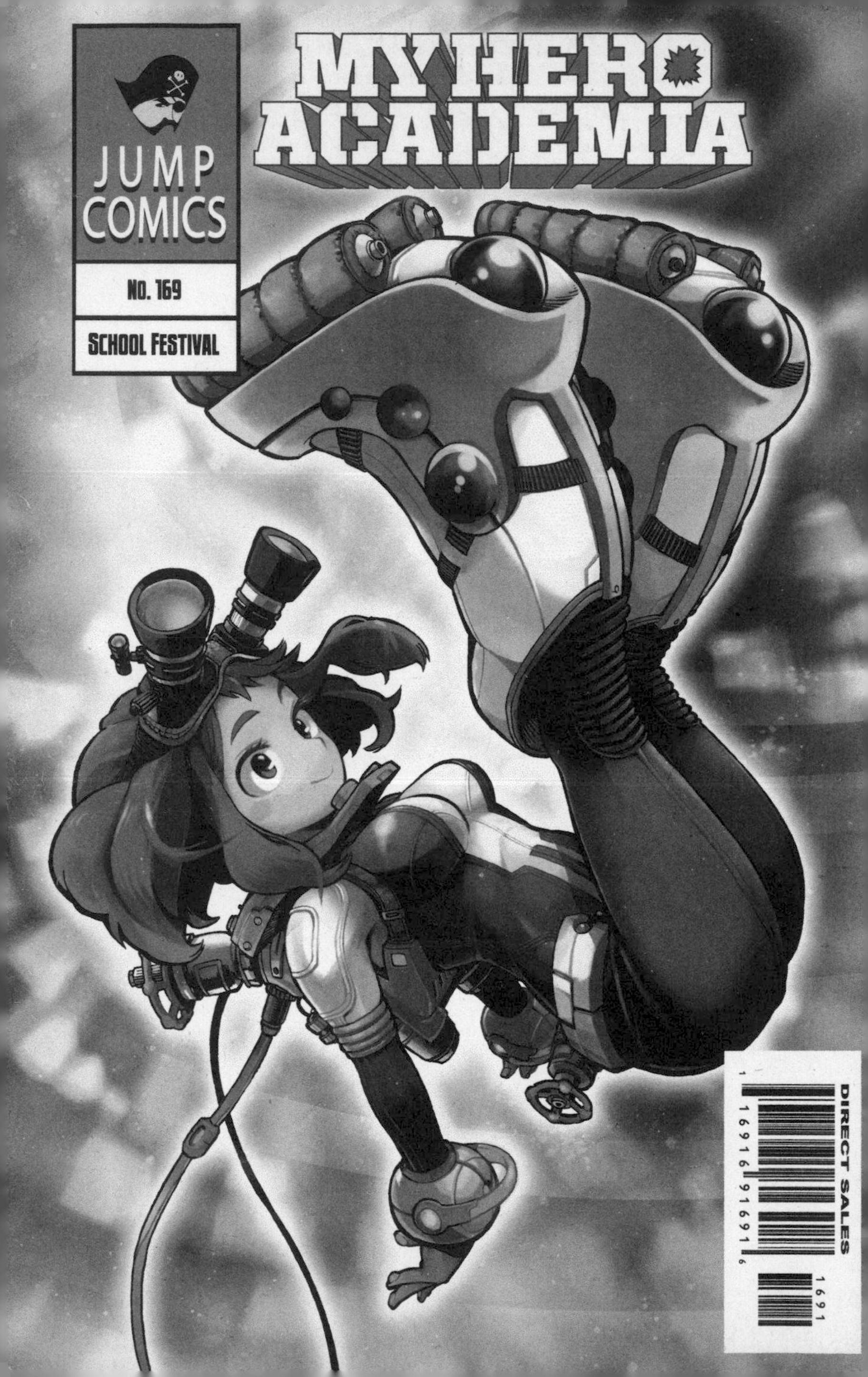
MY HERO ACADEMIA
JUMP COMICS
NO. 169
SCHOOL FESTIVAL
DIRECT SALES

MY HERO
ACADEMIA

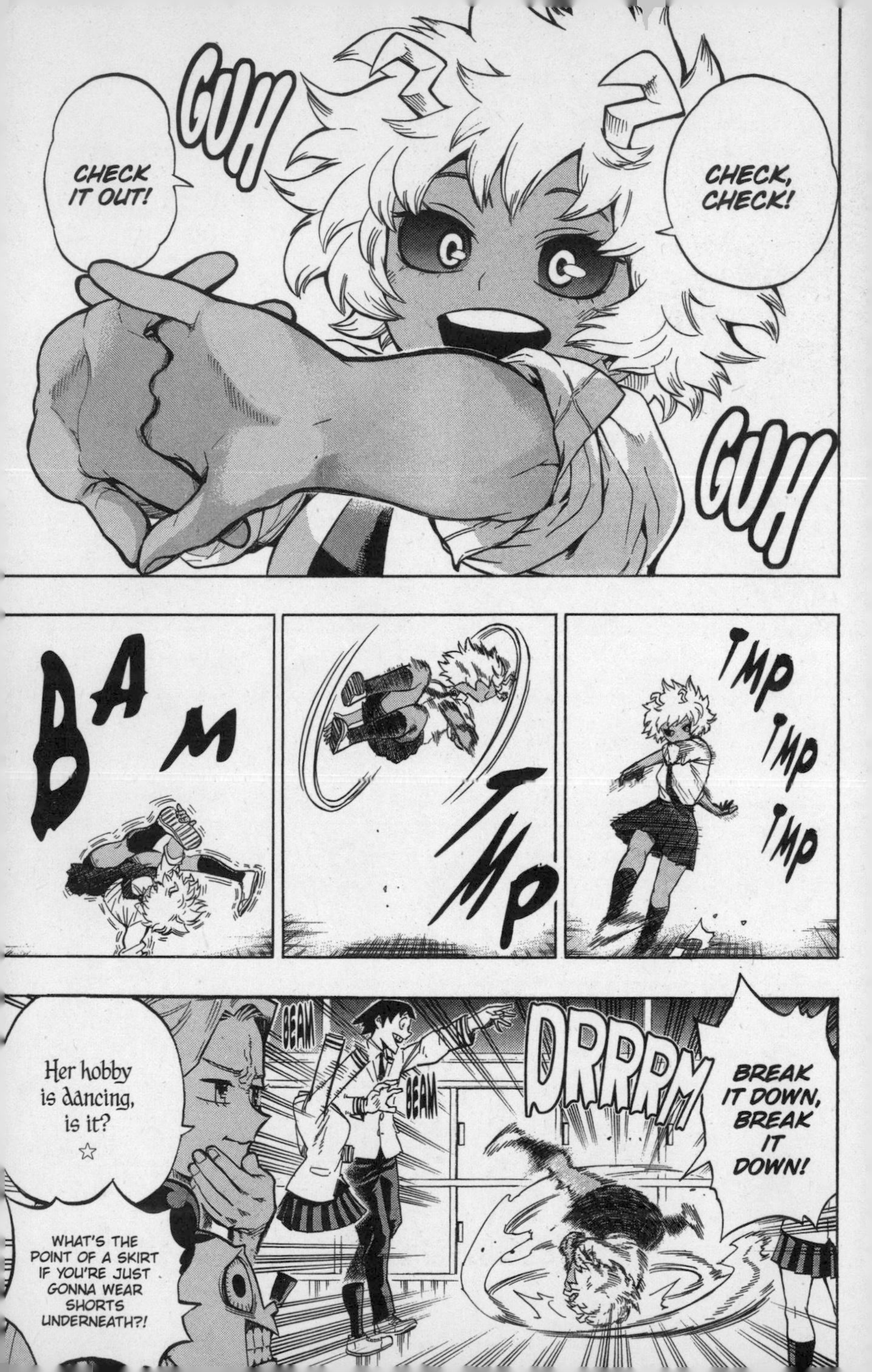
CHECK, CHECK!
GUH
CHECK IT OUT!
GUH
TMP
TMP
TMP
TMP
TMP
BAM
BREAK IT DOWN, BREAK IT DOWN!
DRRRM
BEAM
BEAM
Her hobby is dancing, is it? ☆
WHAT'S THE POINT OF A SKIRT IF YOU'RE JUST GONNA WEAR SHORTS UNDERNEATH?!

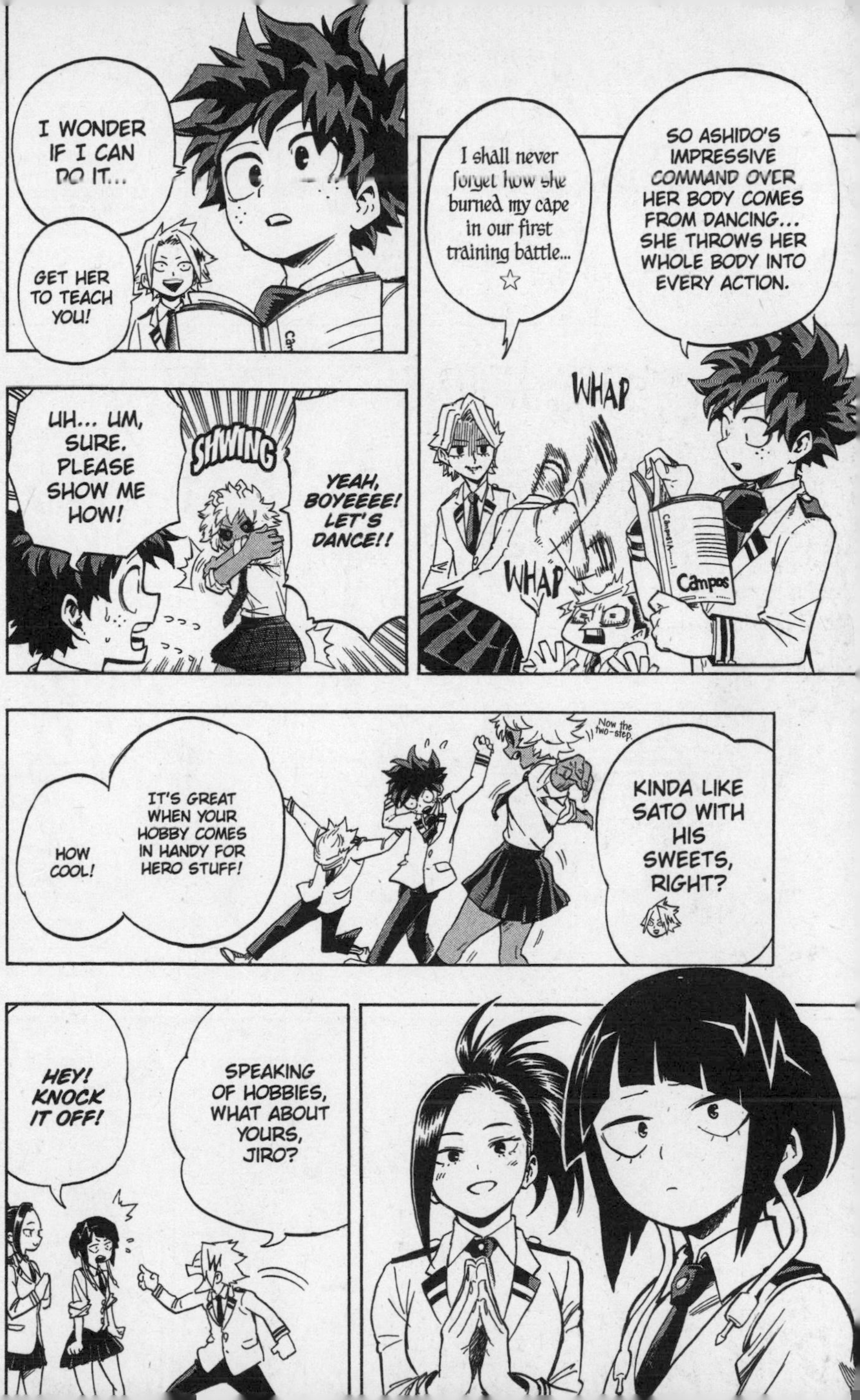
SO ASHIDO'S IMPRESSIVE COMMAND OVER HER BODY COMES FROM DANCING... SHE THROWS HER WHOLE BODY INTO EVERY ACTION.
I shall never forget how she burned my cape in our first training battle... ☆
WHAP
WHAP
Campos
I WONDER IF I CAN DO IT...
GET HER TO TEACH YOU!
SHWING
YEAH, BOYEEEE! LET'S DANCE!!
UH... UM, SURE. PLEASE SHOW ME HOW!
Now the two-step.
KINDA LIKE SATO WITH HIS SWEETS, RIGHT?
IT'S GREAT WHEN YOUR HOBBY COMES IN HANDY FOR HERO STUFF!
HOW COOL!
SPEAKING OF HOBBIES, WHAT ABOUT YOURS, JIRO?
HEY! KNOCK IT OFF!

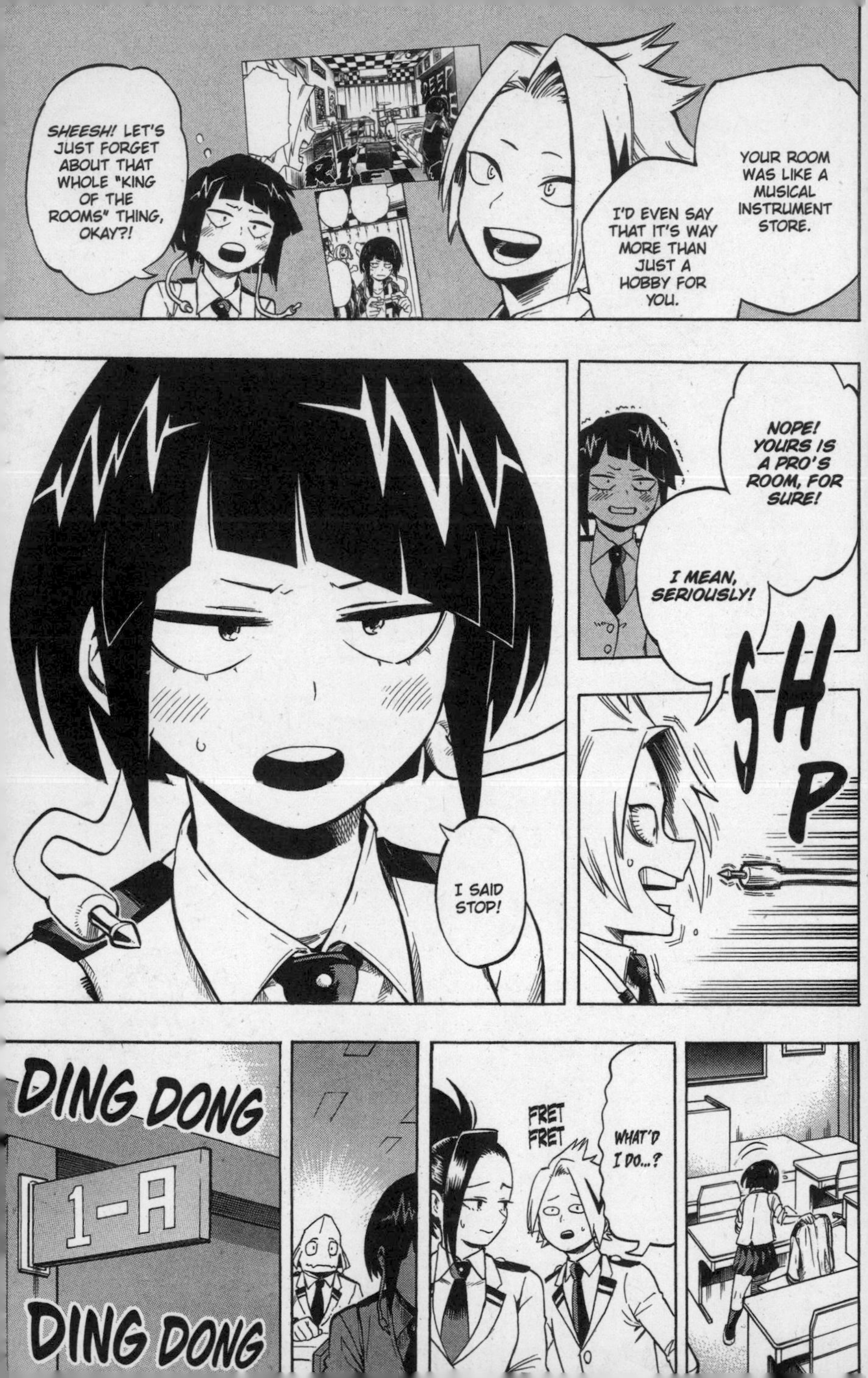
YOUR ROOM WAS LIKE A MUSICAL INSTRUMENT STORE.
I'D EVEN SAY THAT IT'S WAY MORE THAN JUST A HOBBY FOR YOU.
SHEESH! LET'S JUST FORGET ABOUT THAT WHOLE "KING OF THE ROOMS" THING, OKAY?!
NOPE! YOURS IS A PRO'S ROOM, FOR SURE!
I MEAN, SERIOUSLY!
SHP
I SAID STOP!
WHAT'D I DO...?
FRET FRET
DING DONG
1-A
DING DONG

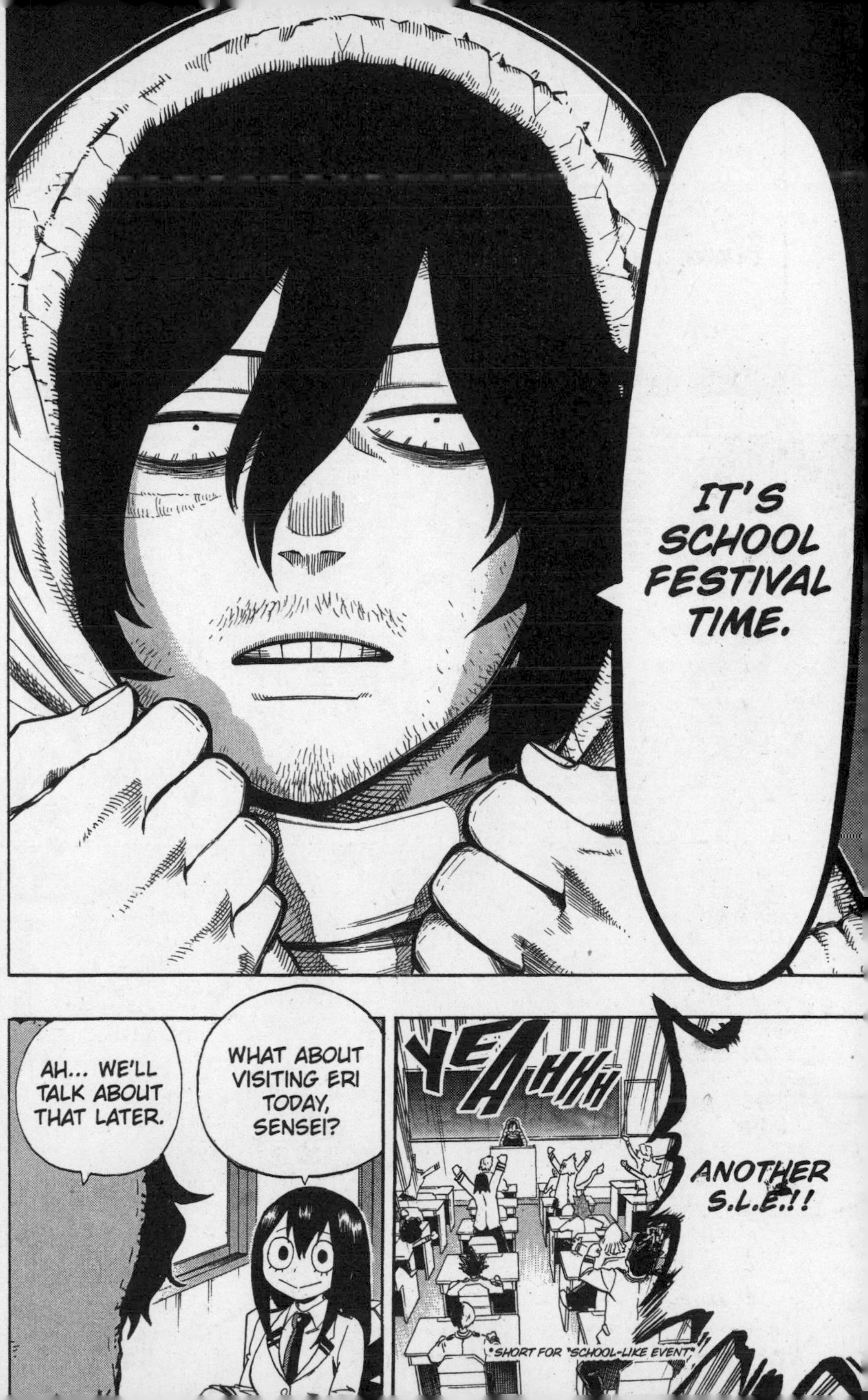
IT'S SCHOOL FESTIVAL TIME.
YEAHHHH
ANOTHER S.L.E.!!
*SHORT FOR "SCHOOL-LIKE EVENT"
WHAT ABOUT VISITING ERI TODAY, SENSEI?
AH... WE'LL TALK ABOUT THAT LATER.

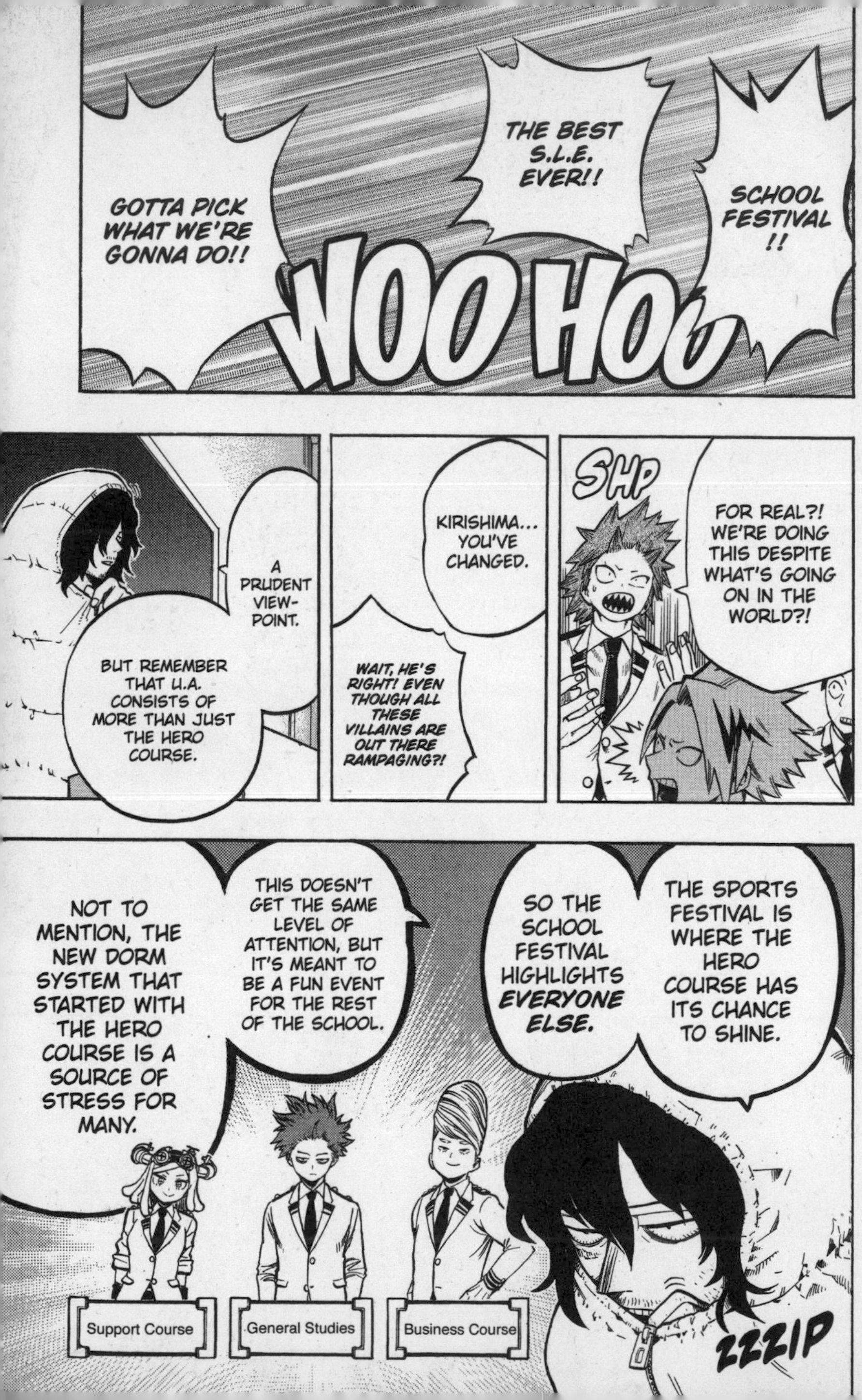
SCHOOL FESTIVAL !!
THE BEST S.L.E. EVER!!
GOTTA PICK WHAT WE'RE GONNA DO!!
WOO HOO
SHP
FOR REAL?! WE'RE DOING THIS DESPITE WHAT'S GOING ON IN THE WORLD?!
KIRISHIMA... YOU'VE CHANGED.
WAIT, HE'S RIGHT! EVEN THOUGH ALL THESE VILLAINS ARE OUT THERE RAMPAGING?!
A PRUDENT VIEW-POINT.
BUT REMEMBER THAT U.A. CONSISTS OF MORE THAN JUST THE HERO COURSE.
THE SPORTS FESTIVAL IS WHERE THE HERO COURSE HAS ITS CHANCE TO SHINE.
SO THE SCHOOL FESTIVAL HIGHLIGHTS EVERYONE ELSE.
THIS DOESN'T GET THE SAME LEVEL OF ATTENTION, BUT IT'S MEANT TO BE A FUN EVENT FOR THE REST OF THE SCHOOL.
NOT TO MENTION, THE NEW DORM SYSTEM THAT STARTED WITH THE HERO COURSE IS A SOURCE OF STRESS FOR MANY.
Business Course
General Studies
Support Course
ZZZIP

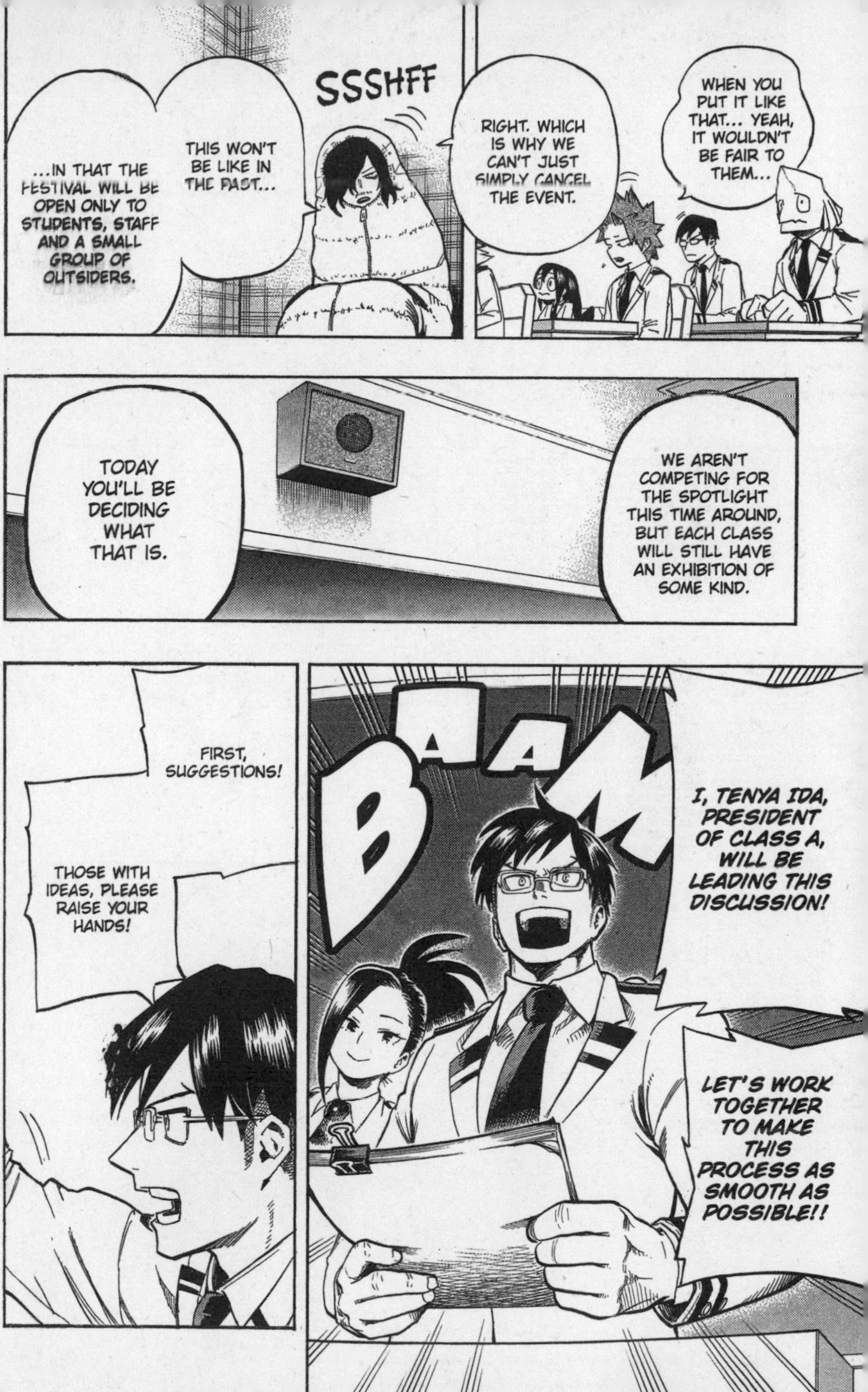
WHEN YOU PUT IT LIKE THAT... YEAH, IT WOULDN'T BE FAIR TO THEM...
RIGHT. WHICH IS WHY WE CAN'T JUST SIMPLY CANCEL THE EVENT.
SSSHFF
THIS WON'T BE LIKE IN THE PAST...
...IN THAT THE FESTIVAL WILL BE OPEN ONLY TO STUDENTS, STAFF AND A SMALL GROUP OF OUTSIDERS.
WE AREN'T COMPETING FOR THE SPOTLIGHT THIS TIME AROUND, BUT EACH CLASS WILL STILL HAVE AN EXHIBITION OF SOME KIND.
TODAY YOU'LL BE DECIDING WHAT THAT IS.
BAAM
I, TENYA IDA, PRESIDENT OF CLASS A, WILL BE LEADING THIS DISCUSSION!
LET'S WORK TOGETHER TO MAKE THIS PROCESS AS SMOOTH AS POSSIBLE!!
FIRST, SUGGESTIONS!
THOSE WITH IDEAS, PLEASE RAISE YOUR HANDS!

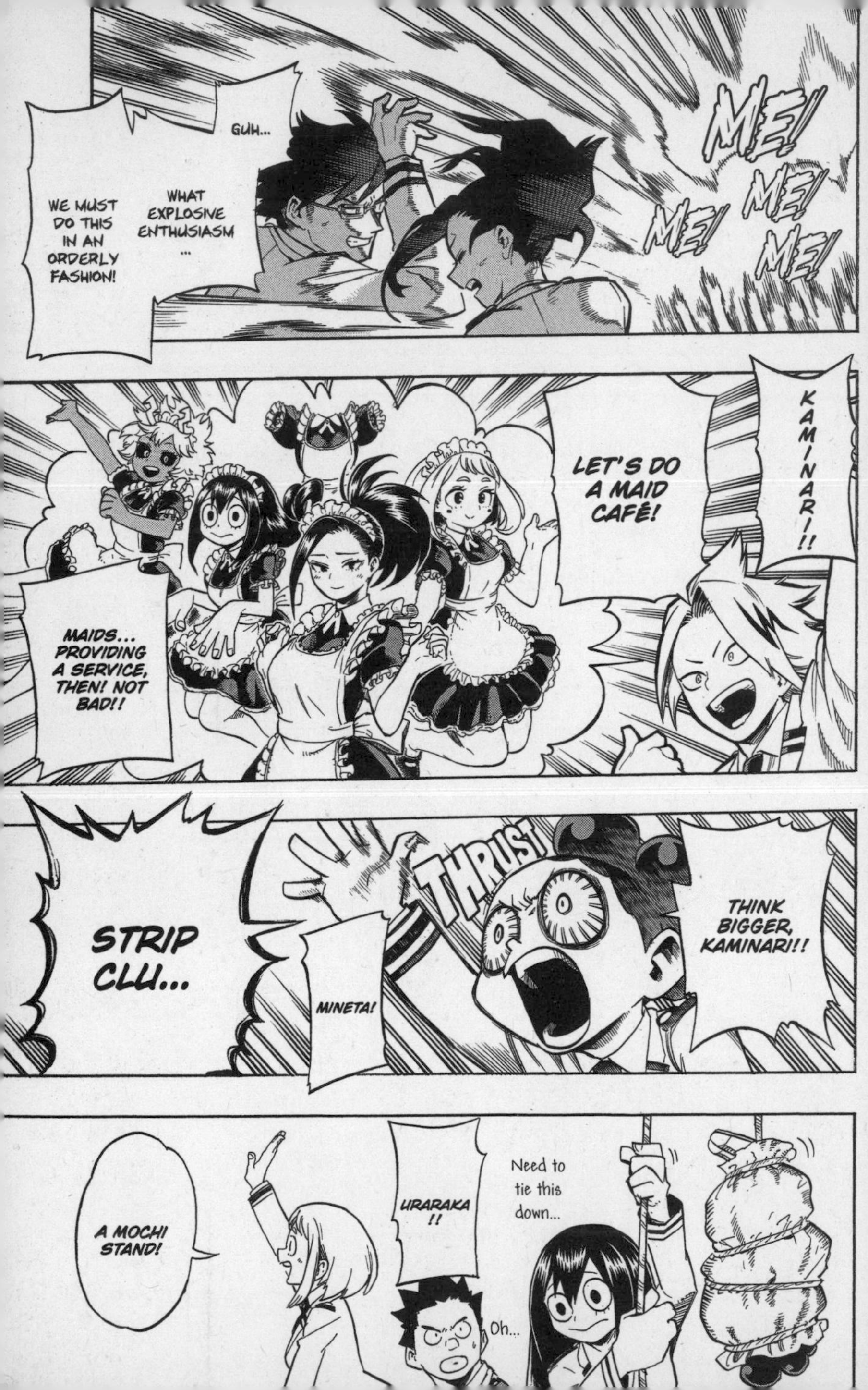
ME! ME! ME! ME! ME!
GUH...
WHAT EXPLOSIVE ENTHUSIASM ...
WE MUST DO THIS IN AN ORDERLY FASHION!
KAMINARI!!
LET'S DO A MAID CAFÉ!
MAIDS... PROVIDING A SERVICE, THEN! NOT BAD!!
THINK BIGGER, KAMINARI!!
THRUST
MINETA!
STRIP CLU...
Need to tie this down...
URARAKA !!
A MOCHI STAND!
Oh...

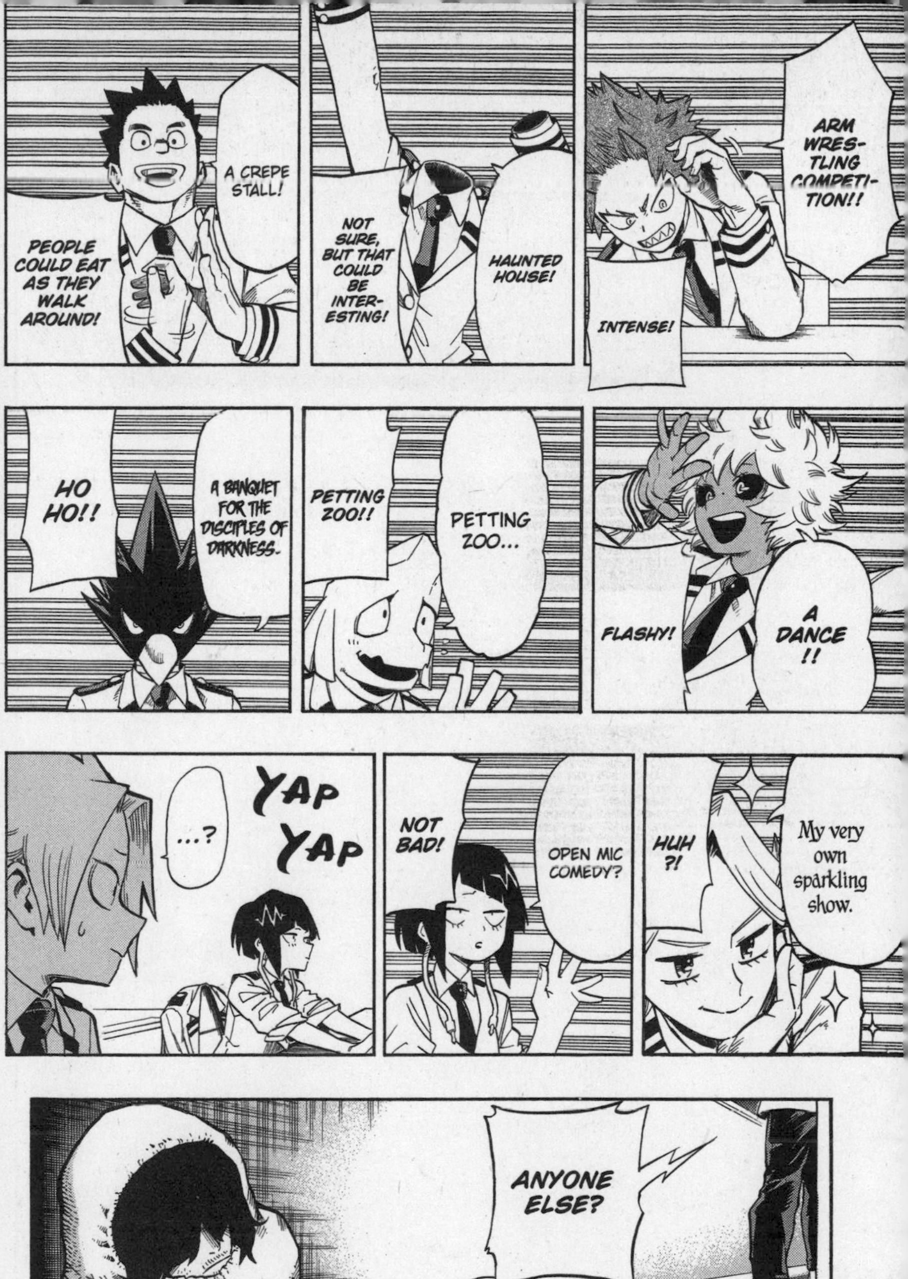
ARM WRESTLING COMPETITION!!
INTENSE!
HAUNTED HOUSE!
NOT SURE, BUT THAT COULD BE INTERESTING!
A CREPE STALL!
PEOPLE COULD EAT AS THEY WALK AROUND!
A DANCE!!
FLASHY!
PETTING ZOO...
PETTING ZOO!!
A BANQUET FOR THE DISCIPLES OF DARKNESS.
HO HO!!
My very own sparkling show.
HUH?!
OPEN MIC COMEDY?
NOT BAD!
YAP YAP
...?
ANYONE ELSE?

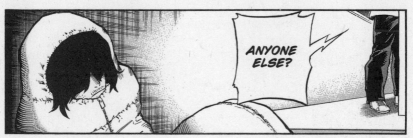

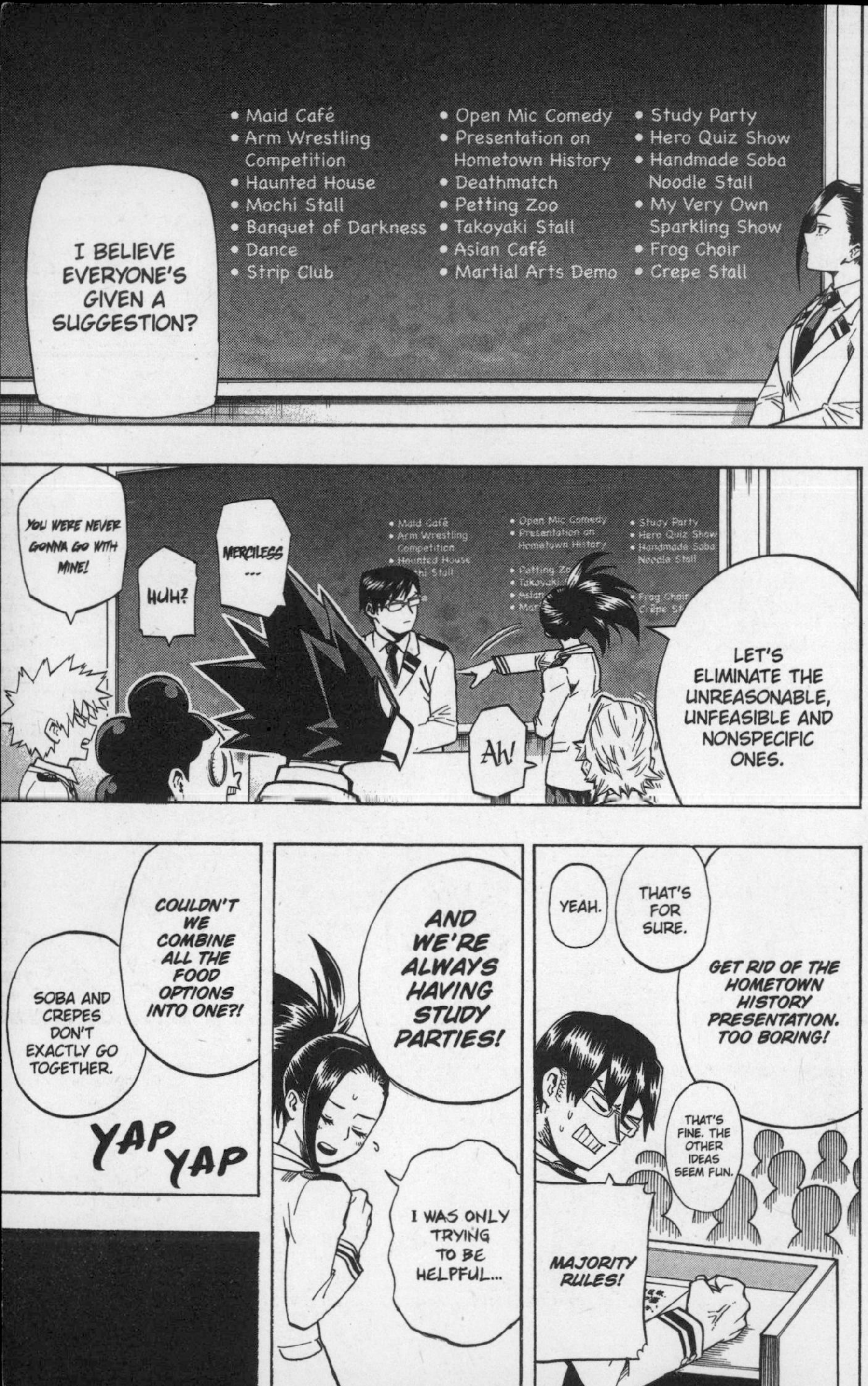

• Maid Café
• Arm Wrestling Competition
• Haunted House
• Mochi Stall
• Banquet of Darkness
• Dance
• Strip Club
• Open Mic Comedy
• Presentation on Hometown History
• Deathmatch
• Petting Zoo
• Takoyaki Stall
• Asian Café
• Martial Arts Demo
• Study Party
• Hero Quiz Show
• Handmade Soba Noodle Stall
• My Very Own Sparkling Show
• Frog Choir
• Crepe Stall
I BELIEVE EVERYONE'S GIVEN A SUGGESTION?
LET'S ELIMINATE THE UNREASONABLE, UNFEASIBLE AND NONSPECIFIC ONES.
Ah!
MERCILESS...
HUH?
YOU WERE NEVER GONNA GO WITH MINE!
THAT'S FOR SURE.
YEAH.
GET RID OF THE HOMETOWN HISTORY PRESENTATION. TOO BORING!
THAT'S FINE. THE OTHER IDEAS SEEM FUN.
MAJORITY RULES!
AND WE'RE ALWAYS HAVING STUDY PARTIES!
I WAS ONLY TRYING TO BE HELPFUL...
COULDN'T WE COMBINE ALL THE FOOD OPTIONS INTO ONE?!
SOBA AND CREPES DON'T EXACTLY GO TOGETHER.
YAP YAP

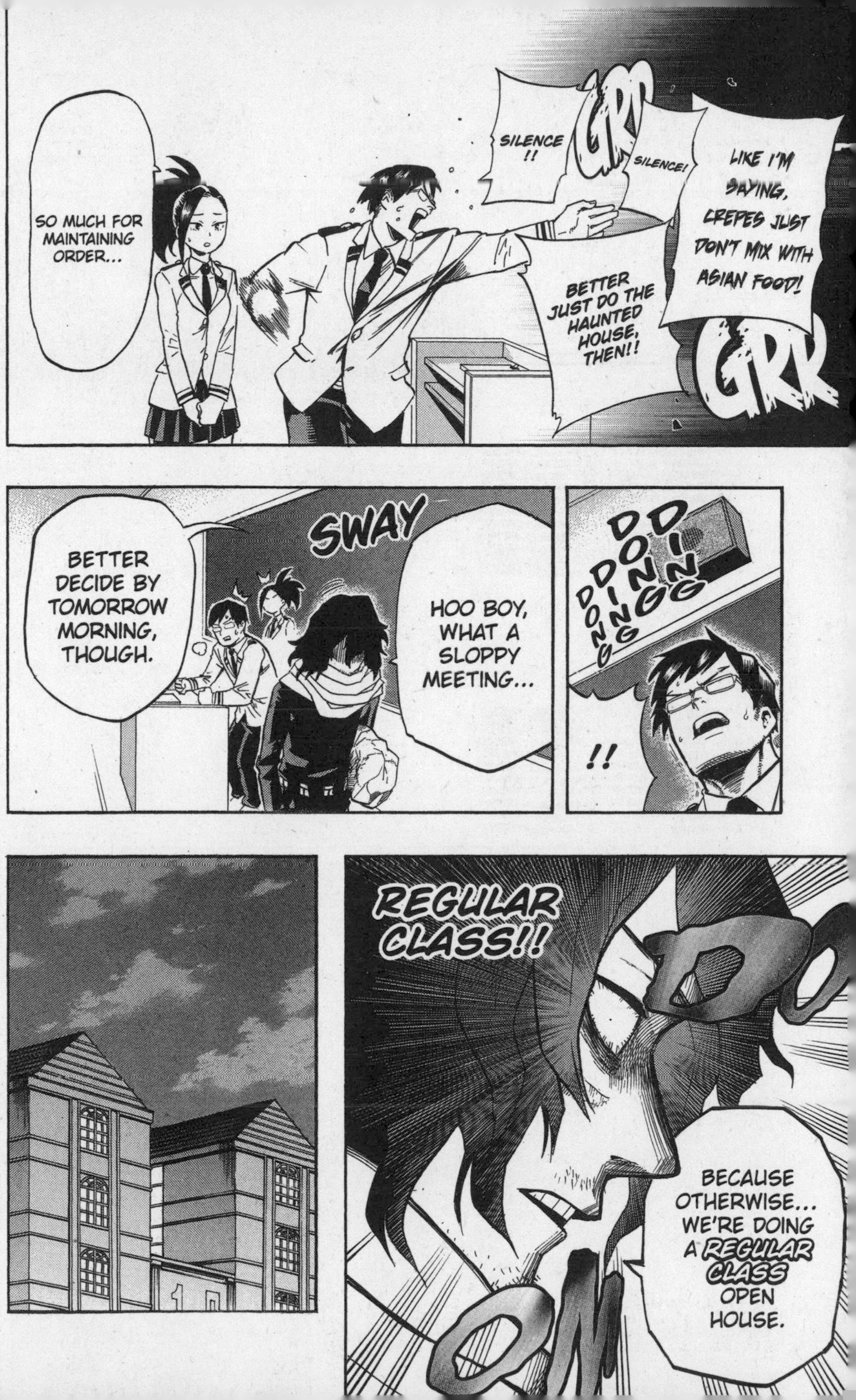
LIKE I'M SAYING, CREPES JUST DON'T MIX WITH ASIAN FOOD!
GRR
SILENCE!
GRR
SILENCE !!
BETTER JUST DO THE HAUNTED HOUSE, THEN!!
SO MUCH FOR MAINTAINING ORDER...
DING DONG DING DONG
!!
SWAY
HOO BOY, WHAT A SLOPPY MEETING...
BETTER DECIDE BY TOMORROW MORNING, THOUGH.
REGULAR CLASS!!
DOOM
BECAUSE OTHERWISE... WE'RE DOING A REGULAR CLASS OPEN HOUSE.

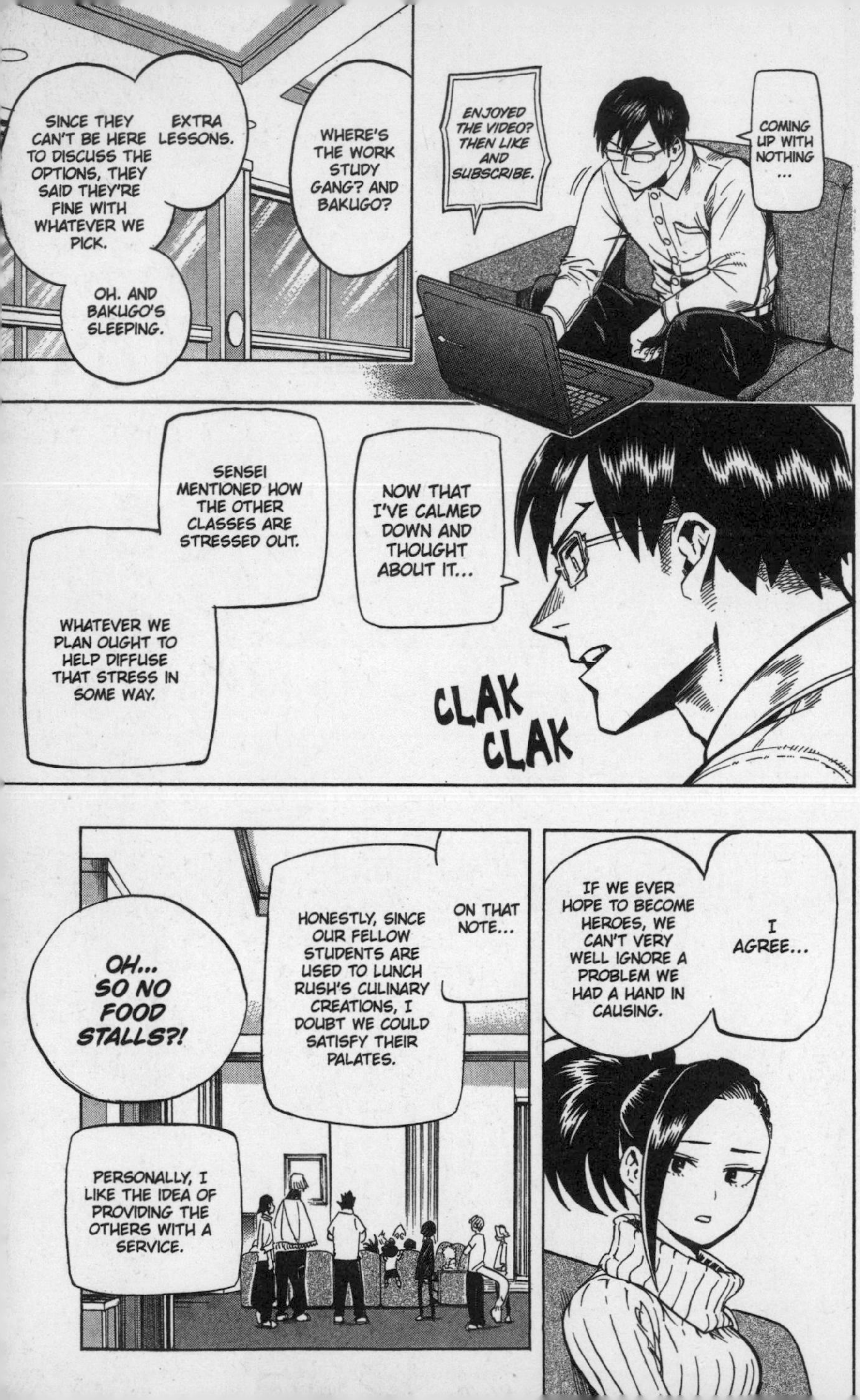
COMING UP WITH NOTHING...
ENJOYED THE VIDEO? THEN LIKE AND SUBSCRIBE.
WHERE'S THE WORK STUDY GANG? AND BAKUGO?
EXTRA LESSONS.
SINCE THEY CAN'T BE HERE TO DISCUSS THE OPTIONS, THEY SAID THEY'RE FINE WITH WHATEVER WE PICK.
OH. AND BAKUGO'S SLEEPING.
NOW THAT I'VE CALMED DOWN AND THOUGHT ABOUT IT...
SENSEI MENTIONED HOW THE OTHER CLASSES ARE STRESSED OUT.
WHATEVER WE PLAN OUGHT TO HELP DIFFUSE THAT STRESS IN SOME WAY.
CLAK CLAK
I AGREE...
IF WE EVER HOPE TO BECOME HEROES, WE CAN'T VERY WELL IGNORE A PROBLEM WE HAD A HAND IN CAUSING.
ON THAT NOTE...
HONESTLY, SINCE OUR FELLOW STUDENTS ARE USED TO LUNCH RUSH'S CULINARY CREATIONS, I DOUBT WE COULD SATISFY THEIR PALATES.
OH... SO NO FOOD STALLS?!
PERSONALLY, I LIKE THE IDEA OF PROVIDING THE OTHERS WITH A SERVICE.

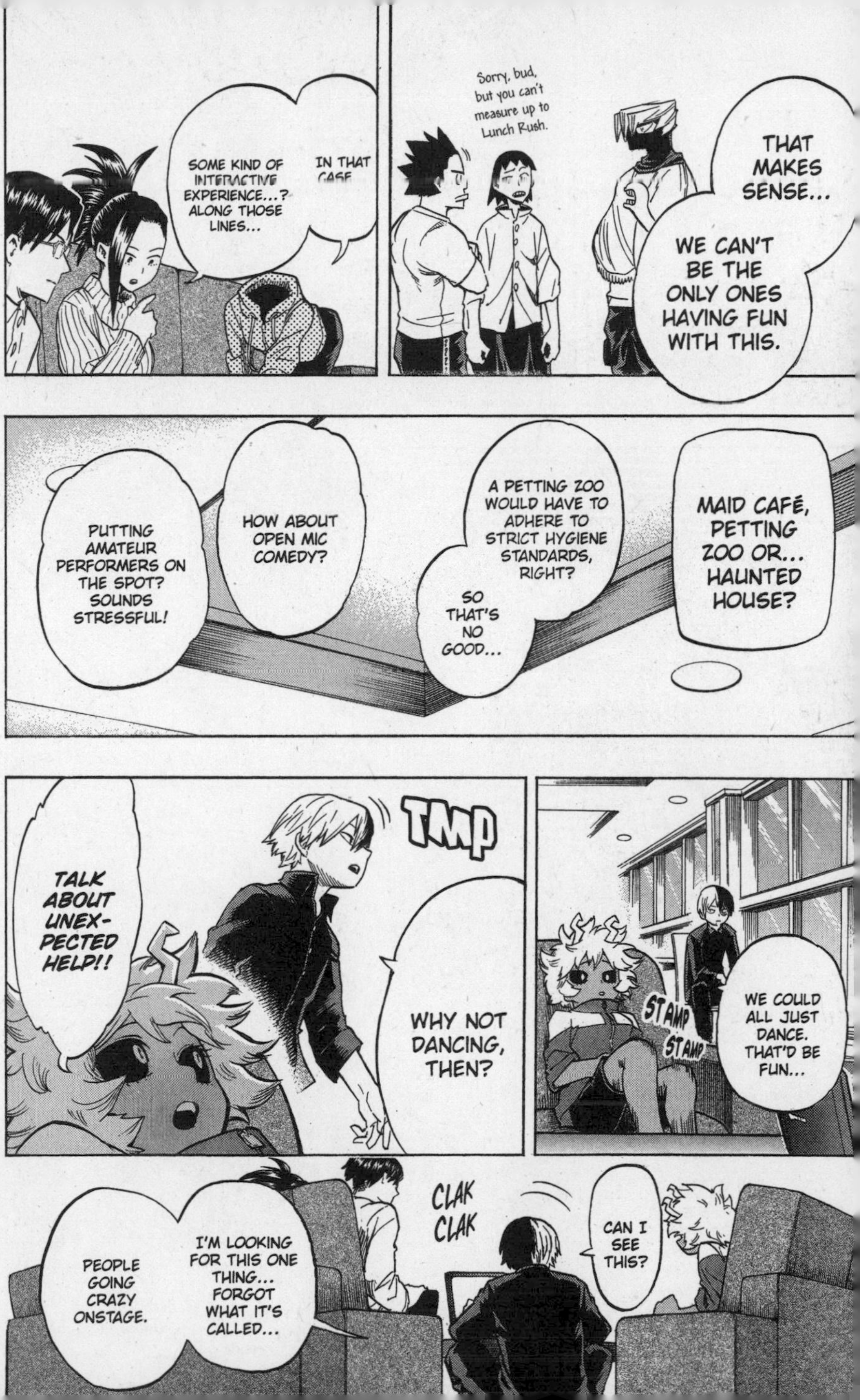
THAT MAKES SENSE...
WE CAN'T BE THE ONLY ONES HAVING FUN WITH THIS.
Sorry, bud, but you can't measure up to Lunch Rush.
IN THAT CASE
SOME KIND OF INTERACTIVE EXPERIENCE...? ALONG THOSE LINES...
MAID CAFÉ, PETTING ZOO OR... HAUNTED HOUSE?
A PETTING ZOO WOULD HAVE TO ADHERE TO STRICT HYGIENE STANDARDS, RIGHT?
SO THAT'S NO GOOD...
HOW ABOUT OPEN MIC COMEDY?
PUTTING AMATEUR PERFORMERS ON THE SPOT? SOUNDS STRESSFUL!
STAMP
STAMP
WE COULD ALL JUST DANCE. THAT'D BE FUN...
TMP
WHY NOT DANCING, THEN?
TALK ABOUT UNEX-PECTED HELP!!
CAN I SEE THIS?
CLAK CLAK
I'M LOOKING FOR THIS ONE THING... FORGOT WHAT IT'S CALLED...
PEOPLE GOING CRAZY ONSTAGE.

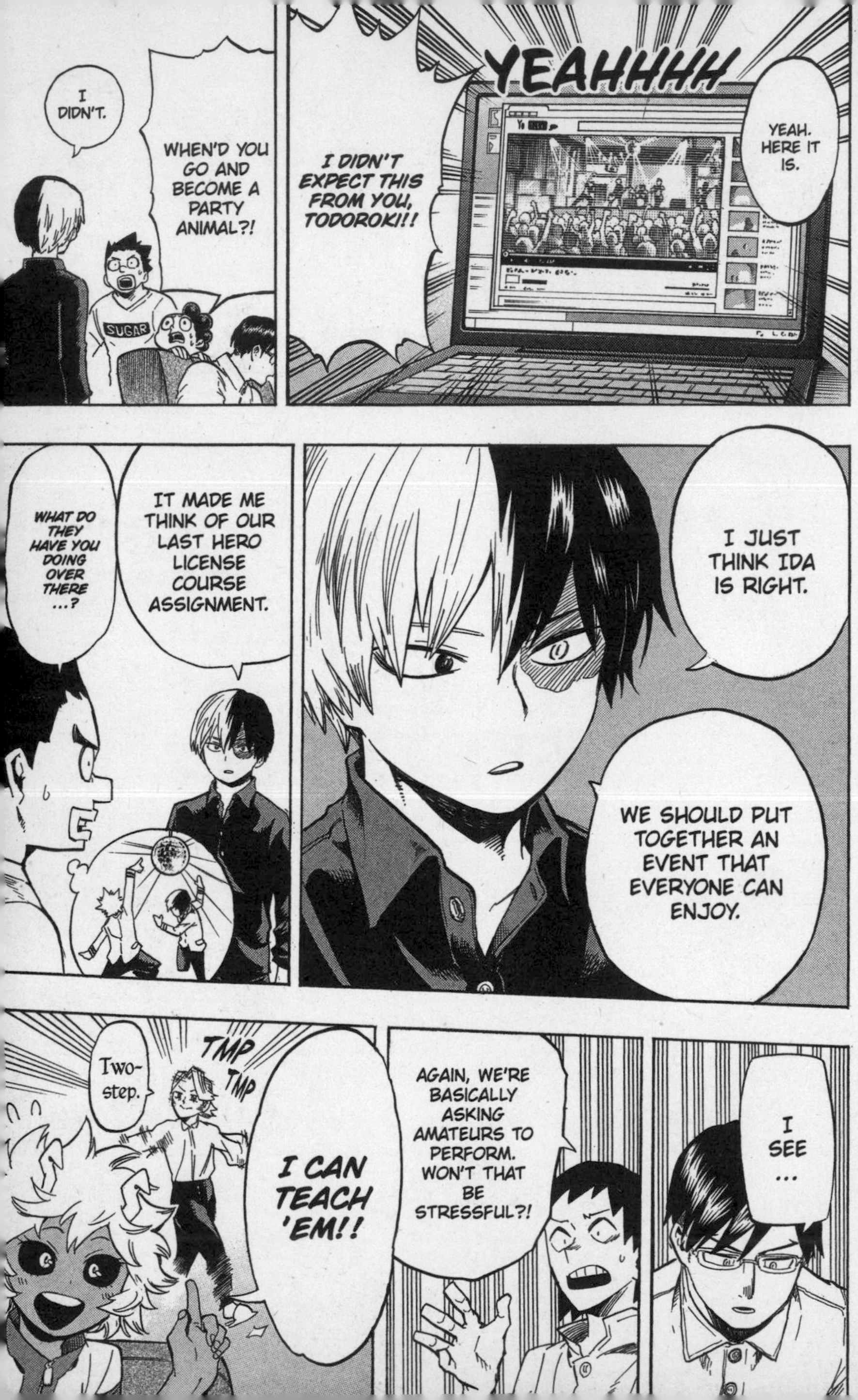
YEAH. HERE IT IS.
YEAHHHH
I DIDN'T EXPECT THIS FROM YOU, TODOROKI!!
WHEN'D YOU GO AND BECOME A PARTY ANIMAL?!
SUGAR
I DIDN'T.
I JUST THINK IDA IS RIGHT.
WE SHOULD PUT TOGETHER AN EVENT THAT EVERYONE CAN ENJOY.
IT MADE ME THINK OF OUR LAST HERO LICENSE COURSE ASSIGNMENT.
WHAT DO THEY HAVE YOU DOING OVER THERE ...?
I SEE ...
AGAIN, WE'RE BASICALLY ASKING AMATEURS TO PERFORM. WON'T THAT BE STRESSFUL?!
I CAN TEACH 'EM!!
TMP TMP
Two-step.

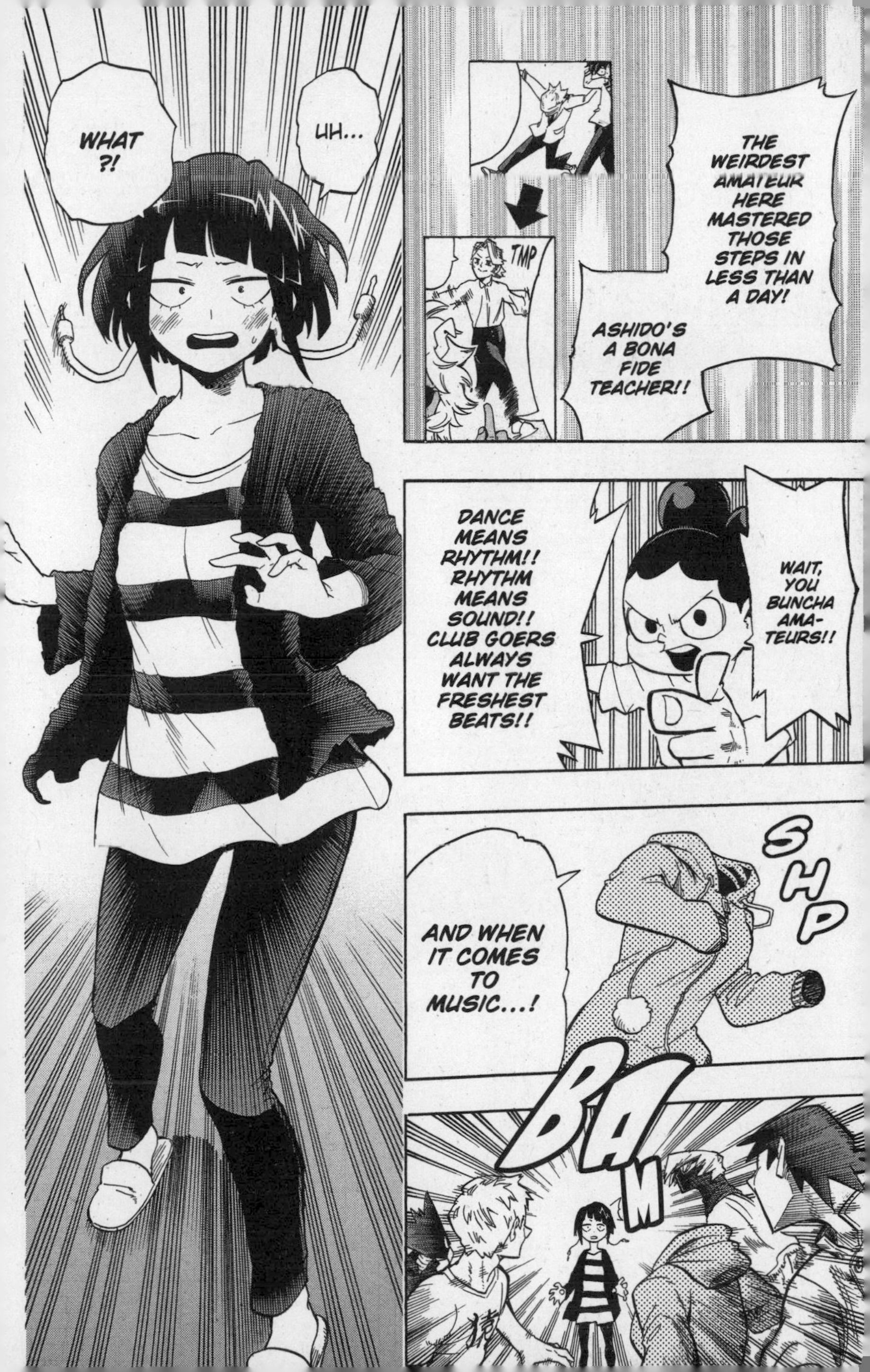
THE WEIRDEST AMATEUR HERE MASTERED THOSE STEPS IN LESS THAN A DAY!
TMP
ASHIDO'S A BONA FIDE TEACHER!!
WAIT, YOU BUNCHA AMA-TEURS!!
DANCE MEANS RHYTHM!! RHYTHM MEANS SOUND!! CLUB GOERS ALWAYS WANT THE FRESHEST BEATS!!
SHP
AND WHEN IT COMES TO MUSIC...!
BAM
UH...
WHAT ?!

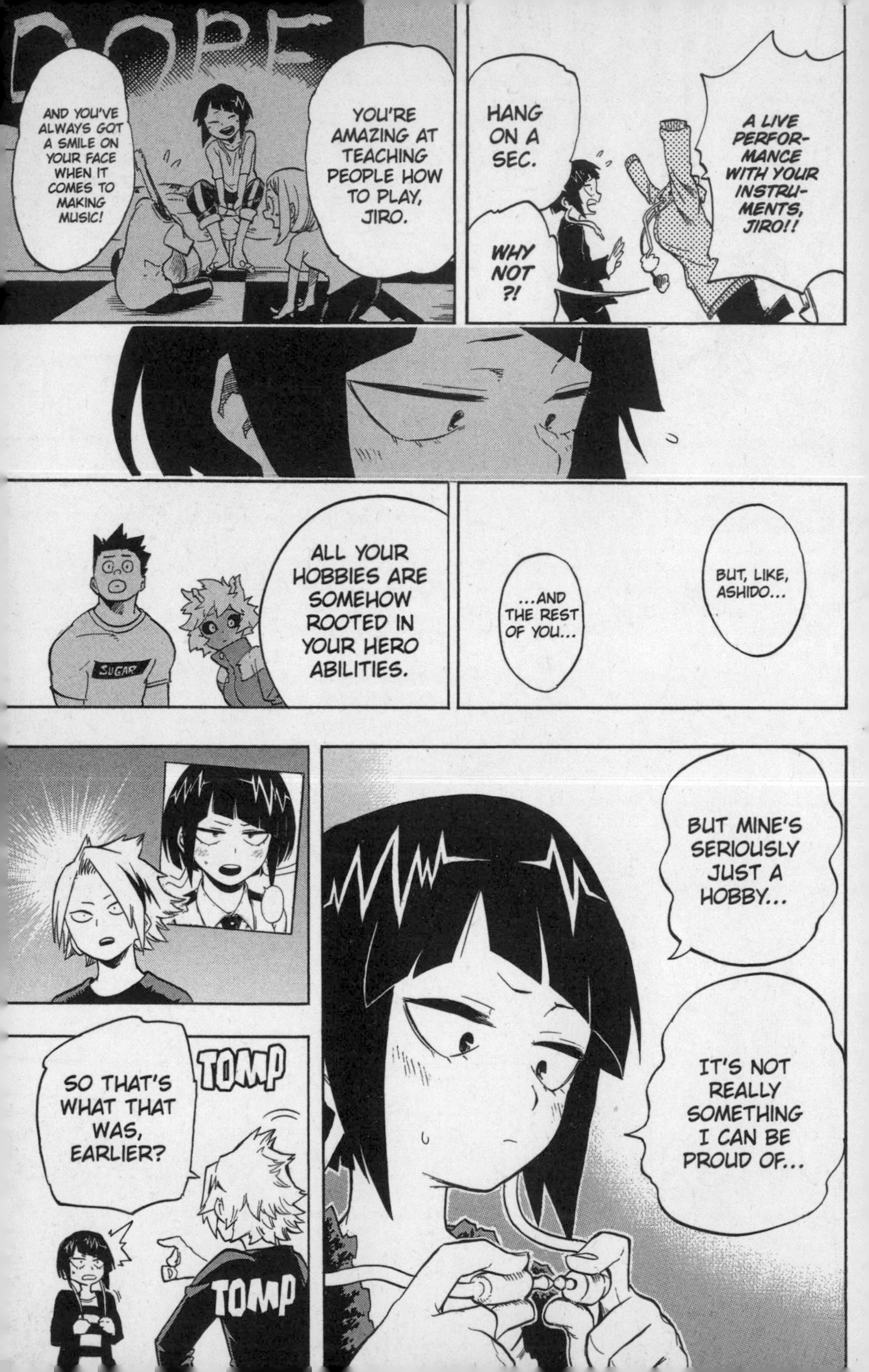
A LIVE PERFORMANCE WITH YOUR INSTRUMENTS, JIRO!!
HANG ON A SEC.
WHY NOT ?!
YOU'RE AMAZING AT TEACHING PEOPLE HOW TO PLAY, JIRO.
AND YOU'VE ALWAYS GOT A SMILE ON YOUR FACE WHEN IT COMES TO MAKING MUSIC!
BUT, LIKE, ASHIDO...
...AND THE REST OF YOU...
ALL YOUR HOBBIES ARE SOMEHOW ROOTED IN YOUR HERO ABILITIES.
SUGAR
BUT MINE'S SERIOUSLY JUST A HOBBY...
IT'S NOT REALLY SOMETHING I CAN BE PROUD OF...
TOMP
SO THAT'S WHAT THAT WAS, EARLIER?
TOMP

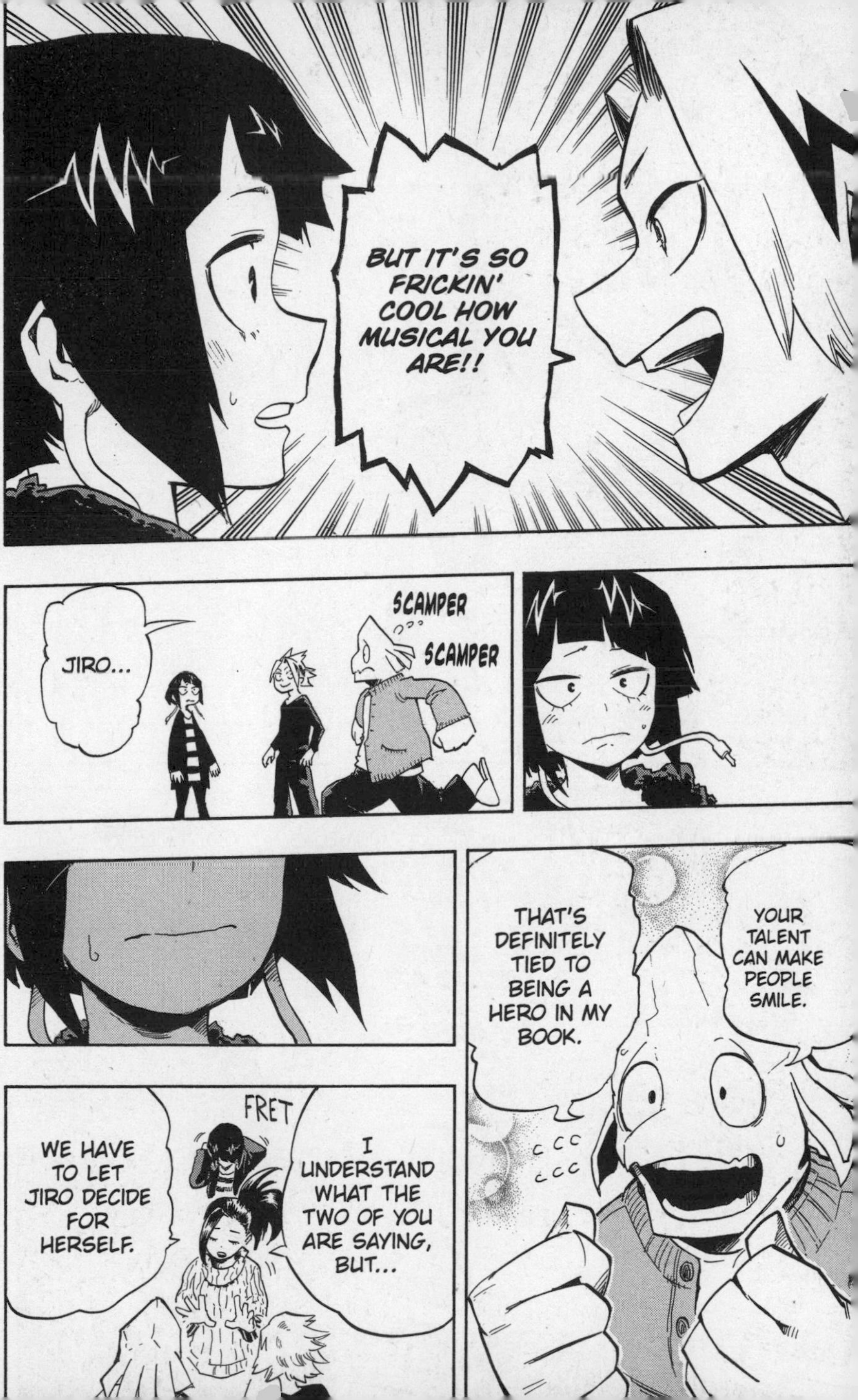
BUT IT'S SO FRICKIN' COOL HOW MUSICAL YOU ARE!!
SCAMPER
SCAMPER
JIRO...
YOUR TALENT CAN MAKE PEOPLE SMILE.
THAT'S DEFINITELY TIED TO BEING A HERO IN MY BOOK.
FRET
I UNDERSTAND WHAT THE TWO OF YOU ARE SAYING, BUT...
WE HAVE TO LET JIRO DECIDE FOR HERSELF.

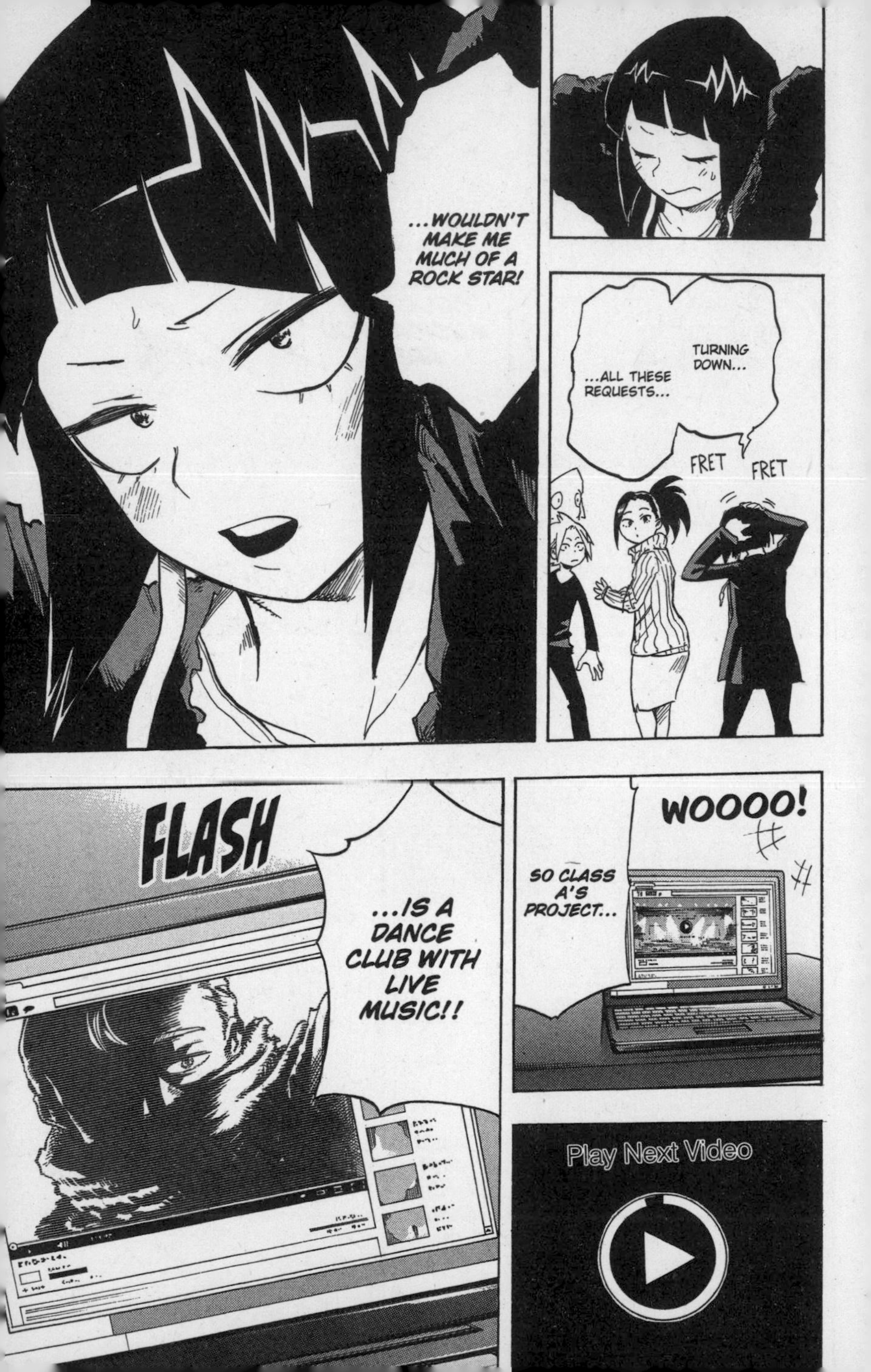
TURNING DOWN...
...ALL THESE REQUESTS...
FRET
FRET
...WOULDN'T MAKE ME MUCH OF A ROCK STAR!
WOOOO!
SO CLASS A'S PROJECT...
Play Next Video
FLASH
...IS A DANCE CLUB WITH LIVE MUSIC!!

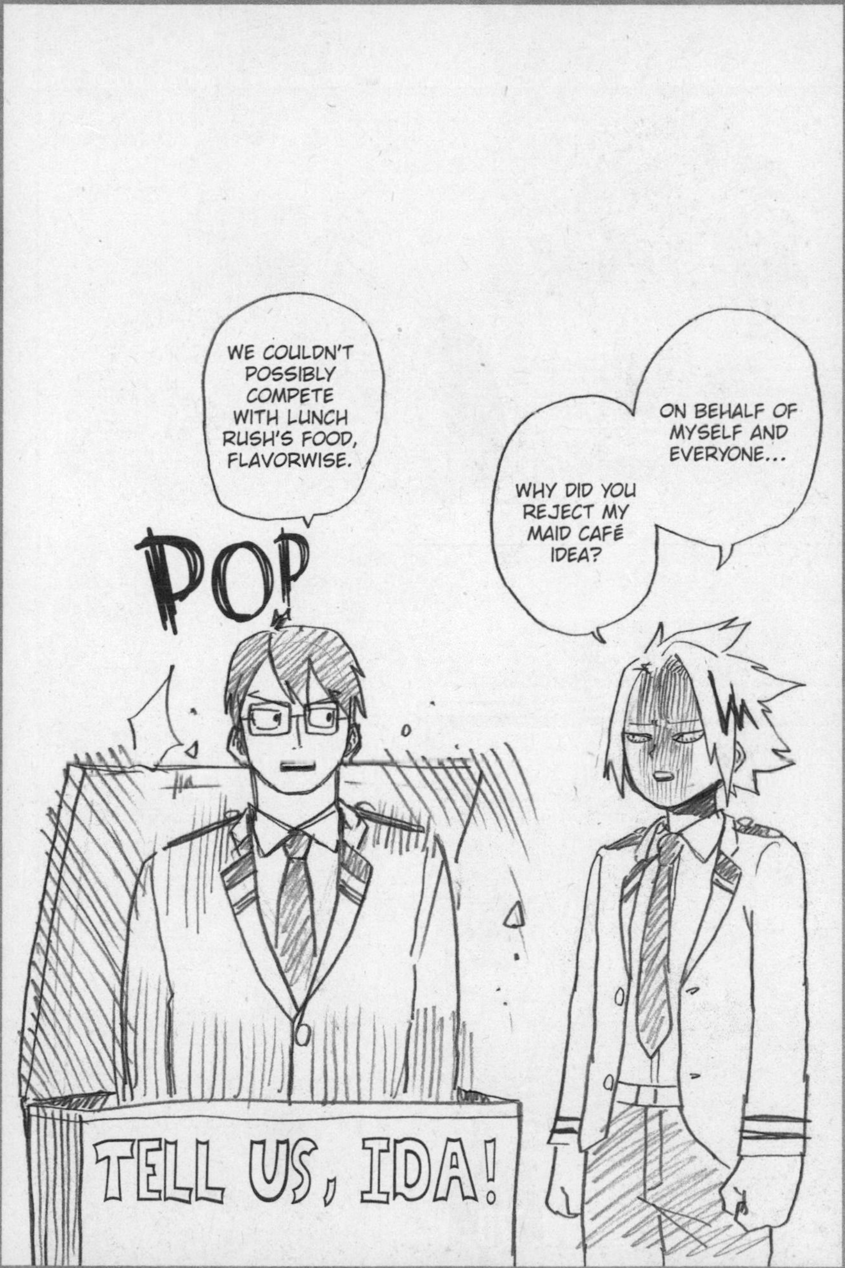
TELL US, IDA!
ON BEHALF OF MYSELF AND EVERYONE...
WHY DID YOU REJECT MY MAID CAFÉ IDEA?
POP
WE COULDN'T POSSIBLY COMPETE WITH LUNCH RUSH'S FOOD, FLAVORWISE.

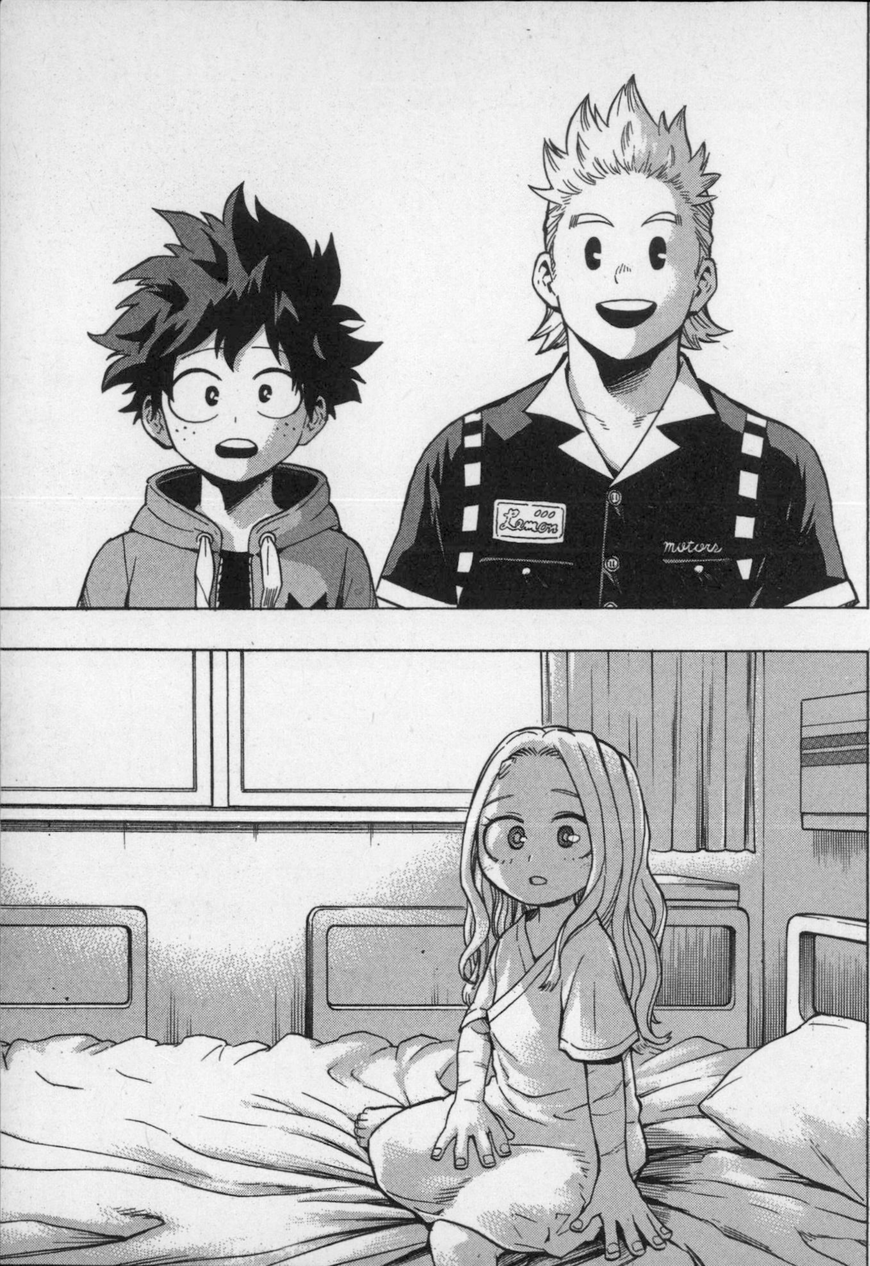
Lemon
motors

NO. 170 - WITH ERI

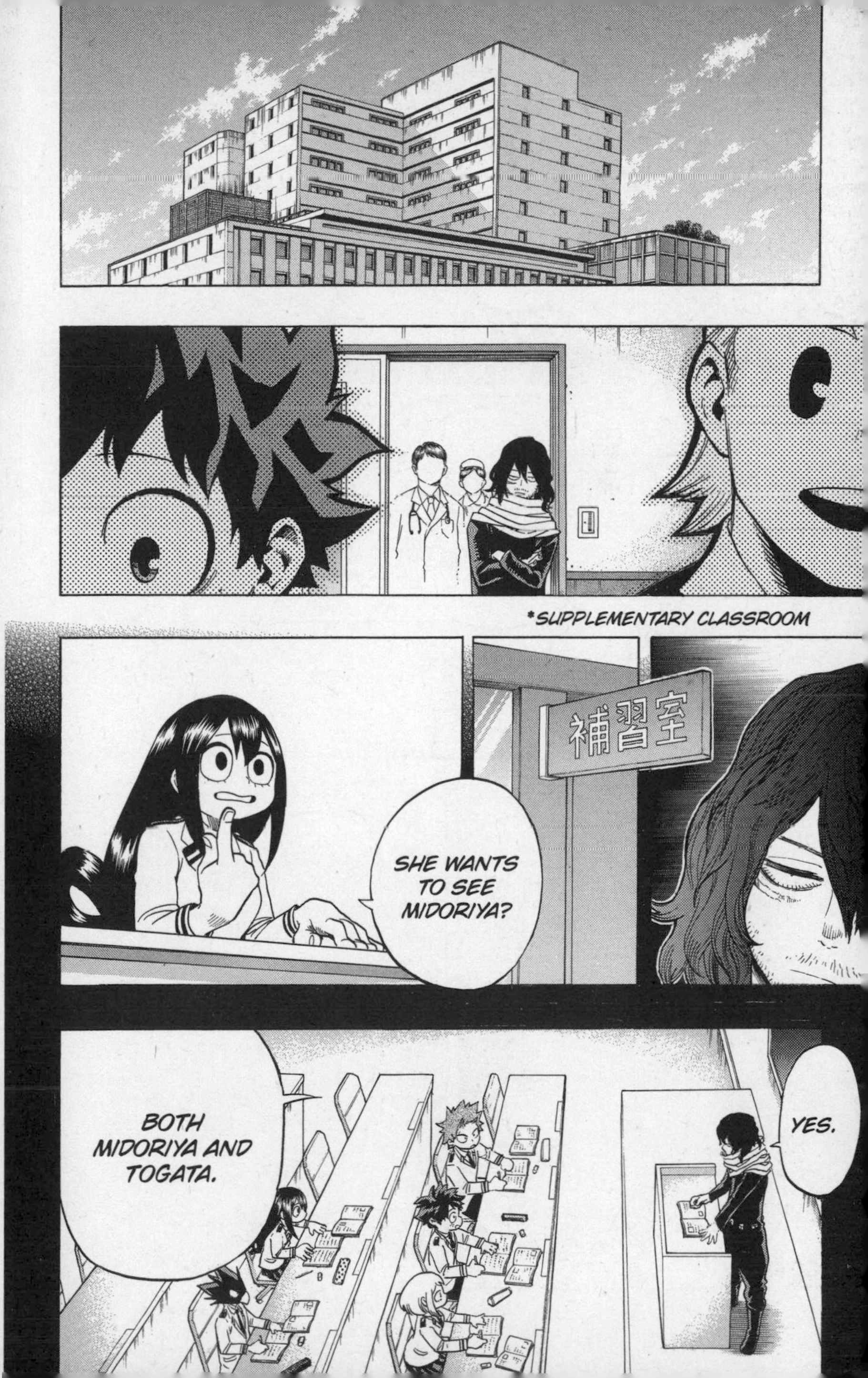
補習室
*SUPPLEMENTARY CLASSROOM
SHE WANTS TO SEE MIDORIYA?
YES.
BOTH MIDORIYA AND TOGATA.

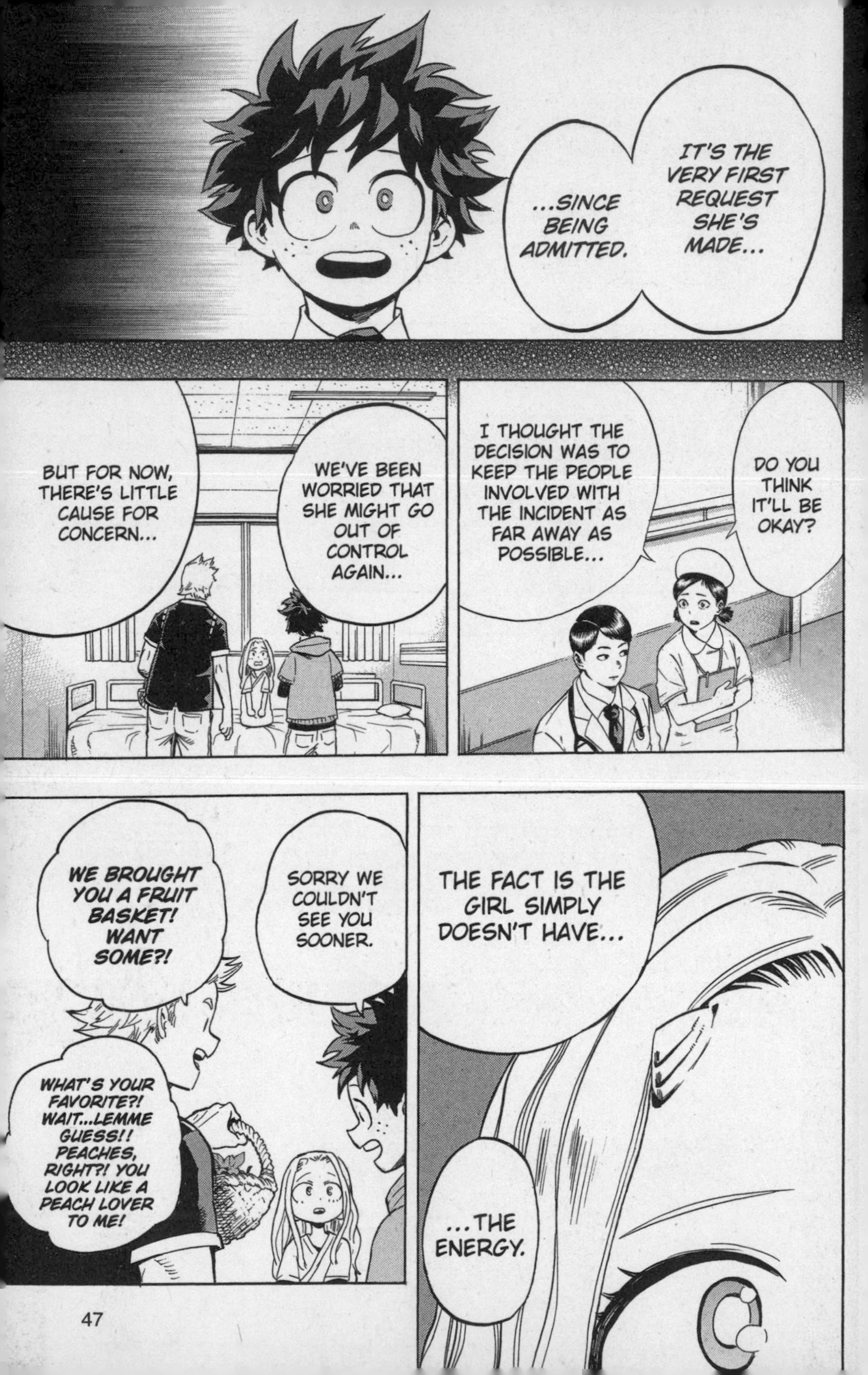
IT'S THE VERY FIRST REQUEST SHE'S MADE...
...SINCE BEING ADMITTED.
DO YOU THINK IT'LL BE OKAY?
I THOUGHT THE DECISION WAS TO KEEP THE PEOPLE INVOLVED WITH THE INCIDENT AS FAR AWAY AS POSSIBLE...
WE'VE BEEN WORRIED THAT SHE MIGHT GO OUT OF CONTROL AGAIN...
BUT FOR NOW, THERE'S LITTLE CAUSE FOR CONCERN...
THE FACT IS THE GIRL SIMPLY DOESN'T HAVE...
...THE ENERGY.
SORRY WE COULDN'T SEE YOU SOONER.
WE BROUGHT YOU A FRUIT BASKET! WANT SOME?!
WHAT'S YOUR FAVORITE?! WAIT...LEMME GUESS!! PEACHES, RIGHT?! YOU LOOK LIKE A PEACH LOVER TO ME!

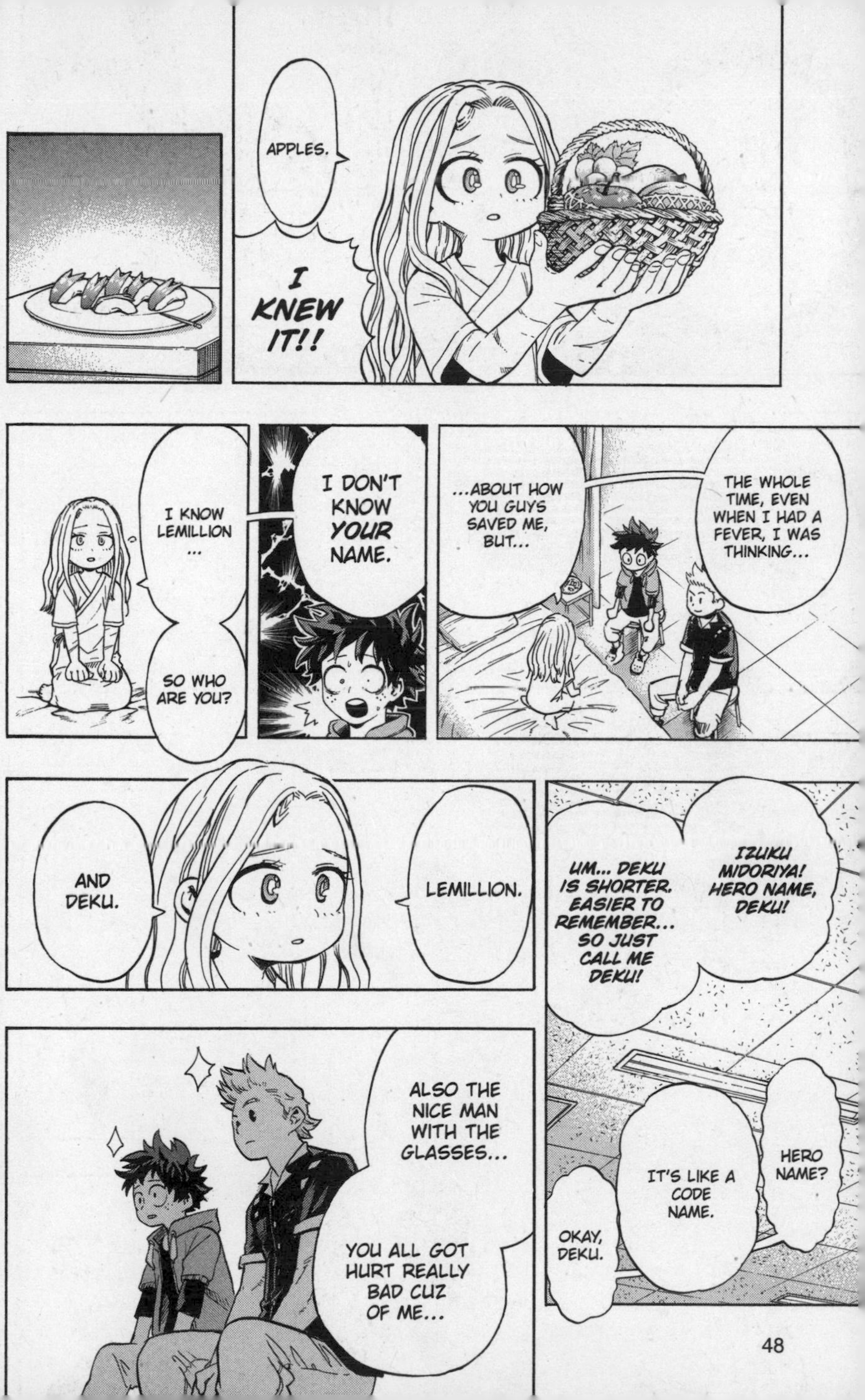
APPLES.
I KNEW IT!!
THE WHOLE TIME, EVEN WHEN I HAD A FEVER, I WAS THINKING...
...ABOUT HOW YOU GUYS SAVED ME, BUT...
I DON'T KNOW YOUR NAME.
I KNOW LEMILLION ...
SO WHO ARE YOU?
IZUKU MIDORIYA! HERO NAME, DEKU!
UM... DEKU IS SHORTER. EASIER TO REMEMBER... SO JUST CALL ME DEKU!
HERO NAME?
IT'S LIKE A CODE NAME.
OKAY, DEKU.
LEMILLION.
AND DEKU.
ALSO THE NICE MAN WITH THE GLASSES...
YOU ALL GOT HURT REALLY BAD CUZ OF ME...

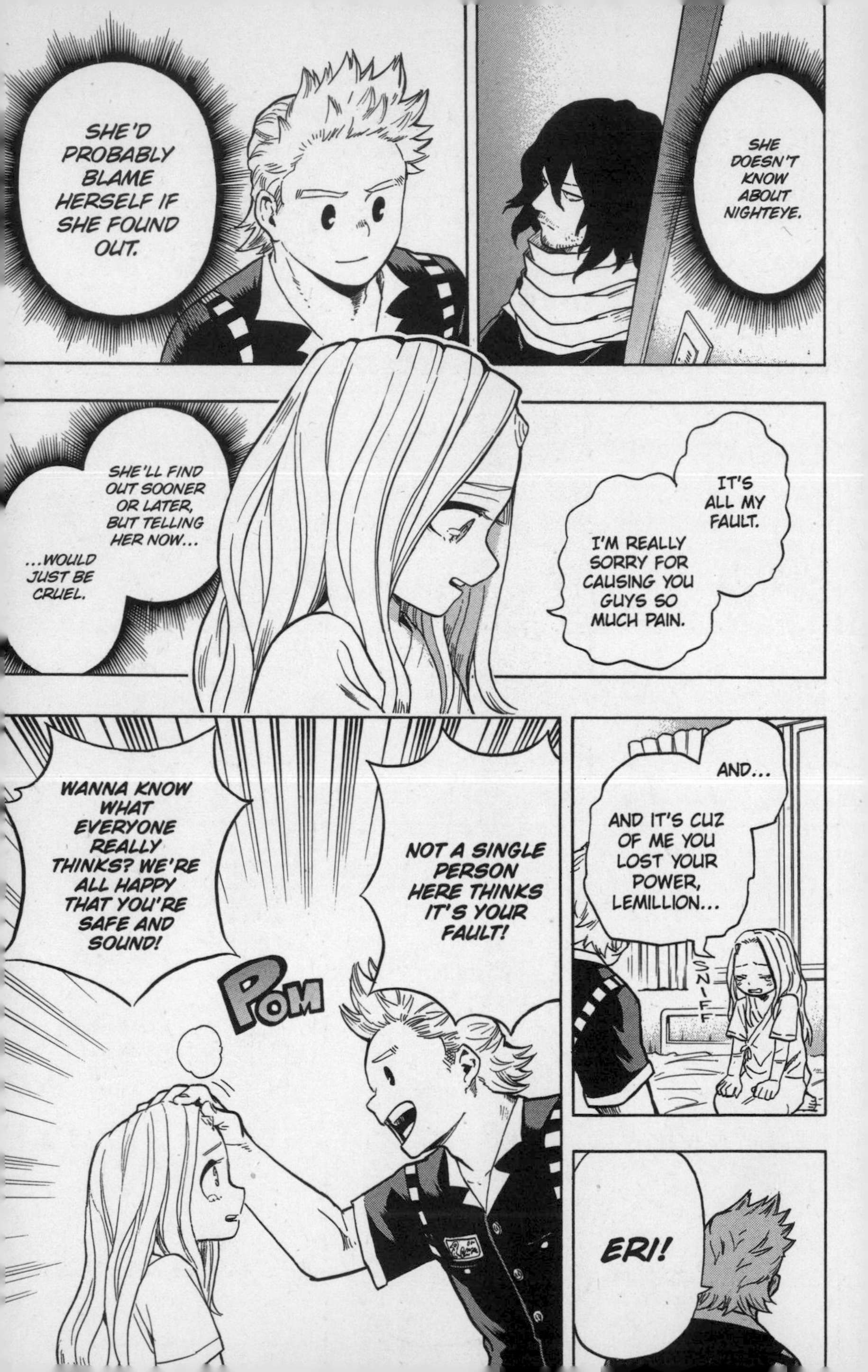
SHE DOESN'T KNOW ABOUT NIGHTEYE.
SHE'D PROBABLY BLAME HERSELF IF SHE FOUND OUT.
IT'S ALL MY FAULT.
I'M REALLY SORRY FOR CAUSING YOU GUYS SO MUCH PAIN.
SHE'LL FIND OUT SOONER OR LATER, BUT TELLING HER NOW...
...WOULD JUST BE CRUEL.
AND...
AND IT'S CUZ OF ME YOU LOST YOUR POWER, LEMILLION...
SNIFF
ERI!
NOT A SINGLE PERSON HERE THINKS IT'S YOUR FAULT!
WANNA KNOW WHAT EVERYONE REALLY THINKS? WE'RE ALL HAPPY THAT YOU'RE SAFE AND SOUND!
POM

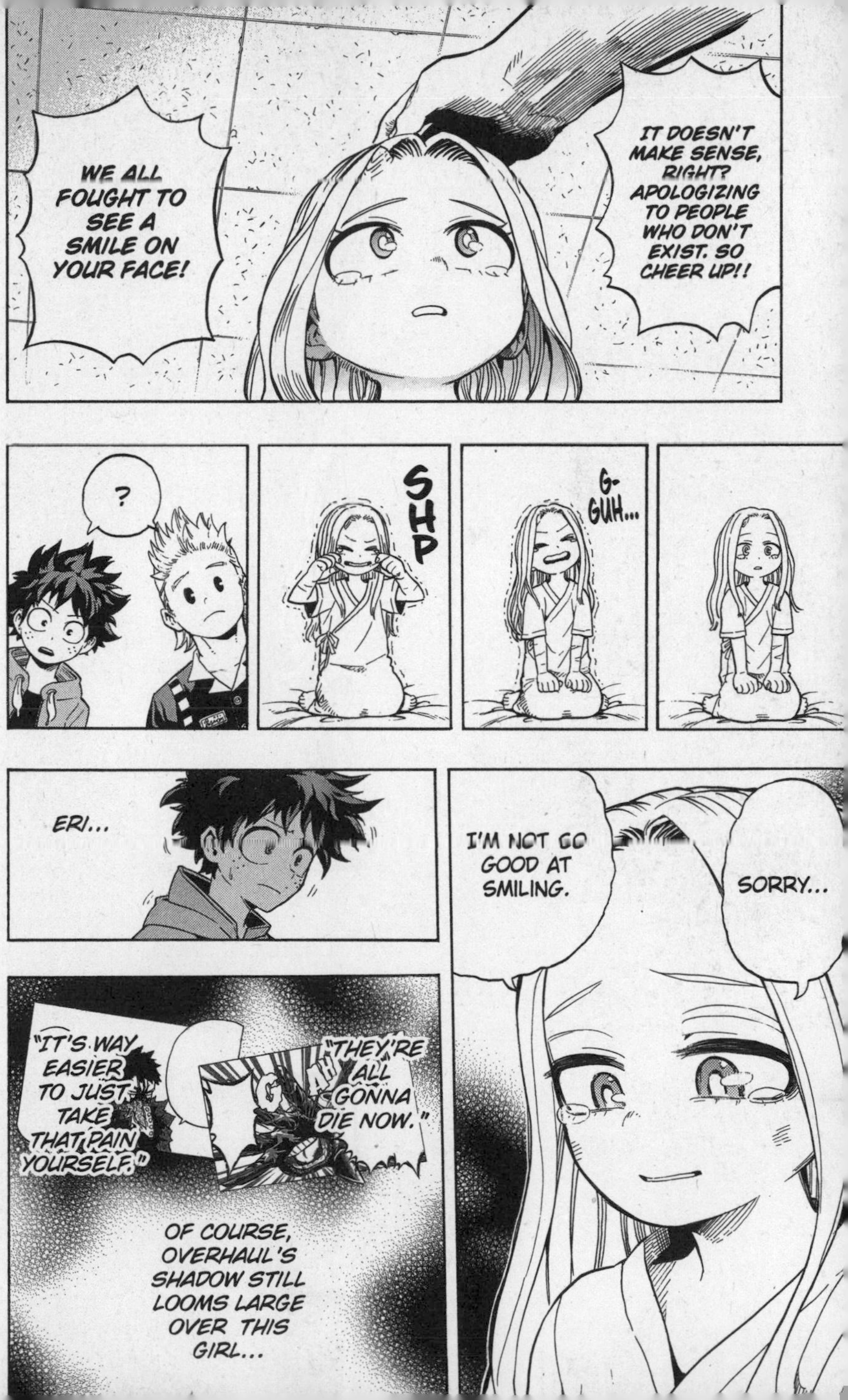
IT DOESN'T MAKE SENSE, RIGHT? APOLOGIZING TO PEOPLE WHO DON'T EXIST. SO CHEER UP!!
WE ALL FOUGHT TO SEE A SMILE ON YOUR FACE!
G-GUH...
SHP
?
SORRY...
I'M NOT SO GOOD AT SMILING.
ERI...
"THEY'RE ALL GONNA DIE NOW."
"IT'S WAY EASIER TO JUST TAKE THAT PAIN YOURSELF."
OF COURSE, OVERHAUL'S SHADOW STILL LOOMS LARGE OVER THIS GIRL...

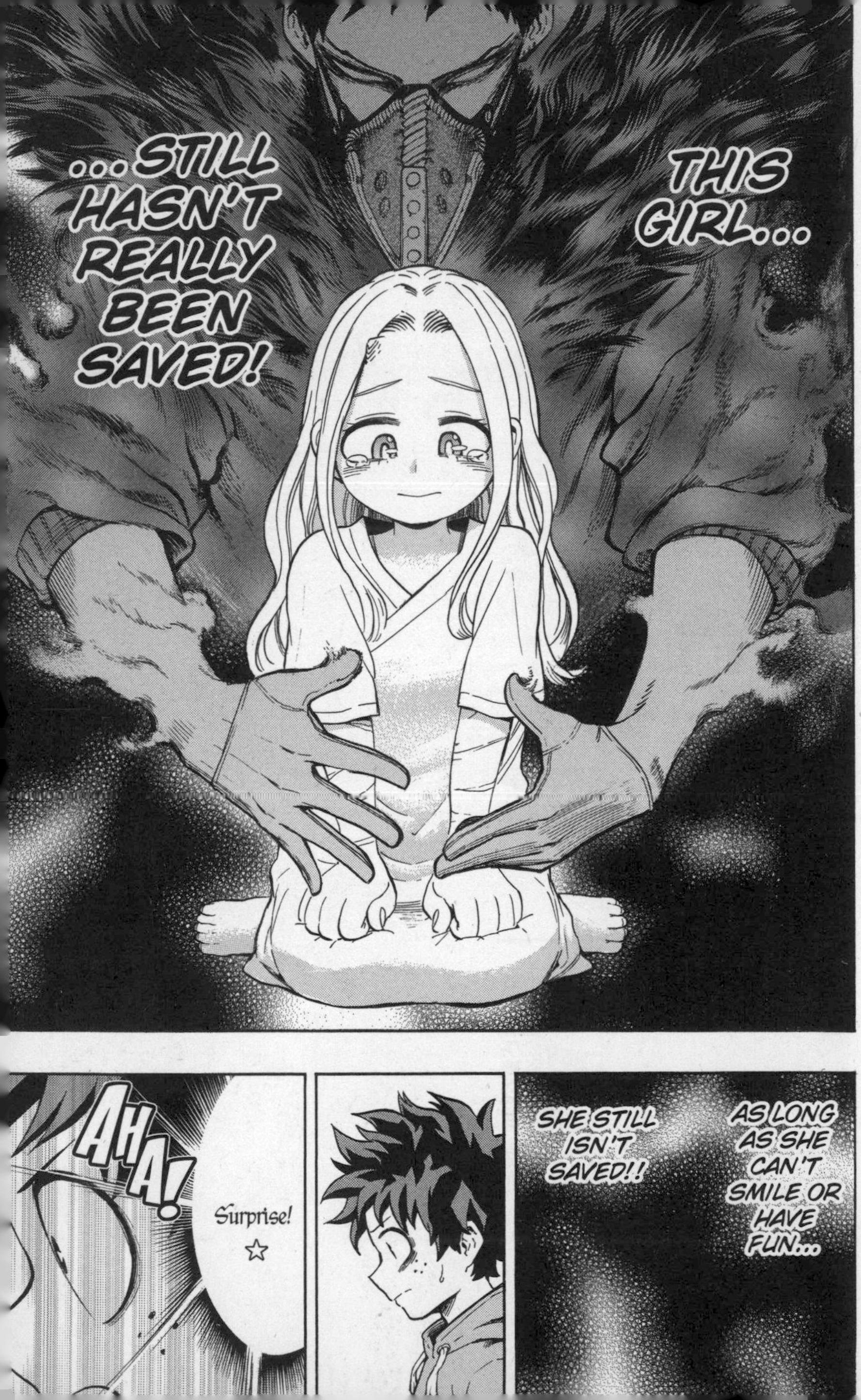
THIS GIRL...
...STILL HASN'T REALLY BEEN SAVED!
AS LONG AS SHE CAN'T SMILE OR HAVE FUN...
SHE STILL ISN'T SAVED!!
AHA!
Surprise! ☆

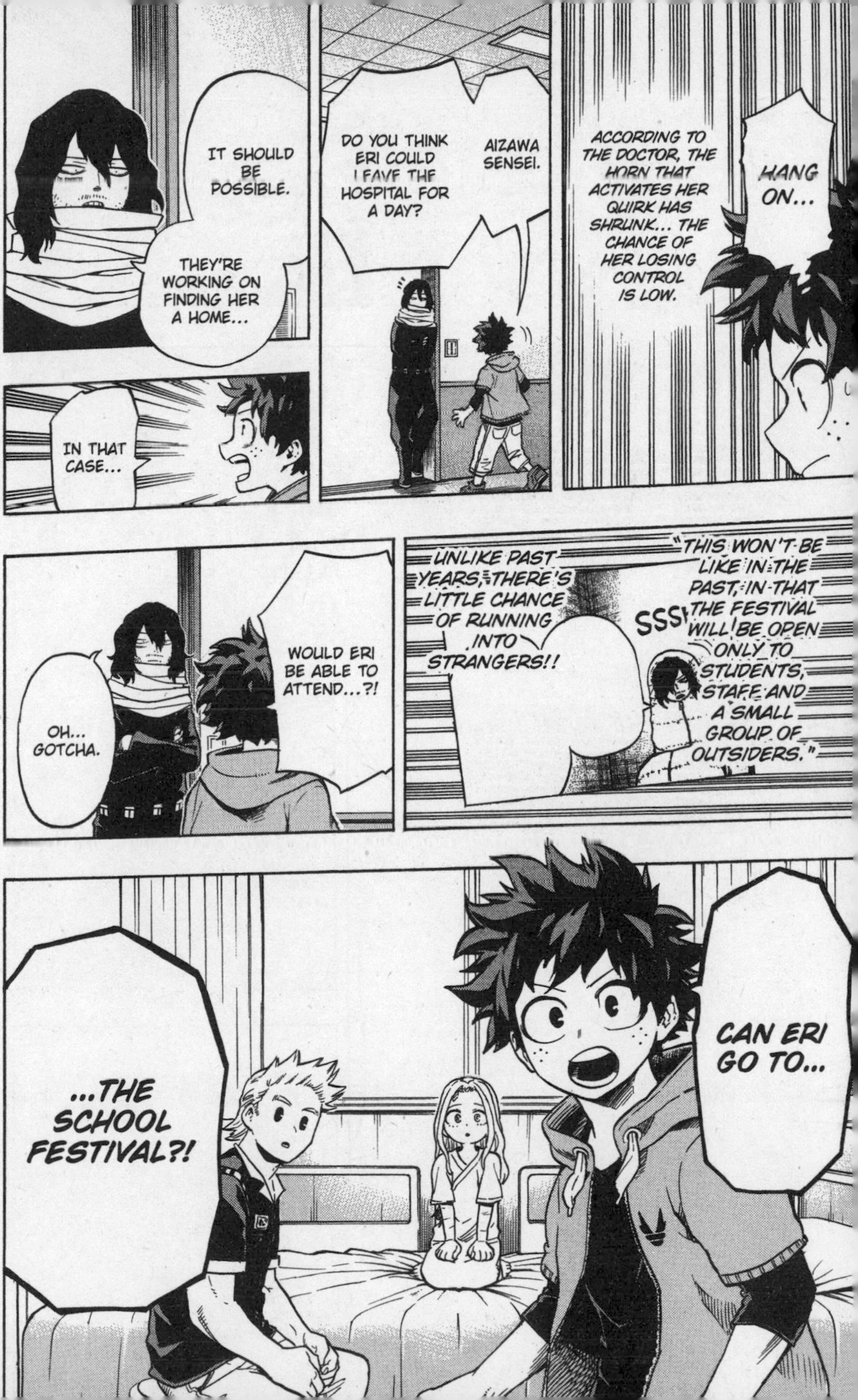
HANG ON...
ACCORDING TO THE DOCTOR, THE HORN THAT ACTIVATES HER QUIRK HAS SHRUNK... THE CHANCE OF HER LOSING CONTROL IS LOW.
AIZAWA SENSEI.
DO YOU THINK ERI COULD LEAVE THE HOSPITAL FOR A DAY?
IT SHOULD BE POSSIBLE.
THEY'RE WORKING ON FINDING HER A HOME...
IN THAT CASE...
"THIS WON'T BE LIKE IN THE PAST, IN THAT THE FESTIVAL WILL BE OPEN ONLY TO STUDENTS, STAFF AND A SMALL GROUP OF OUTSIDERS."
SSS
UNLIKE PAST YEARS, THERE'S LITTLE CHANCE OF RUNNING INTO STRANGERS!!
WOULD ERI BE ABLE TO ATTEND...?!
OH... GOTCHA.
CAN ERI GO TO...
...THE SCHOOL FESTIVAL?!

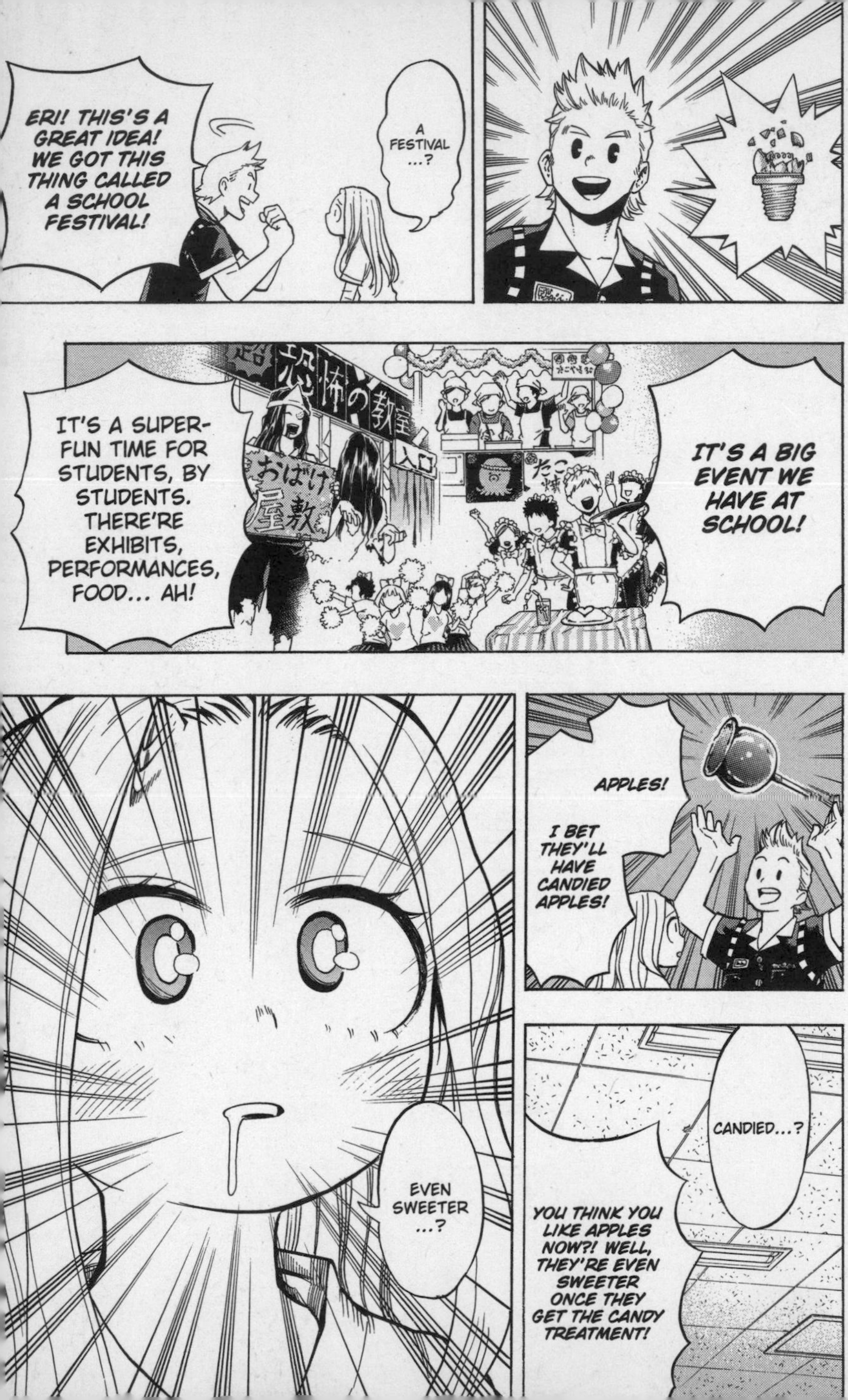
A FESTIVAL …?
ERI! THIS'S A GREAT IDEA! WE GOT THIS THING CALLED A SCHOOL FESTIVAL!
IT'S A BIG EVENT WE HAVE AT SCHOOL!
恐怖の教室
入口
たこ焼
おばけ屋敷
IT'S A SUPER-FUN TIME FOR STUDENTS, BY STUDENTS. THERE'RE EXHIBITS, PERFORMANCES, FOOD… AH!
APPLES!
I BET THEY'LL HAVE CANDIED APPLES!
CANDIED…?
YOU THINK YOU LIKE APPLES NOW?! WELL, THEY'RE EVEN SWEETER ONCE THEY GET THE CANDY TREATMENT!
EVEN SWEETER …?

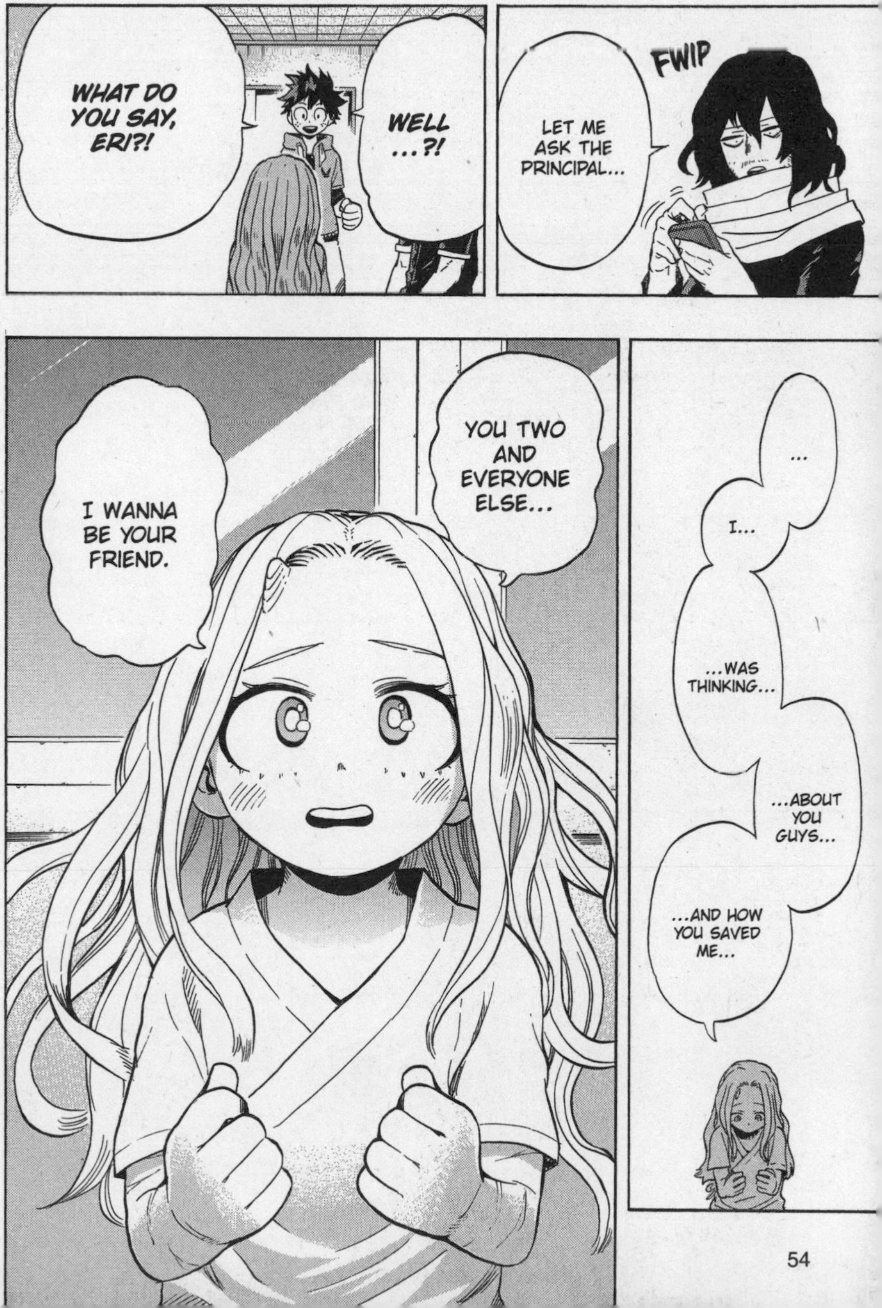
FWIP
LET ME ASK THE PRINCIPAL...
WELL ...?!
WHAT DO YOU SAY, ERI?!
...
I...
...WAS THINKING...
...ABOUT YOU GUYS...
...AND HOW YOU SAVED ME...
YOU TWO AND EVERYONE ELSE...
I WANNA BE YOUR FRIEND.

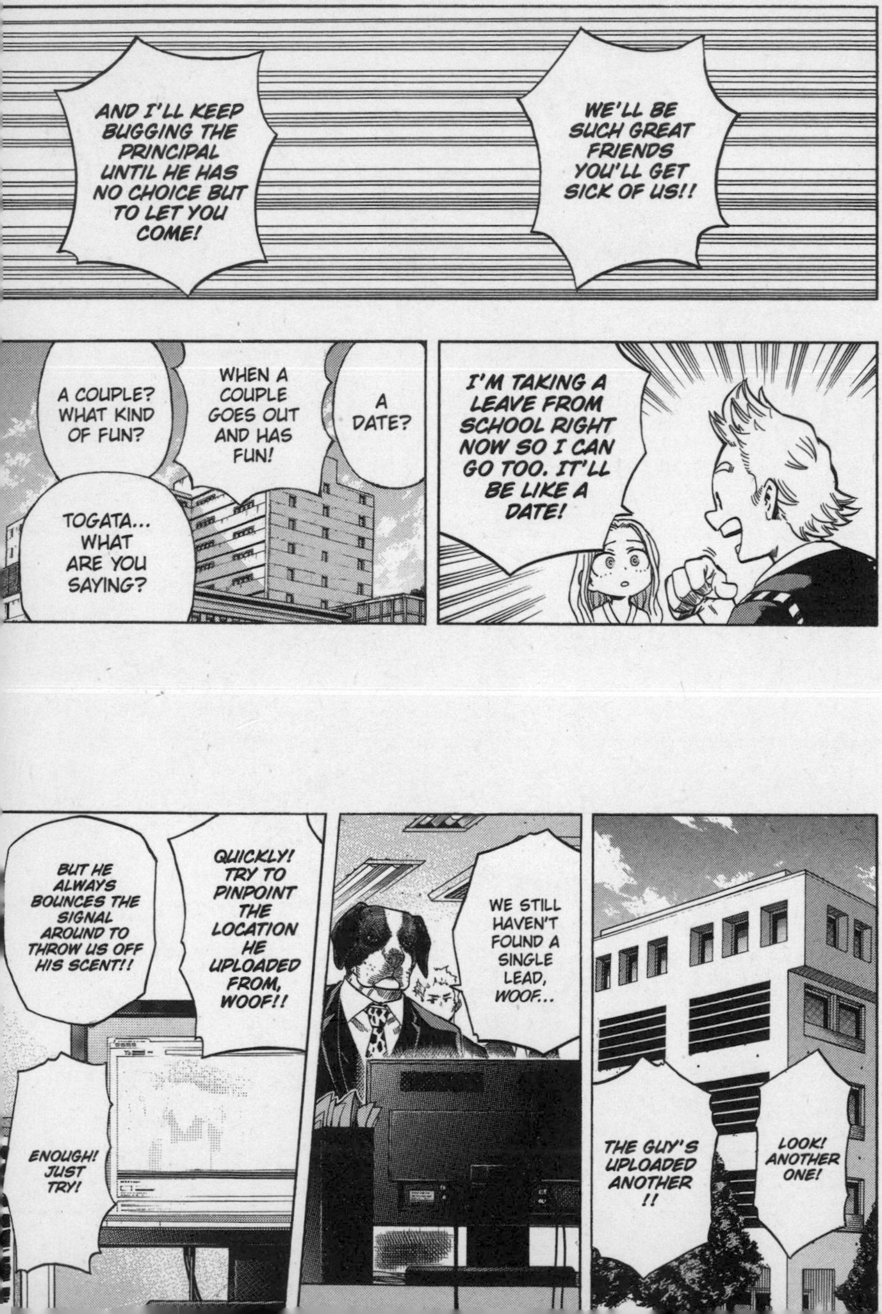
WE'LL BE SUCH GREAT FRIENDS YOU'LL GET SICK OF US!!
AND I'LL KEEP BUGGING THE PRINCIPAL UNTIL HE HAS NO CHOICE BUT TO LET YOU COME!
I'M TAKING A LEAVE FROM SCHOOL RIGHT NOW SO I CAN GO TOO. IT'LL BE LIKE A DATE!
A DATE?
WHEN A COUPLE GOES OUT AND HAS FUN!
A COUPLE? WHAT KIND OF FUN?
TOGATA... WHAT ARE YOU SAYING?
LOOK! ANOTHER ONE!
THE GUY'S UPLOADED ANOTHER!!
WE STILL HAVEN'T FOUND A SINGLE LEAD, WOOF...
QUICKLY! TRY TO PINPOINT THE LOCATION HE UPLOADED FROM, WOOF!!
BUT HE ALWAYS BOUNCES THE SIGNAL AROUND TO THROW US OFF HIS SCENT!!
ENOUGH! JUST TRY!

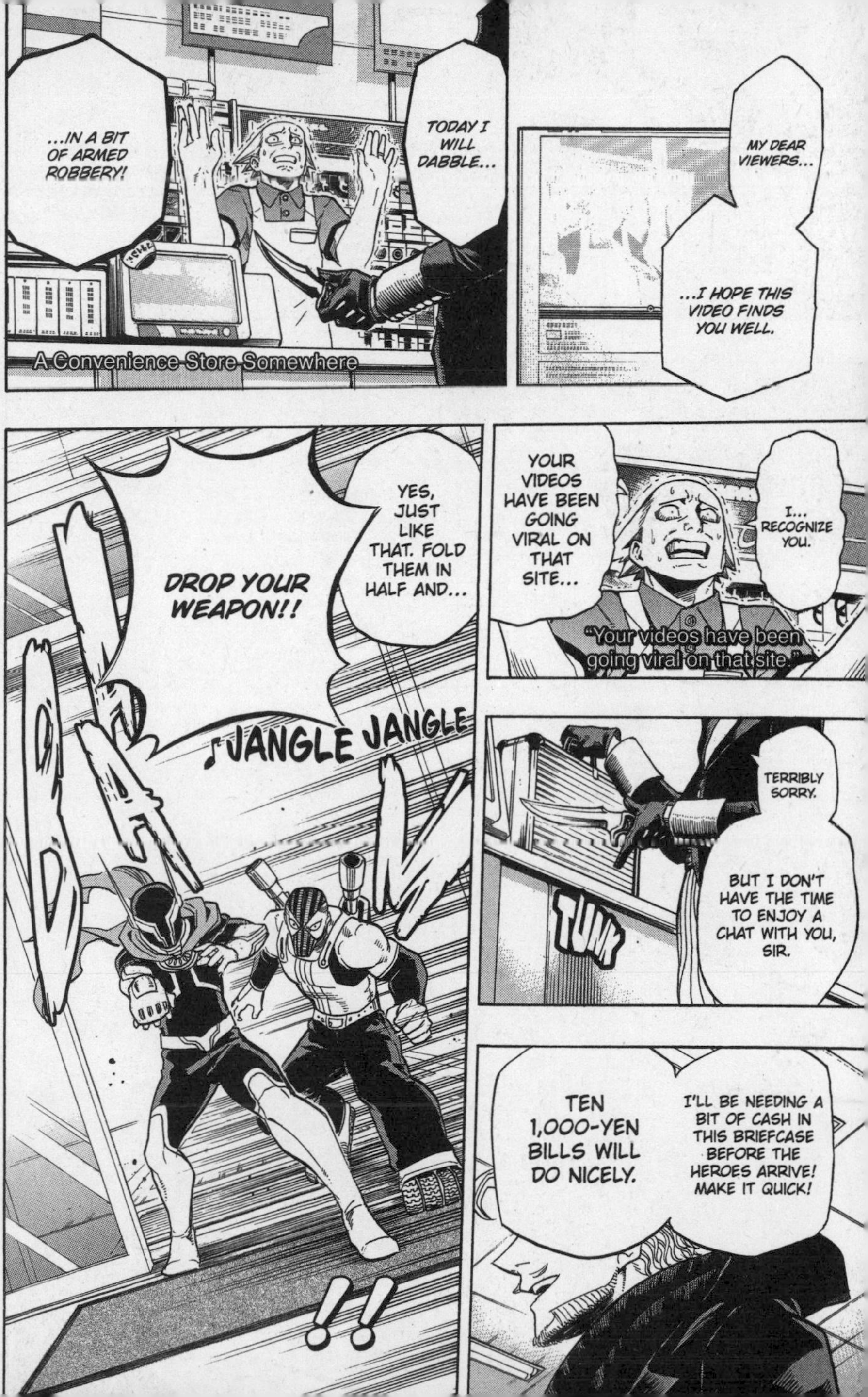
MY DEAR VIEWERS...
...I HOPE THIS VIDEO FINDS YOU WELL.
TODAY I WILL DABBLE...
...IN A BIT OF ARMED ROBBERY!
A Convenience Store Somewhere
I... RECOGNIZE YOU.
YOUR VIDEOS HAVE BEEN GOING VIRAL ON THAT SITE...
"Your videos have been going viral on that site."
TERRIBLY SORRY.
BUT I DON'T HAVE THE TIME TO ENJOY A CHAT WITH YOU, SIR.
TUNK
I'LL BE NEEDING A BIT OF CASH IN THIS BRIEFCASE BEFORE THE HEROES ARRIVE! MAKE IT QUICK!
TEN 1,000-YEN BILLS WILL DO NICELY.
YES, JUST LIKE THAT. FOLD THEM IN HALF AND...
DROP YOUR WEAPON!!
JANGLE JANGLE
!!

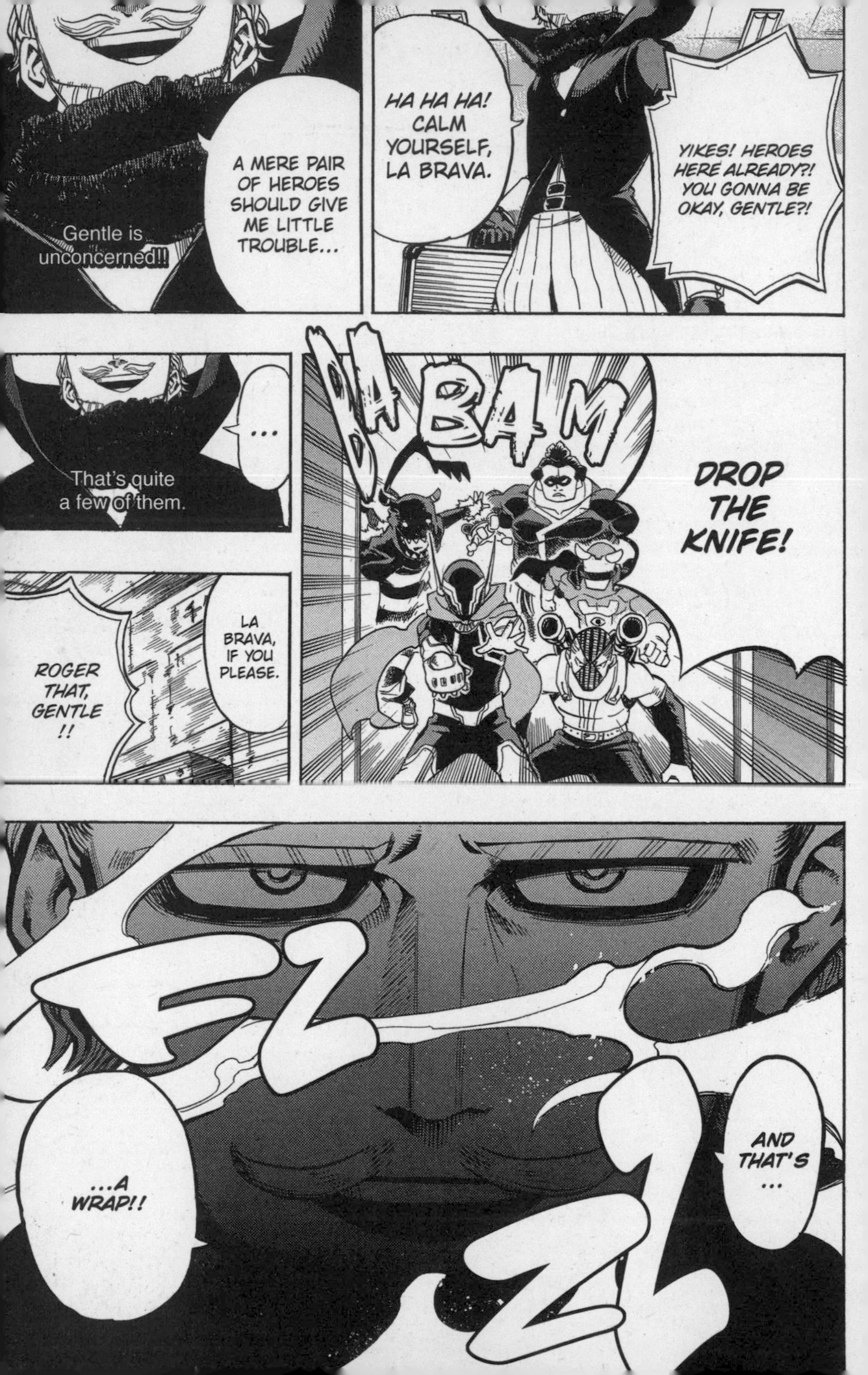
YIKES! HEROES HERE ALREADY?! YOU GONNA BE OKAY, GENTLE?!
HA HA HA! CALM YOURSELF, LA BRAVA.
A MERE PAIR OF HEROES SHOULD GIVE ME LITTLE TROUBLE...
Gentle is unconcerned!!
DABAM
DROP THE KNIFE!
...
That's quite a few of them.
LA BRAVA, IF YOU PLEASE.
ROGER THAT, GENTLE!!
FZZZ
AND THAT'S...
...A WRAP!!

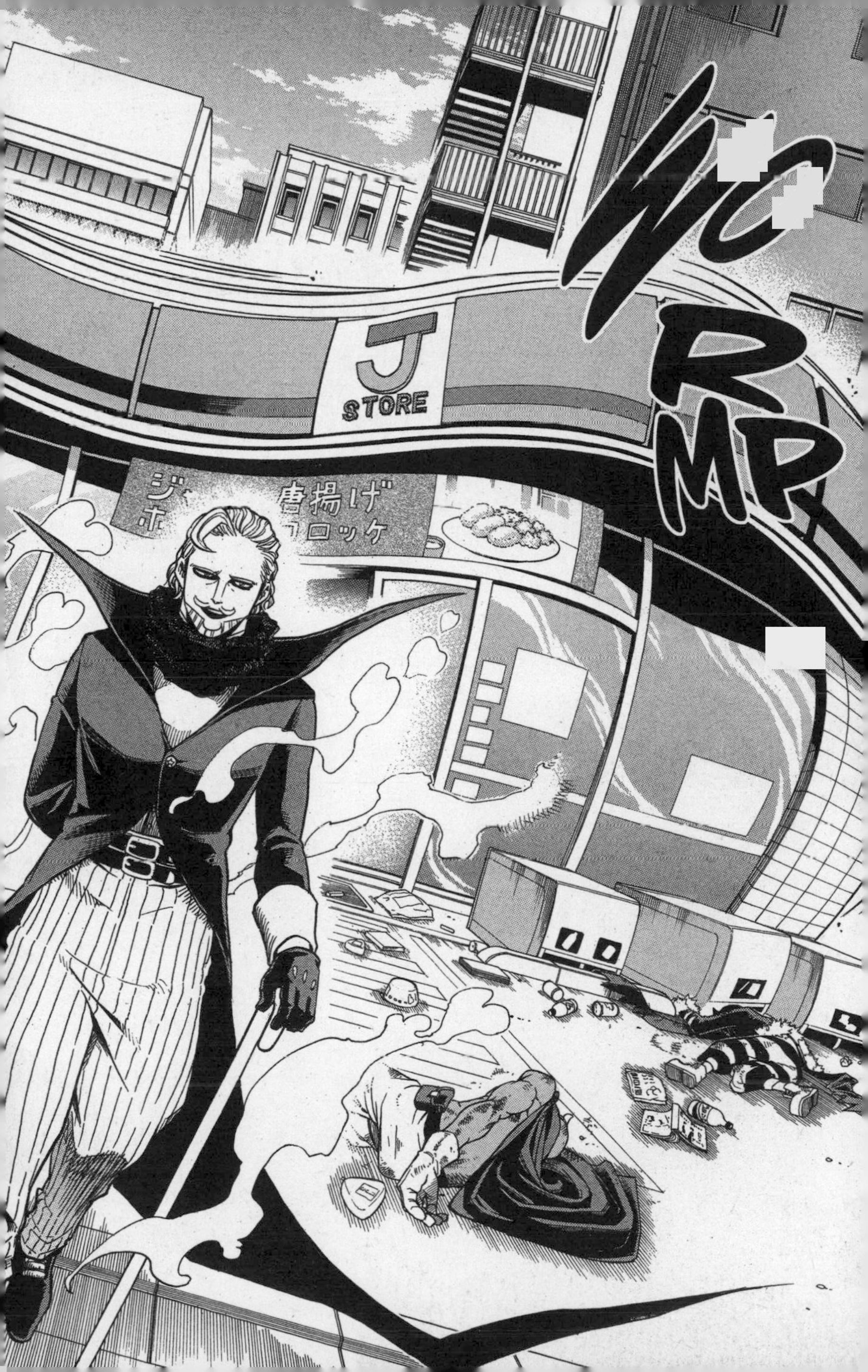
J
STORE
唐揚げ
コロッケ

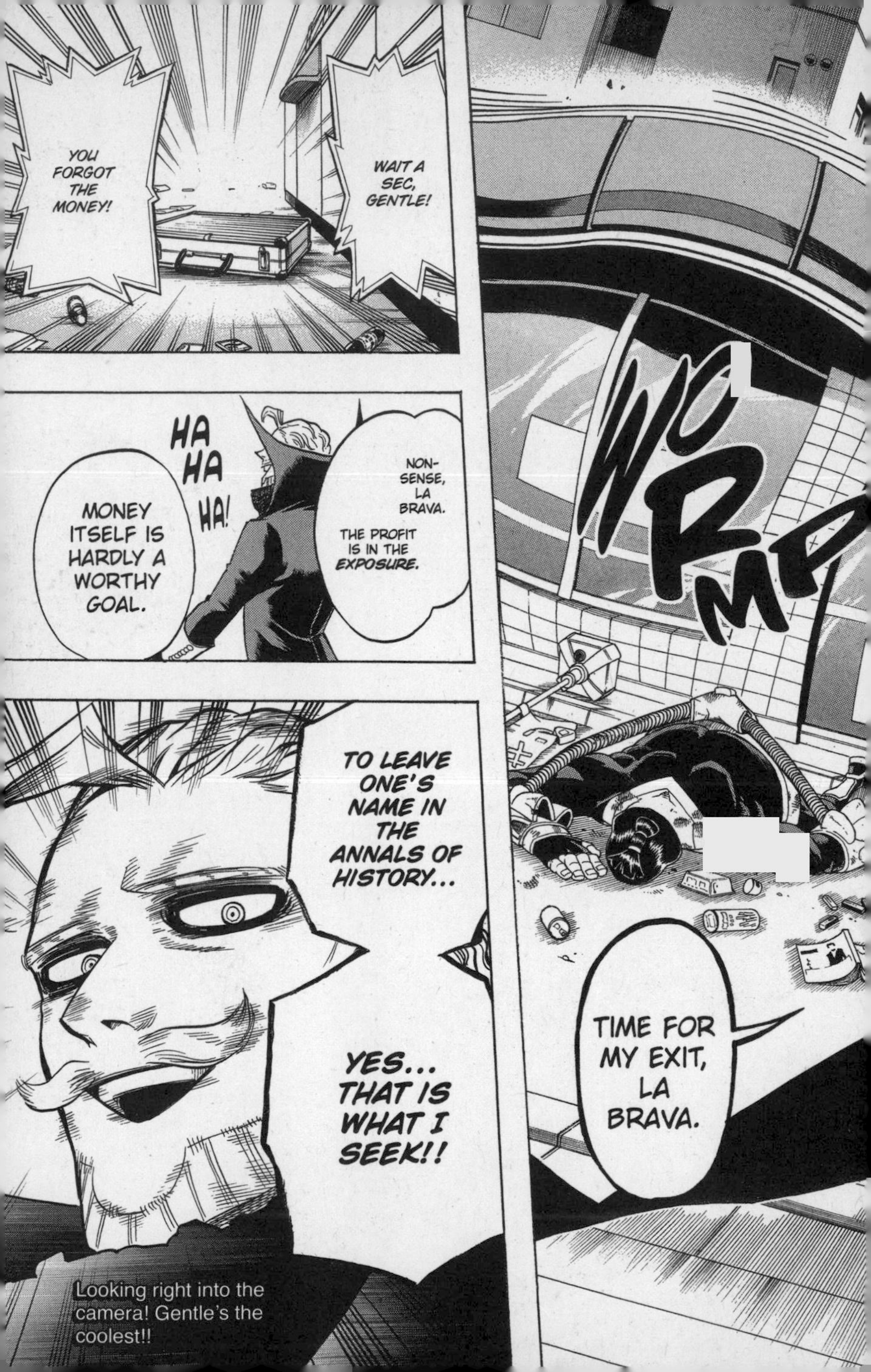
WORMP
TIME FOR MY EXIT, LA BRAVA.
WAIT A SEC, GENTLE!
YOU FORGOT THE MONEY!
NON-SENSE, LA BRAVA.
THE PROFIT IS IN THE *EXPOSURE.*
HA HA HA!
MONEY ITSELF IS HARDLY A WORTHY GOAL.
TO LEAVE ONE'S NAME IN THE ANNALS OF HISTORY...
YES... THAT IS WHAT I SEEK!!
Looking right into the camera! Gentle's the coolest!!

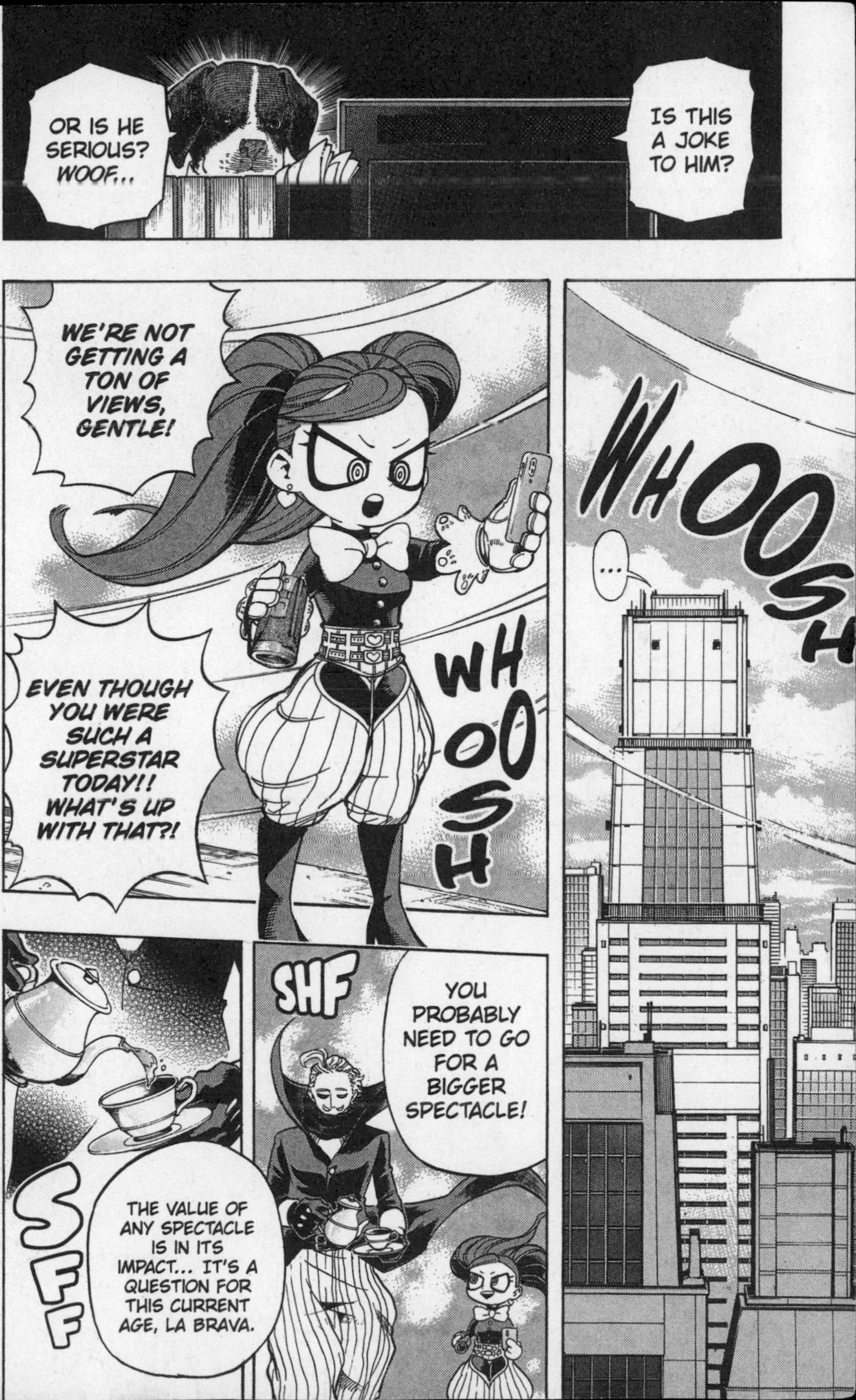
IS THIS A JOKE TO HIM?
OR IS HE SERIOUS? WOOF...
WHOOSH
...
WE'RE NOT GETTING A TON OF VIEWS, GENTLE!
EVEN THOUGH YOU WERE SUCH A SUPERSTAR TODAY!! WHAT'S UP WITH THAT?!
WHOOSH
SHF
YOU PROBABLY NEED TO GO FOR A BIGGER SPECTACLE!
SFF
THE VALUE OF ANY SPECTACLE IS IN ITS IMPACT... IT'S A QUESTION FOR THIS CURRENT AGE, LA BRAVA.

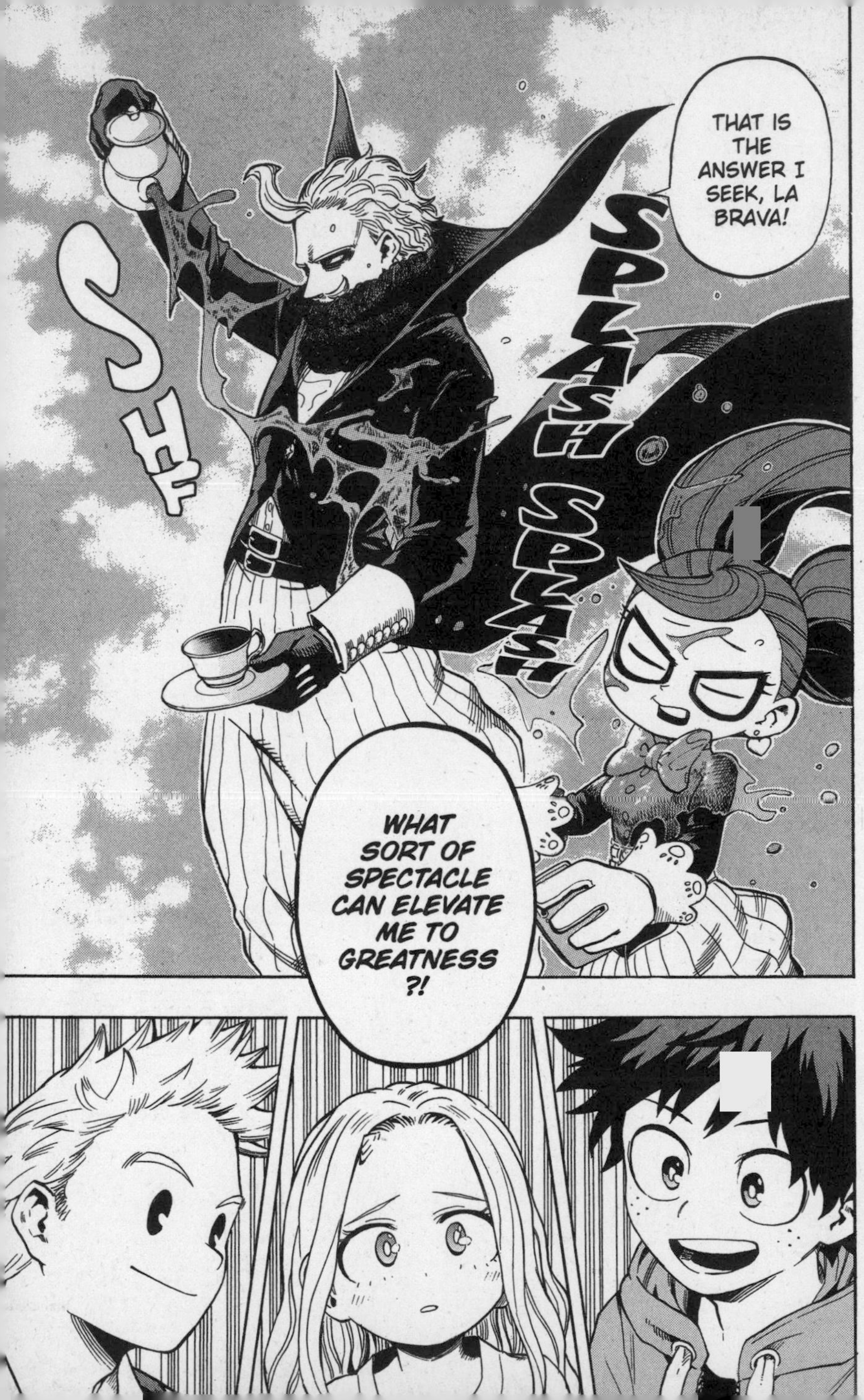
THAT IS THE ANSWER I SEEK, LA BRAVA!
SPLASH SPLASH
SHF
WHAT SORT OF SPECTACLE CAN ELEVATE ME TO GREATNESS ?!

Apple

ERI (6)

STYLISH LITTLE ONE

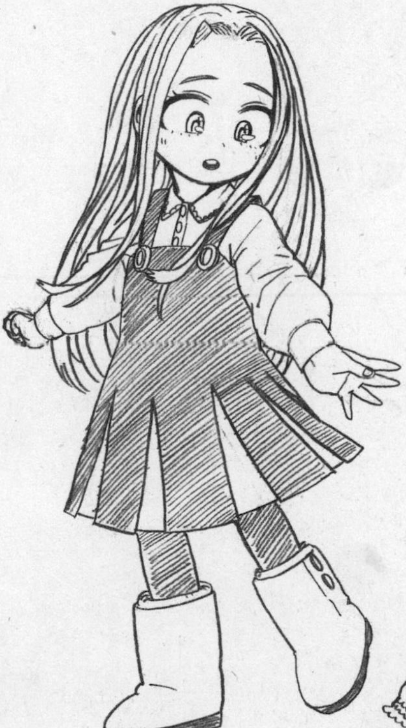

Birthday: 12/21
Height: 110 cm
Favorite Thing: Apples

BEHIND THE SCENES

I didn't manage to include the whole sequence of events, but in light of the visit in this chapter... Aizawa bought Eri some new clothes for going out and about, but the sweater was really unfashionable, so her nurse picked out something more stylish. Good job, Nurse. Walk it off, Aizawa.

Since she loves apples, I'd like to have her interact with Tokoyami at some point (who also loves apples).

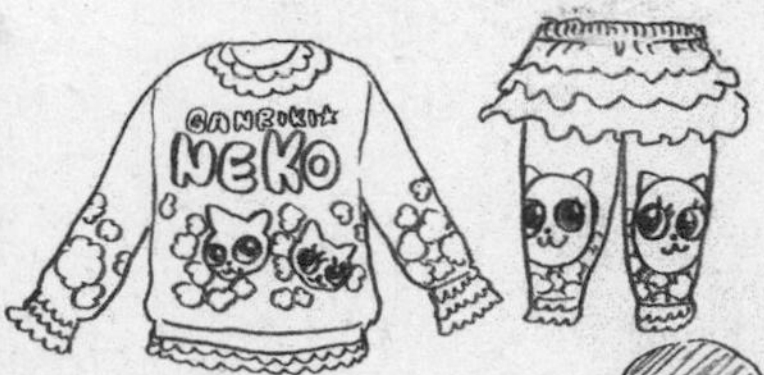
NEKO

For reference: extremely unfashionable sweater (with bottoms)

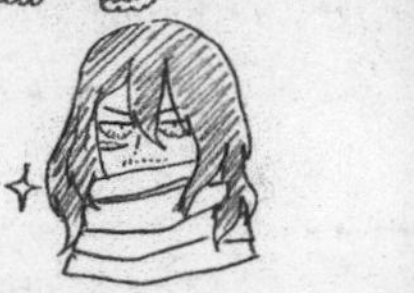

MyHeroAcademia

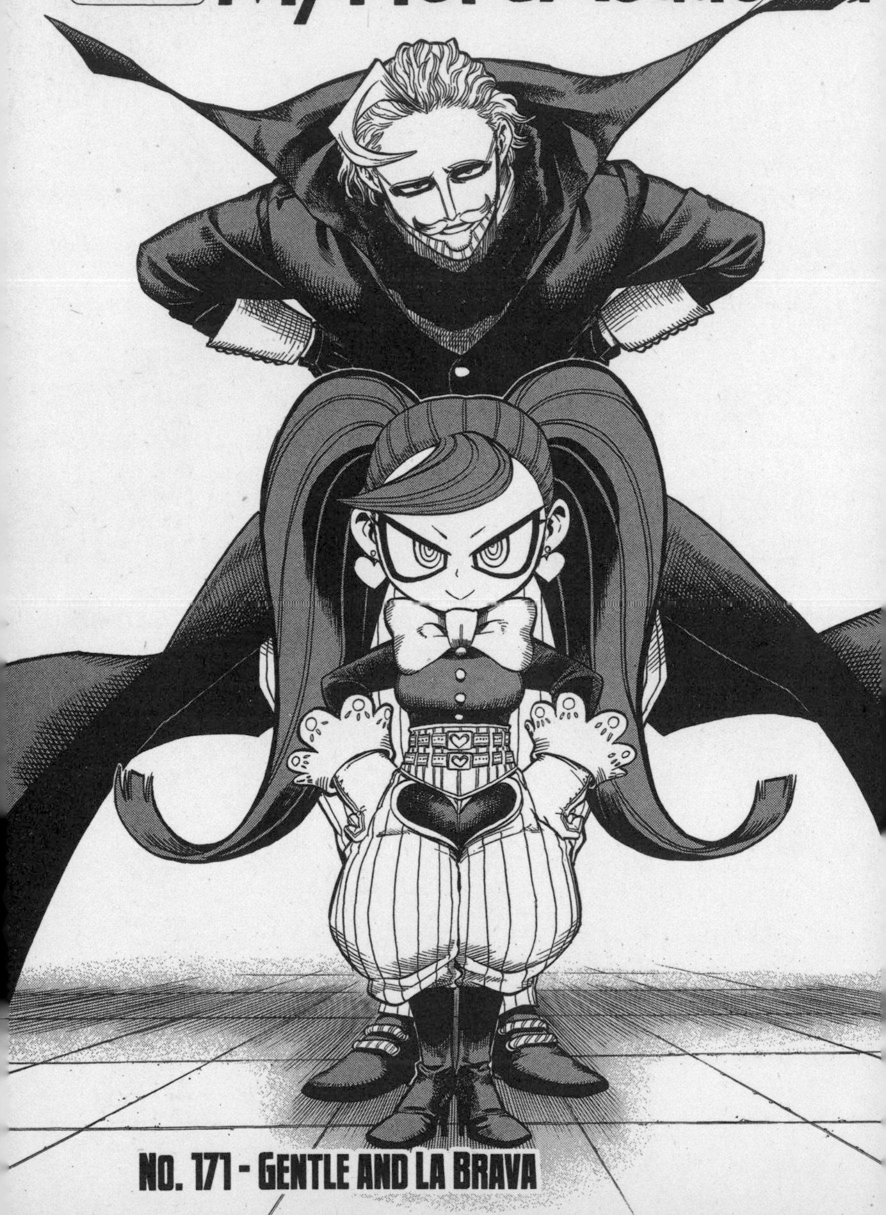

No. 171 - Gentle and La Brava

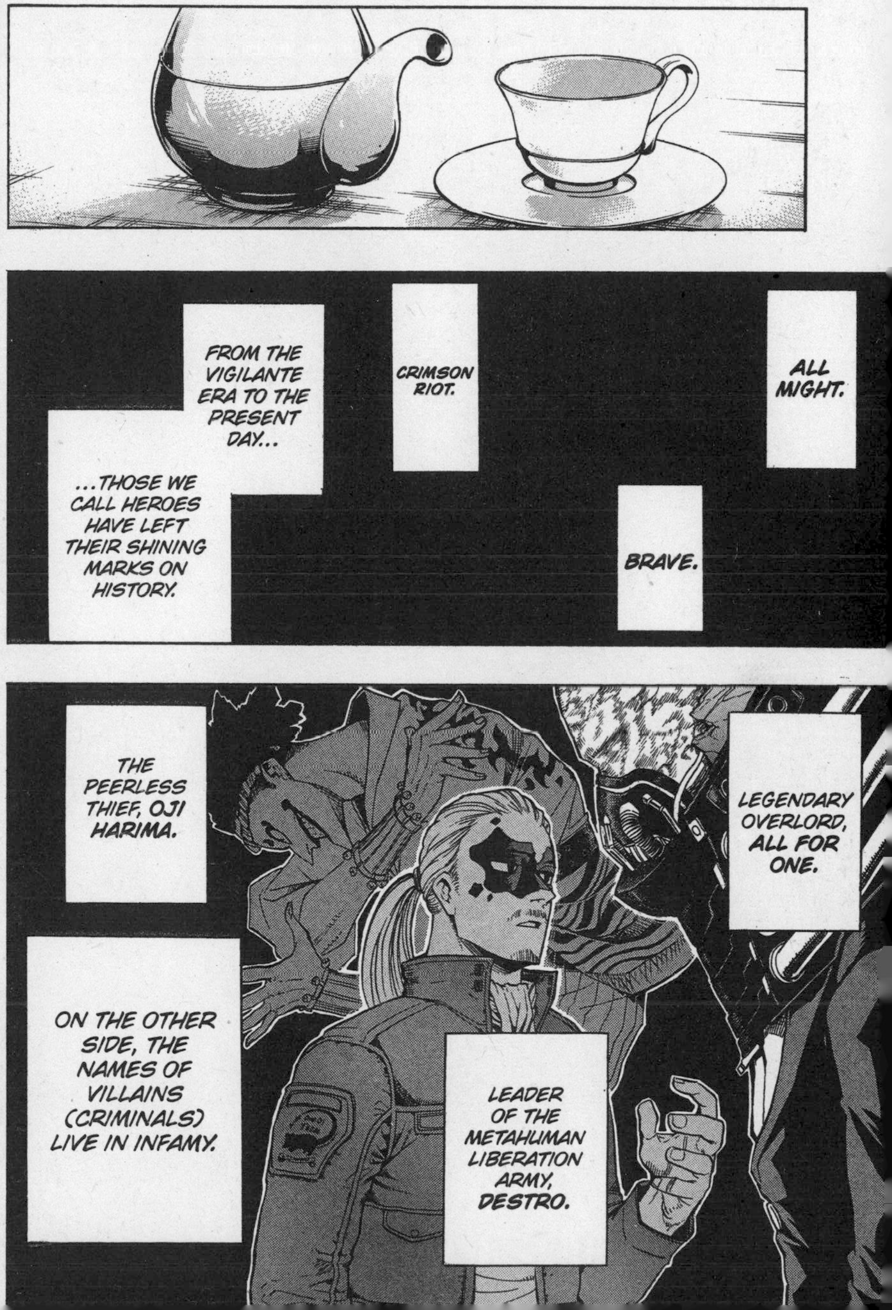
ALL MIGHT.
CRIMSON RIOT.
FROM THE VIGILANTE ERA TO THE PRESENT DAY...
BRAVE.
...THOSE WE CALL HEROES HAVE LEFT THEIR SHINING MARKS ON HISTORY.
LEGENDARY OVERLORD, ALL FOR ONE.
THE PEERLESS THIEF, OJI HARIMA.
LEADER OF THE METAHUMAN LIBERATION ARMY, DESTRO.
ON THE OTHER SIDE, THE NAMES OF VILLAINS (CRIMINALS) LIVE IN INFAMY.

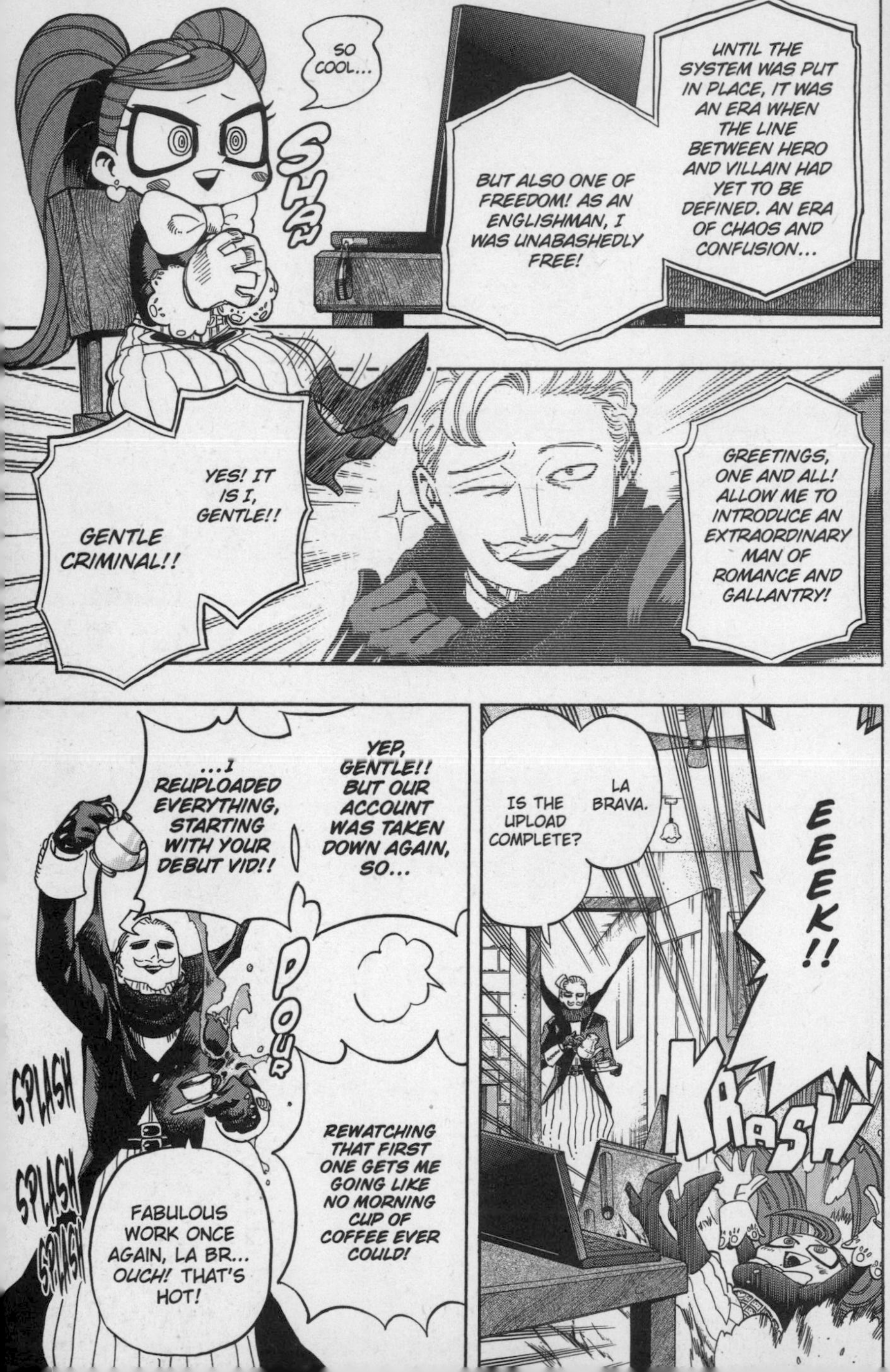
UNTIL THE SYSTEM WAS PUT IN PLACE, IT WAS AN ERA WHEN THE LINE BETWEEN HERO AND VILLAIN HAD YET TO BE DEFINED. AN ERA OF CHAOS AND CONFUSION...
BUT ALSO ONE OF FREEDOM! AS AN ENGLISHMAN, I WAS UNABASHEDLY FREE!
SO COOL...
SHAH
GREETINGS, ONE AND ALL! ALLOW ME TO INTRODUCE AN EXTRAORDINARY MAN OF ROMANCE AND GALLANTRY!
YES! IT IS I, GENTLE!!
GENTLE CRIMINAL!!
LA BRAVA.
IS THE UPLOAD COMPLETE?
EEEK!!
KRASH
YEP, GENTLE!! BUT OUR ACCOUNT WAS TAKEN DOWN AGAIN, SO...
...I REUPLOADED EVERYTHING, STARTING WITH YOUR DEBUT VID!!
POUR
REWATCHING THAT FIRST ONE GETS ME GOING LIKE NO MORNING CUP OF COFFEE EVER COULD!
FABULOUS WORK ONCE AGAIN, LA BR... OUCH! THAT'S HOT!
SPLASH
SPLASH
SPLASH

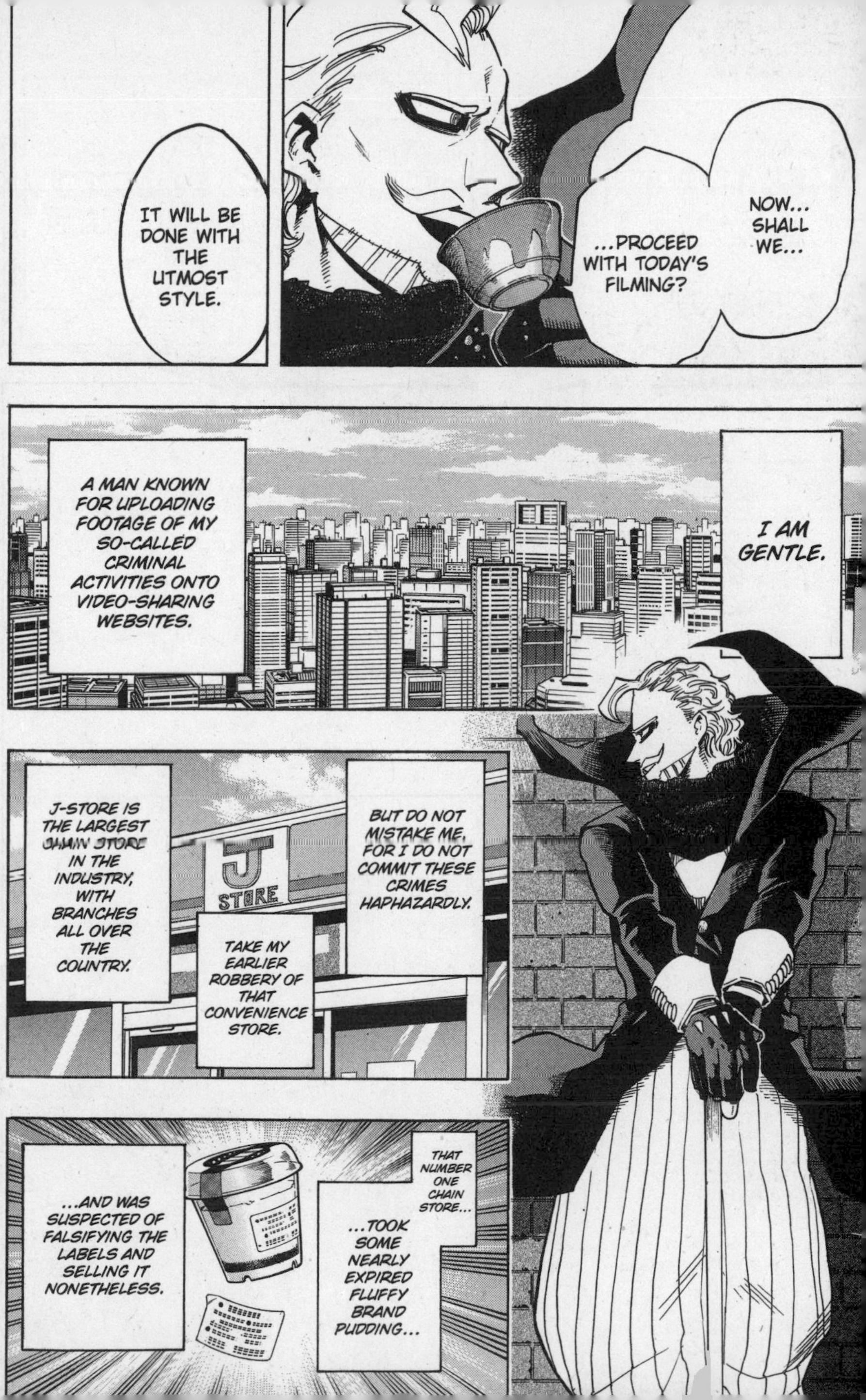
NOW... SHALL WE...
...PROCEED WITH TODAY'S FILMING?
IT WILL BE DONE WITH THE UTMOST STYLE.
I AM GENTLE.
A MAN KNOWN FOR UPLOADING FOOTAGE OF MY SO-CALLED CRIMINAL ACTIVITIES ONTO VIDEO-SHARING WEBSITES.
BUT DO NOT MISTAKE ME, FOR I DO NOT COMMIT THESE CRIMES HAPHAZARDLY.
TAKE MY EARLIER ROBBERY OF THAT CONVENIENCE STORE.
J-STORE IS THE LARGEST CHAIN STORE IN THE INDUSTRY, WITH BRANCHES ALL OVER THE COUNTRY.
J STORE
THAT NUMBER ONE CHAIN STORE...
...TOOK SOME NEARLY EXPIRED FLUFFY BRAND PUDDING...
...AND WAS SUSPECTED OF FALSIFYING THE LABELS AND SELLING IT NONETHELESS.

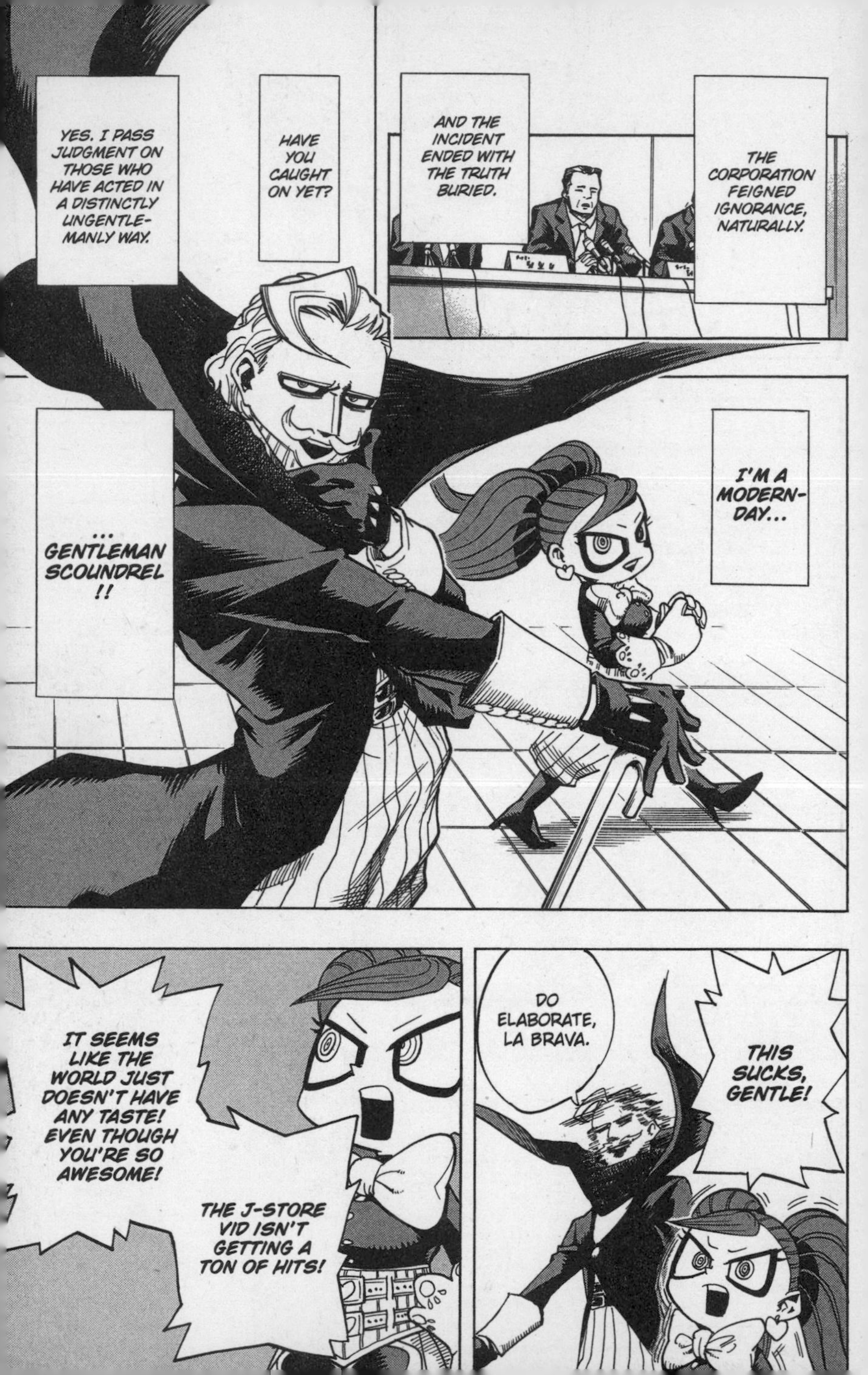
THE CORPORATION FEIGNED IGNORANCE, NATURALLY.
AND THE INCIDENT ENDED WITH THE TRUTH BURIED.
HAVE YOU CAUGHT ON YET?
YES. I PASS JUDGMENT ON THOSE WHO HAVE ACTED IN A DISTINCTLY UNGENTLE-MANLY WAY.
I'M A MODERN-DAY...
...GENTLEMAN SCOUNDREL !!
THIS SUCKS, GENTLE!
DO ELABORATE, LA BRAVA.
IT SEEMS LIKE THE WORLD JUST DOESN'T HAVE ANY TASTE! EVEN THOUGH YOU'RE SO AWESOME!
THE J-STORE VID ISN'T GETTING A TON OF HITS!

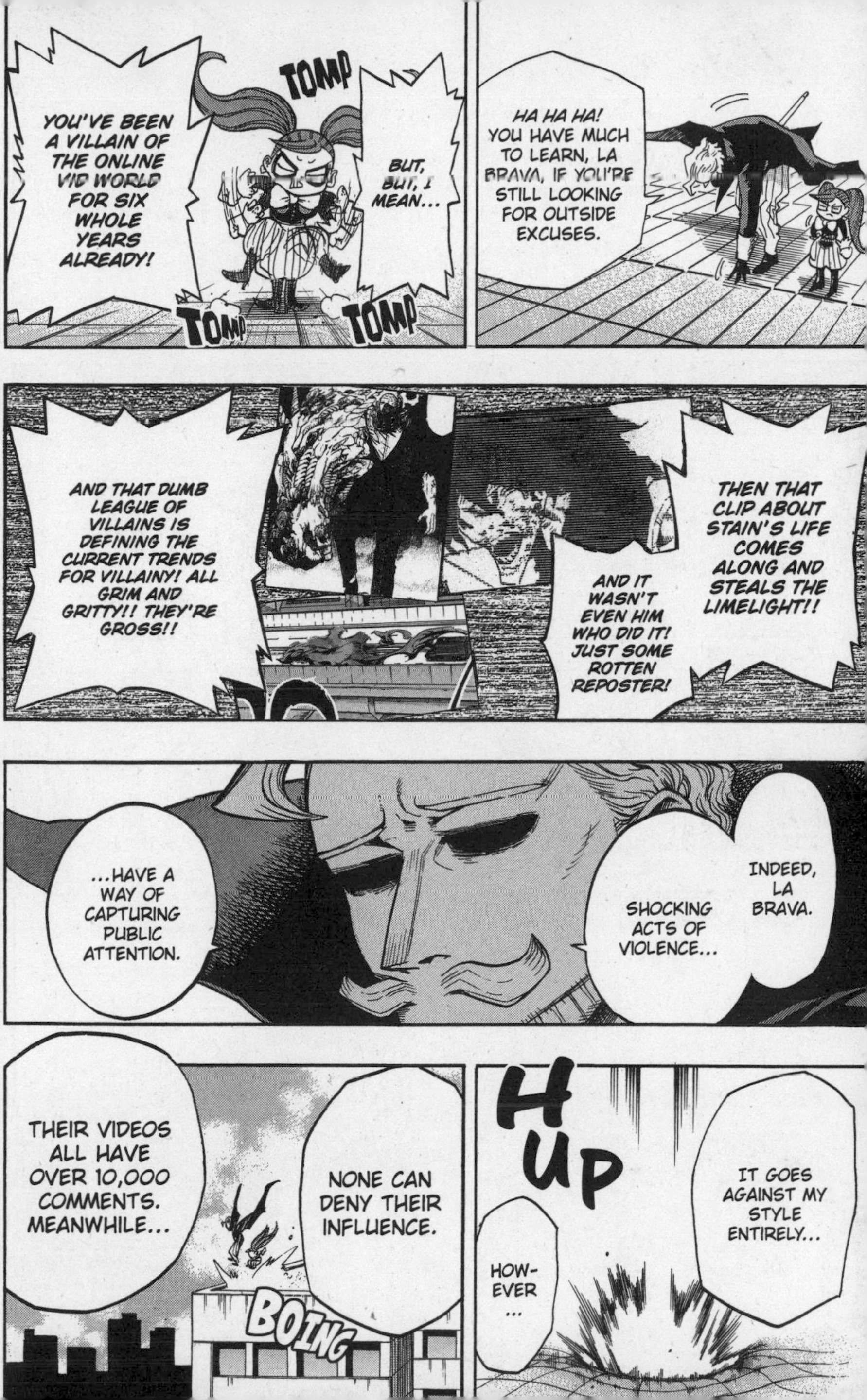
HA HA HA! YOU HAVE MUCH TO LEARN, LA BRAVA, IF YOU'RE STILL LOOKING FOR OUTSIDE EXCUSES.
TOMP
BUT, BUT, I MEAN...
YOU'VE BEEN A VILLAIN OF THE ONLINE VID WORLD FOR SIX WHOLE YEARS ALREADY!
TOMP
TOMP
THEN THAT CLIP ABOUT STAIN'S LIFE COMES ALONG AND STEALS THE LIMELIGHT!!
AND IT WASN'T EVEN HIM WHO DID IT! JUST SOME ROTTEN REPOSTER!
AND THAT DUMB LEAGUE OF VILLAINS IS DEFINING THE CURRENT TRENDS FOR VILLAINY! ALL GRIM AND GRITTY!! THEY'RE GROSS!!
INDEED, LA BRAVA.
SHOCKING ACTS OF VIOLENCE...
...HAVE A WAY OF CAPTURING PUBLIC ATTENTION.
HUP
IT GOES AGAINST MY STYLE ENTIRELY...
HOW-EVER...
NONE CAN DENY THEIR INFLUENCE.
THEIR VIDEOS ALL HAVE OVER 10,000 COMMENTS. MEANWHILE...
BOING

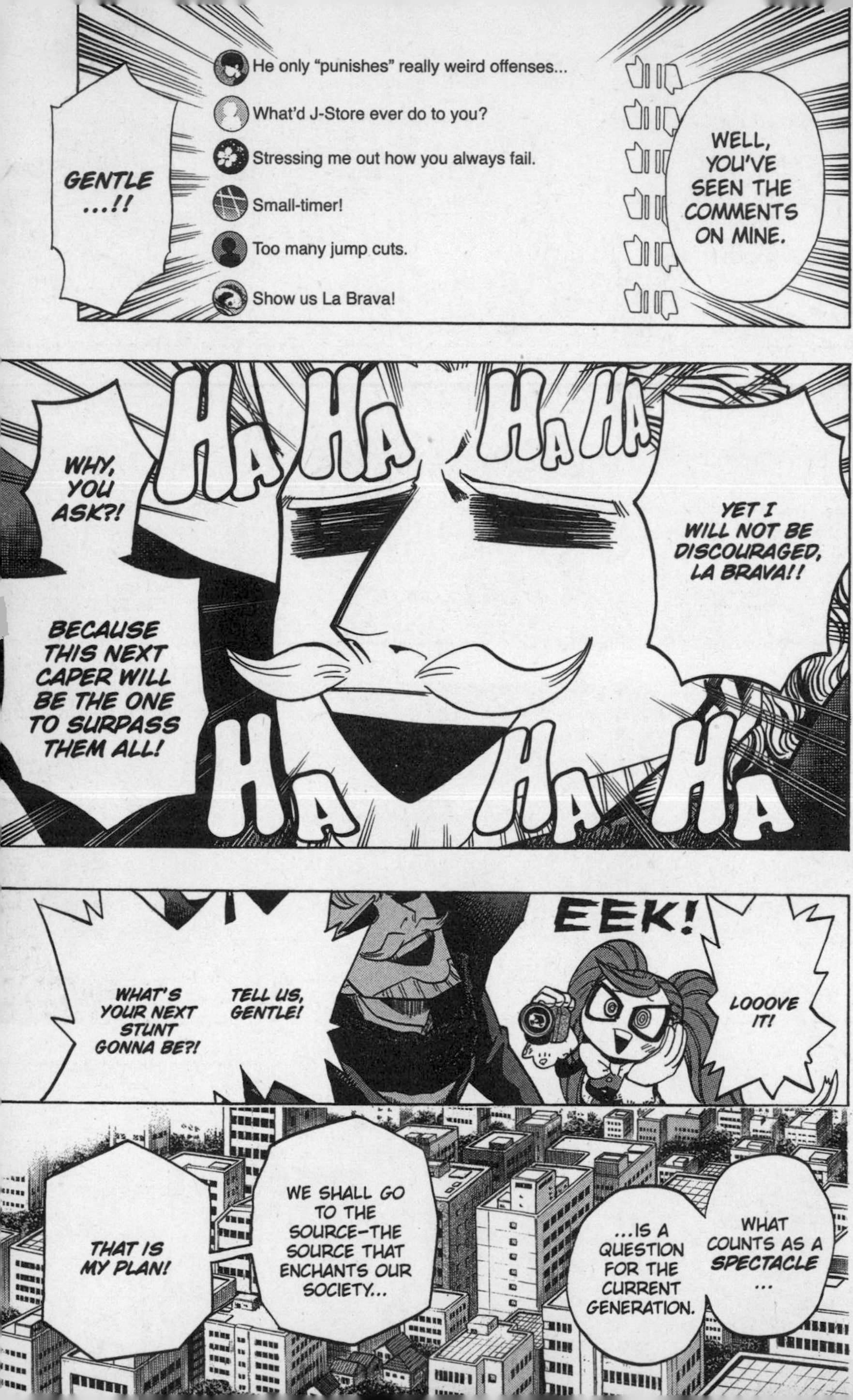
WELL, YOU'VE SEEN THE COMMENTS ON MINE.
He only "punishes" really weird offenses...
What'd J-Store ever do to you?
Stressing me out how you always fail.
Small-timer!
Too many jump cuts.
Show us La Brava!
GENTLE ...!!
YET I WILL NOT BE DISCOURAGED, LA BRAVA!!
HA HA HA HA
WHY, YOU ASK?!
BECAUSE THIS NEXT CAPER WILL BE THE ONE TO SURPASS THEM ALL!
HA HA HA
EEK!
LOOOVE IT!
TELL US, GENTLE!
WHAT'S YOUR NEXT STUNT GONNA BE?!
WHAT COUNTS AS A SPECTACLE ...
...IS A QUESTION FOR THE CURRENT GENERATION.
WE SHALL GO TO THE SOURCE—THE SOURCE THAT ENCHANTS OUR SOCIETY...
THAT IS MY PLAN!

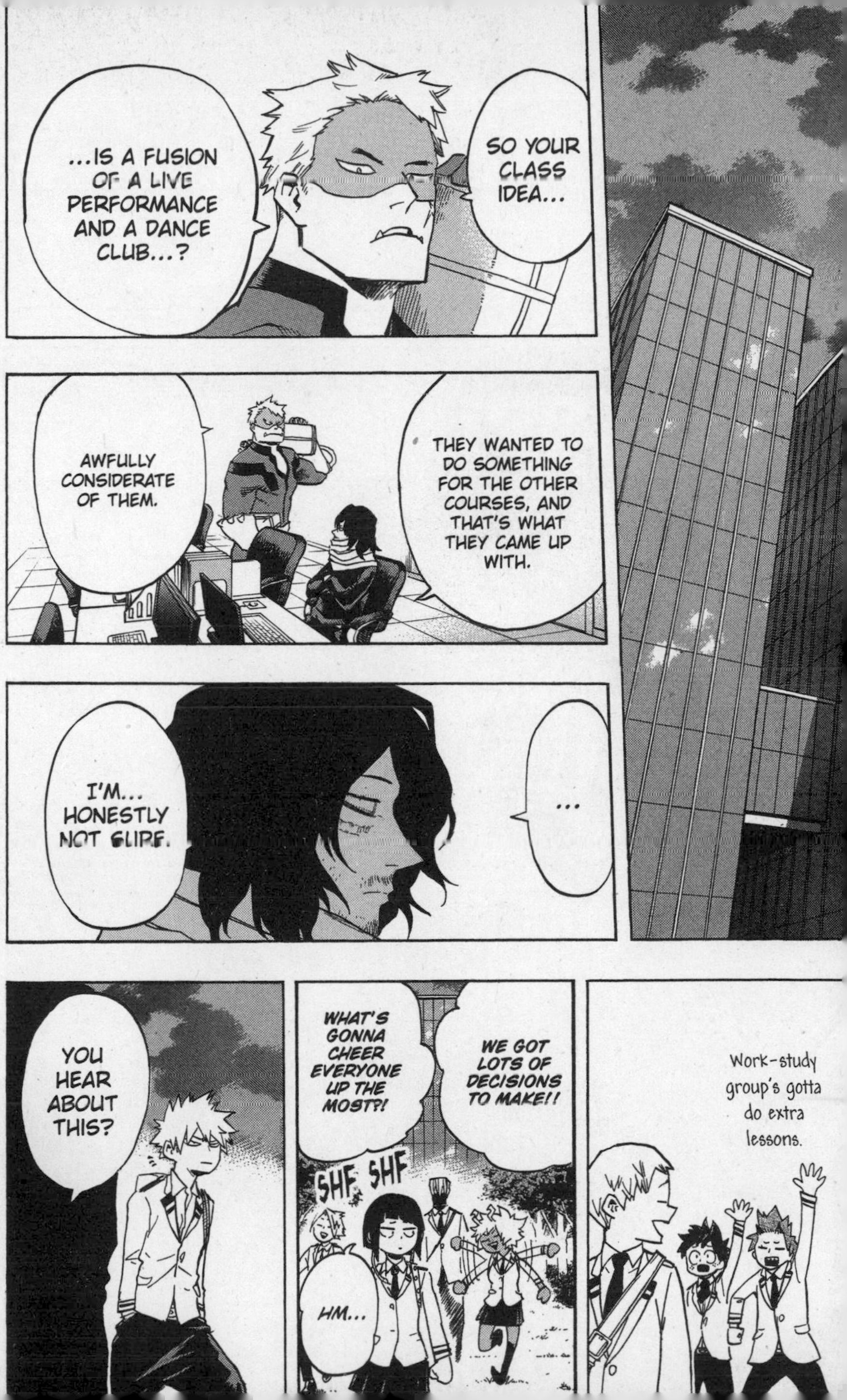
SO YOUR CLASS IDEA...
...IS A FUSION OF A LIVE PERFORMANCE AND A DANCE CLUB...?
THEY WANTED TO DO SOMETHING FOR THE OTHER COURSES, AND THAT'S WHAT THEY CAME UP WITH.
AWFULLY CONSIDERATE OF THEM.
...
I'M... HONESTLY NOT SURE.
Work-study group's gotta do extra lessons.
WE GOT LOTS OF DECISIONS TO MAKE!!
WHAT'S GONNA CHEER EVERYONE UP THE MOST?!
SHF SHF
HM...
YOU HEAR ABOUT THIS?

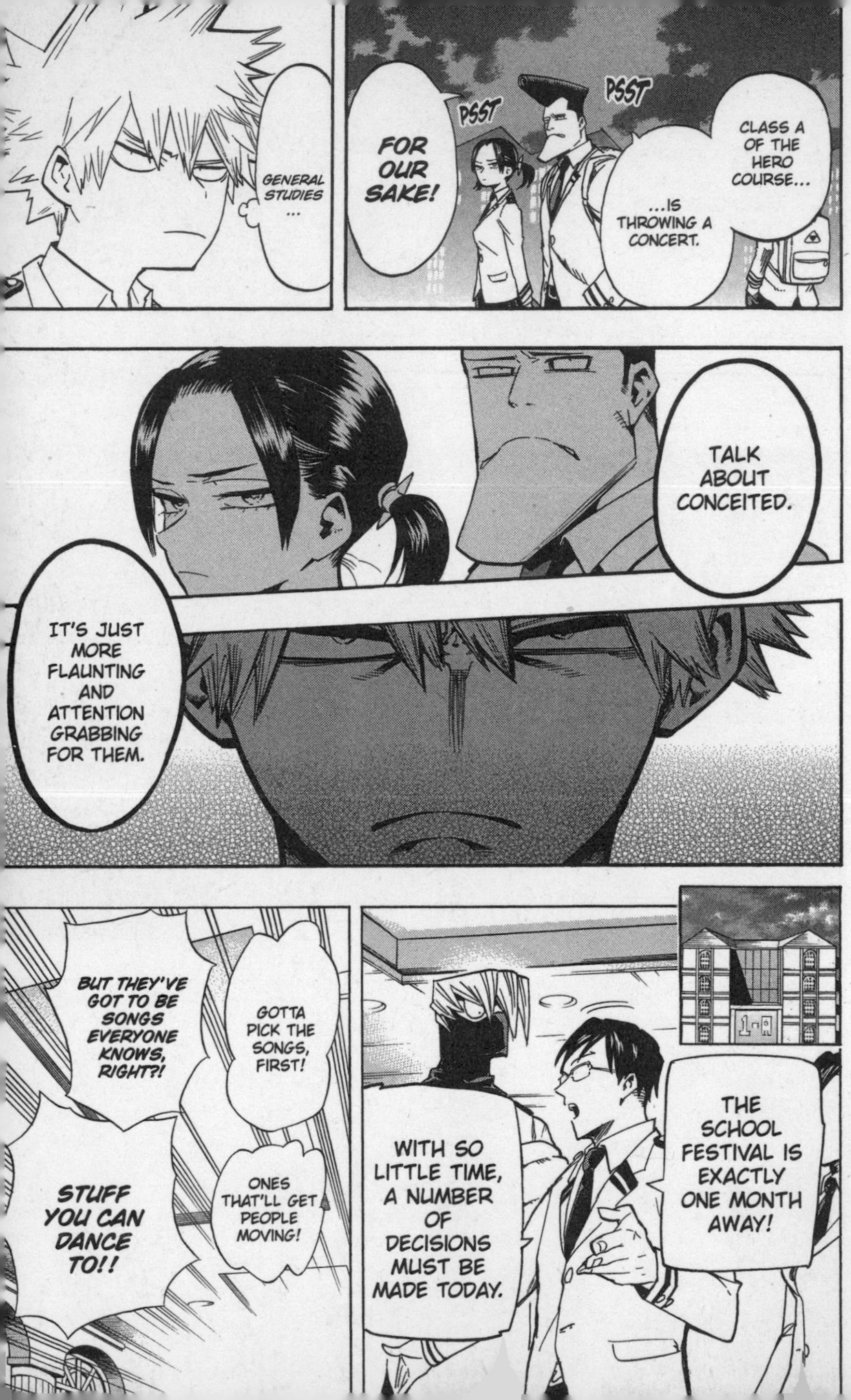
CLASS A OF THE HERO COURSE...
...IS THROWING A CONCERT.
PSST
PSST
FOR OUR SAKE!
GENERAL STUDIES ...
TALK ABOUT CONCEITED.
IT'S JUST MORE FLAUNTING AND ATTENTION GRABBING FOR THEM.
1-A
THE SCHOOL FESTIVAL IS EXACTLY ONE MONTH AWAY!
WITH SO LITTLE TIME, A NUMBER OF DECISIONS MUST BE MADE TODAY.
GOTTA PICK THE SONGS, FIRST!
BUT THEY'VE GOT TO BE SONGS EVERYONE KNOWS, RIGHT?!
ONES THAT'LL GET PEOPLE MOVING!
STUFF YOU CAN DANCE TO!!

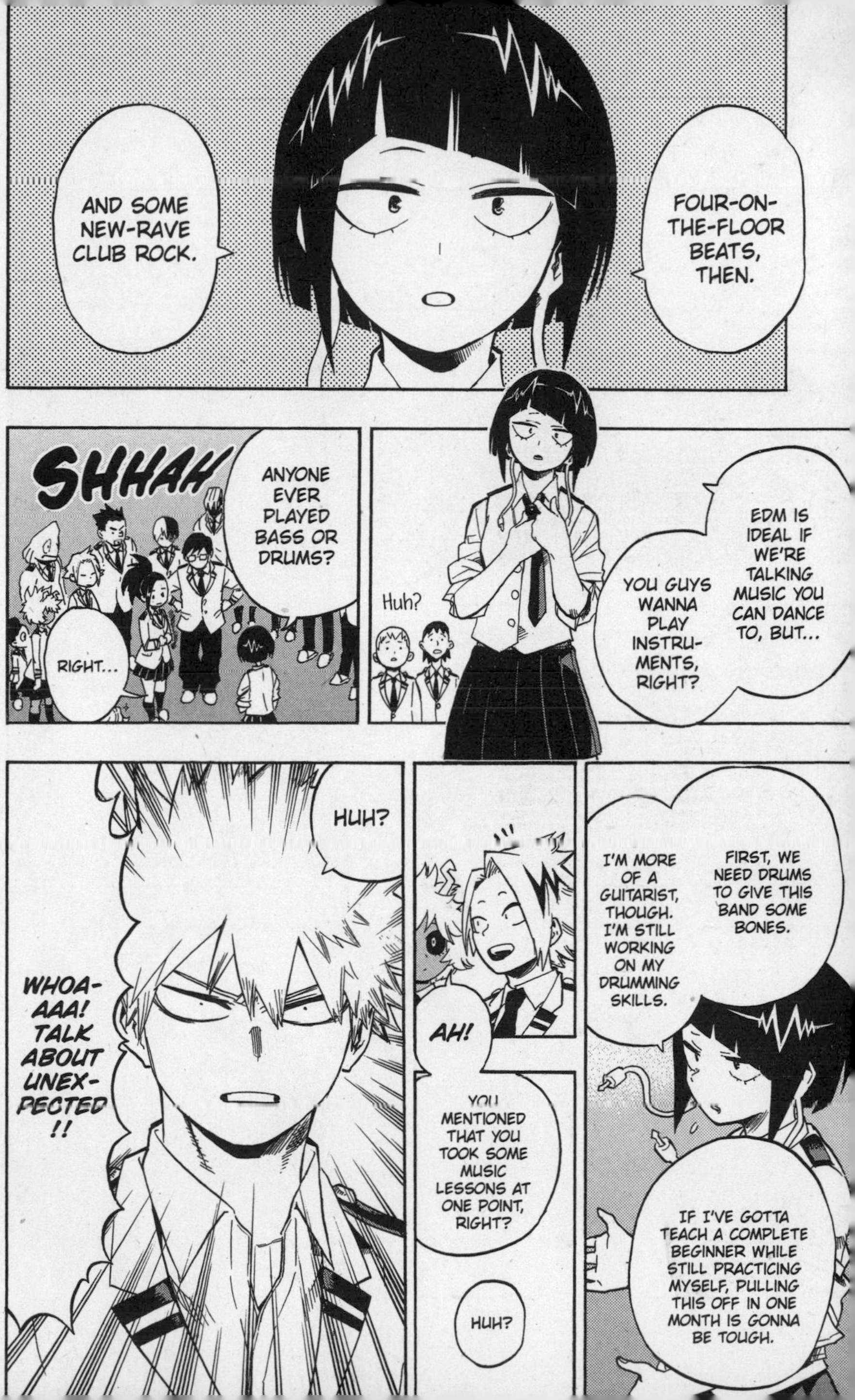
FOUR-ON-THE-FLOOR BEATS, THEN.
AND SOME NEW-RAVE CLUB ROCK.
EDM IS IDEAL IF WE'RE TALKING MUSIC YOU CAN DANCE TO, BUT...
YOU GUYS WANNA PLAY INSTRU-MENTS, RIGHT?
Huh?
SHHAH
ANYONE EVER PLAYED BASS OR DRUMS?
RIGHT...
FIRST, WE NEED DRUMS TO GIVE THIS BAND SOME BONES.
I'M MORE OF A GUITARIST, THOUGH. I'M STILL WORKING ON MY DRUMMING SKILLS.
IF I'VE GOTTA TEACH A COMPLETE BEGINNER WHILE STILL PRACTICING MYSELF, PULLING THIS OFF IN ONE MONTH IS GONNA BE TOUGH.
AH!
YOU MENTIONED THAT YOU TOOK SOME MUSIC LESSONS AT ONE POINT, RIGHT?
HUH?
HUH?
WHOA-AAA! TALK ABOUT UNEX-PECTED!!

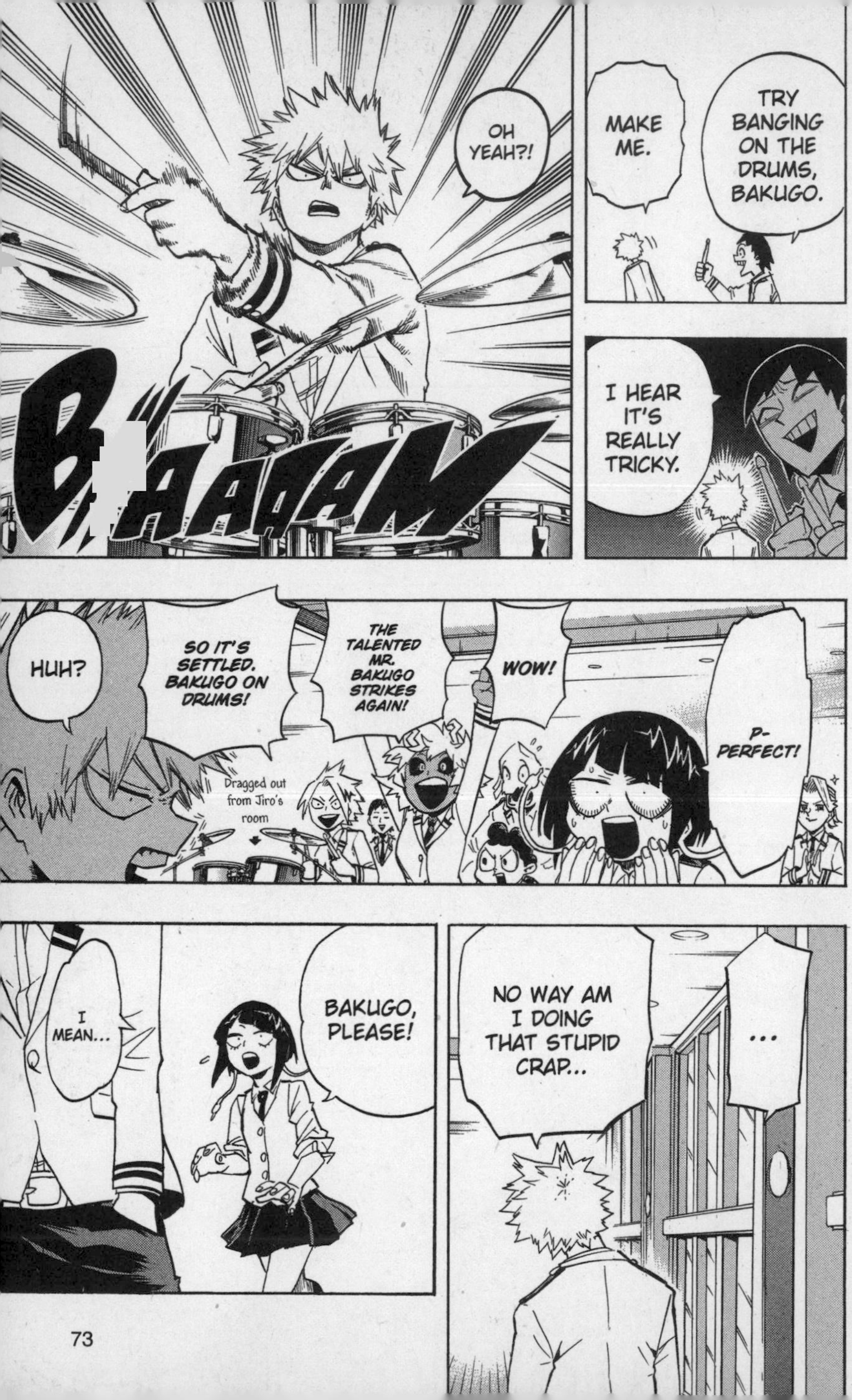
TRY BANGING ON THE DRUMS, BAKUGO.
MAKE ME.
I HEAR IT'S REALLY TRICKY.
OH YEAH?!
P-PERFECT!
WOW!
THE TALENTED MR. BAKUGO STRIKES AGAIN!
SO IT'S SETTLED. BAKUGO ON DRUMS!
HUH?
Dragged out from Jiro's room
...
NO WAY AM I DOING THAT STUPID CRAP...
BAKUGO, PLEASE!
I MEAN...

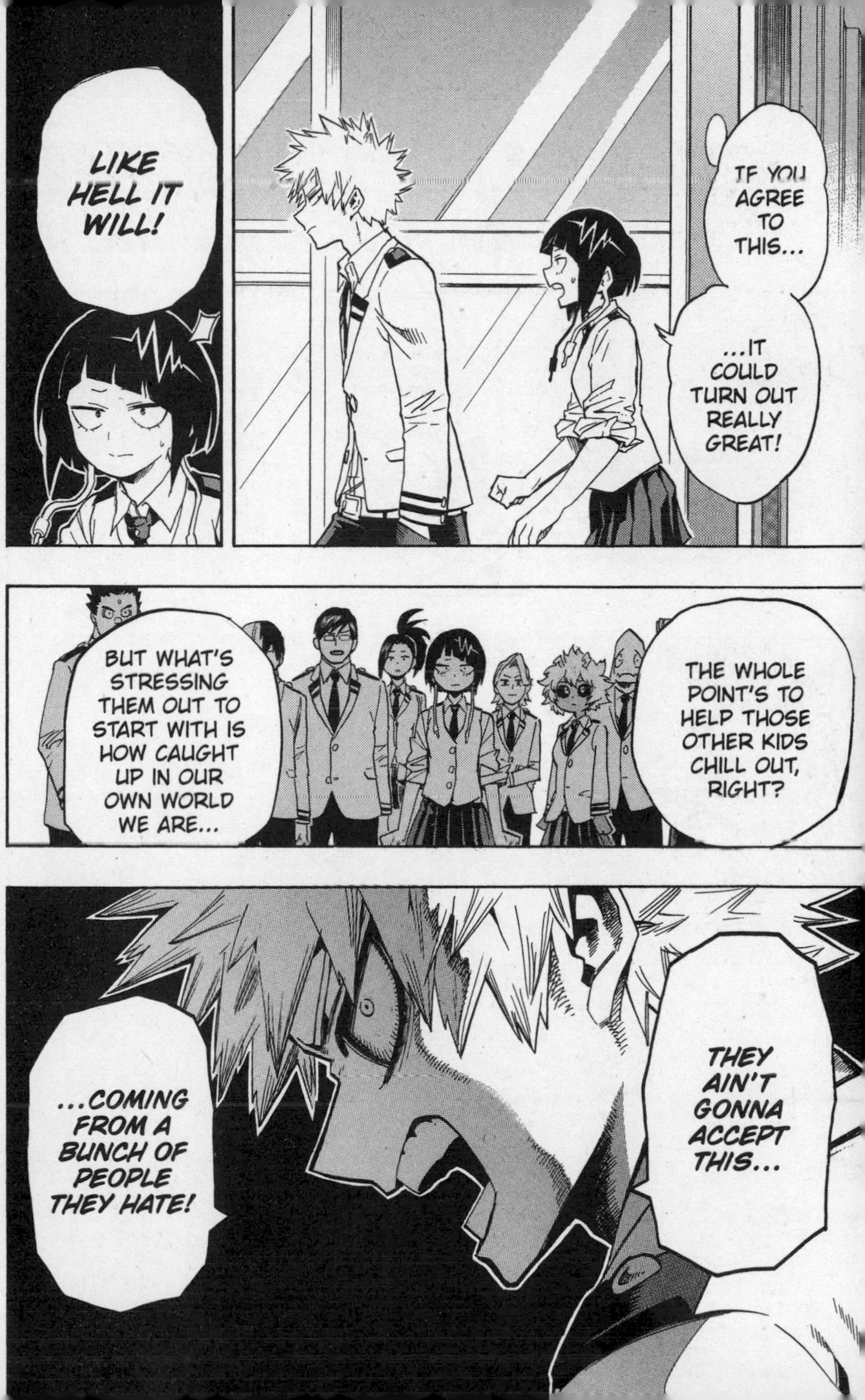
IF YOU AGREE TO THIS...
...IT COULD TURN OUT REALLY GREAT!
LIKE HELL IT WILL!
THE WHOLE POINT'S TO HELP THOSE OTHER KIDS CHILL OUT, RIGHT?
BUT WHAT'S STRESSING THEM OUT TO START WITH IS HOW CAUGHT UP IN OUR OWN WORLD WE ARE...
THEY AIN'T GONNA ACCEPT THIS...
...COMING FROM A BUNCH OF PEOPLE THEY HATE!

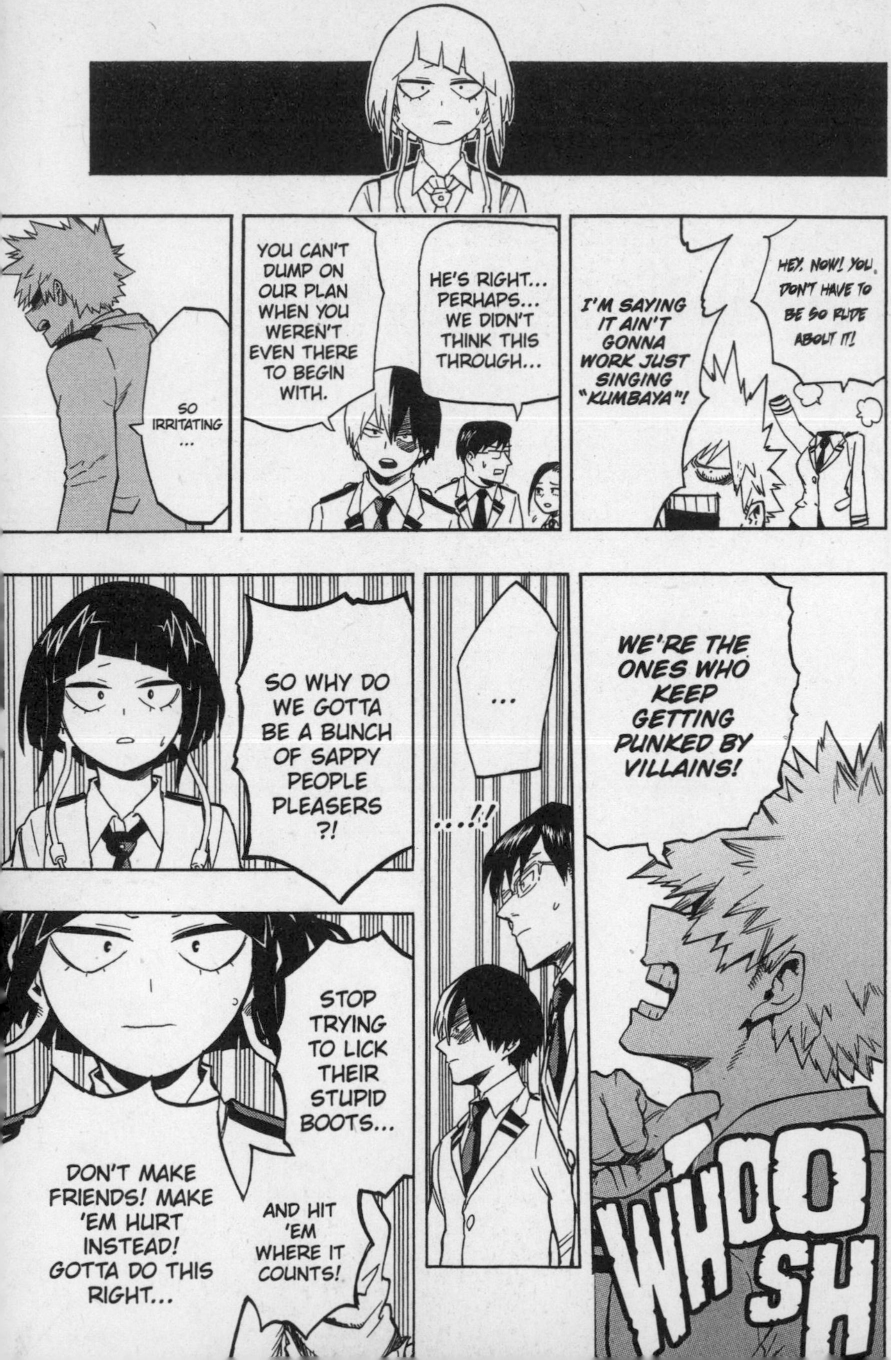
HEY, NOW! YOU DON'T HAVE TO BE SO RUDE ABOUT IT!
I'M SAYING IT AIN'T GONNA WORK JUST SINGING "KUMBAYA"!
HE'S RIGHT... PERHAPS... WE DIDN'T THINK THIS THROUGH...
YOU CAN'T DUMP ON OUR PLAN WHEN YOU WEREN'T EVEN THERE TO BEGIN WITH.
SO IRRITATING...
WE'RE THE ONES WHO KEEP GETTING PUNKED BY VILLAINS!
WHOOSH
...
...!!
SO WHY DO WE GOTTA BE A BUNCH OF SAPPY PEOPLE PLEASERS?!
STOP TRYING TO LICK THEIR STUPID BOOTS...
AND HIT 'EM WHERE IT COUNTS!
DON'T MAKE FRIENDS! MAKE 'EM HURT INSTEAD! GOTTA DO THIS RIGHT...

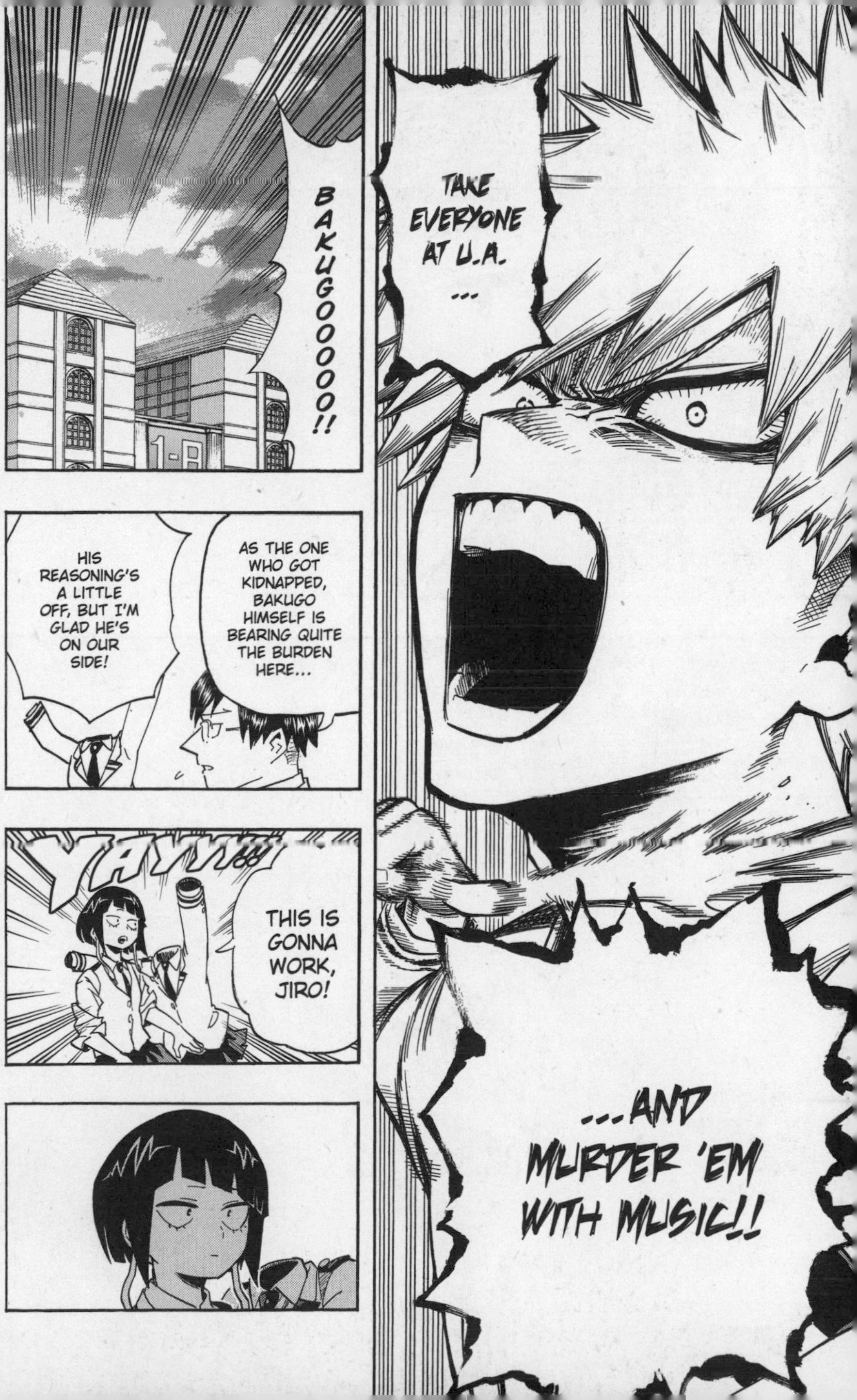

TAKE EVERYONE AT U.A. ...
...AND MURDER 'EM WITH MUSIC!!
BAKUGOOOOOOO!!
AS THE ONE WHO GOT KIDNAPPED, BAKUGO HIMSELF IS BEARING QUITE THE BURDEN HERE...
HIS REASONING'S A LITTLE OFF, BUT I'M GLAD HE'S ON OUR SIDE!
THIS IS GONNA WORK, JIRO!

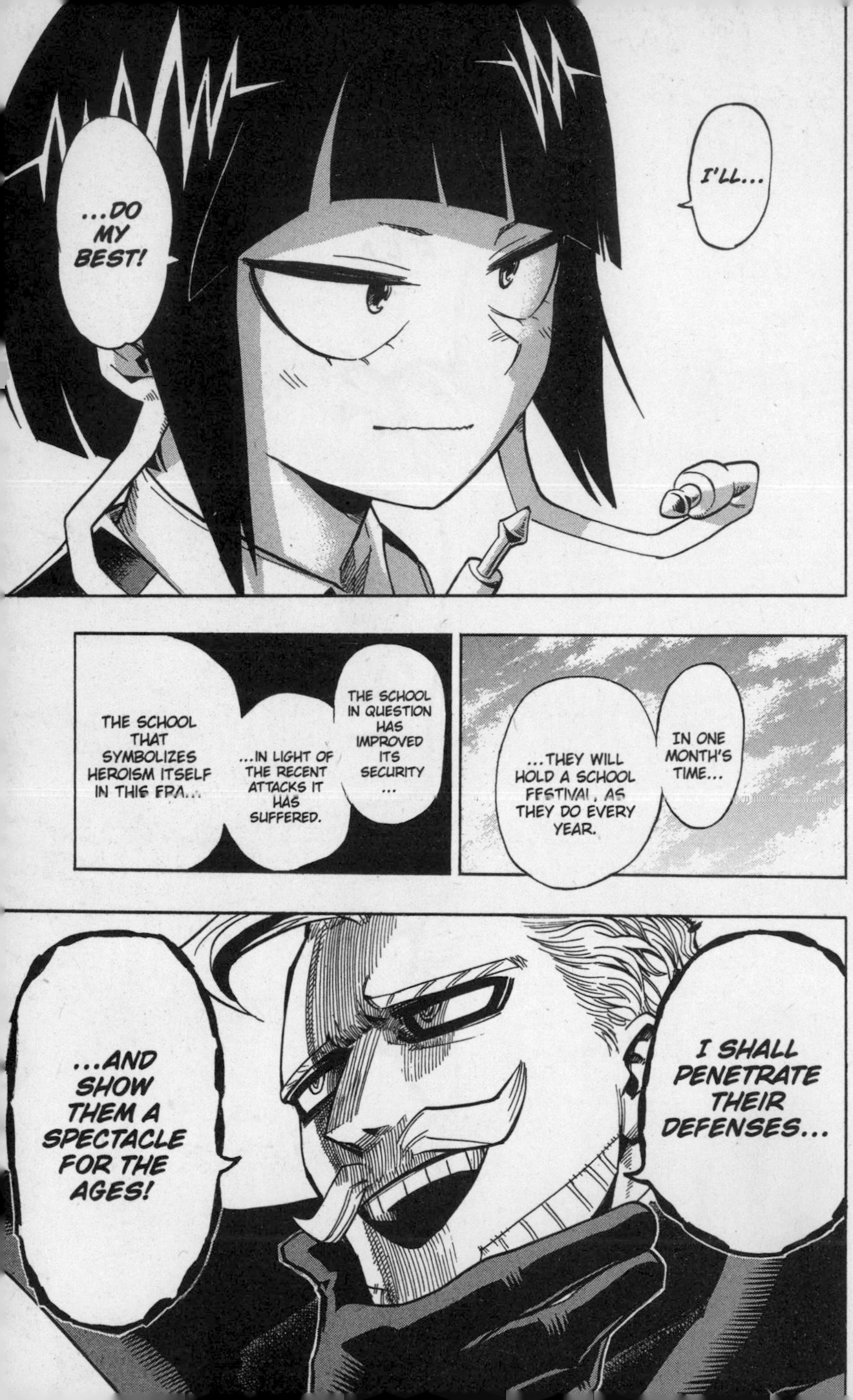
I'LL...
...DO MY BEST!
IN ONE MONTH'S TIME...
...THEY WILL HOLD A SCHOOL FESTIVAL, AS THEY DO EVERY YEAR.
THE SCHOOL IN QUESTION HAS IMPROVED ITS SECURITY...
...IN LIGHT OF THE RECENT ATTACKS IT HAS SUFFERED.
THE SCHOOL THAT SYMBOLIZES HEROISM ITSELF IN THIS ERA...
I SHALL PENETRATE THEIR DEFENSES...
...AND SHOW THEM A SPECTACLE FOR THE AGES!

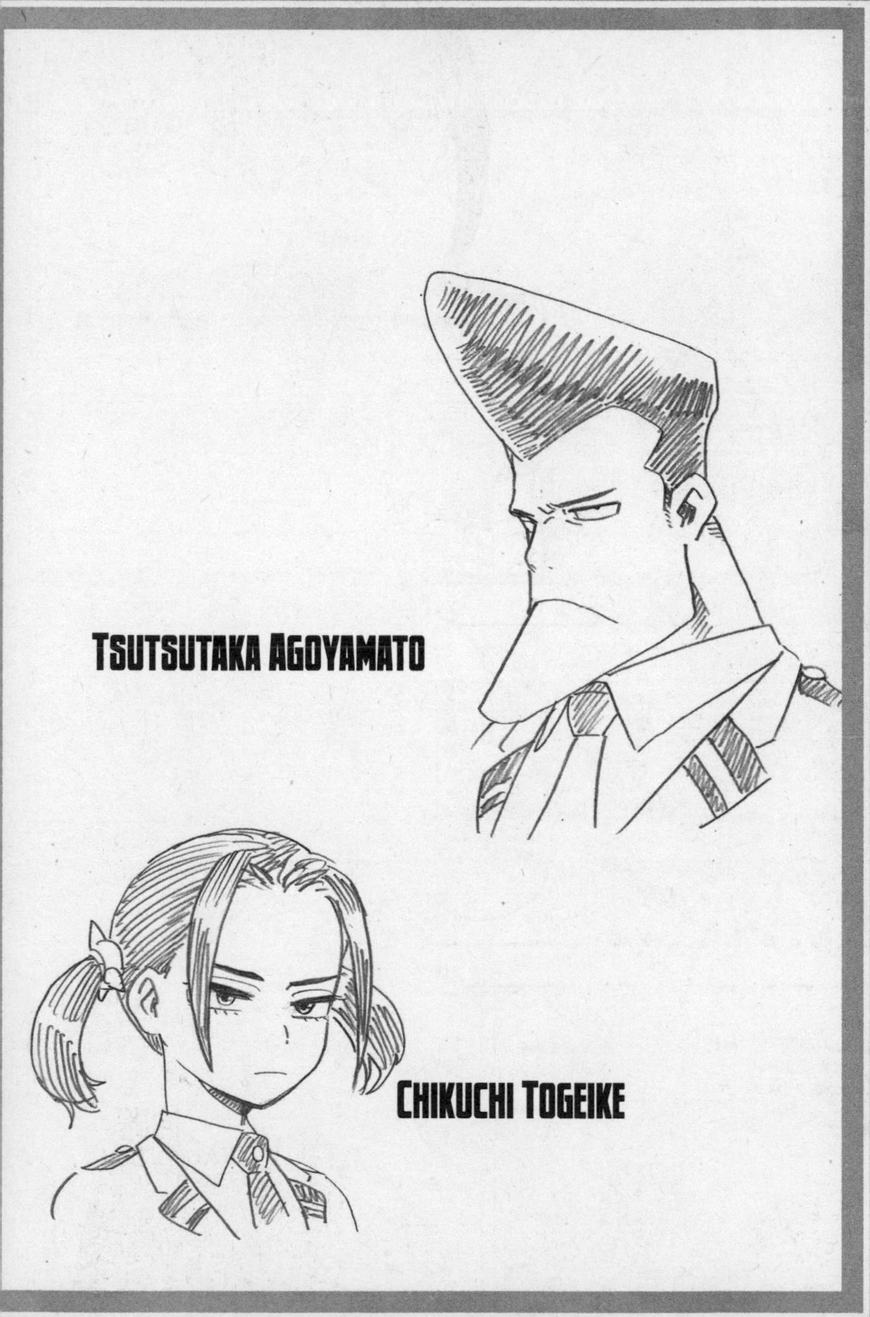
TSUTSUTAKA AGOYAMATO
CHIKUCHI TOGEIKE

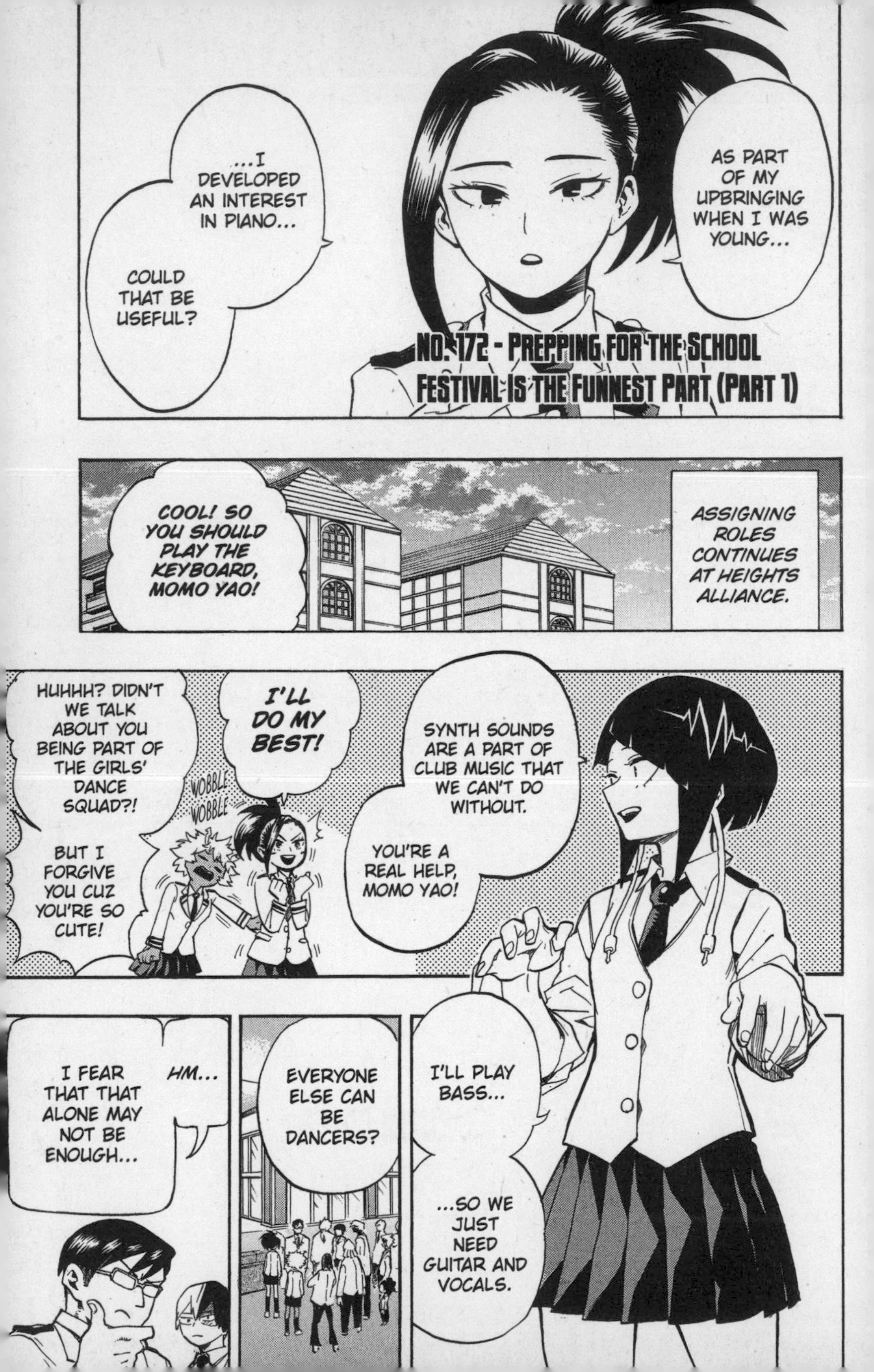
AS PART OF MY UPBRINGING WHEN I WAS YOUNG...
...I DEVELOPED AN INTEREST IN PIANO...
COULD THAT BE USEFUL?
NO. 172 - PREPPING FOR THE SCHOOL FESTIVAL IS THE FUNNEST PART (PART 1)
ASSIGNING ROLES CONTINUES AT HEIGHTS ALLIANCE.
COOL! SO YOU SHOULD PLAY THE KEYBOARD, MOMO YAO!
SYNTH SOUNDS ARE A PART OF CLUB MUSIC THAT WE CAN'T DO WITHOUT.
YOU'RE A REAL HELP, MOMO YAO!
I'LL DO MY BEST!
HUHHH? DIDN'T WE TALK ABOUT YOU BEING PART OF THE GIRLS' DANCE SQUAD?!
BUT I FORGIVE YOU CUZ YOU'RE SO CUTE!
WOBBLE WOBBLE
I'LL PLAY BASS...
...SO WE JUST NEED GUITAR AND VOCALS.
EVERYONE ELSE CAN BE DANCERS?
HM...
I FEAR THAT THAT ALONE MAY NOT BE ENOUGH...

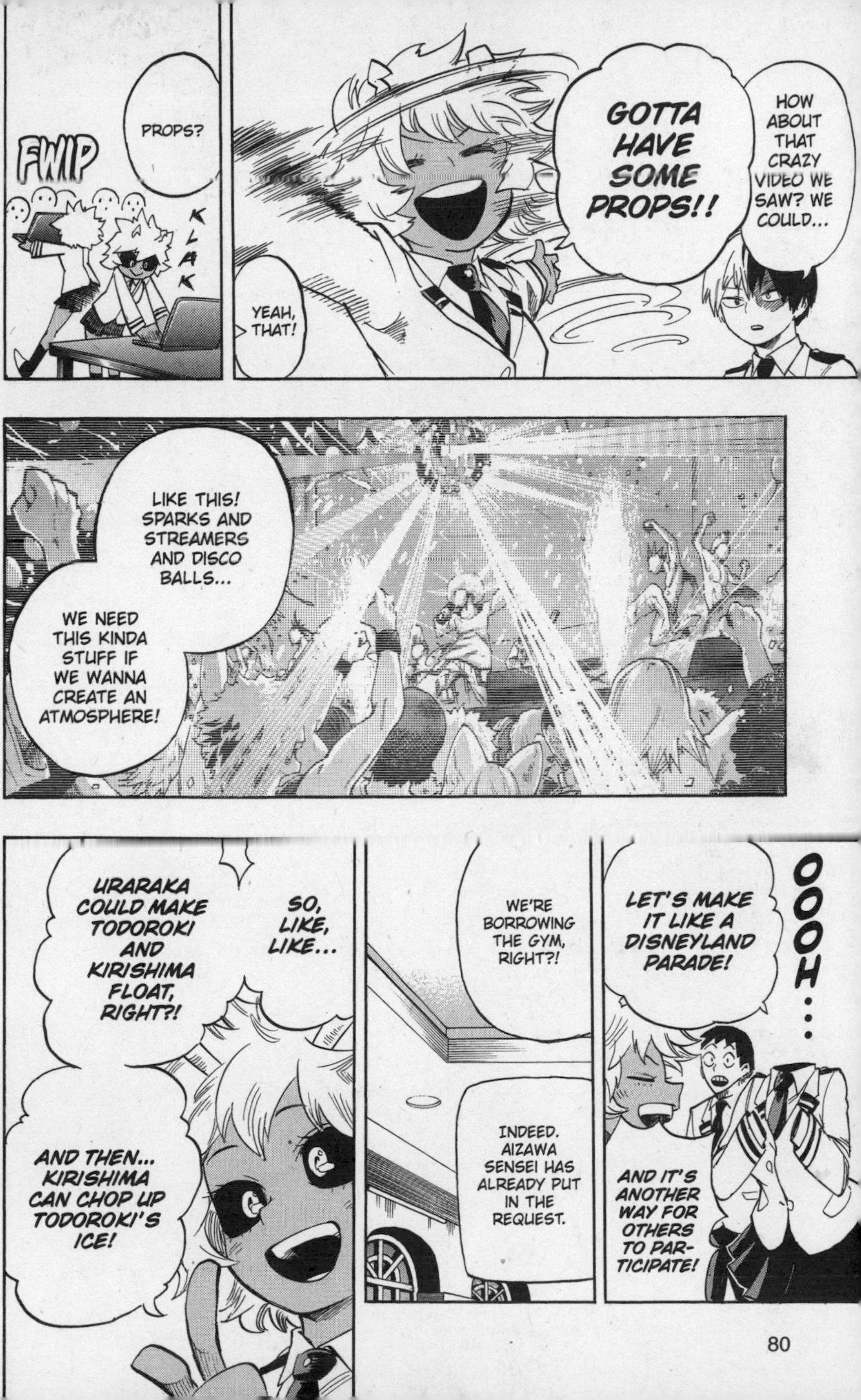
HOW ABOUT THAT CRAZY VIDEO WE SAW? WE COULD...
GOTTA HAVE SOME PROPS!!
YEAH, THAT!
PROPS?
FWIP
KLAK
LIKE THIS! SPARKS AND STREAMERS AND DISCO BALLS...
WE NEED THIS KINDA STUFF IF WE WANNA CREATE AN ATMOSPHERE!
OOOH...
LET'S MAKE IT LIKE A DISNEYLAND PARADE!
AND IT'S ANOTHER WAY FOR OTHERS TO PAR-TICIPATE!
WE'RE BORROWING THE GYM, RIGHT?!
INDEED. AIZAWA SENSEI HAS ALREADY PUT IN THE REQUEST.
SO, LIKE, LIKE...
URARAKA COULD MAKE TODOROKI AND KIRISHIMA FLOAT, RIGHT?!
AND THEN... KIRISHIMA CAN CHOP UP TODOROKI'S ICE!

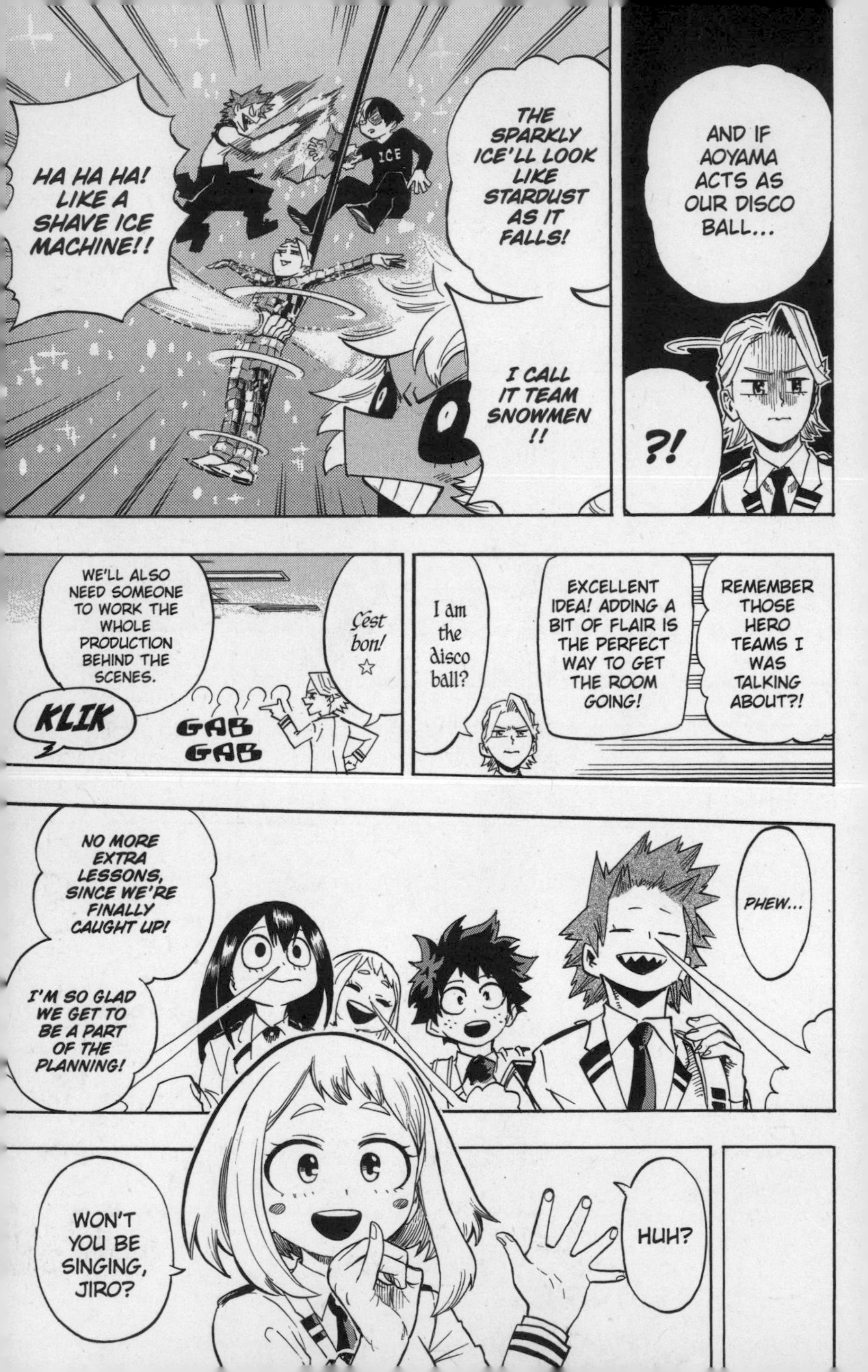
AND IF AOYAMA ACTS AS OUR DISCO BALL...
?!
THE SPARKLY ICE'LL LOOK LIKE STARDUST AS IT FALLS!
I CALL IT TEAM SNOWMEN!!
HA HA HA! LIKE A SHAVE ICE MACHINE!!
REMEMBER THOSE HERO TEAMS I WAS TALKING ABOUT?!
EXCELLENT IDEA! ADDING A BIT OF FLAIR IS THE PERFECT WAY TO GET THE ROOM GOING!
I am the disco ball?
Çest bon! ☆
WE'LL ALSO NEED SOMEONE TO WORK THE WHOLE PRODUCTION BEHIND THE SCENES.
KLIK
GAB GAB
PHEW...
NO MORE EXTRA LESSONS, SINCE WE'RE FINALLY CAUGHT UP!
I'M SO GLAD WE GET TO BE A PART OF THE PLANNING!
HUH?
WON'T YOU BE SINGING, JIRO?

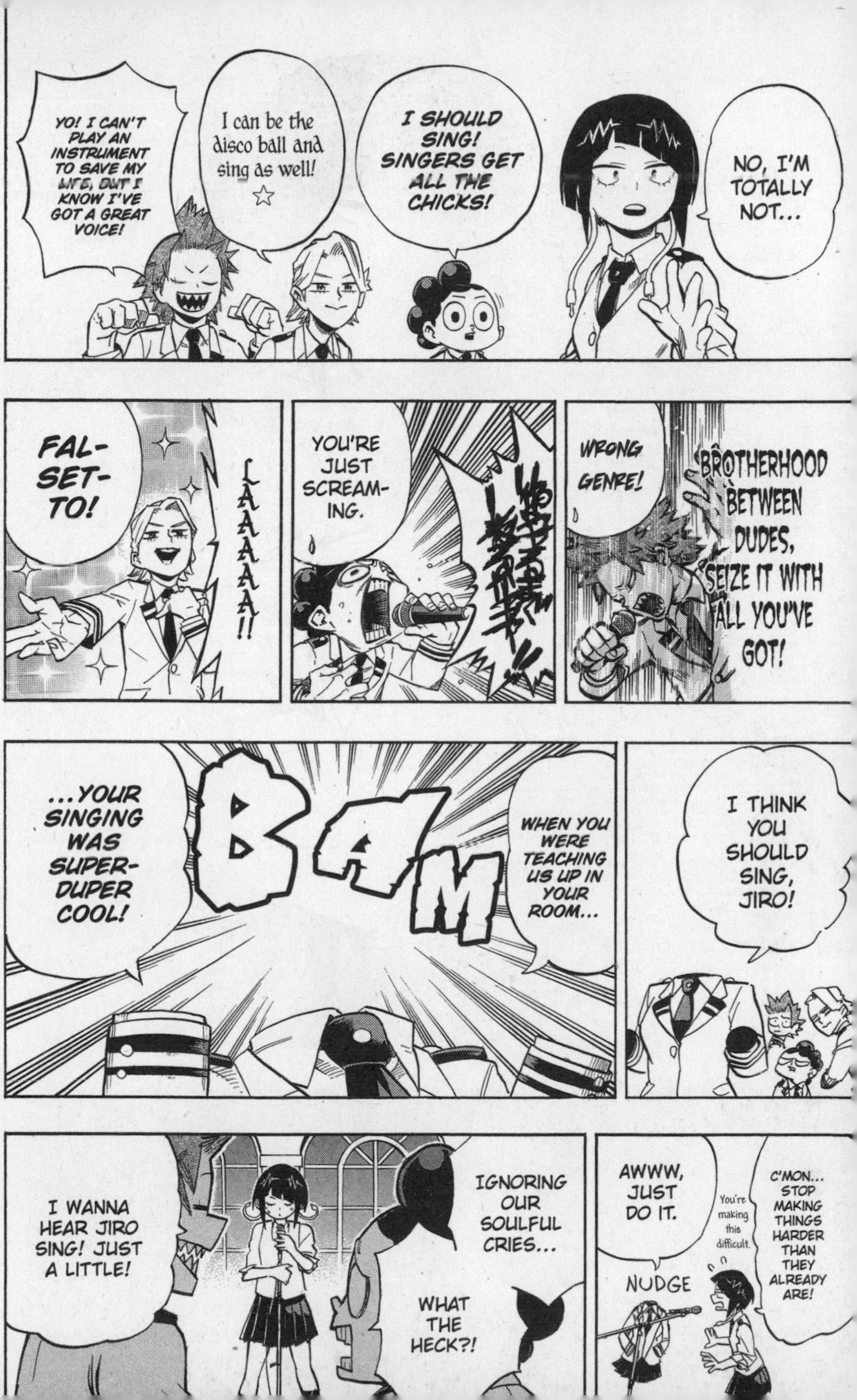
NO, I'M TOTALLY NOT...
I SHOULD SING! SINGERS GET ALL THE CHICKS!
I can be the disco ball and sing as well! ☆
YO! I CAN'T PLAY AN INSTRUMENT TO SAVE MY LIFE, BUT I KNOW I'VE GOT A GREAT VOICE!
BROTHERHOOD BETWEEN DUDES, SEIZE IT WITH ALL YOU'VE GOT!
WRONG GENRE!
YOU'RE JUST SCREAM-ING.
LAAAAAA!!
FAL-SET-TO!
I THINK YOU SHOULD SING, JIRO!
WHEN YOU WERE TEACHING US UP IN YOUR ROOM...
BAM
...YOUR SINGING WAS SUPER-DUPER COOL!
C'MON... STOP MAKING THINGS HARDER THAN THEY ALREADY ARE!
You're making this difficult.
AWWW, JUST DO IT.
NUDGE
IGNORING OUR SOULFUL CRIES...
WHAT THE HECK?!
I WANNA HEAR JIRO SING! JUST A LITTLE!

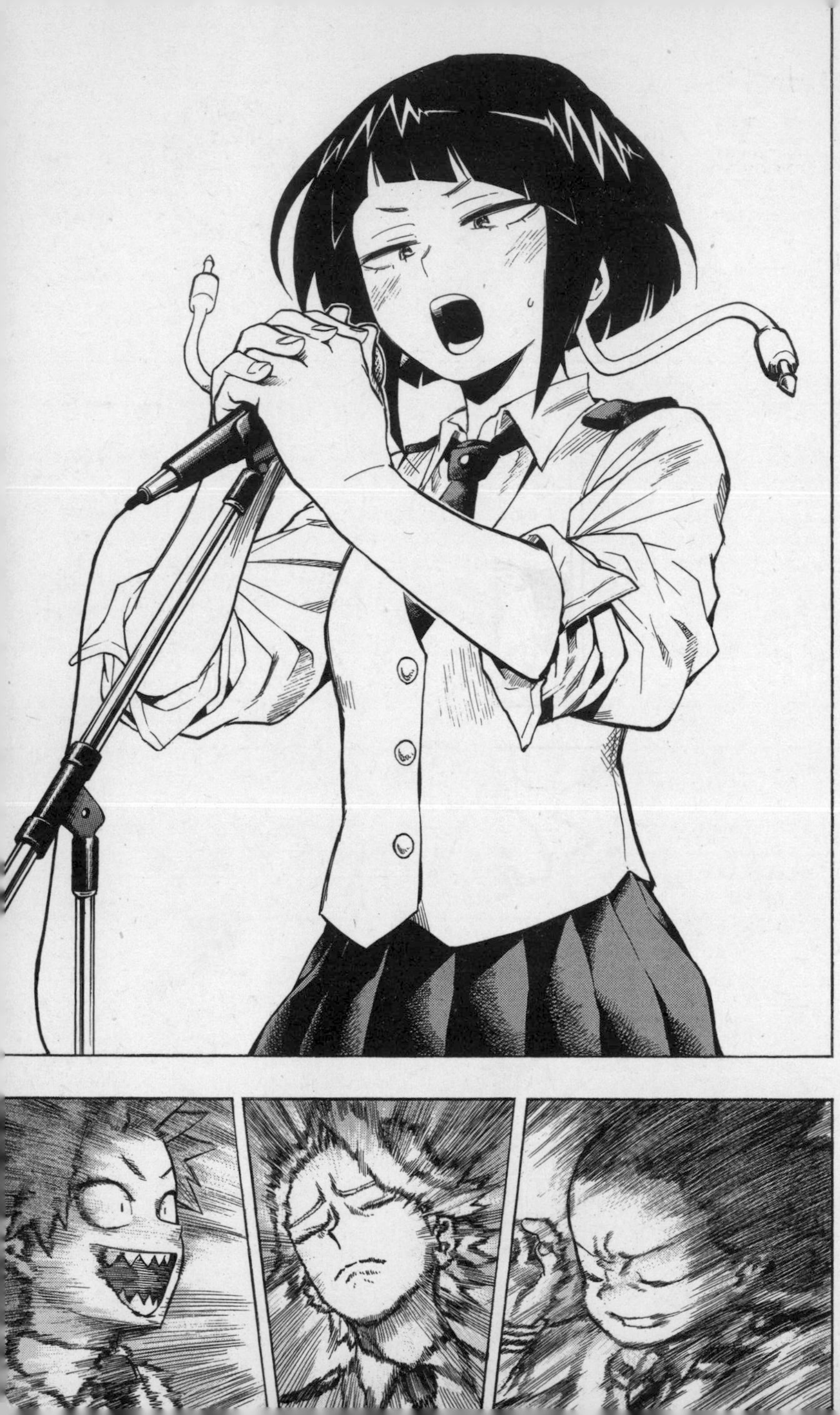

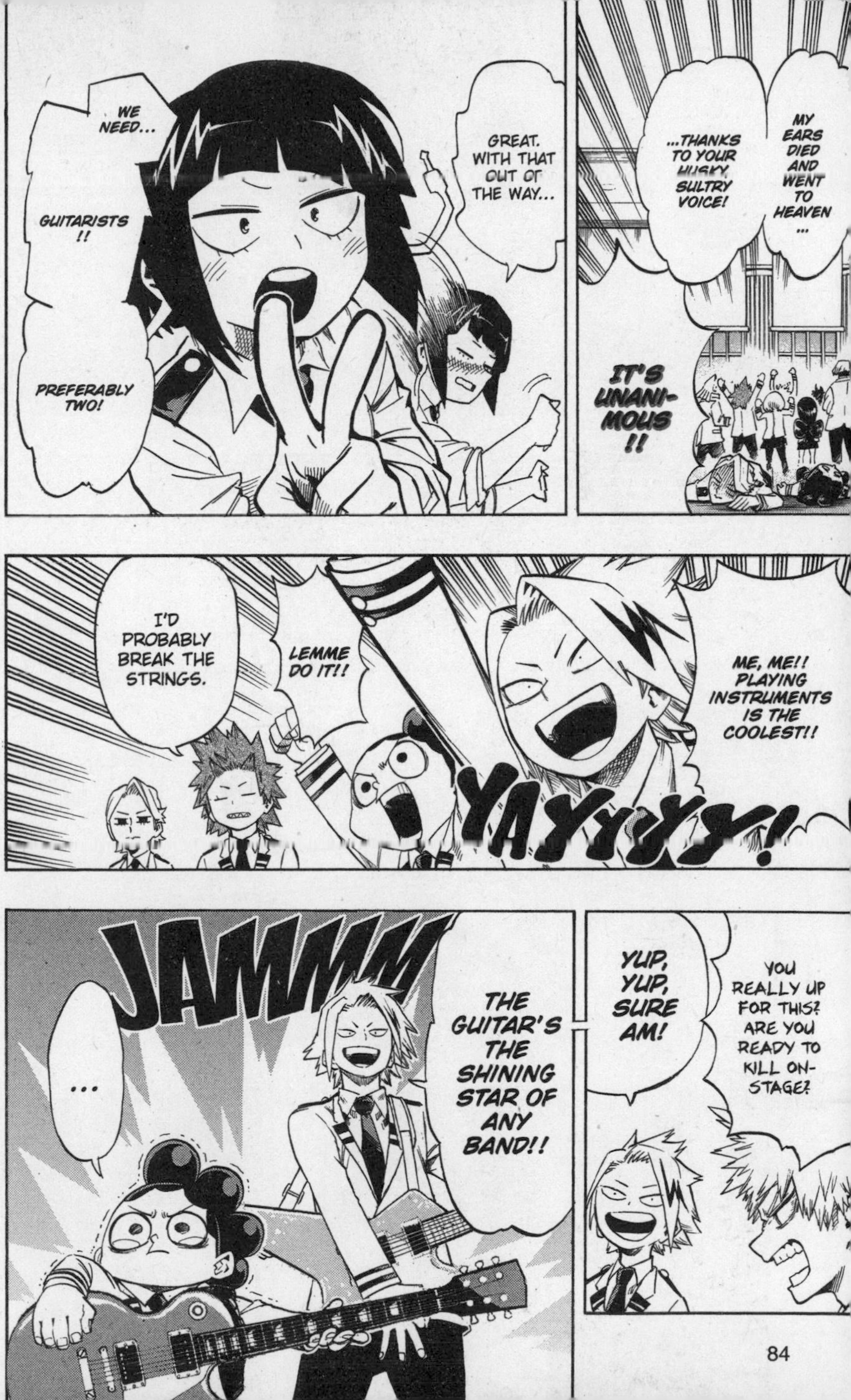
MY EARS DIED AND WENT TO HEAVEN ...
...THANKS TO YOUR HUSKY, SULTRY VOICE!
IT'S UNANIMOUS!!
GREAT. WITH THAT OUT OF THE WAY...
WE NEED...
GUITARISTS!!
PREFERABLY TWO!
ME, ME!! PLAYING INSTRUMENTS IS THE COOLEST!!
YAYYYYY!
LEMME DO IT!!
I'D PROBABLY BREAK THE STRINGS.
YOU REALLY UP FOR THIS? ARE YOU READY TO KILL ON-STAGE?
YUP, YUP, SURE AM!
THE GUITAR'S THE SHINING STAR OF ANY BAND!!
JAMMM
...

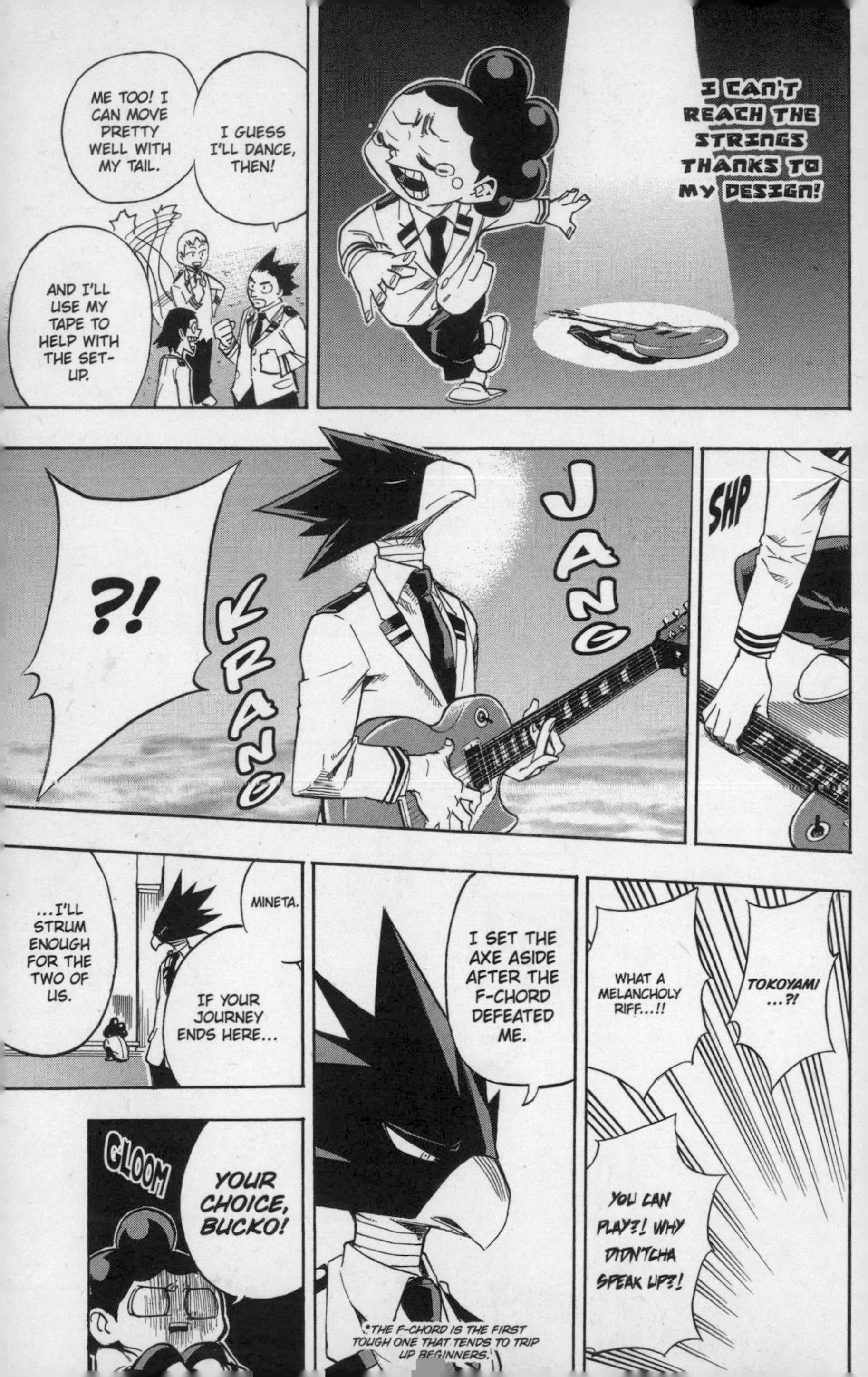
I CAN'T REACH THE STRINGS THANKS TO MY DESIGN!
I GUESS I'LL DANCE, THEN!
ME TOO! I CAN MOVE PRETTY WELL WITH MY TAIL.
AND I'LL USE MY TAPE TO HELP WITH THE SET-UP.
SHP
JANG
KRANG
?!
TOKOYAMI ...?!
WHAT A MELANCHOLY RIFF...!!
YOU CAN PLAY?! WHY DIDN'TCHA SPEAK UP?!
I SET THE AXE ASIDE AFTER THE F-CHORD DEFEATED ME.
*THE F-CHORD IS THE FIRST TOUGH ONE THAT TENDS TO TRIP UP BEGINNERS.
MINETA.
IF YOUR JOURNEY ENDS HERE...
...I'LL STRUM ENOUGH FOR THE TWO OF US.
YOUR CHOICE, BUCKO!
GLOOM

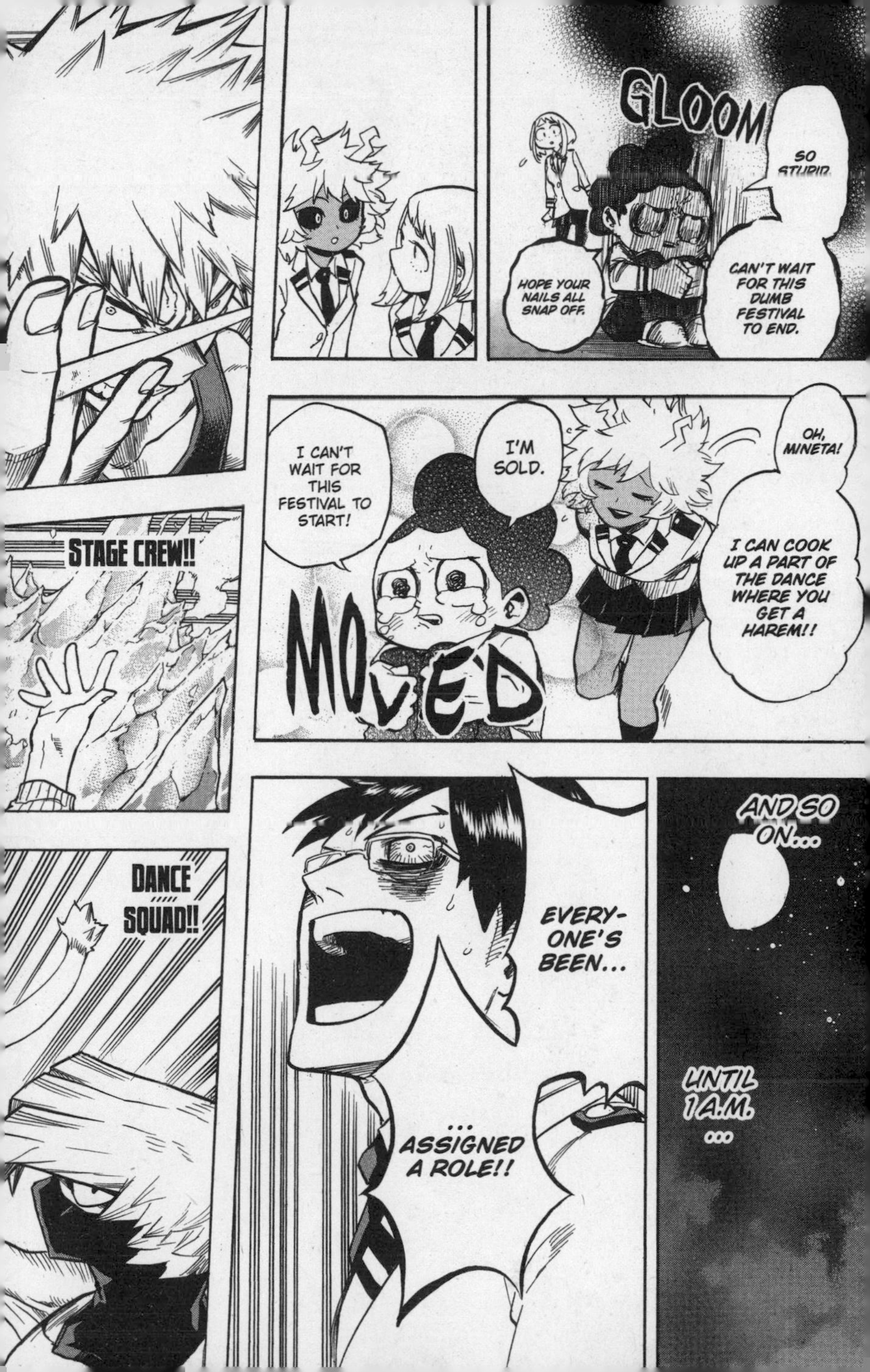
GLOOM
SO STUPID.
CAN'T WAIT FOR THIS DUMB FESTIVAL TO END.
HOPE YOUR NAILS ALL SNAP OFF.
OH, MINETA!
I CAN COOK UP A PART OF THE DANCE WHERE YOU GET A HAREM!!
I'M SOLD.
I CAN'T WAIT FOR THIS FESTIVAL TO START!
MOVED
STAGE CREW!!
AND SO ON...
UNTIL 1 A.M. ...
EVERY-ONE'S BEEN...
... ASSIGNED A ROLE!!
DANCE SQUAD!!

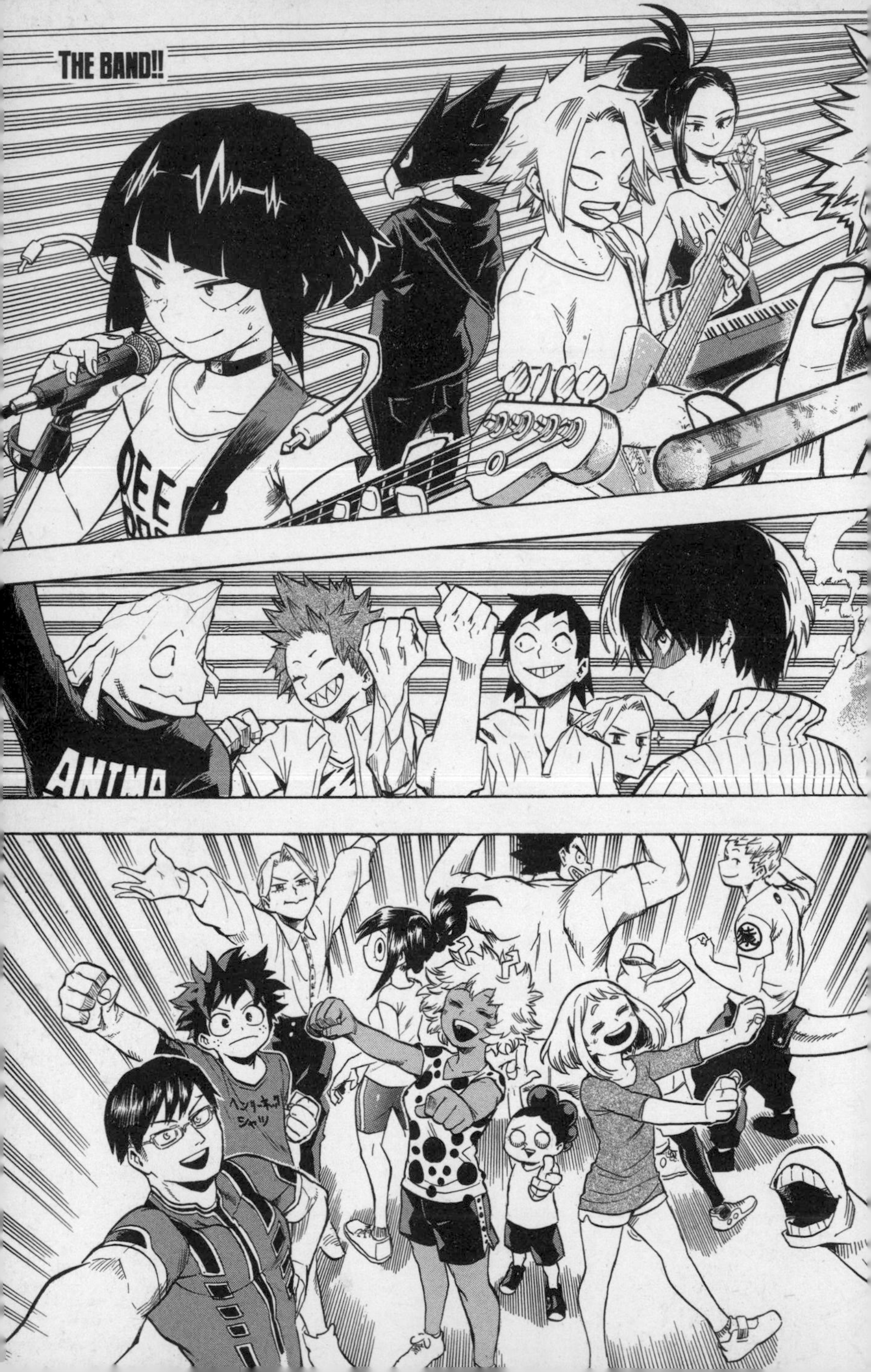
THE BAND!!

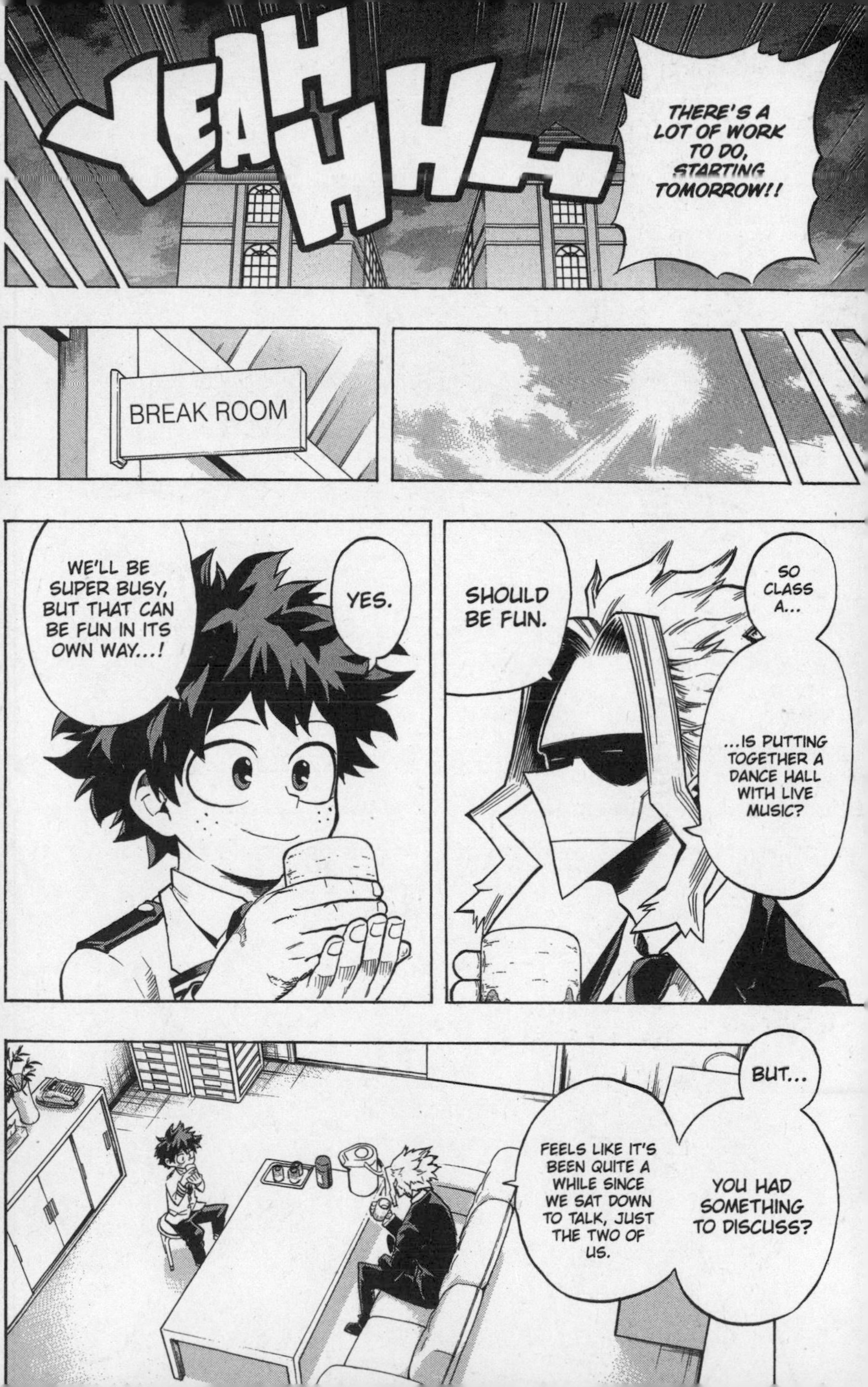
THERE'S A LOT OF WORK TO DO, STARTING TOMORROW!!
YEAHHH--
BREAK ROOM
SO CLASS A...
...IS PUTTING TOGETHER A DANCE HALL WITH LIVE MUSIC?
SHOULD BE FUN.
YES.
WE'LL BE SUPER BUSY, BUT THAT CAN BE FUN IN ITS OWN WAY...!
BUT...
YOU HAD SOMETHING TO DISCUSS?
FEELS LIKE IT'S BEEN QUITE A WHILE SINCE WE SAT DOWN TO TALK, JUST THE TWO OF US.

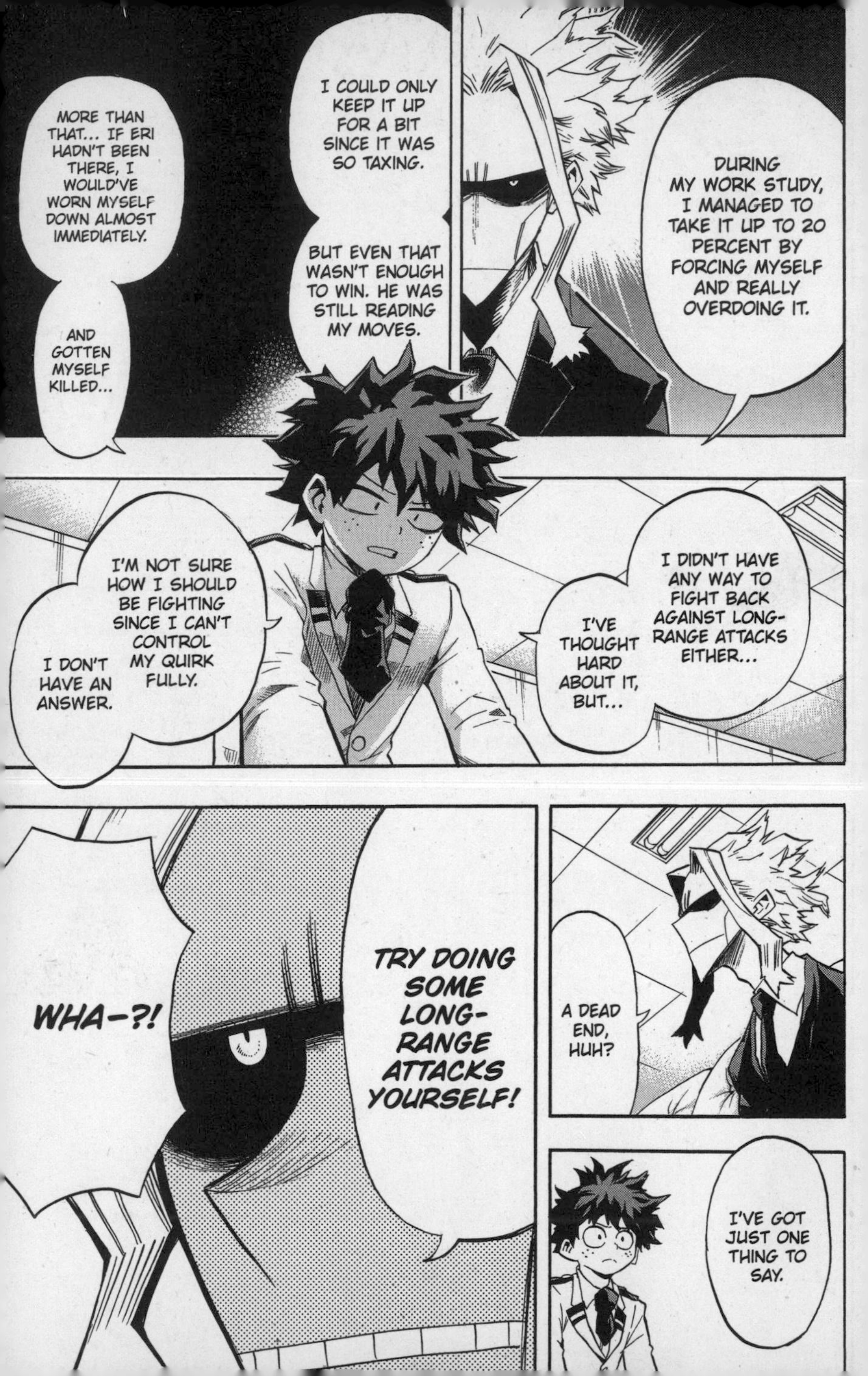
DURING MY WORK STUDY, I MANAGED TO TAKE IT UP TO 20 PERCENT BY FORCING MYSELF AND REALLY OVERDOING IT.
I COULD ONLY KEEP IT UP FOR A BIT SINCE IT WAS SO TAXING.
BUT EVEN THAT WASN'T ENOUGH TO WIN. HE WAS STILL READING MY MOVES.
MORE THAN THAT... IF ERI HADN'T BEEN THERE, I WOULD'VE WORN MYSELF DOWN ALMOST IMMEDIATELY.
AND GOTTEN MYSELF KILLED...
I DIDN'T HAVE ANY WAY TO FIGHT BACK AGAINST LONG-RANGE ATTACKS EITHER...
I'VE THOUGHT HARD ABOUT IT, BUT...
I'M NOT SURE HOW I SHOULD BE FIGHTING SINCE I CAN'T CONTROL MY QUIRK FULLY.
I DON'T HAVE AN ANSWER.
A DEAD END, HUH?
I'VE GOT JUST ONE THING TO SAY.
TRY DOING SOME LONG-RANGE ATTACKS YOURSELF!
WHA-?!

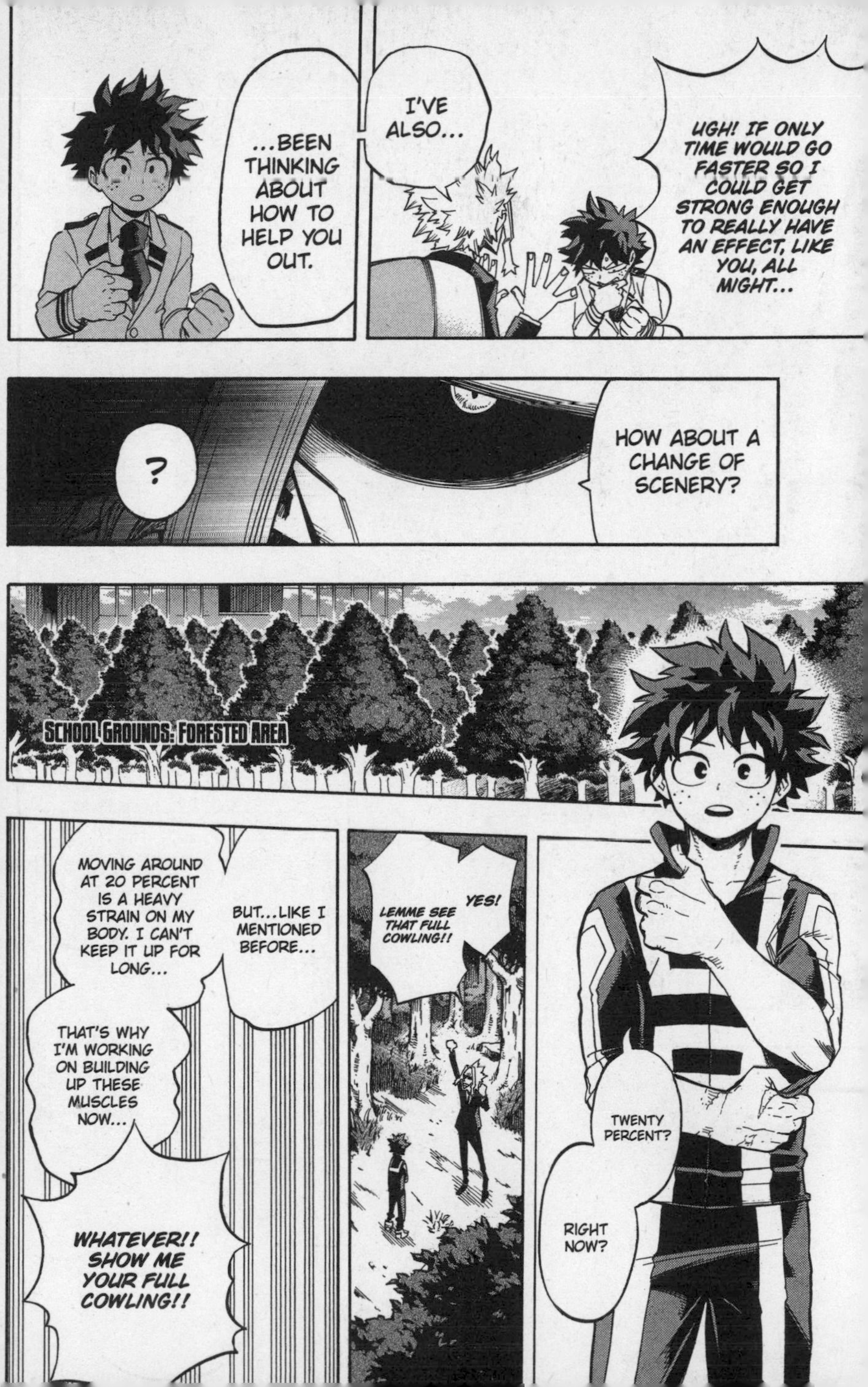
UGH! IF ONLY TIME WOULD GO FASTER SO I COULD GET STRONG ENOUGH TO REALLY HAVE AN EFFECT, LIKE YOU, ALL MIGHT...
I'VE ALSO...
...BEEN THINKING ABOUT HOW TO HELP YOU OUT.
HOW ABOUT A CHANGE OF SCENERY?
?
SCHOOL GROUNDS: FORESTED AREA
TWENTY PERCENT?
RIGHT NOW?
YES!
LEMME SEE THAT FULL COWLING!!
BUT...LIKE I MENTIONED BEFORE...
MOVING AROUND AT 20 PERCENT IS A HEAVY STRAIN ON MY BODY. I CAN'T KEEP IT UP FOR LONG...
THAT'S WHY I'M WORKING ON BUILDING UP THESE MUSCLES NOW...
WHATEVER!! SHOW ME YOUR FULL COWLING!!

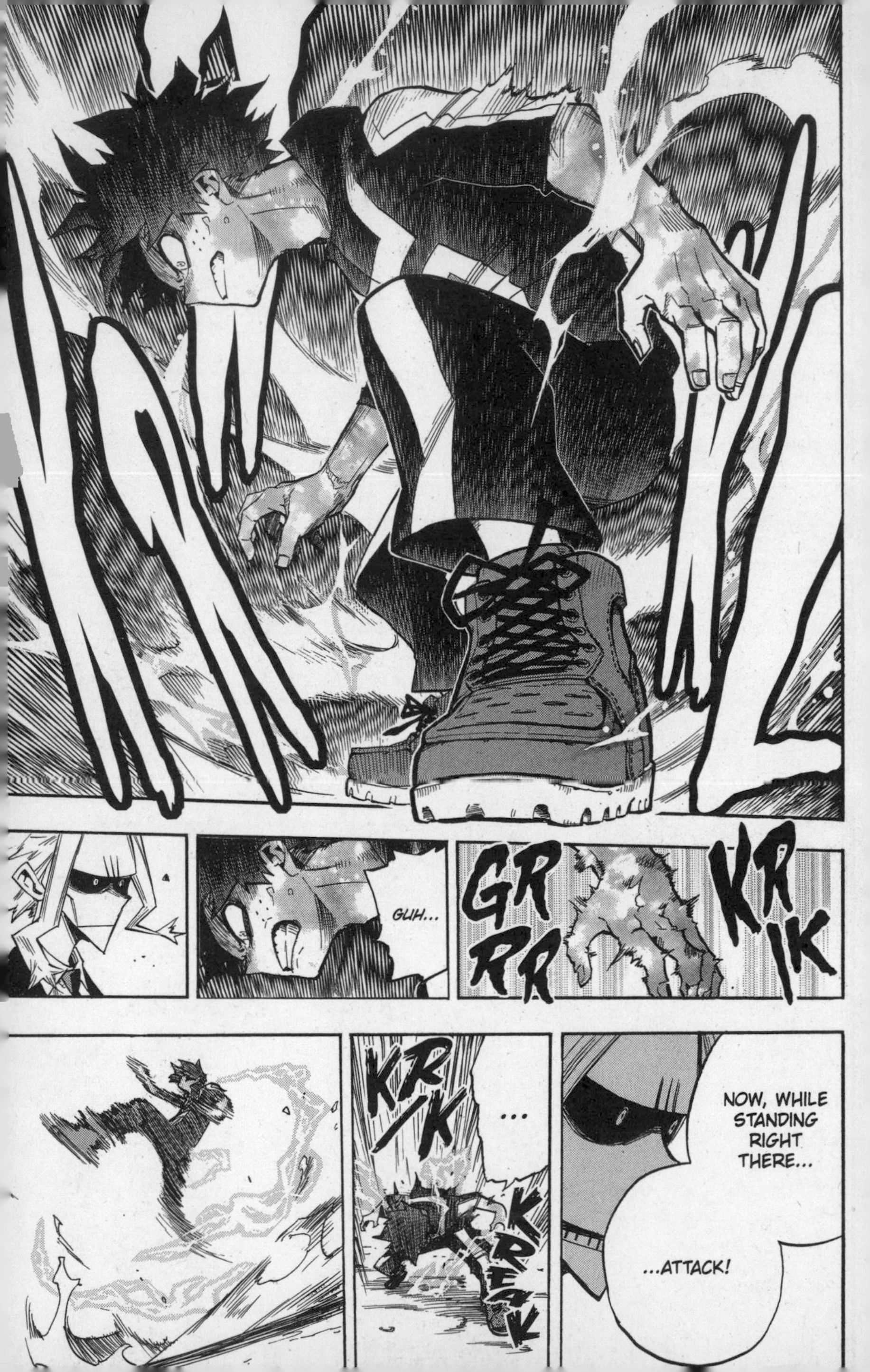
KRIK
GRRR
GUH...
NOW, WHILE STANDING RIGHT THERE...
...ATTACK!
KRK
...
KREAK

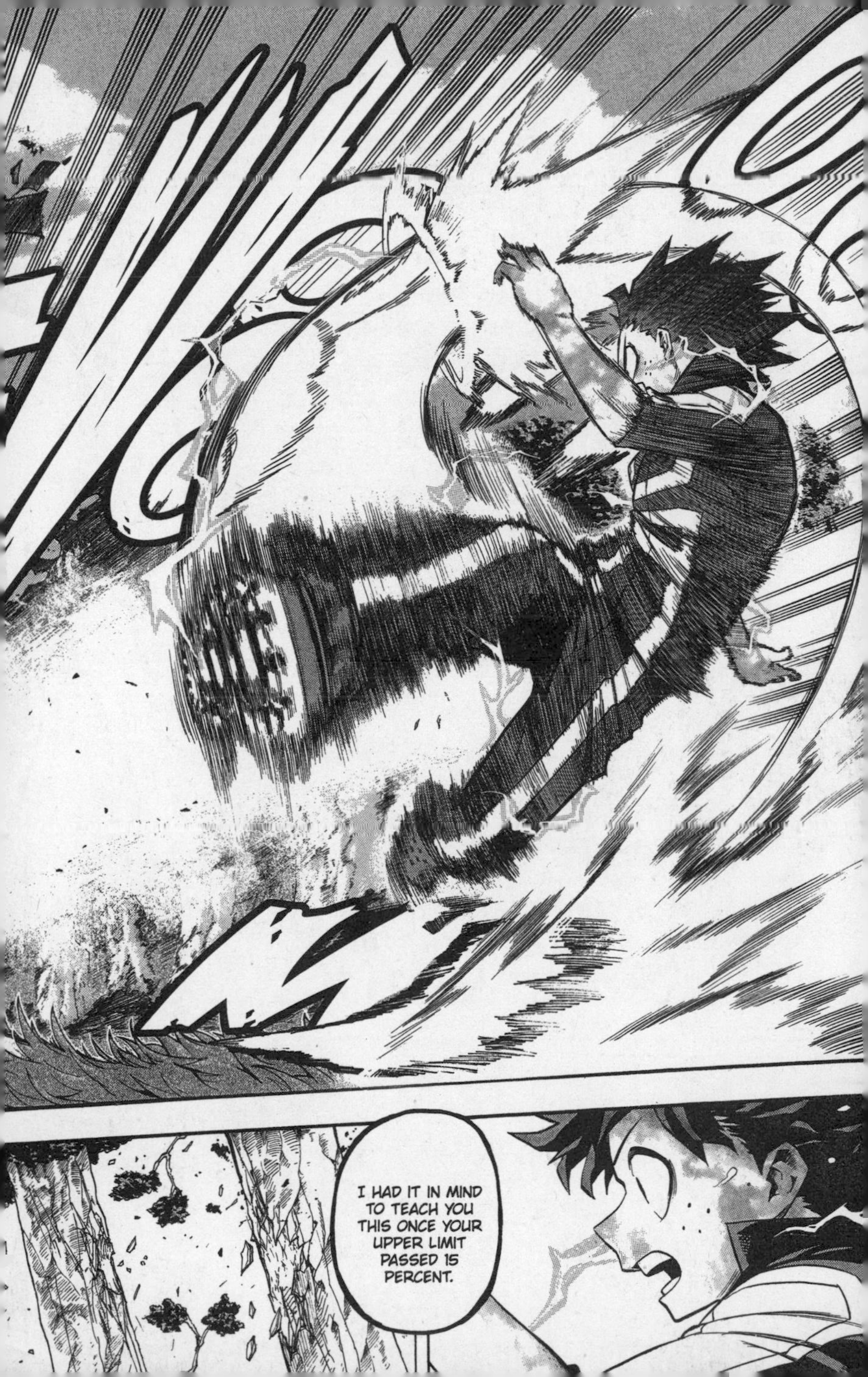
I HAD IT IN MIND TO TEACH YOU THIS ONCE YOUR UPPER LIMIT PASSED 15 PERCENT.

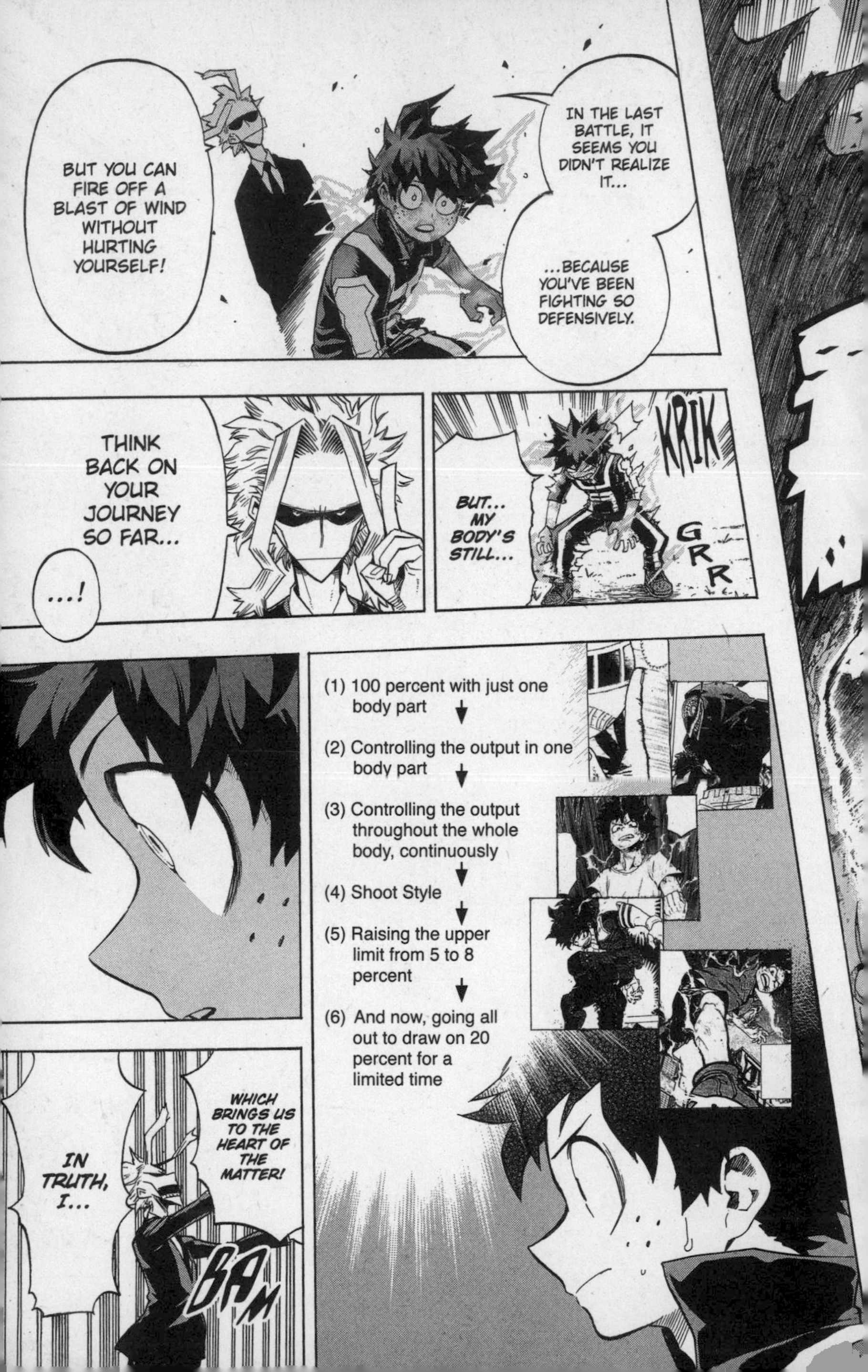
IN THE LAST BATTLE, IT SEEMS YOU DIDN'T REALIZE IT...
...BECAUSE YOU'VE BEEN FIGHTING SO DEFENSIVELY.
BUT YOU CAN FIRE OFF A BLAST OF WIND WITHOUT HURTING YOURSELF!
KRIK
BUT... MY BODY'S STILL...
GRR
THINK BACK ON YOUR JOURNEY SO FAR...
...!
(1) 100 percent with just one body part
(2) Controlling the output in one body part
(3) Controlling the output throughout the whole body, continuously
(4) Shoot Style
(5) Raising the upper limit from 5 to 8 percent
(6) And now, going all out to draw on 20 percent for a limited time
WHICH BRINGS US TO THE HEART OF THE MATTER!
IN TRUTH, I...
BAM

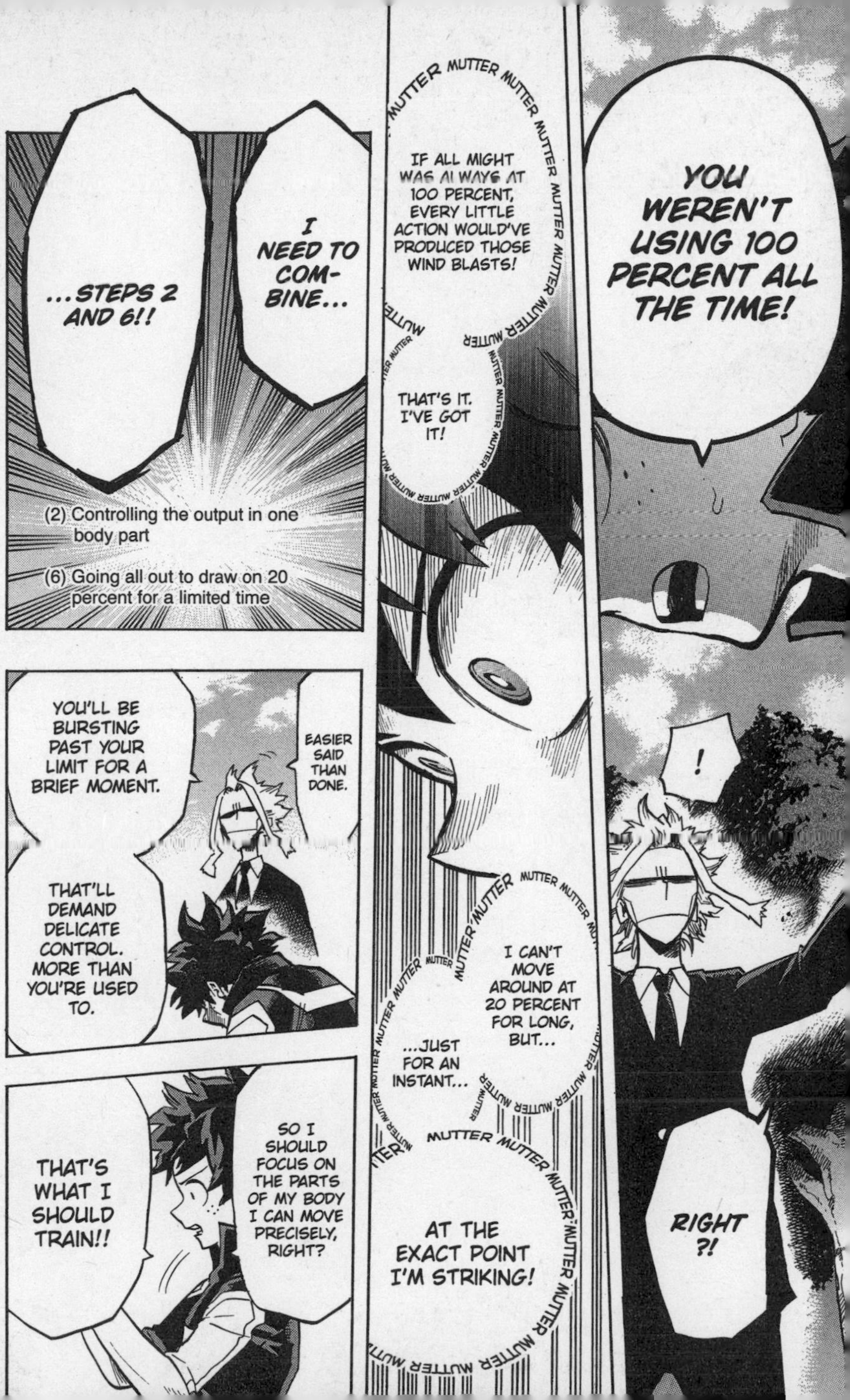
YOU WEREN'T USING 100 PERCENT ALL THE TIME!
!
RIGHT?!
MUTTER MUTTER MUTTER MUTTER MUTTER MUTTER
IF ALL MIGHT WAS ALWAYS AT 100 PERCENT, EVERY LITTLE ACTION WOULD'VE PRODUCED THOSE WIND BLASTS!
THAT'S IT. I'VE GOT IT!
I CAN'T MOVE AROUND AT 20 PERCENT FOR LONG, BUT...
...JUST FOR AN INSTANT...
AT THE EXACT POINT I'M STRIKING!
I NEED TO COMBINE...
...STEPS 2 AND 6!!
(2) Controlling the output in one body part
(6) Going all out to draw on 20 percent for a limited time
EASIER SAID THAN DONE.
YOU'LL BE BURSTING PAST YOUR LIMIT FOR A BRIEF MOMENT.
THAT'LL DEMAND DELICATE CONTROL. MORE THAN YOU'RE USED TO.
SO I SHOULD FOCUS ON THE PARTS OF MY BODY I CAN MOVE PRECISELY, RIGHT?
THAT'S WHAT I SHOULD TRAIN!!

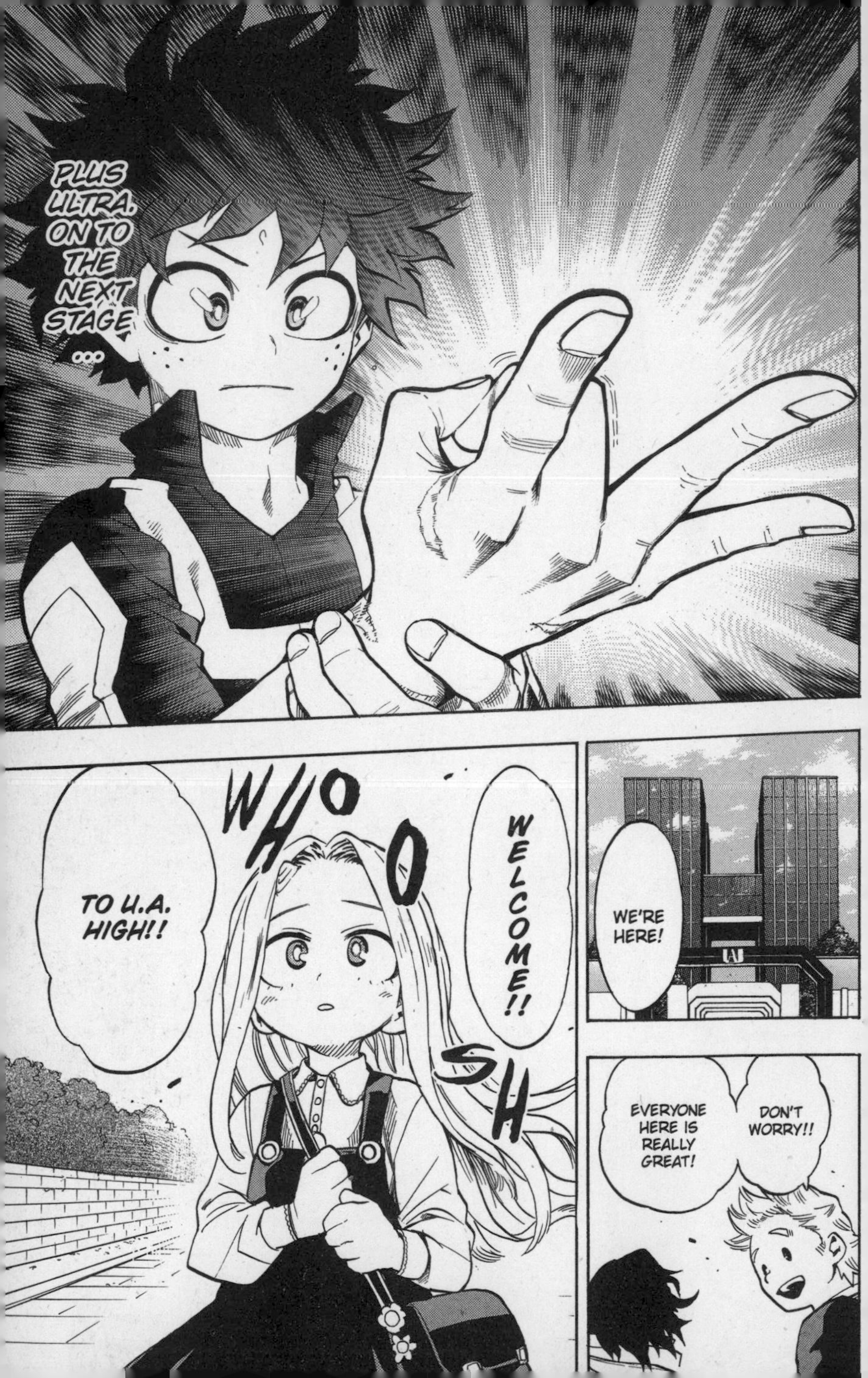
PLUS ULTRA. ON TO THE NEXT STAGE...
WE'RE HERE!
DON'T WORRY!!
EVERYONE HERE IS REALLY GREAT!
WELCOME!!
TO U.A. HIGH!!
WHOOOSH

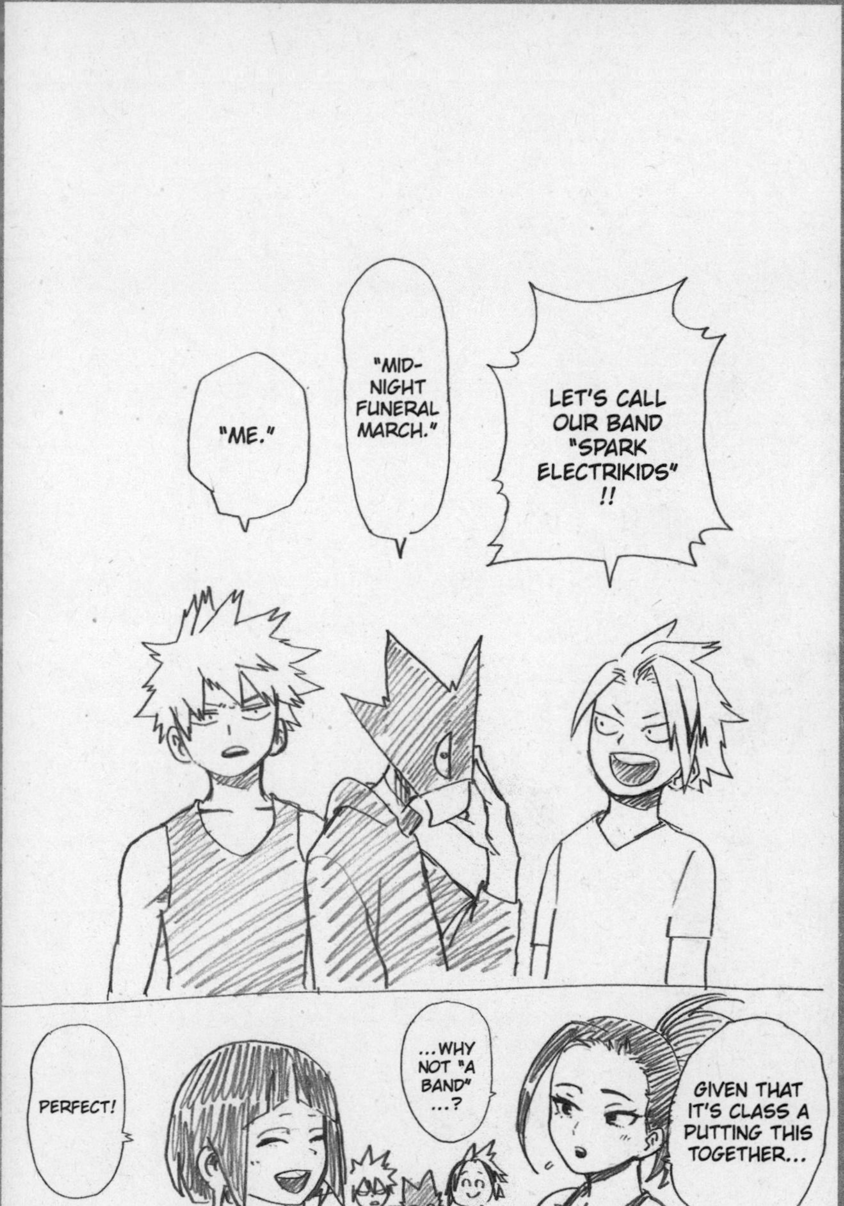
LET'S CALL OUR BAND "SPARK ELECTRIKIDS" !!
"MID-NIGHT FUNERAL MARCH."
"ME."
GIVEN THAT IT'S CLASS A PUTTING THIS TOGETHER...
...WHY NOT "A BAND" ...?
PERFECT!
That's cute.

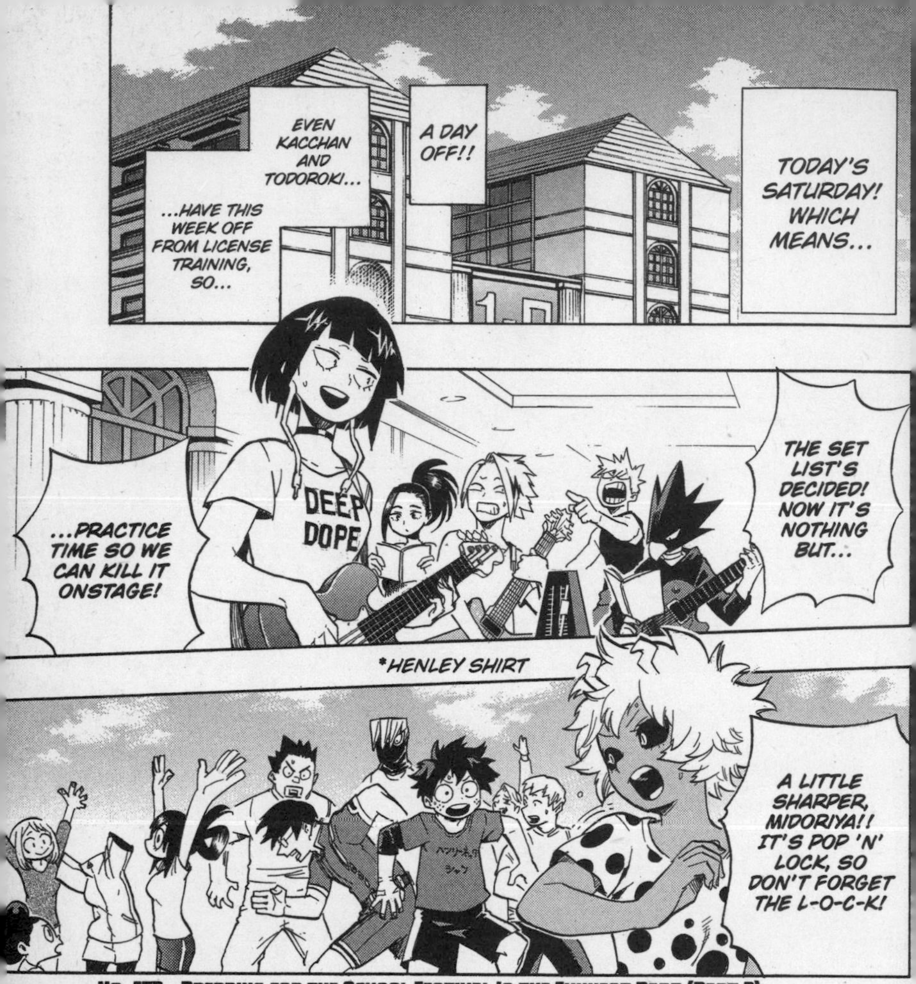
TODAY'S SATURDAY! WHICH MEANS...
A DAY OFF!!
EVEN KACCHAN AND TODOROKI...
...HAVE THIS WEEK OFF FROM LICENSE TRAINING, SO...
THE SET LIST'S DECIDED! NOW IT'S NOTHING BUT...
DEEP DOPE
...PRACTICE TIME SO WE CAN KILL IT ONSTAGE!
*HENLEY SHIRT
A LITTLE SHARPER, MIDORIYA!! IT'S POP 'N' LOCK, SO DON'T FORGET THE L-O-C-K!

No. 173 - Prepping for the School Festival Is the Funnest Part (Part 2)

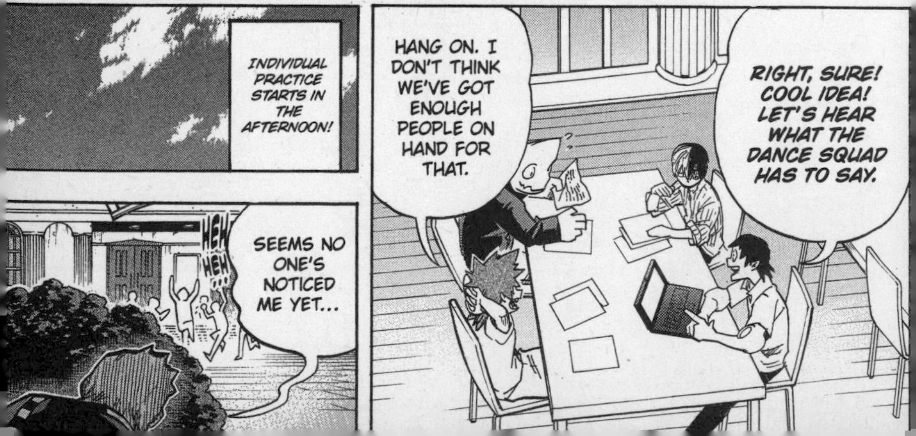
RIGHT, SURE! COOL IDEA! LET'S HEAR WHAT THE DANCE SQUAD HAS TO SAY.
HANG ON. I DON'T THINK WE'VE GOT ENOUGH PEOPLE ON HAND FOR THAT.
INDIVIDUAL PRACTICE STARTS IN THE AFTERNOON!
HEH HEH
SEEMS NO ONE'S NOTICED ME YET...

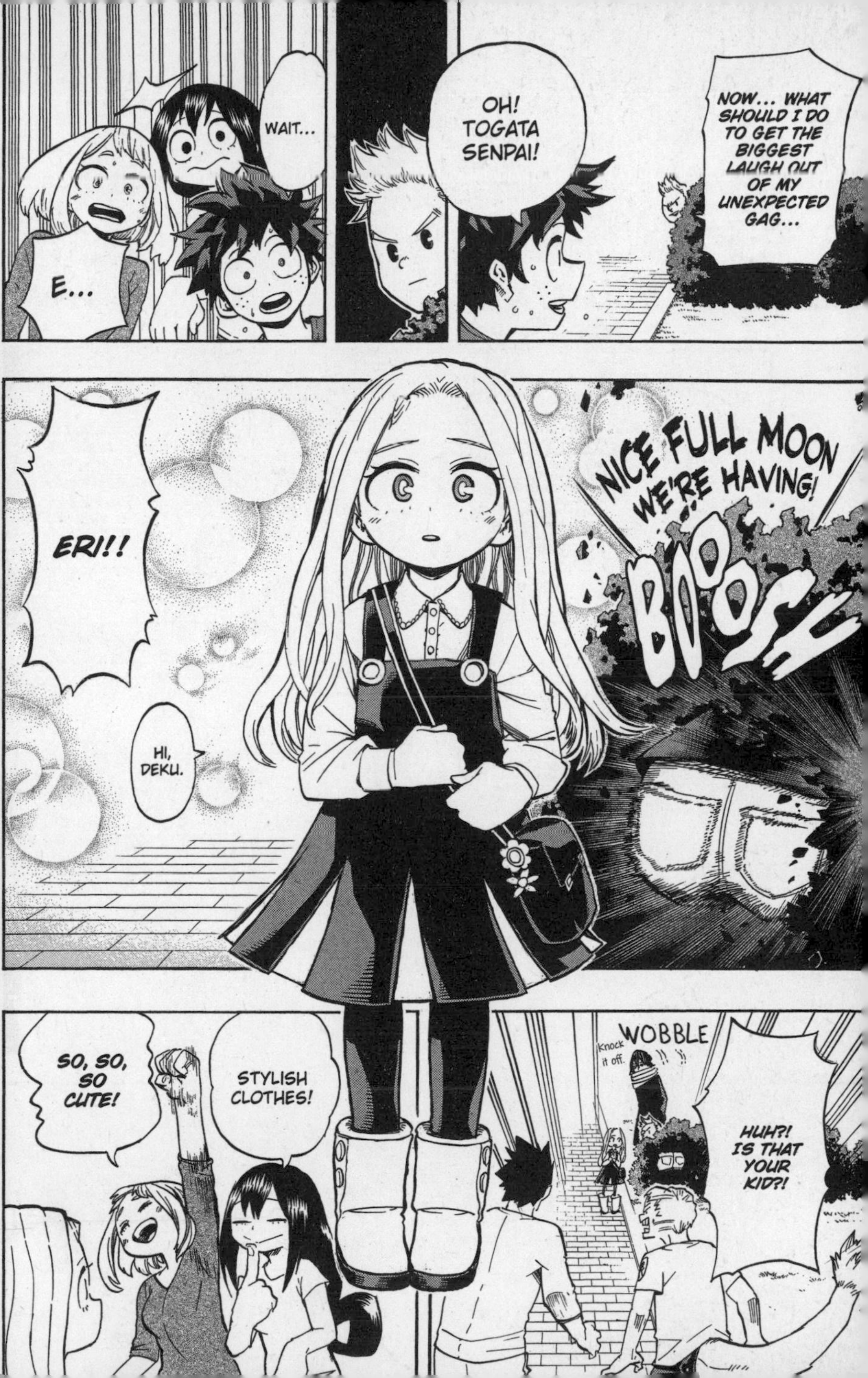
NOW... WHAT SHOULD I DO TO GET THE BIGGEST LAUGH OUT OF MY UNEXPECTED GAG...
OH! TOGATA SENPAI!
WAIT...
E...
NICE FULL MOON WE'RE HAVING!
BOOSH
ERI!!
HI, DEKU.
HUH?! IS THAT YOUR KID?!
WOBBLE
Knock it off.
STYLISH CLOTHES!
SO, SO, SO CUTE!

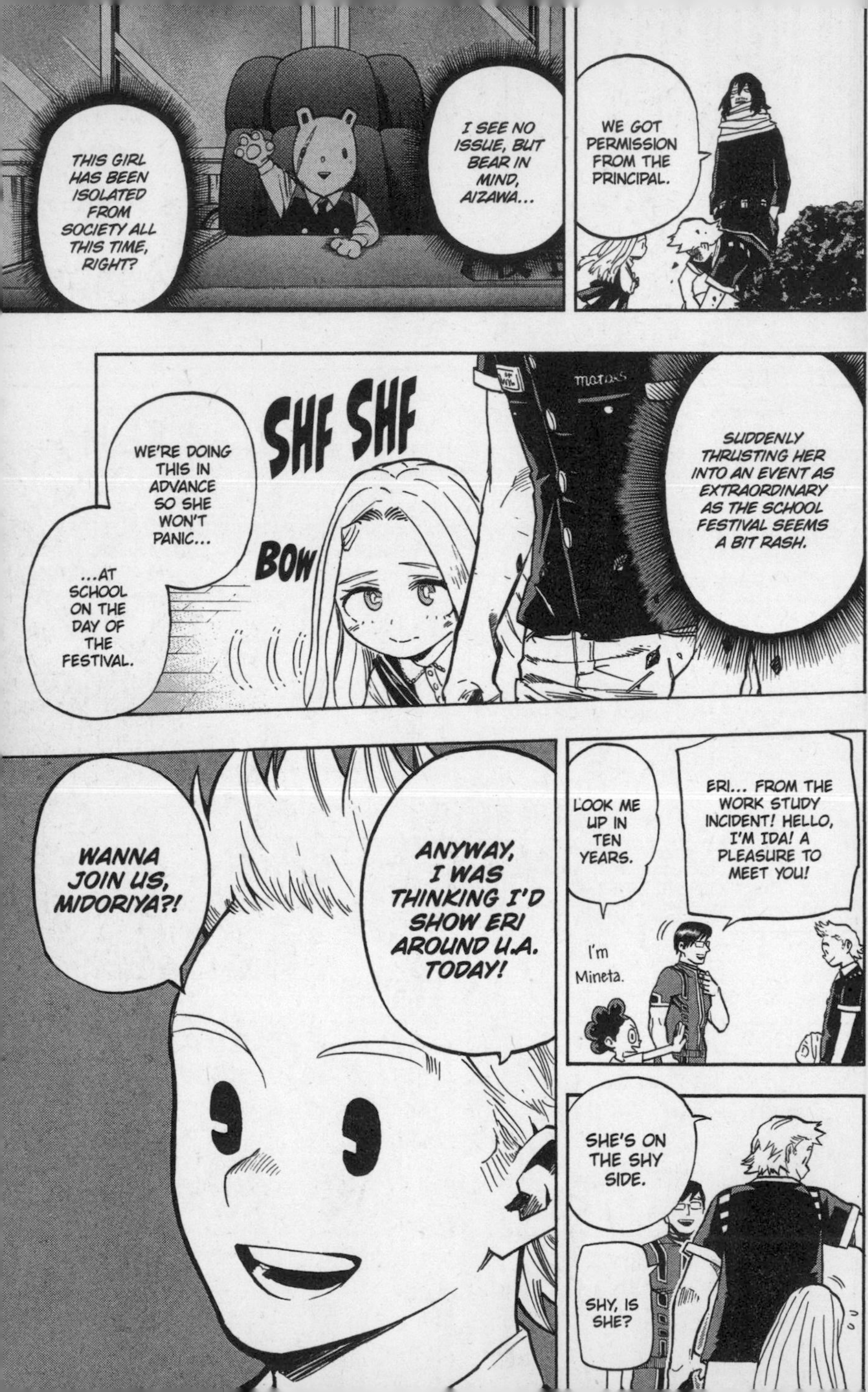
WE GOT PERMISSION FROM THE PRINCIPAL.
I SEE NO ISSUE, BUT BEAR IN MIND, AIZAWA...
THIS GIRL HAS BEEN ISOLATED FROM SOCIETY ALL THIS TIME, RIGHT?
SUDDENLY THRUSTING HER INTO AN EVENT AS EXTRAORDINARY AS THE SCHOOL FESTIVAL SEEMS A BIT RASH.
SHF SHF
BOW
WE'RE DOING THIS IN ADVANCE SO SHE WON'T PANIC...
...AT SCHOOL ON THE DAY OF THE FESTIVAL.
ERI... FROM THE WORK STUDY INCIDENT! HELLO, I'M IDA! A PLEASURE TO MEET YOU!
LOOK ME UP IN TEN YEARS.
I'm Mineta.
SHE'S ON THE SHY SIDE.
SHY, IS SHE?
ANYWAY, I WAS THINKING I'D SHOW ERI AROUND U.A. TODAY!
WANNA JOIN US, MIDORIYA?!

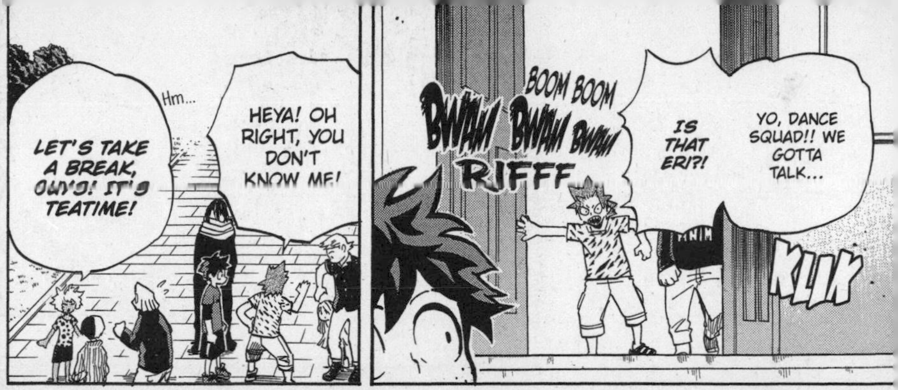
YO, DANCE SQUAD!! WE GOTTA TALK...
IS THAT ERI?!
BOOM BOOM
BWAM BWAM BWAM
RIFFF
KLIK
HEYA! OH RIGHT, YOU DON'T KNOW ME!
Hm...
LET'S TAKE A BREAK, GUYS! IT'S TEATIME!

No. 173 - Prepping for the School Festival Is the Funnest Part (Part 2)

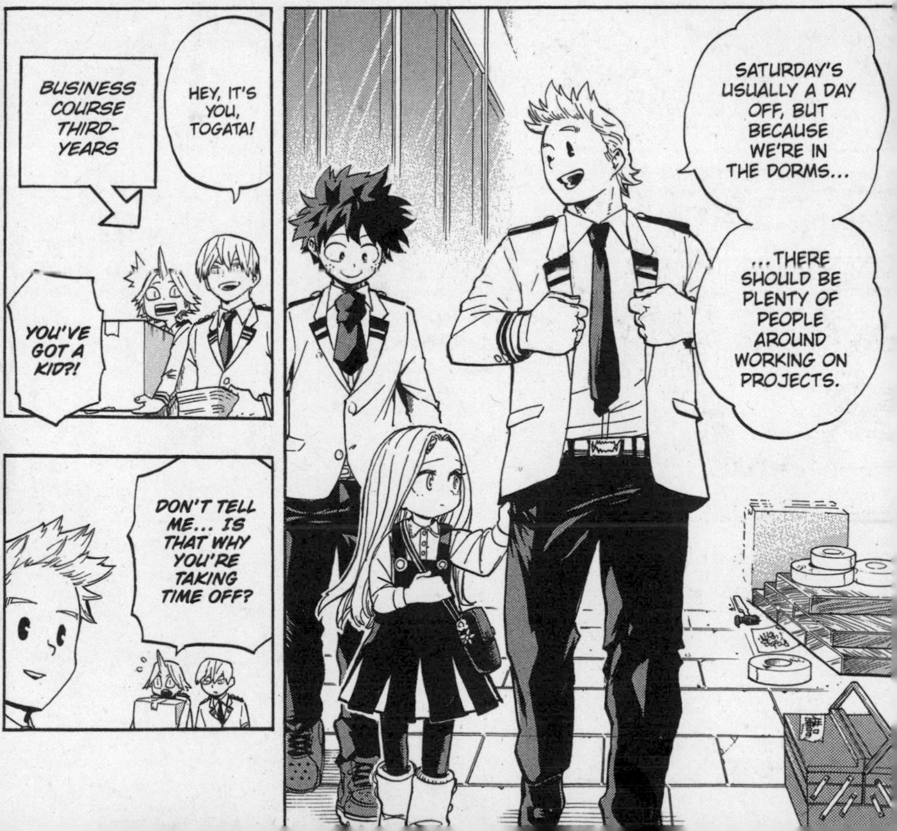
SATURDAY'S USUALLY A DAY OFF, BUT BECAUSE WE'RE IN THE DORMS...
...THERE SHOULD BE PLENTY OF PEOPLE AROUND WORKING ON PROJECTS.
HEY, IT'S YOU, TOGATA!
BUSINESS COURSE THIRD-YEARS
YOU'VE GOT A KID?!
DON'T TELL ME... IS THAT WHY YOU'RE TAKING TIME OFF?

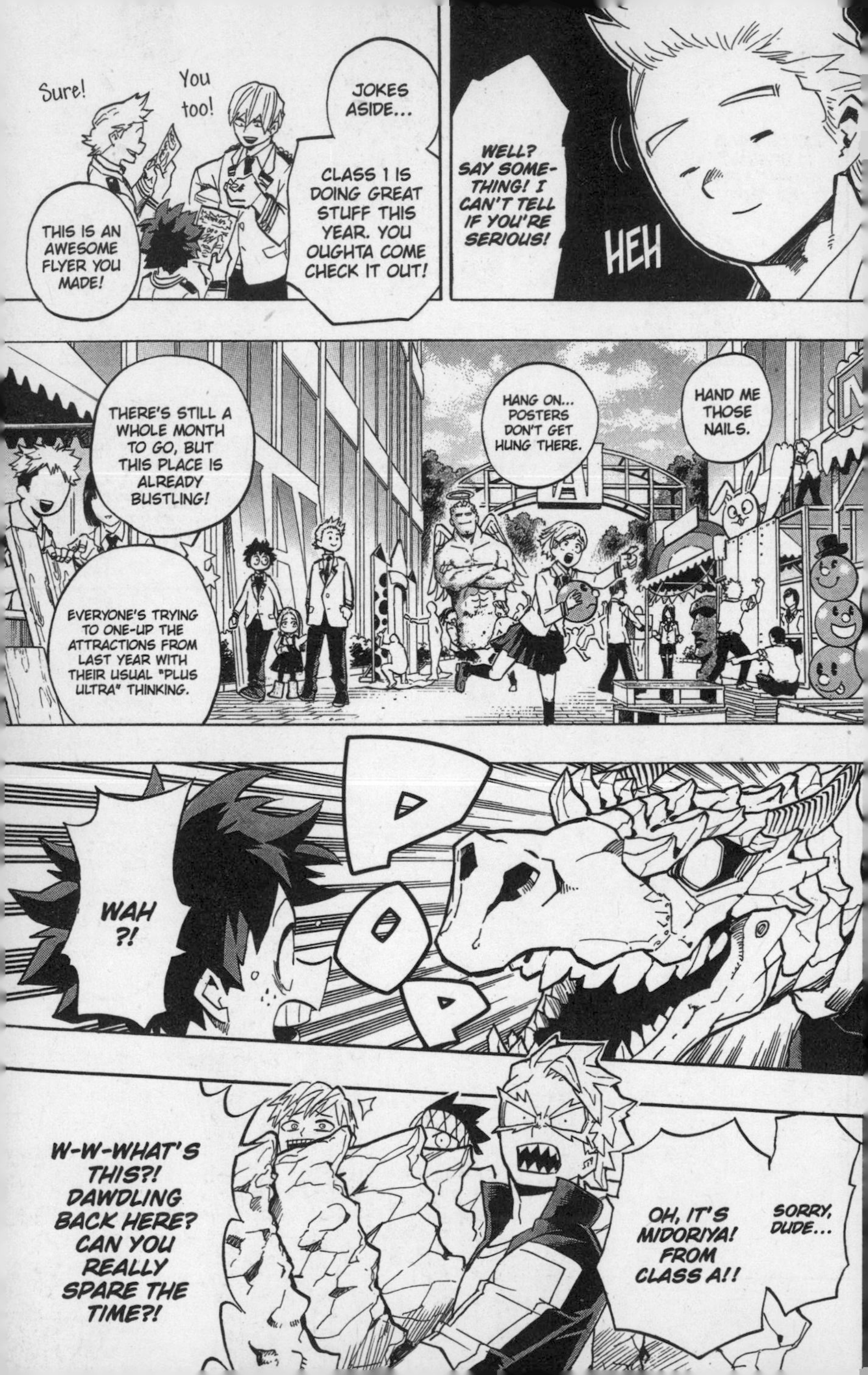
THIS IS AN AWESOME FLYER YOU MADE!
Sure!
You too!
JOKES ASIDE...
CLASS 1 IS DOING GREAT STUFF THIS YEAR. YOU OUGHTA COME CHECK IT OUT!
WELL? SAY SOME-THING! I CAN'T TELL IF YOU'RE SERIOUS!
HEH
THERE'S STILL A WHOLE MONTH TO GO, BUT THIS PLACE IS ALREADY BUSTLING!
EVERYONE'S TRYING TO ONE-UP THE ATTRACTIONS FROM LAST YEAR WITH THEIR USUAL "PLUS ULTRA" THINKING.
HANG ON... POSTERS DON'T GET HUNG THERE.
HAND ME THOSE NAILS.
WAH ?!
POP
W-W-WHAT'S THIS?! DAWDLING BACK HERE? CAN YOU REALLY SPARE THE TIME?!
OH, IT'S MIDORIYA! FROM CLASS A!!
SORRY, DUDE...

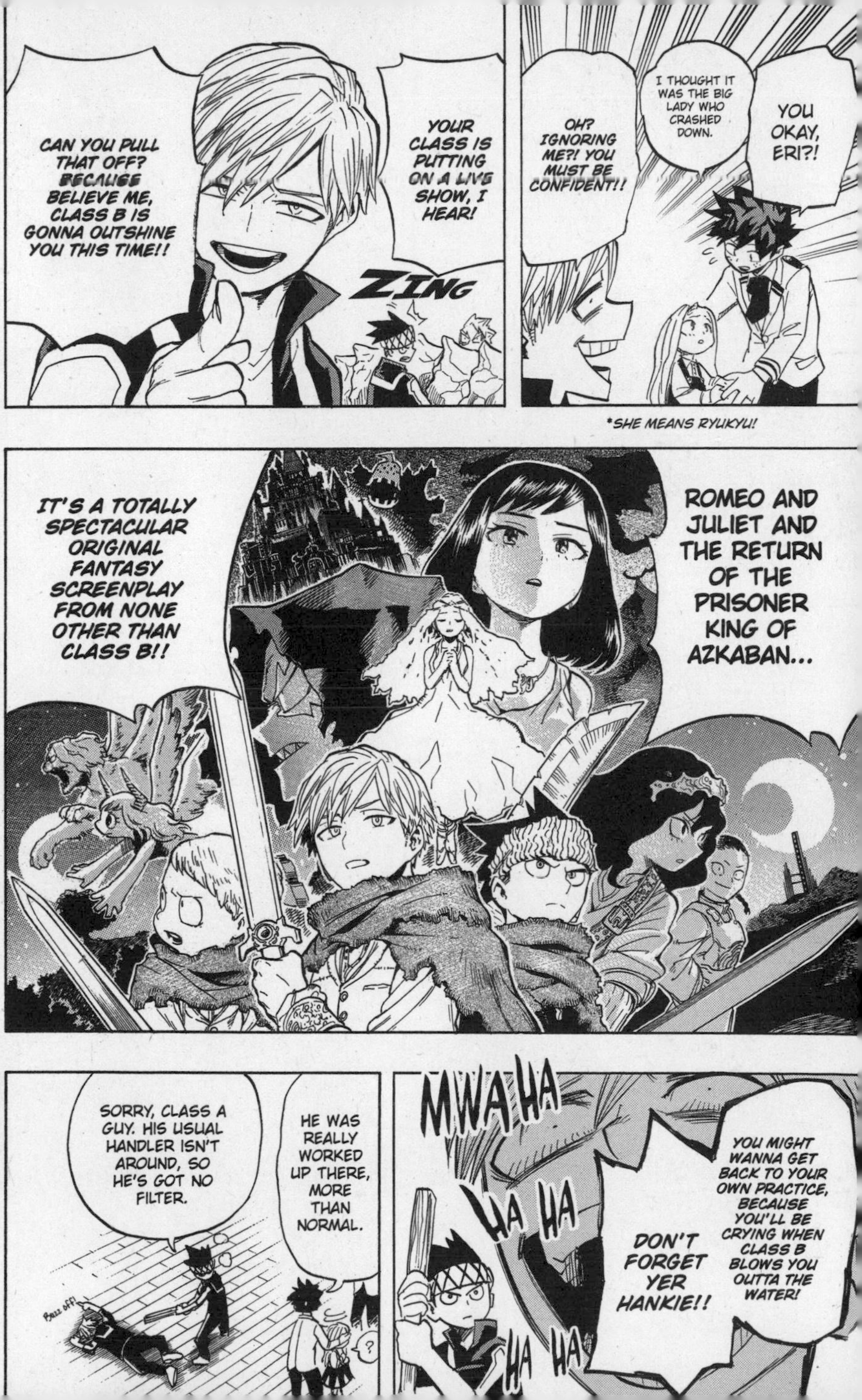
YOU OKAY, ERI?!
I THOUGHT IT WAS THE BIG LADY WHO CRASHED DOWN.
OH? IGNORING ME?! YOU MUST BE CONFIDENT!!
YOUR CLASS IS PUTTING ON A LIVE SHOW, I HEAR!
CAN YOU PULL THAT OFF? BECAUSE BELIEVE ME, CLASS B IS GONNA OUTSHINE YOU THIS TIME!!
ZING
*SHE MEANS RYUKYU!
ROMEO AND JULIET AND THE RETURN OF THE PRISONER KING OF AZKABAN...
IT'S A TOTALLY SPECTACULAR ORIGINAL FANTASY SCREENPLAY FROM NONE OTHER THAN CLASS B!!
MWA HA
HA HA
HA HA
YOU MIGHT WANNA GET BACK TO YOUR OWN PRACTICE, BECAUSE YOU'LL BE CRYING WHEN CLASS B BLOWS YOU OUTTA THE WATER!
DON'T FORGET YER HANKIE!!
HE WAS REALLY WORKED UP THERE, MORE THAN NORMAL.
SORRY, CLASS A GUY. HIS USUAL HANDLER ISN'T AROUND, SO HE'S GOT NO FILTER.
?

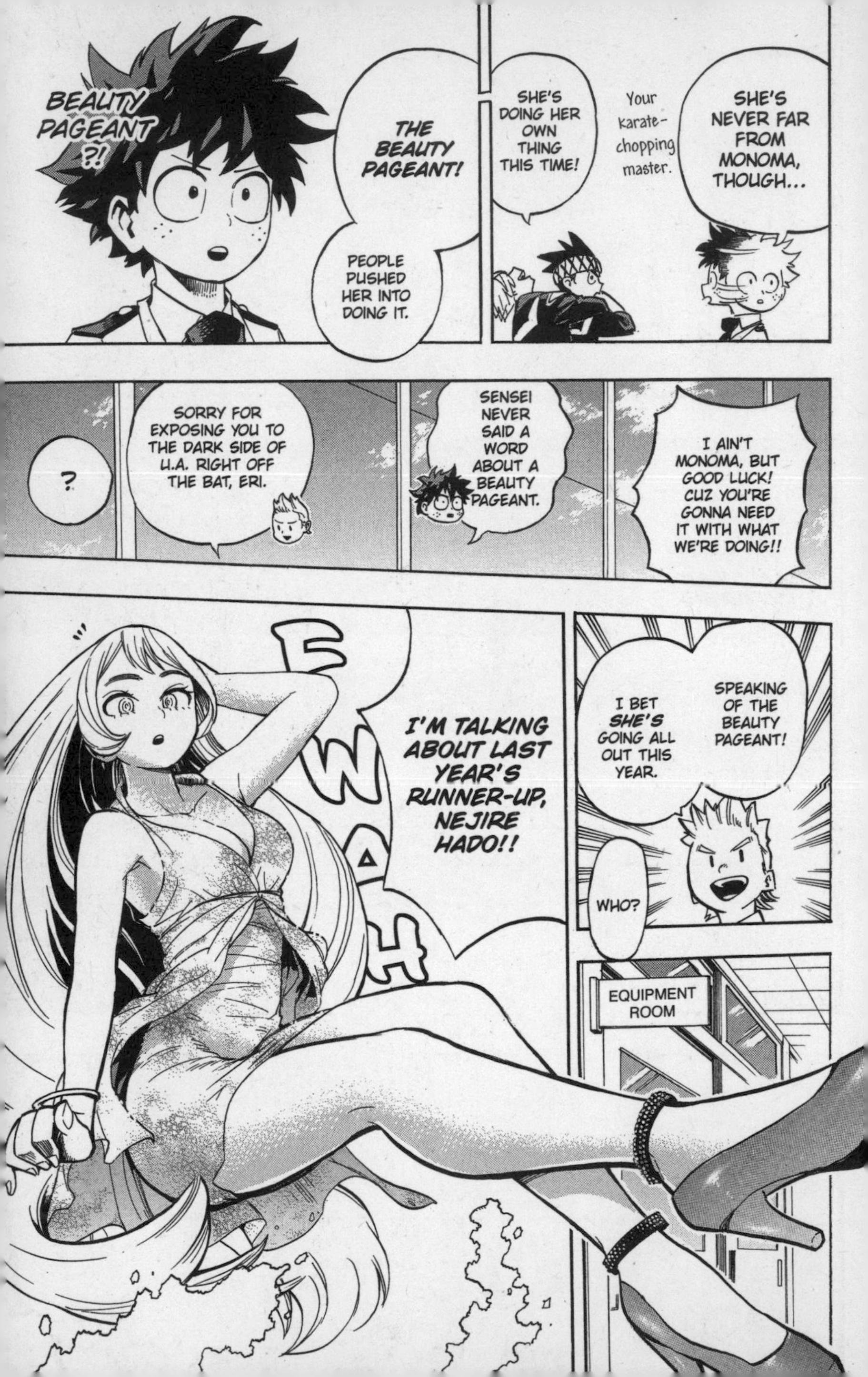
SHE'S NEVER FAR FROM MONOMA, THOUGH...
Your karate-chopping master.
SHE'S DOING HER OWN THING THIS TIME!
THE BEAUTY PAGEANT!
PEOPLE PUSHED HER INTO DOING IT.
BEAUTY PAGEANT ?!
I AIN'T MONOMA, BUT GOOD LUCK! CUZ YOU'RE GONNA NEED IT WITH WHAT WE'RE DOING!!
SENSEI NEVER SAID A WORD ABOUT A BEAUTY PAGEANT.
SORRY FOR EXPOSING YOU TO THE DARK SIDE OF U.A. RIGHT OFF THE BAT, ERI.
?
SPEAKING OF THE BEAUTY PAGEANT!
I BET SHE'S GOING ALL OUT THIS YEAR.
WHO?
EQUIPMENT ROOM
I'M TALKING ABOUT LAST YEAR'S RUNNER-UP, NEJIRE HADO!!

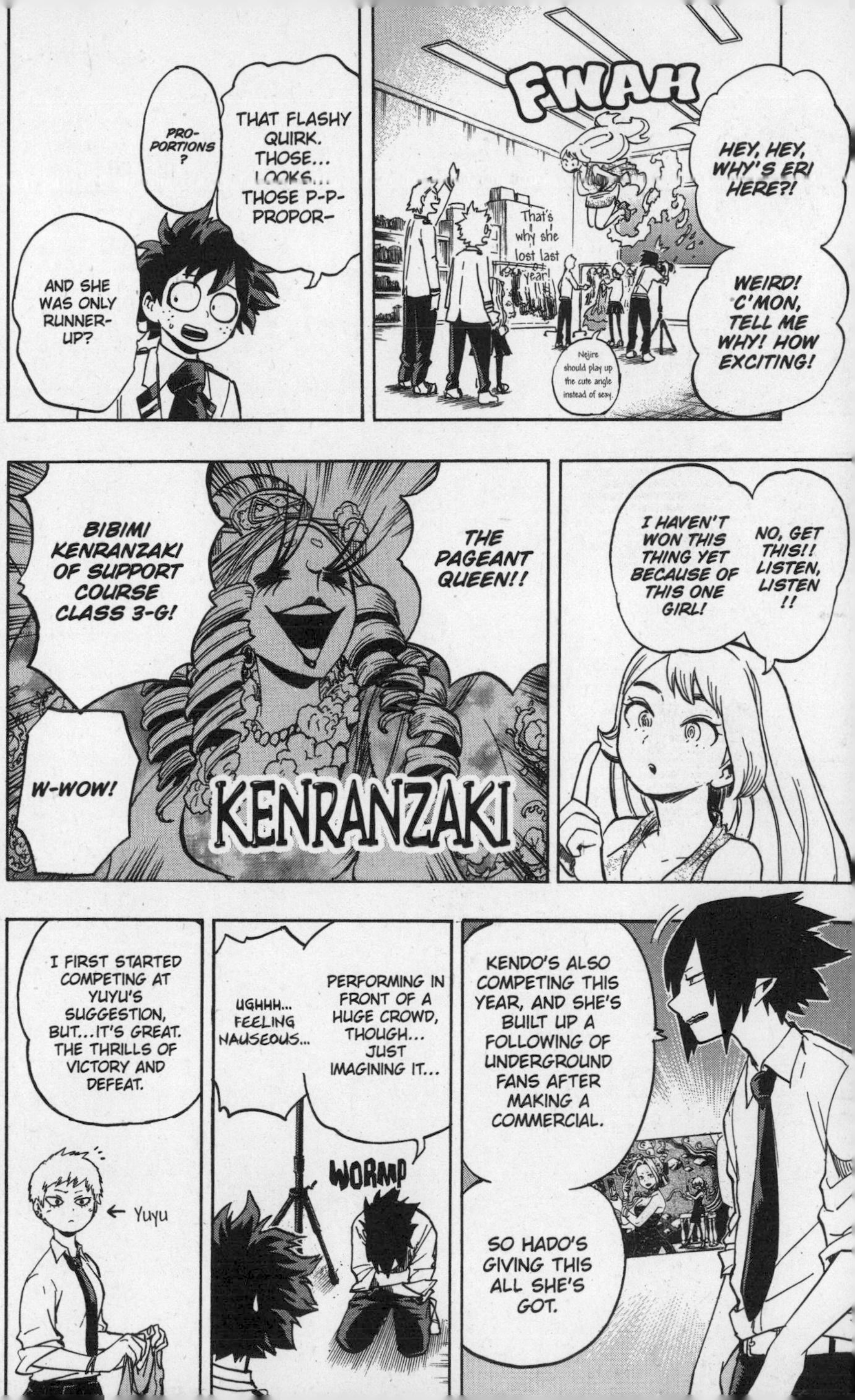
FWAH
HEY, HEY, WHY'S ERI HERE?!
WEIRD! C'MON, TELL ME WHY! HOW EXCITING!
That's why she lost last year!
Nejire should play up the cute angle instead of sexy.
THAT FLASHY QUIRK. THOSE... LOOKS... THOSE P-P-PROPOR-
PRO-PORTIONS?
AND SHE WAS ONLY RUNNER-UP?
NO, GET THIS!! LISTEN, LISTEN!!
I HAVEN'T WON THIS THING YET BECAUSE OF THIS ONE GIRL!
THE PAGEANT QUEEN!!
BIBIMI KENRANZAKI OF SUPPORT COURSE CLASS 3-G!
KENRANZAKI
W-WOW!
KENDO'S ALSO COMPETING THIS YEAR, AND SHE'S BUILT UP A FOLLOWING OF UNDERGROUND FANS AFTER MAKING A COMMERCIAL.
SO HADO'S GIVING THIS ALL SHE'S GOT.
PERFORMING IN FRONT OF A HUGE CROWD, THOUGH... JUST IMAGINING IT...
UGHHH... FEELING NAUSEOUS...
WORMP
I FIRST STARTED COMPETING AT YUYU'S SUGGESTION, BUT...IT'S GREAT. THE THRILLS OF VICTORY AND DEFEAT.
Yuyu

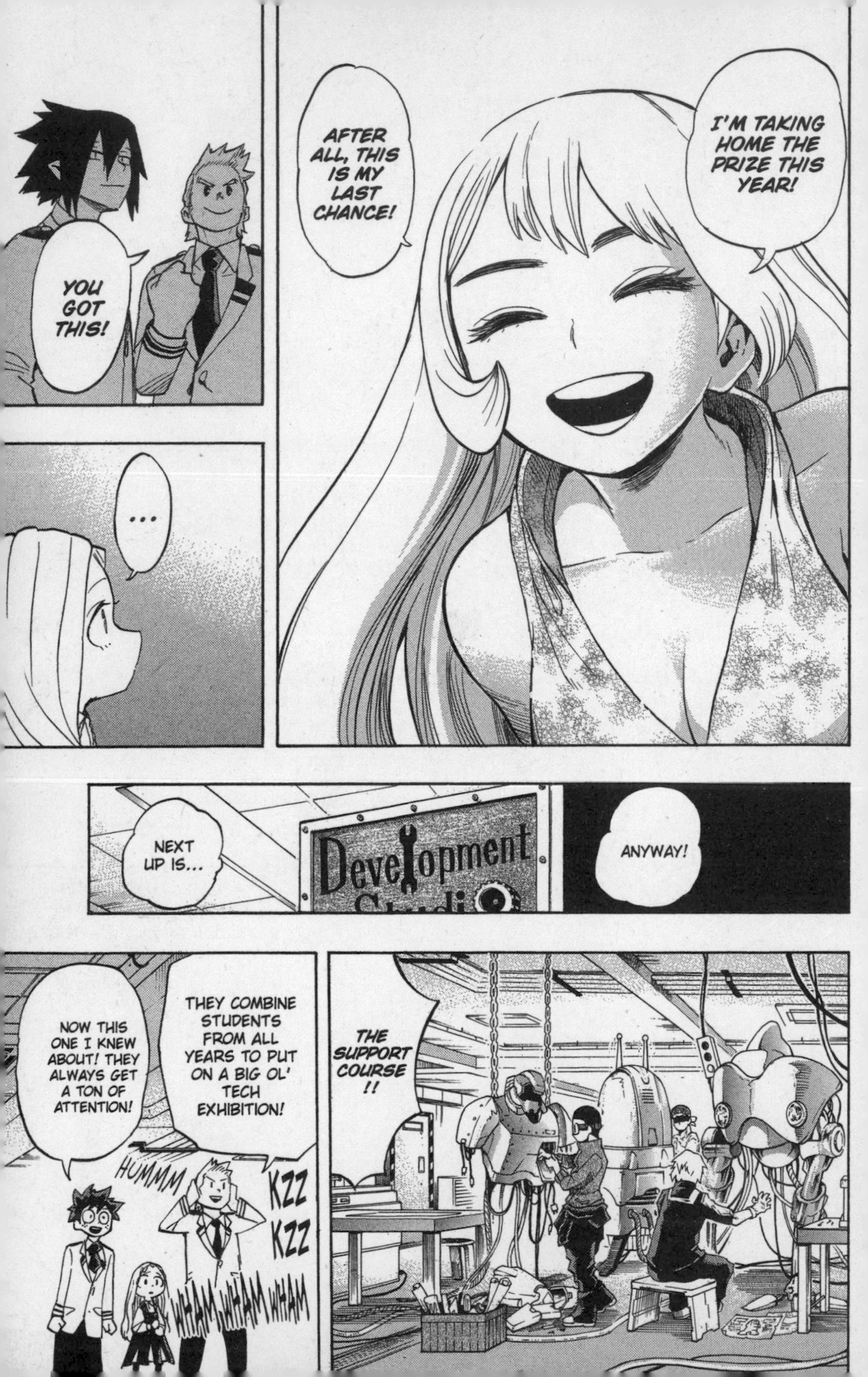
I'M TAKING HOME THE PRIZE THIS YEAR!
AFTER ALL, THIS IS MY LAST CHANCE!
YOU GOT THIS!
...
ANYWAY!
Development
NEXT UP IS...
THE SUPPORT COURSE !!
THEY COMBINE STUDENTS FROM ALL YEARS TO PUT ON A BIG OL' TECH EXHIBITION!
NOW THIS ONE I KNEW ABOUT! THEY ALWAYS GET A TON OF ATTENTION!
KZZ KZZ
HUMMM
WHAM WHAM WHAM

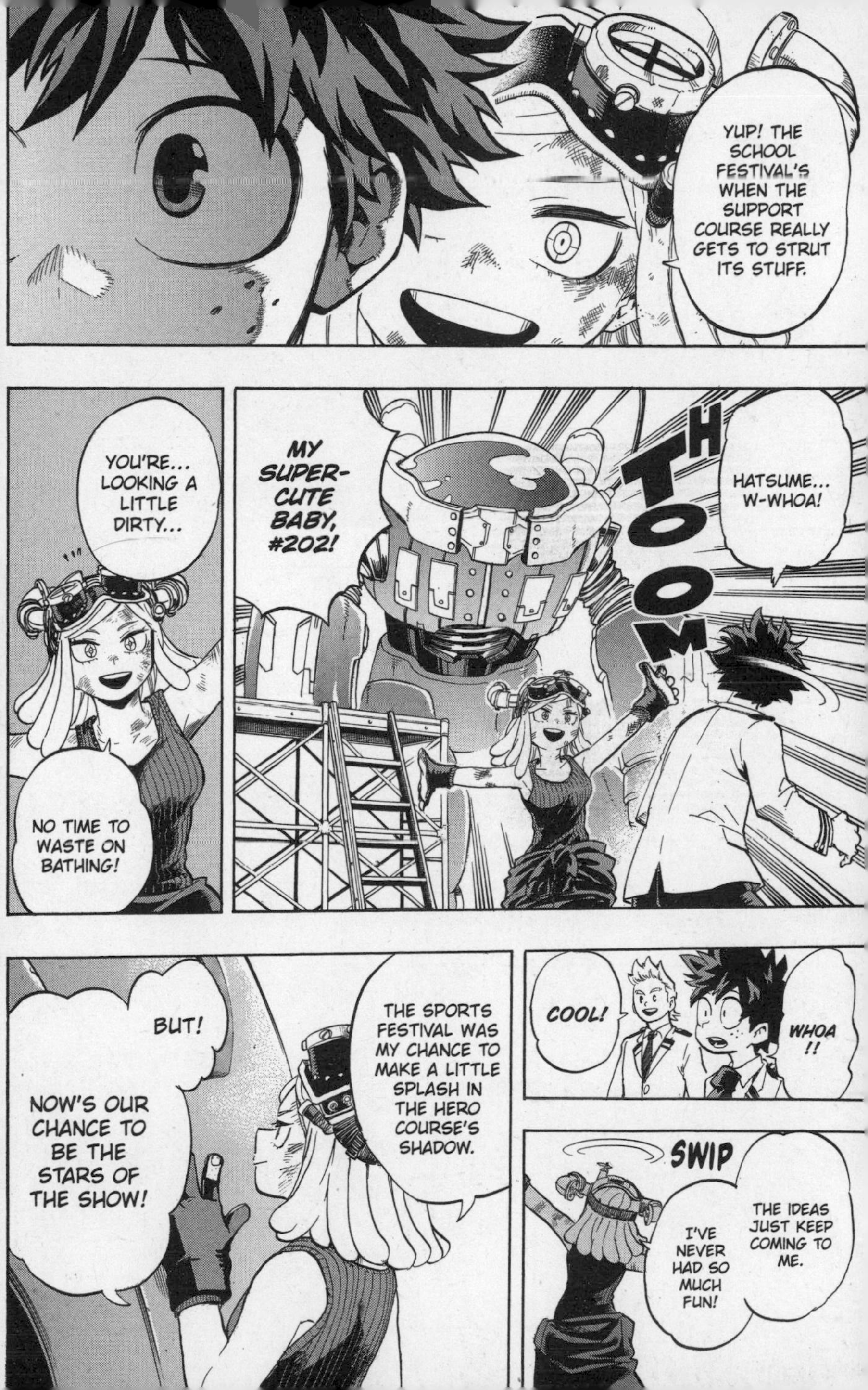
YUP! THE SCHOOL FESTIVAL'S WHEN THE SUPPORT COURSE REALLY GETS TO STRUT ITS STUFF.
HATSUME... W-WHOA!
THOOM
MY SUPER-CUTE BABY, #202!
YOU'RE... LOOKING A LITTLE DIRTY...
NO TIME TO WASTE ON BATHING!
WHOA!!
COOL!
SWIP
THE IDEAS JUST KEEP COMING TO ME.
I'VE NEVER HAD SO MUCH FUN!
THE SPORTS FESTIVAL WAS MY CHANCE TO MAKE A LITTLE SPLASH IN THE HERO COURSE'S SHADOW.
BUT!
NOW'S OUR CHANCE TO BE THE STARS OF THE SHOW!

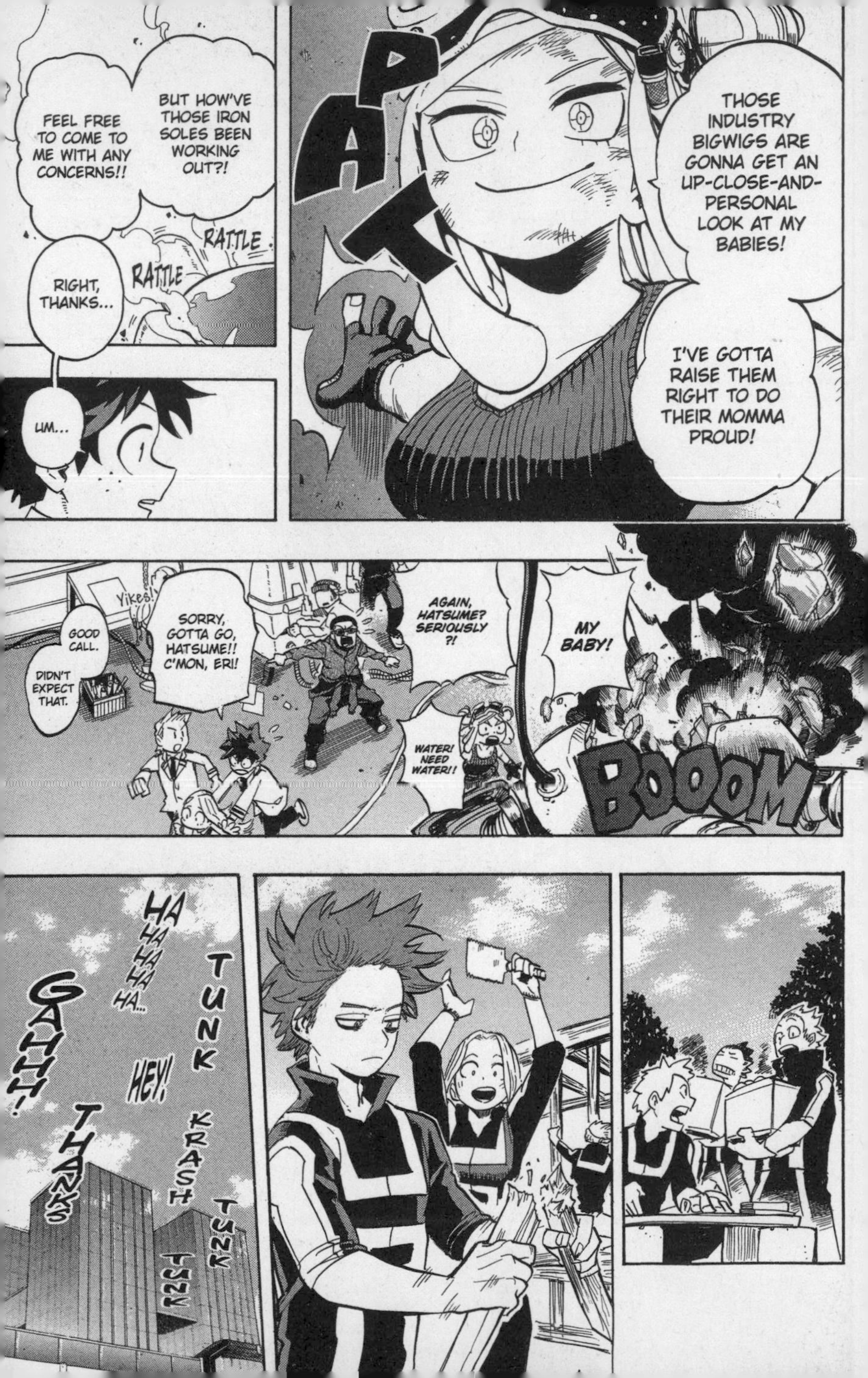
THOSE INDUSTRY BIGWIGS ARE GONNA GET AN UP-CLOSE-AND-PERSONAL LOOK AT MY BABIES!
I'VE GOTTA RAISE THEM RIGHT TO DO THEIR MOMMA PROUD!
BUT HOW'VE THOSE IRON SOLES BEEN WORKING OUT?!
FEEL FREE TO COME TO ME WITH ANY CONCERNS!!
RATTLE
RATTLE
RIGHT, THANKS...
UM...
BOOOM
MY BABY!
WATER! NEED WATER!!
AGAIN, HATSUME? SERIOUSLY?!
SORRY, GOTTA GO, HATSUME!! C'MON, ERI!
Yikes!
GOOD CALL.
DIDN'T EXPECT THAT.
HAHAHAHA...
TUNK
HEY!
KRASH
TUNK
GAHHH!
THANKS
TUNK

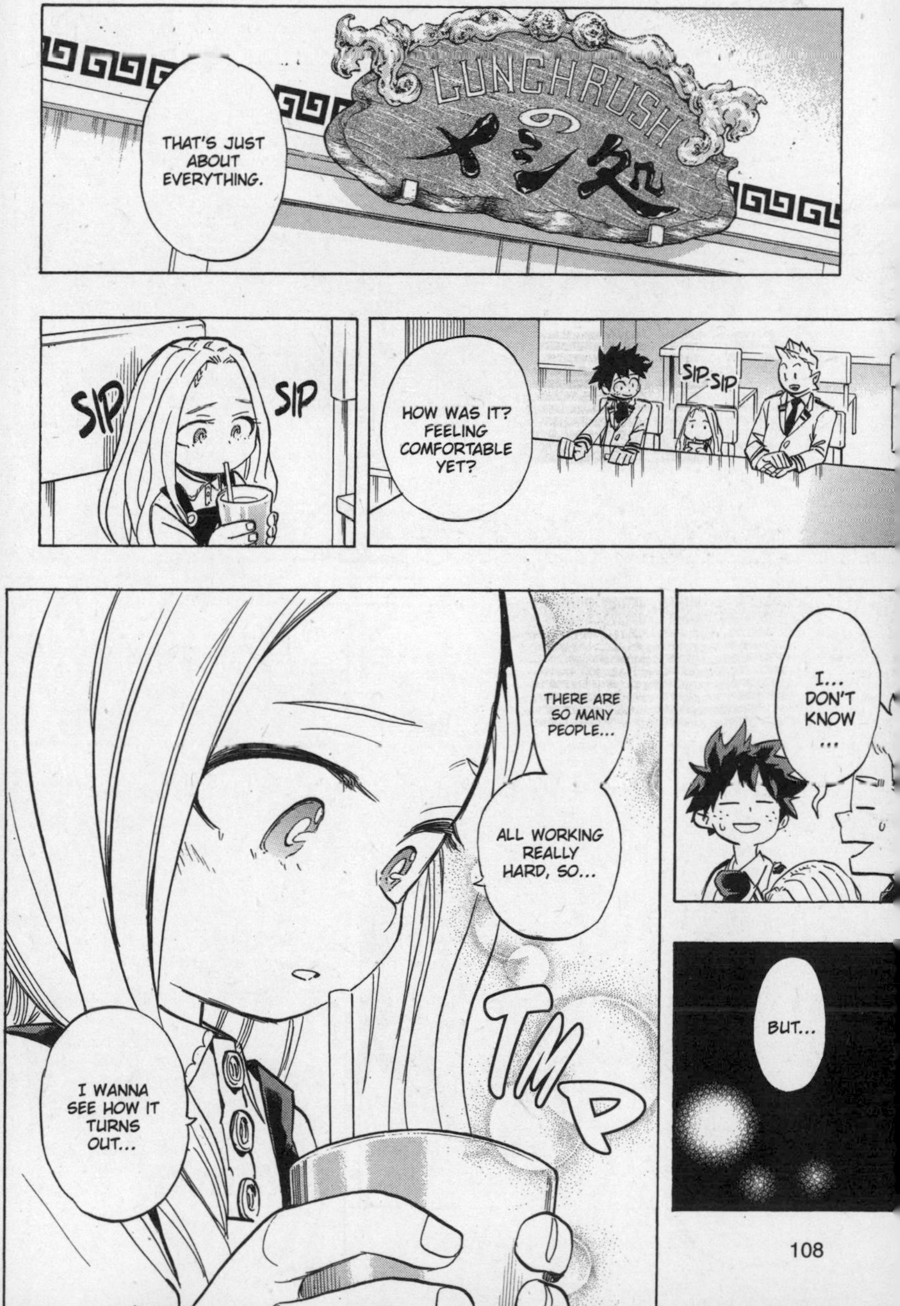
LUNCHRUSH
のメシ処
THAT'S JUST ABOUT EVERYTHING.
SIP SIP
HOW WAS IT? FEELING COMFORTABLE YET?
SIP SIP
I... DON'T KNOW ...
BUT...
THERE ARE SO MANY PEOPLE...
ALL WORKING REALLY HARD, SO...
TMP
I WANNA SEE HOW IT TURNS OUT...

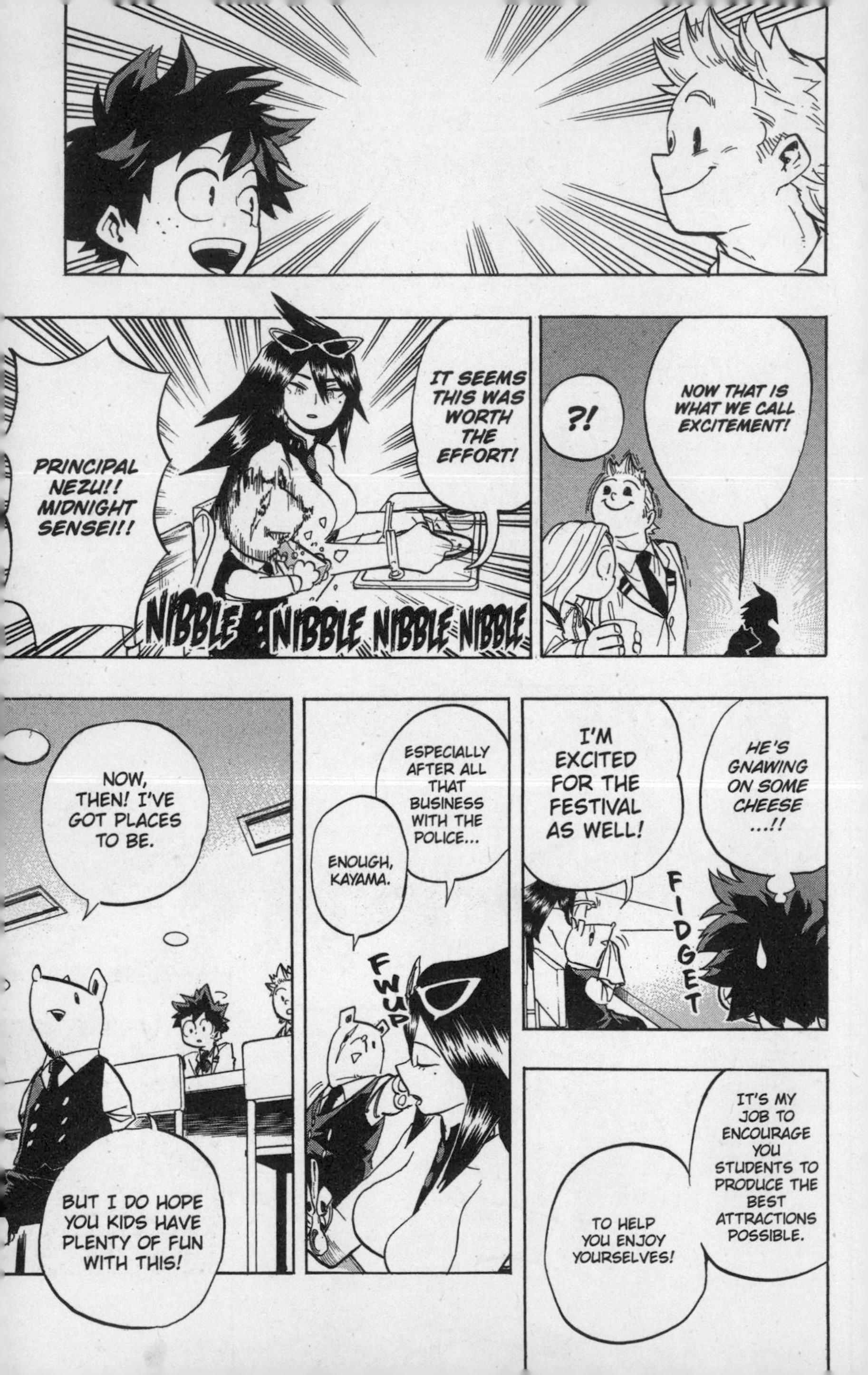

NOW THAT IS WHAT WE CALL EXCITEMENT!
?!
IT SEEMS THIS WAS WORTH THE EFFORT!
PRINCIPAL NEZU!! MIDNIGHT SENSEI!!
NIBBLE NIBBLE NIBBLE NIBBLE
HE'S GNAWING ON SOME CHEESE ...!!
I'M EXCITED FOR THE FESTIVAL AS WELL!
FIDGET
IT'S MY JOB TO ENCOURAGE YOU STUDENTS TO PRODUCE THE BEST ATTRACTIONS POSSIBLE.
TO HELP YOU ENJOY YOURSELVES!
ESPECIALLY AFTER ALL THAT BUSINESS WITH THE POLICE...
ENOUGH, KAYAMA.
FWUP
NOW, THEN! I'VE GOT PLACES TO BE.
BUT I DO HOPE YOU KIDS HAVE PLENTY OF FUN WITH THIS!

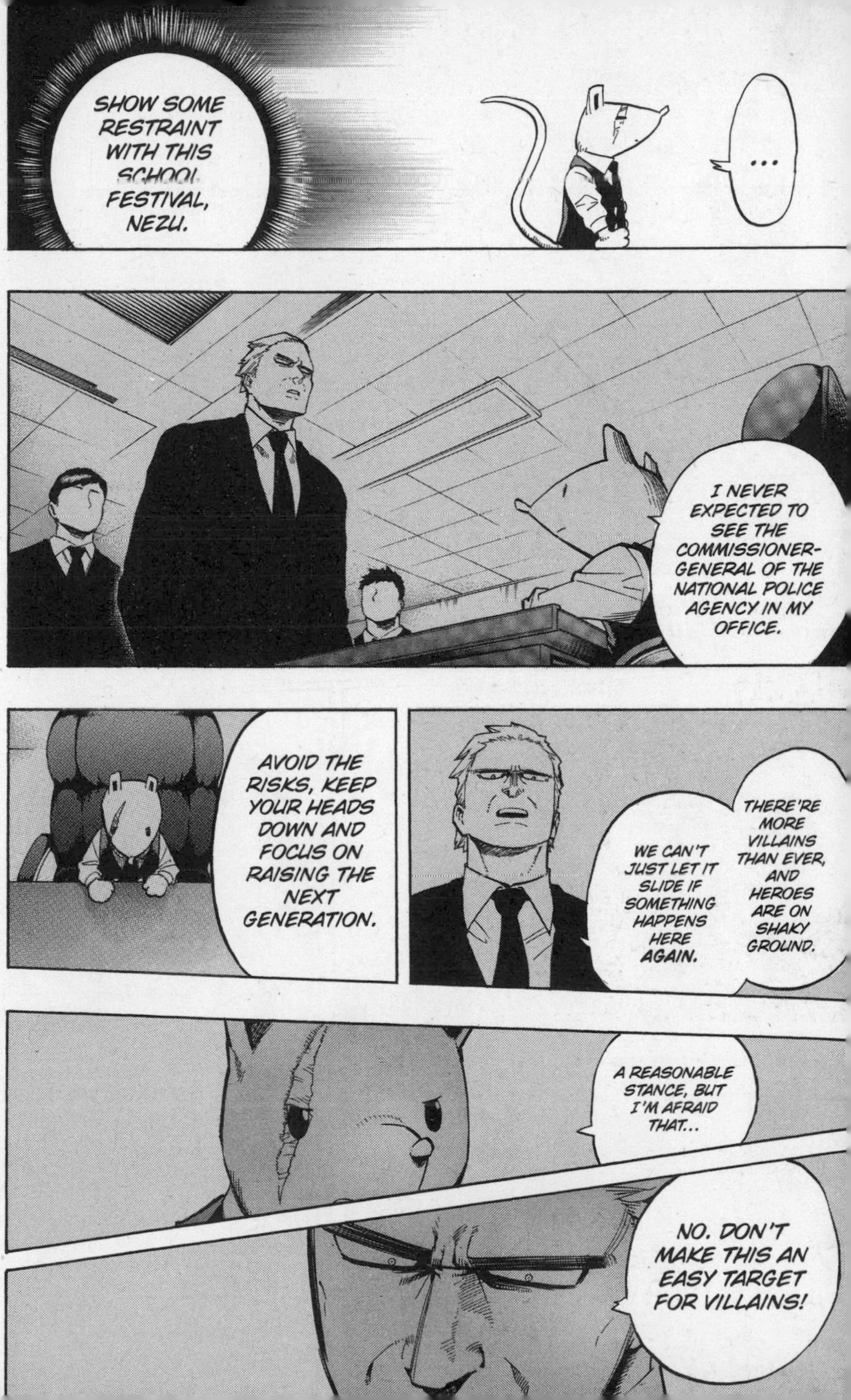
...
SHOW SOME RESTRAINT WITH THIS SCHOOL FESTIVAL, NEZU.
I NEVER EXPECTED TO SEE THE COMMISSIONER-GENERAL OF THE NATIONAL POLICE AGENCY IN MY OFFICE.
THERE'RE MORE VILLAINS THAN EVER, AND HEROES ARE ON SHAKY GROUND.
WE CAN'T JUST LET IT SLIDE IF SOMETHING HAPPENS HERE AGAIN.
AVOID THE RISKS, KEEP YOUR HEADS DOWN AND FOCUS ON RAISING THE NEXT GENERATION.
A REASONABLE STANCE, BUT I'M AFRAID THAT...
NO. DON'T MAKE THIS AN EASY TARGET FOR VILLAINS!

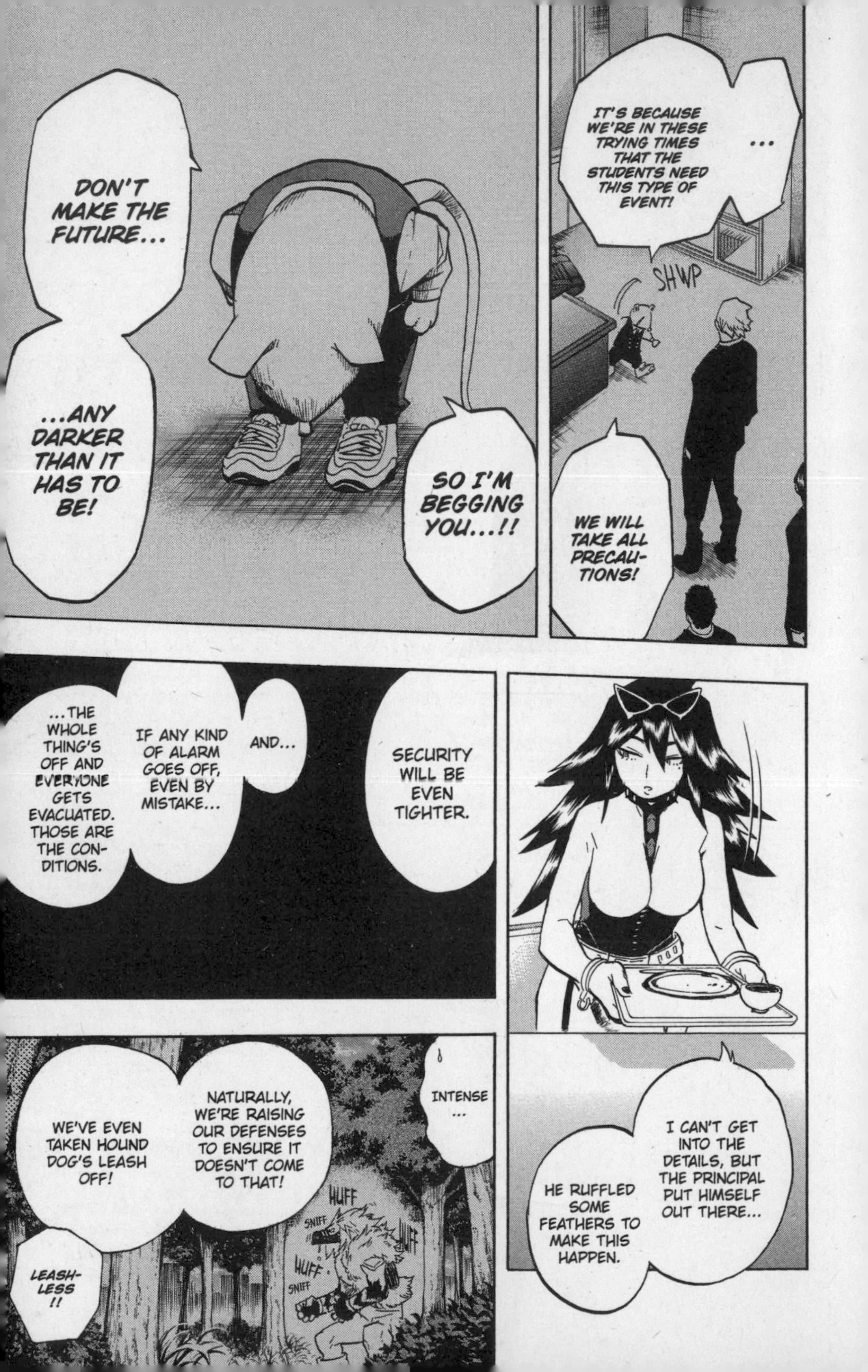
IT'S BECAUSE WE'RE IN THESE TRYING TIMES THAT THE STUDENTS NEED THIS TYPE OF EVENT!
...
SHWP
WE WILL TAKE ALL PRECAUTIONS!
DON'T MAKE THE FUTURE...
...ANY DARKER THAN IT HAS TO BE!
SO I'M BEGGING YOU...!!
SECURITY WILL BE EVEN TIGHTER.
AND...
IF ANY KIND OF ALARM GOES OFF, EVEN BY MISTAKE...
...THE WHOLE THING'S OFF AND EVERYONE GETS EVACUATED. THOSE ARE THE CONDITIONS.
I CAN'T GET INTO THE DETAILS, BUT THE PRINCIPAL PUT HIMSELF OUT THERE...
HE RUFFLED SOME FEATHERS TO MAKE THIS HAPPEN.
INTENSE...
NATURALLY, WE'RE RAISING OUR DEFENSES TO ENSURE IT DOESN'T COME TO THAT!
WE'VE EVEN TAKEN HOUND DOG'S LEASH OFF!
HUFF
SNIFF
HUFF
HUFF
SNIFF
LEASH-LESS!!

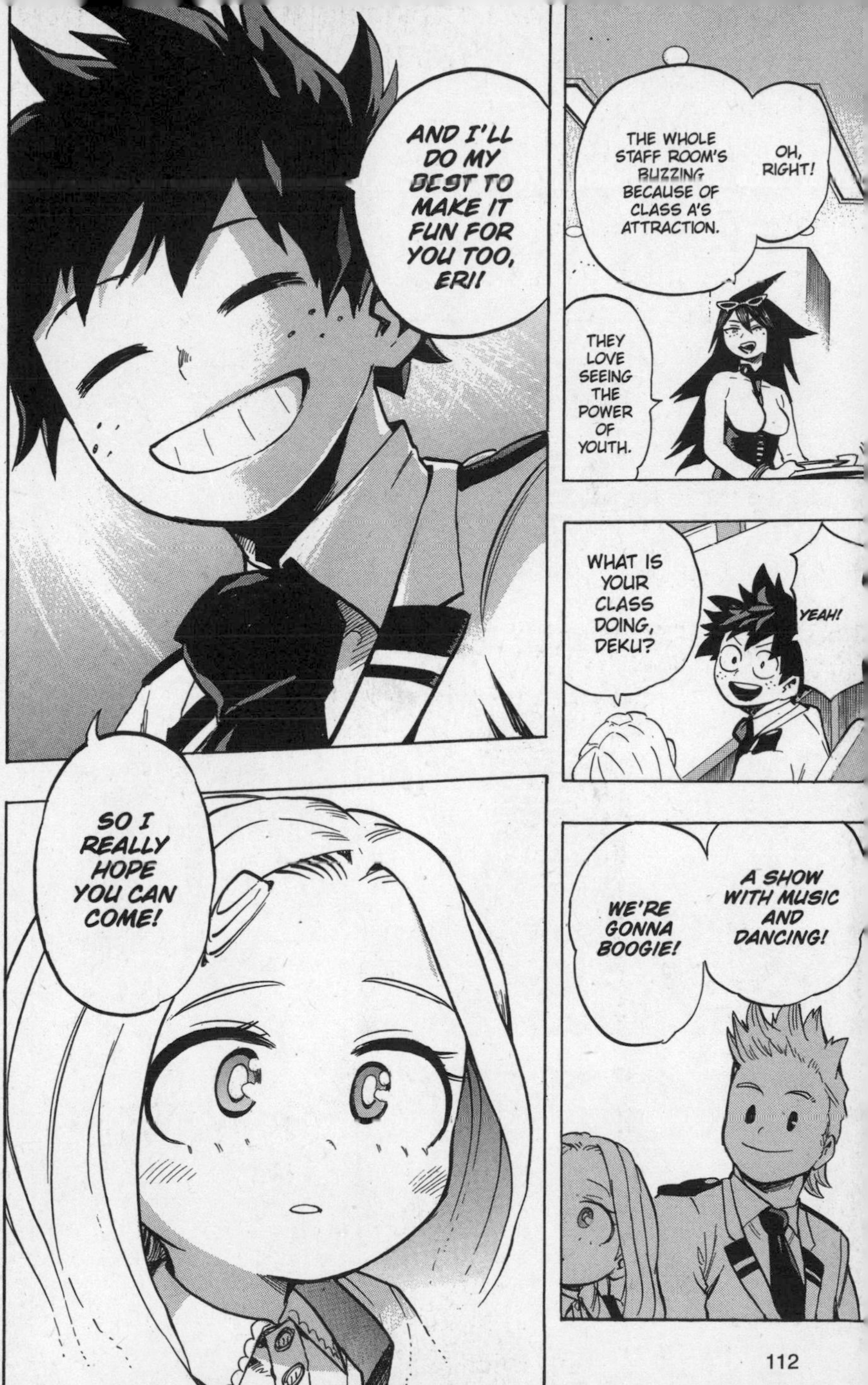
OH, RIGHT!
THE WHOLE STAFF ROOM'S BUZZING BECAUSE OF CLASS A'S ATTRACTION.
THEY LOVE SEEING THE POWER OF YOUTH.
WHAT IS YOUR CLASS DOING, DEKU?
YEAH!
A SHOW WITH MUSIC AND DANCING!
WE'RE GONNA BOOGIE!
AND I'LL DO MY BEST TO MAKE IT FUN FOR YOU TOO, ERI!
SO I REALLY HOPE YOU CAN COME!

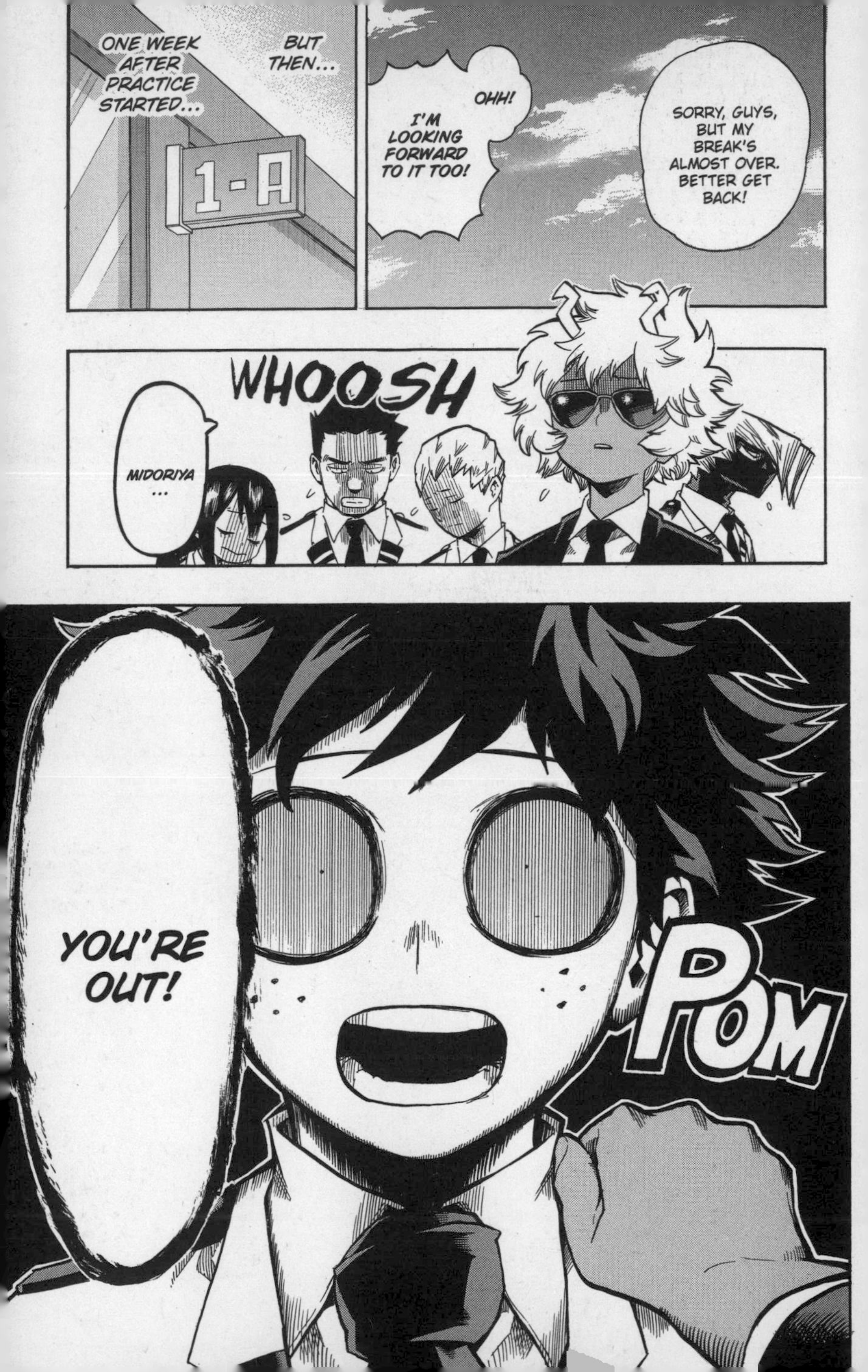
SORRY, GUYS, BUT MY BREAK'S ALMOST OVER. BETTER GET BACK!
OHH! I'M LOOKING FORWARD TO IT TOO!
BUT THEN...
ONE WEEK AFTER PRACTICE STARTED...
1-A
WHOOSH
MIDORIYA...
POM
YOU'RE OUT!

DILIGENT ABOUT PRODUCTION VALUES!

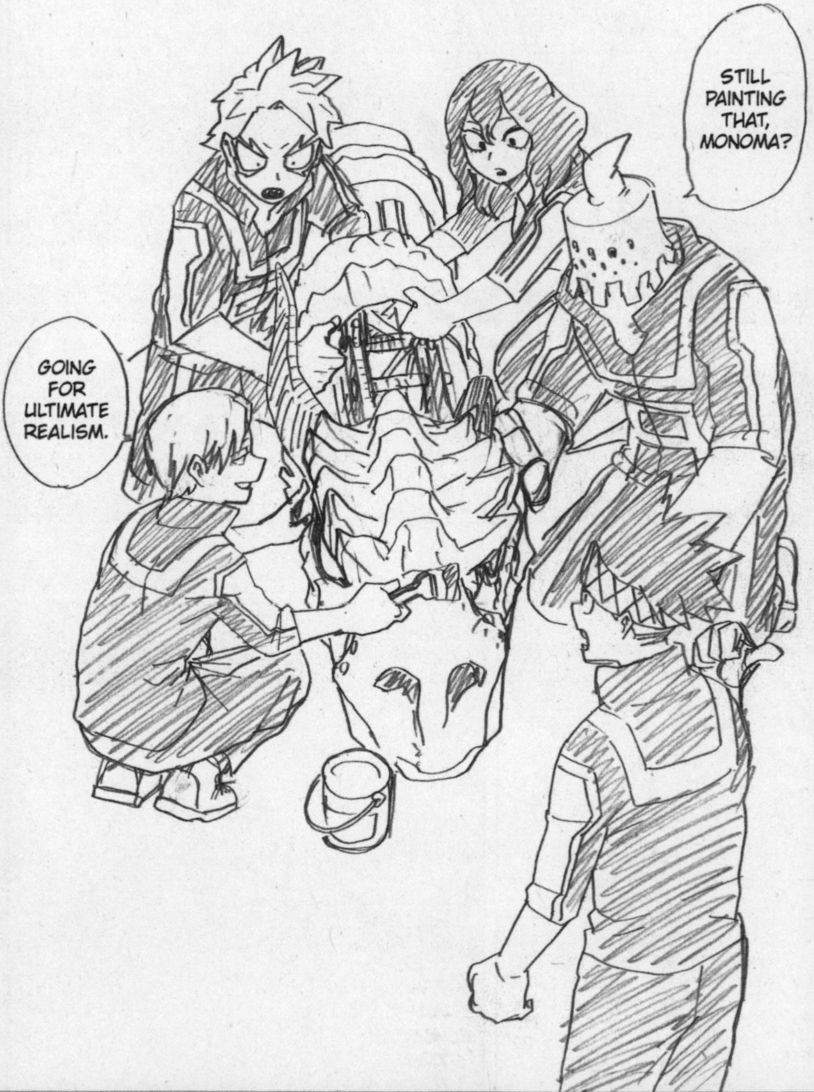

STILL PAINTING THAT, MONOMA?
GOING FOR ULTIMATE REALISM.

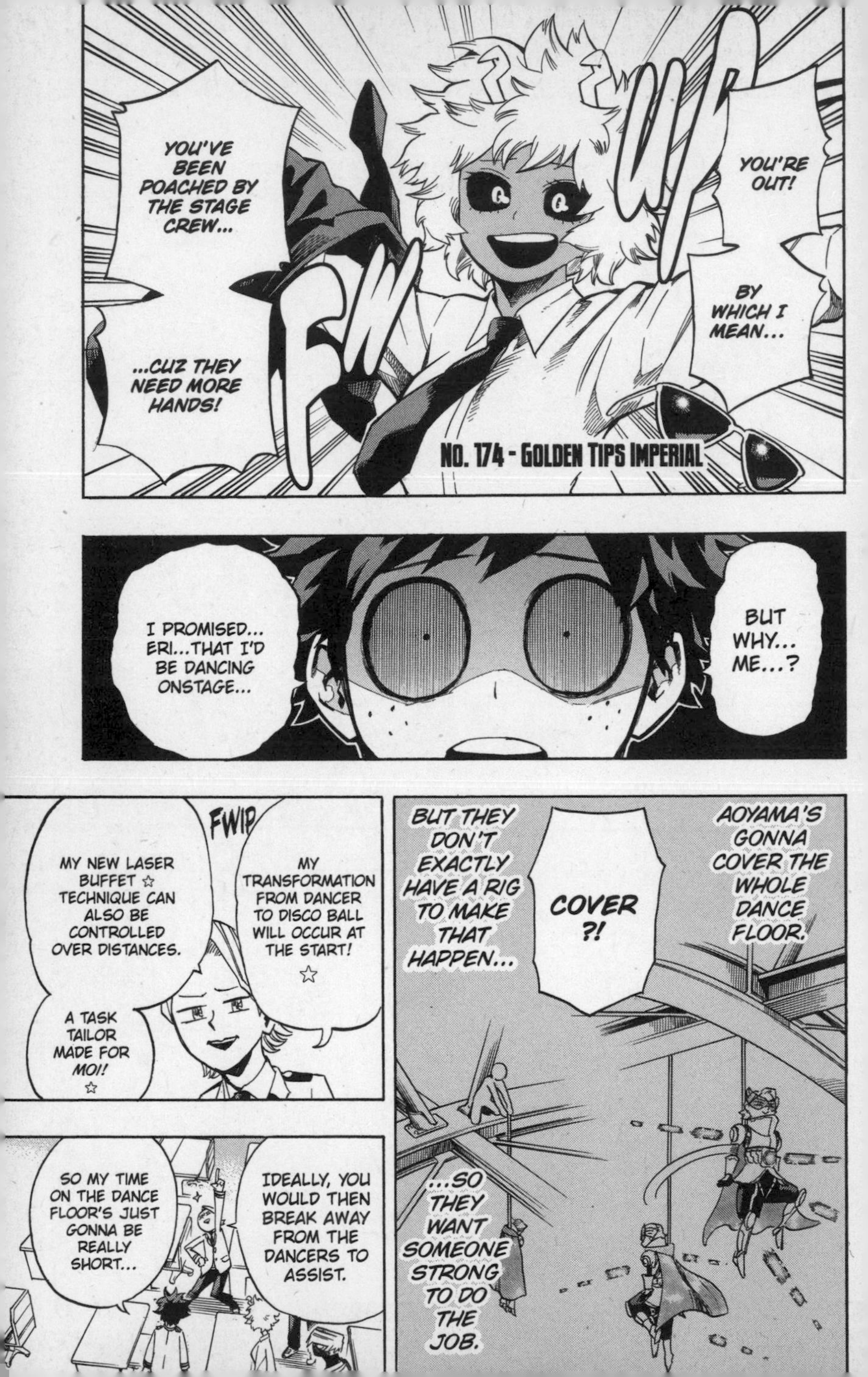
YOU'RE OUT!
BY WHICH I MEAN...
YOU'VE BEEN POACHED BY THE STAGE CREW...
...CUZ THEY NEED MORE HANDS!
No. 174 - Golden Tips Imperial
BUT WHY... ME...?
I PROMISED... ERI...THAT I'D BE DANCING ONSTAGE...
AOYAMA'S GONNA COVER THE WHOLE DANCE FLOOR.
COVER ?!
BUT THEY DON'T EXACTLY HAVE A RIG TO MAKE THAT HAPPEN...
...SO THEY WANT SOMEONE STRONG TO DO THE JOB.
FWIP
MY TRANSFORMATION FROM DANCER TO DISCO BALL WILL OCCUR AT THE START! ☆
MY NEW LASER BUFFET ☆ TECHNIQUE CAN ALSO BE CONTROLLED OVER DISTANCES.
A TASK TAILOR MADE FOR MOI! ☆
IDEALLY, YOU WOULD THEN BREAK AWAY FROM THE DANCERS TO ASSIST.
SO MY TIME ON THE DANCE FLOOR'S JUST GONNA BE REALLY SHORT...

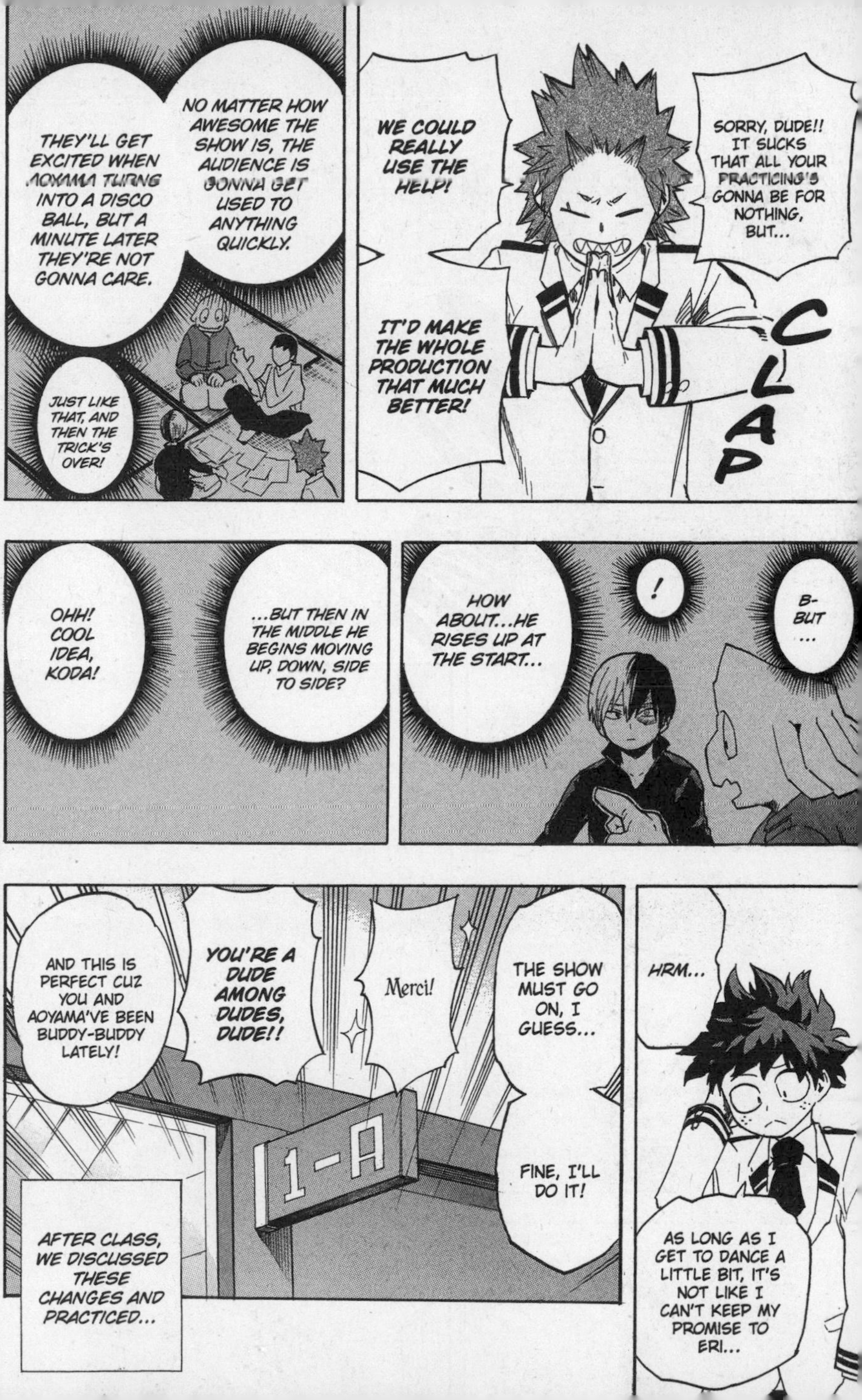
SORRY, DUDE!! IT SUCKS THAT ALL YOUR PRACTICING'S GONNA BE FOR NOTHING, BUT...
WE COULD REALLY USE THE HELP!
IT'D MAKE THE WHOLE PRODUCTION THAT MUCH BETTER!
CLAP
NO MATTER HOW AWESOME THE SHOW IS, THE AUDIENCE IS GONNA GET USED TO ANYTHING QUICKLY.
THEY'LL GET EXCITED WHEN AOYAMA TURNS INTO A DISCO BALL, BUT A MINUTE LATER THEY'RE NOT GONNA CARE.
JUST LIKE THAT, AND THEN THE TRICK'S OVER!
B-BUT...
!
HOW ABOUT...HE RISES UP AT THE START...
...BUT THEN IN THE MIDDLE HE BEGINS MOVING UP, DOWN, SIDE TO SIDE?
OHH! COOL IDEA, KODA!
HRM...
AS LONG AS I GET TO DANCE A LITTLE BIT, IT'S NOT LIKE I CAN'T KEEP MY PROMISE TO ERI...
THE SHOW MUST GO ON, I GUESS...
FINE, I'LL DO IT!
Merci!
YOU'RE A DUDE AMONG DUDES, DUDE!!
AND THIS IS PERFECT CUZ YOU AND AOYAMA'VE BEEN BUDDY-BUDDY LATELY!
1-A
AFTER CLASS, WE DISCUSSED THESE CHANGES AND PRACTICED...

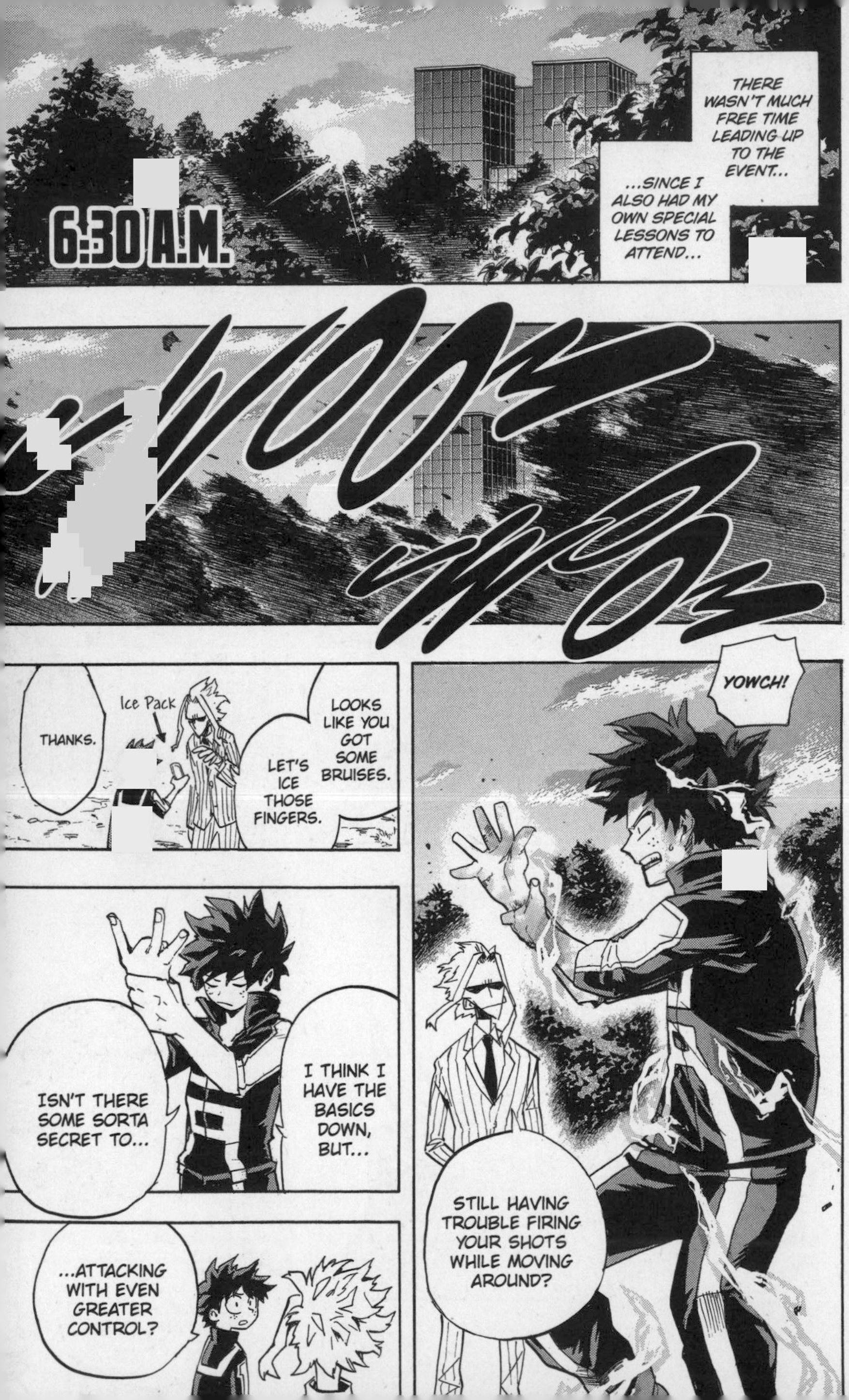
THERE WASN'T MUCH FREE TIME LEADING UP TO THE EVENT...
...SINCE I ALSO HAD MY OWN SPECIAL LESSONS TO ATTEND...
6:30 A.M.
YOWCH!
STILL HAVING TROUBLE FIRING YOUR SHOTS WHILE MOVING AROUND?
LOOKS LIKE YOU GOT SOME BRUISES.
LET'S ICE THOSE FINGERS.
Ice Pack
THANKS.
I THINK I HAVE THE BASICS DOWN, BUT...
ISN'T THERE SOME SORTA SECRET TO...
...ATTACKING WITH EVEN GREATER CONTROL?

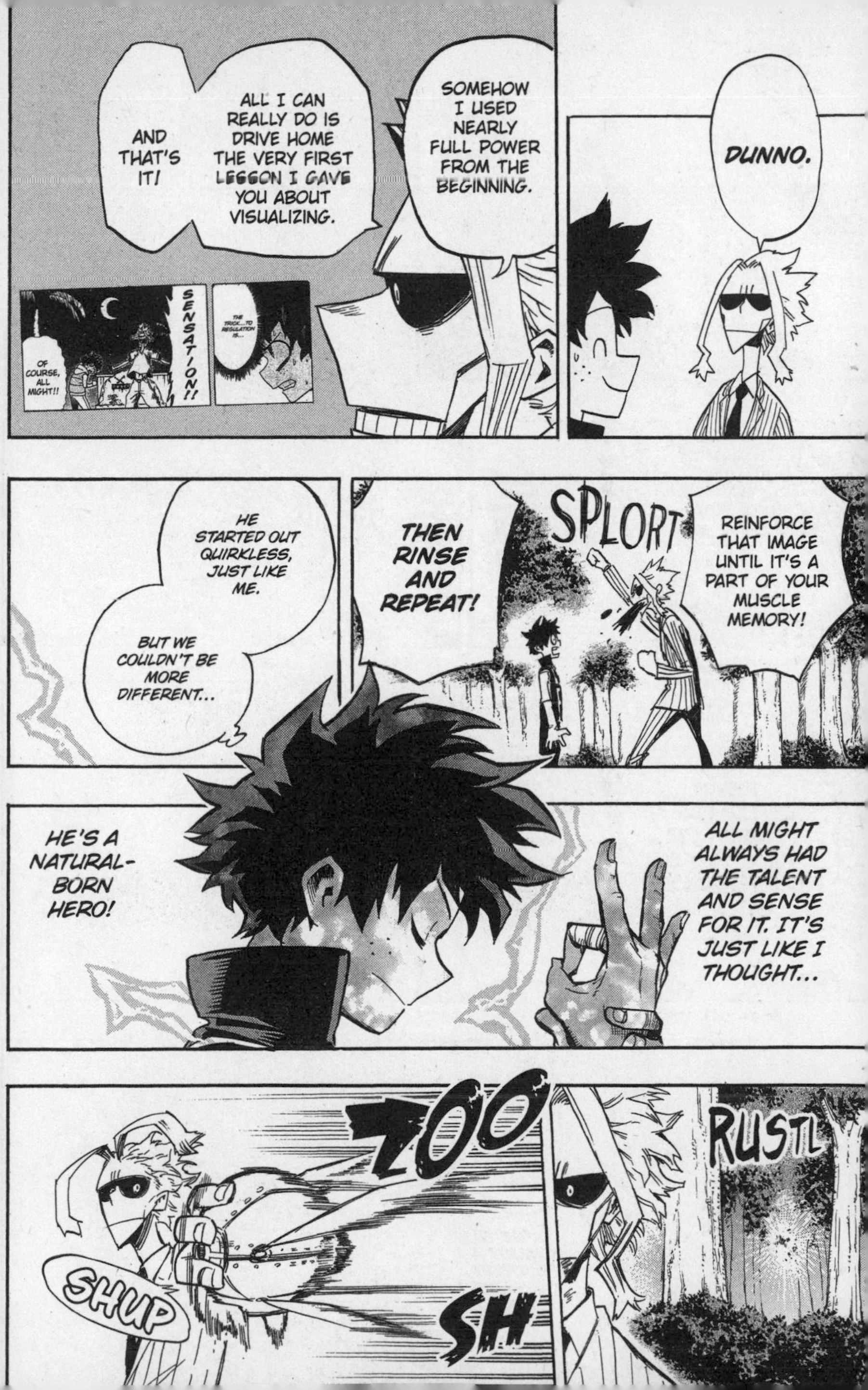
DUNNO.
SOMEHOW I USED NEARLY FULL POWER FROM THE BEGINNING.
ALL I CAN REALLY DO IS DRIVE HOME THE VERY FIRST LESSON I GAVE YOU ABOUT VISUALIZING.
AND THAT'S IT!
THE TRICK... TO REGULATION IS...
SENSATION!!
OF COURSE, ALL MIGHT!!
REINFORCE THAT IMAGE UNTIL IT'S A PART OF YOUR MUSCLE MEMORY!
SPLORT
THEN RINSE AND REPEAT!
HE STARTED OUT QUIRKLESS, JUST LIKE ME.
BUT WE COULDN'T BE MORE DIFFERENT...
ALL MIGHT ALWAYS HAD THE TALENT AND SENSE FOR IT. IT'S JUST LIKE I THOUGHT...
HE'S A NATURAL-BORN HERO!
RUSTL
ZOO
SH
SHUP

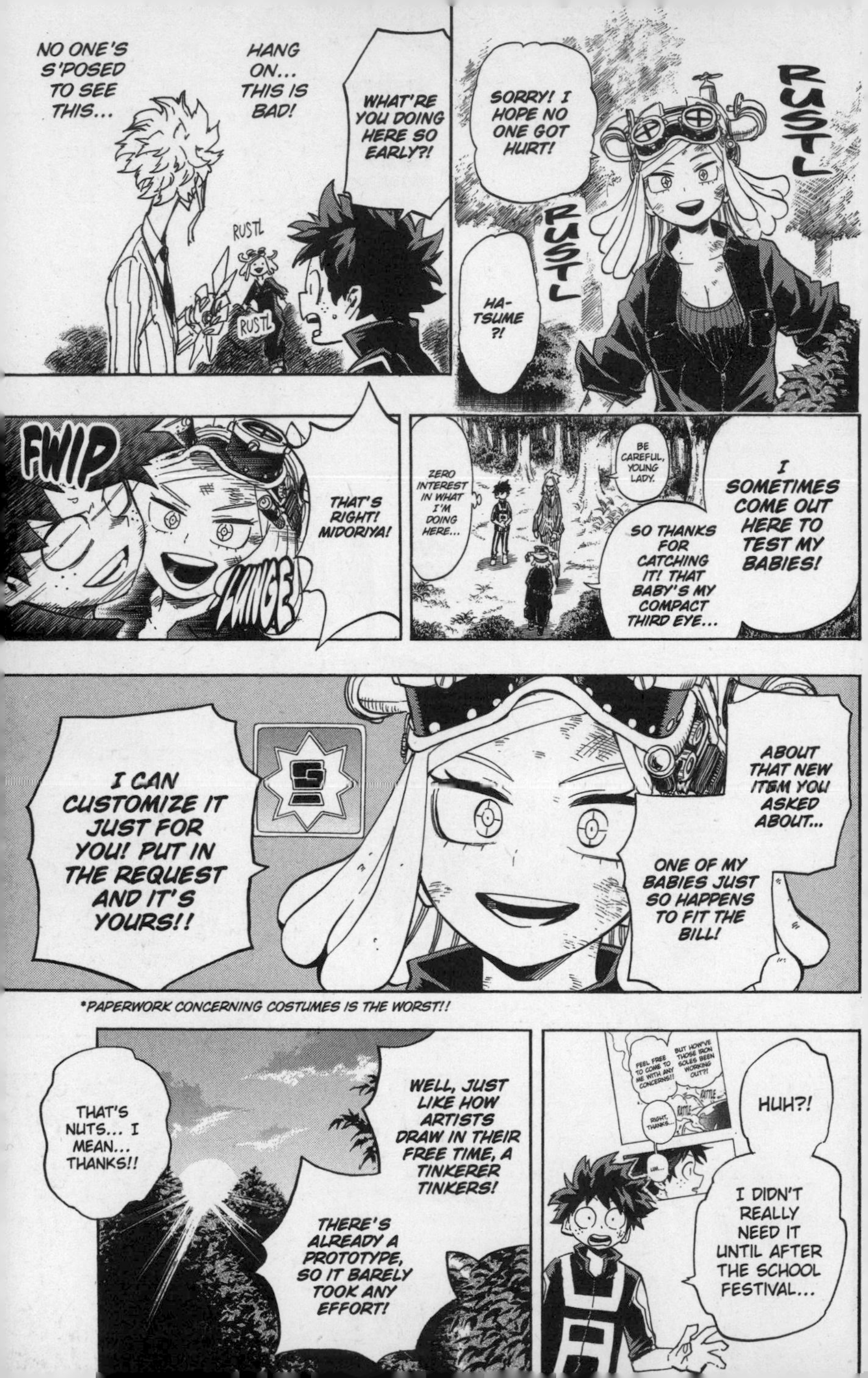
RUSTL
SORRY! I HOPE NO ONE GOT HURT!
RUSTL
HA-TSUME?!
WHAT'RE YOU DOING HERE SO EARLY?!
HANG ON... THIS IS BAD!
NO ONE'S S'POSED TO SEE THIS...
RUSTL
RUSTL
I SOMETIMES COME OUT HERE TO TEST MY BABIES!
BE CAREFUL, YOUNG LADY.
SO THANKS FOR CATCHING IT! THAT BABY'S MY COMPACT THIRD EYE...
ZERO INTEREST IN WHAT I'M DOING HERE...
THAT'S RIGHT! MIDORIYA!
FWIP
LUNGE
ABOUT THAT NEW ITEM YOU ASKED ABOUT...
ONE OF MY BABIES JUST SO HAPPENS TO FIT THE BILL!
I CAN CUSTOMIZE IT JUST FOR YOU! PUT IN THE REQUEST AND IT'S YOURS!!
*PAPERWORK CONCERNING COSTUMES IS THE WORST!!
HUH?!
BUT HOW'VE THOSE IRON SOLES BEEN WORKING OUT?!
FEEL FREE TO COME TO ME WITH ANY CONCERNS!!
RATTLE
RATTLE
RIGHT, THANKS...
UM...
I DIDN'T REALLY NEED IT UNTIL AFTER THE SCHOOL FESTIVAL...
WELL, JUST LIKE HOW ARTISTS DRAW IN THEIR FREE TIME, A TINKERER TINKERS!
THERE'S ALREADY A PROTOTYPE, SO IT BARELY TOOK ANY EFFORT!
THAT'S NUTS... I MEAN... THANKS!!

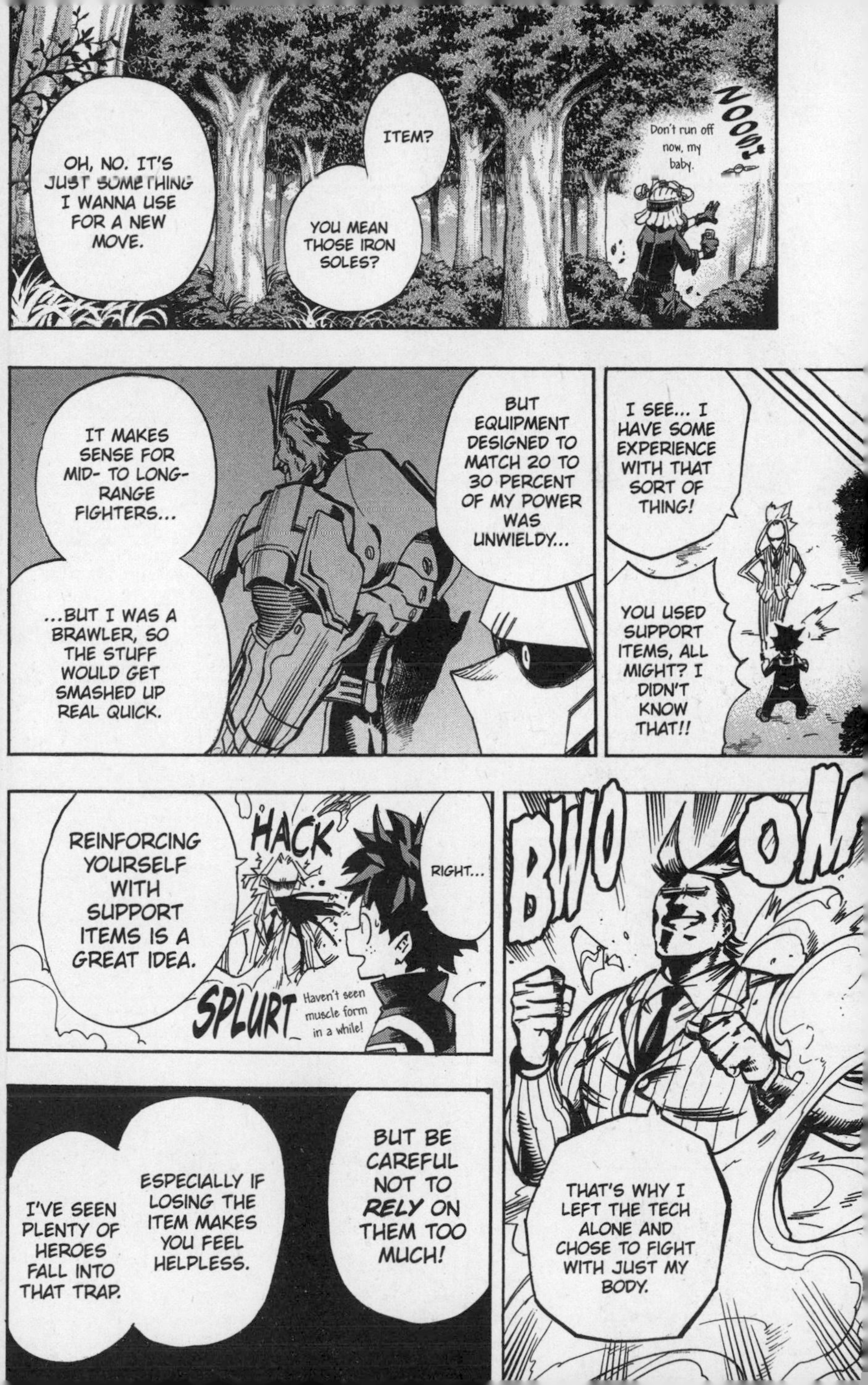
Don't run off now, my baby.
ITEM?
YOU MEAN THOSE IRON SOLES?
OH, NO. IT'S JUST SOMETHING I WANNA USE FOR A NEW MOVE.
I SEE... I HAVE SOME EXPERIENCE WITH THAT SORT OF THING!
YOU USED SUPPORT ITEMS, ALL MIGHT? I DIDN'T KNOW THAT!!
BUT EQUIPMENT DESIGNED TO MATCH 20 TO 30 PERCENT OF MY POWER WAS UNWIELDY...
IT MAKES SENSE FOR MID- TO LONG-RANGE FIGHTERS...
...BUT I WAS A BRAWLER, SO THE STUFF WOULD GET SMASHED UP REAL QUICK.
BWOOM
THAT'S WHY I LEFT THE TECH ALONE AND CHOSE TO FIGHT WITH JUST MY BODY.
RIGHT...
HACK
REINFORCING YOURSELF WITH SUPPORT ITEMS IS A GREAT IDEA.
SPLURT
Haven't seen muscle form in a while!
BUT BE CAREFUL NOT TO *RELY* ON THEM TOO MUCH!
ESPECIALLY IF LOSING THE ITEM MAKES YOU FEEL HELPLESS.
I'VE SEEN PLENTY OF HEROES FALL INTO THAT TRAP.

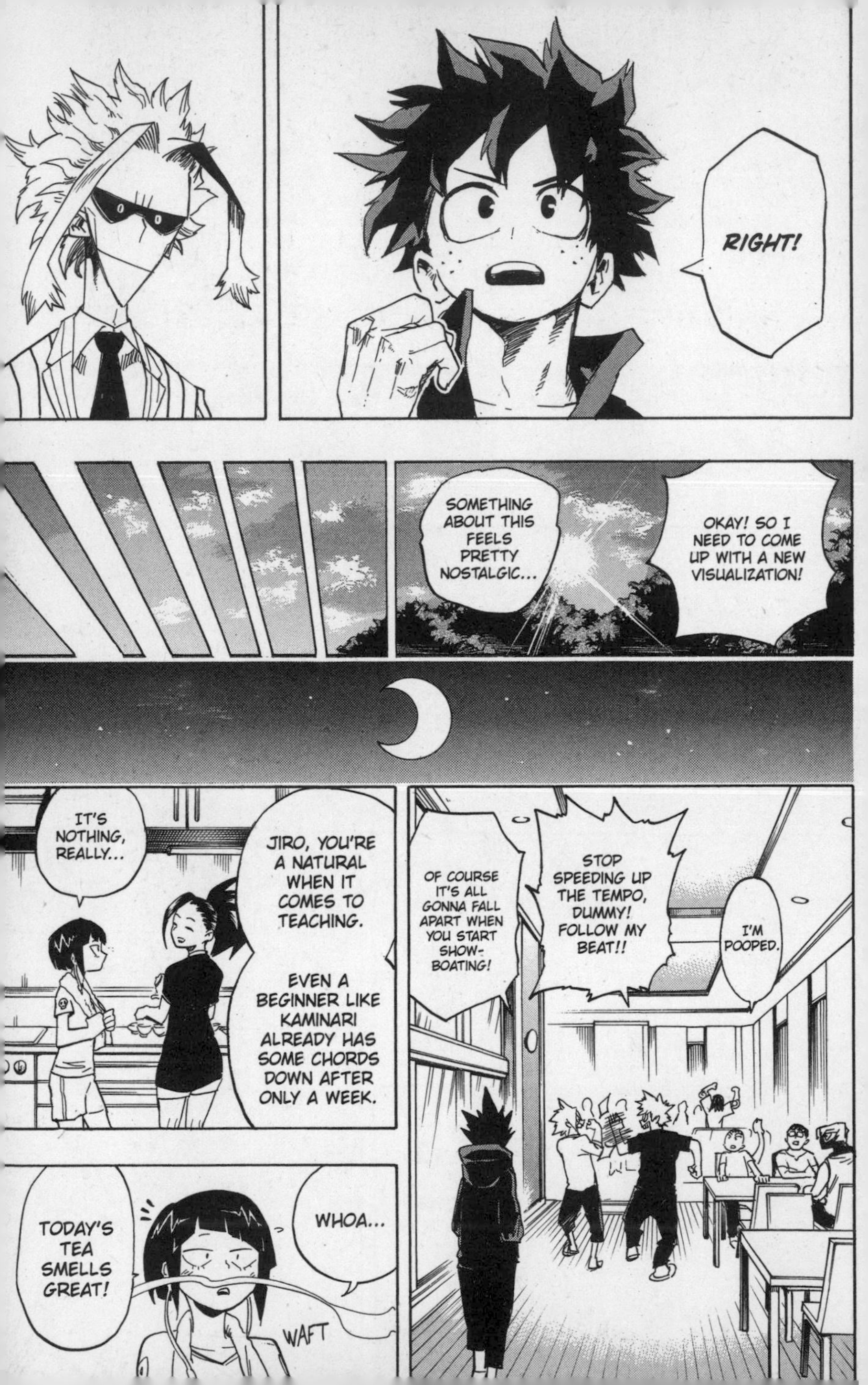
RIGHT!
OKAY! SO I NEED TO COME UP WITH A NEW VISUALIZATION!
SOMETHING ABOUT THIS FEELS PRETTY NOSTALGIC...
I'M POOPED.
STOP SPEEDING UP THE TEMPO, DUMMY! FOLLOW MY BEAT!!
OF COURSE IT'S ALL GONNA FALL APART WHEN YOU START SHOW-BOATING!
JIRO, YOU'RE A NATURAL WHEN IT COMES TO TEACHING.
EVEN A BEGINNER LIKE KAMINARI ALREADY HAS SOME CHORDS DOWN AFTER ONLY A WEEK.
IT'S NOTHING, REALLY...
WHOA...
TODAY'S TEA SMELLS GREAT!
WAFT

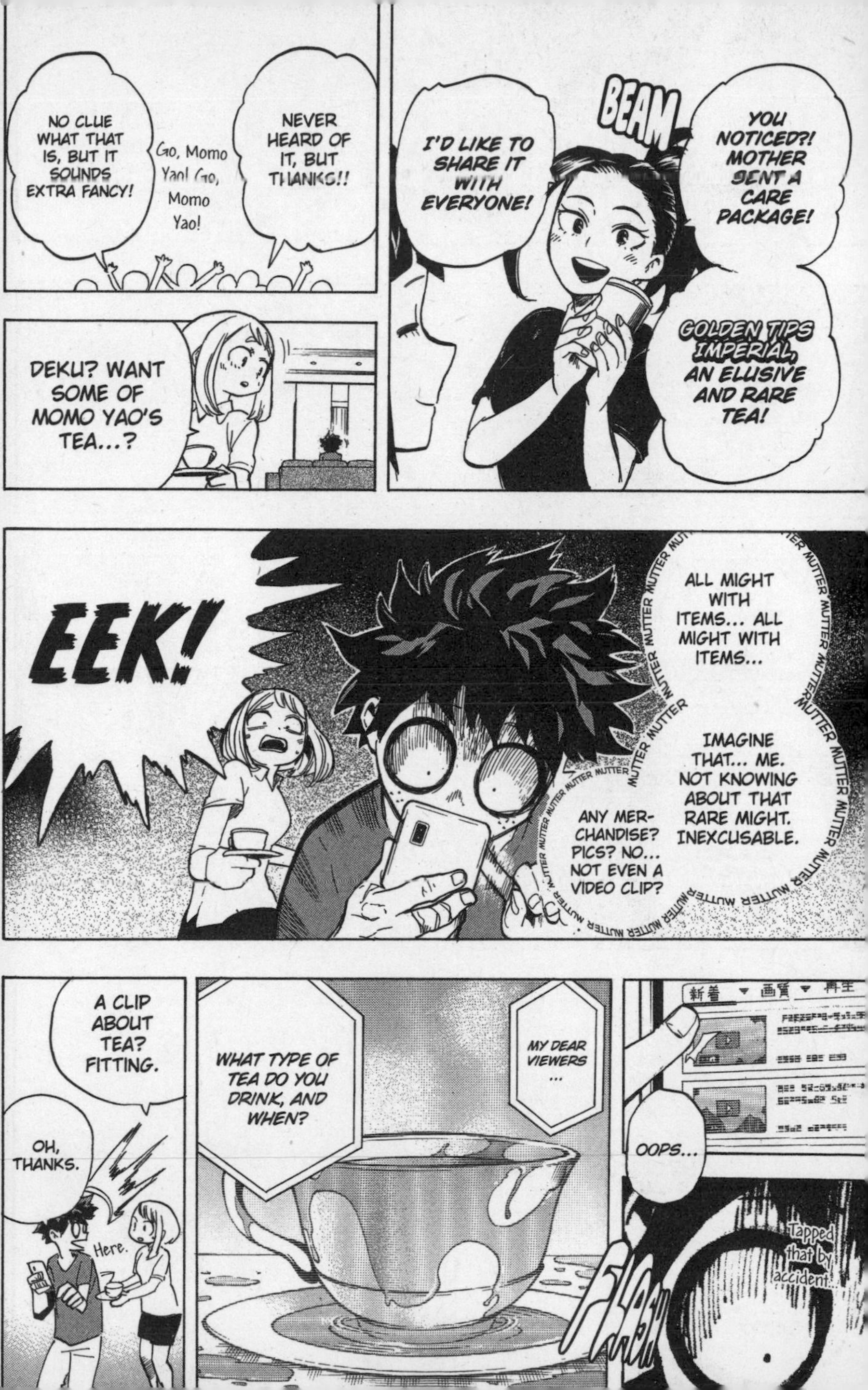
BEAM
YOU NOTICED?! MOTHER SENT A CARE PACKAGE!
GOLDEN TIPS IMPERIAL, AN ELUSIVE AND RARE TEA!
I'D LIKE TO SHARE IT WITH EVERYONE!
NEVER HEARD OF IT, BUT THANKS!!
Go, Momo Yao! Go, Momo Yao!
NO CLUE WHAT THAT IS, BUT IT SOUNDS EXTRA FANCY!
DEKU? WANT SOME OF MOMO YAO'S TEA...?
MUTTER MUTTER
ALL MIGHT WITH ITEMS... ALL MIGHT WITH ITEMS...
IMAGINE THAT... ME. NOT KNOWING ABOUT THAT RARE MIGHT. INEXCUSABLE.
ANY MERCHANDISE? PICS? NO... NOT EVEN A VIDEO CLIP?
EEK!
OOPS...
Tapped that by accident...
MY DEAR VIEWERS ...
WHAT TYPE OF TEA DO YOU DRINK, AND WHEN?
A CLIP ABOUT TEA? FITTING.
OH, THANKS.
Here.

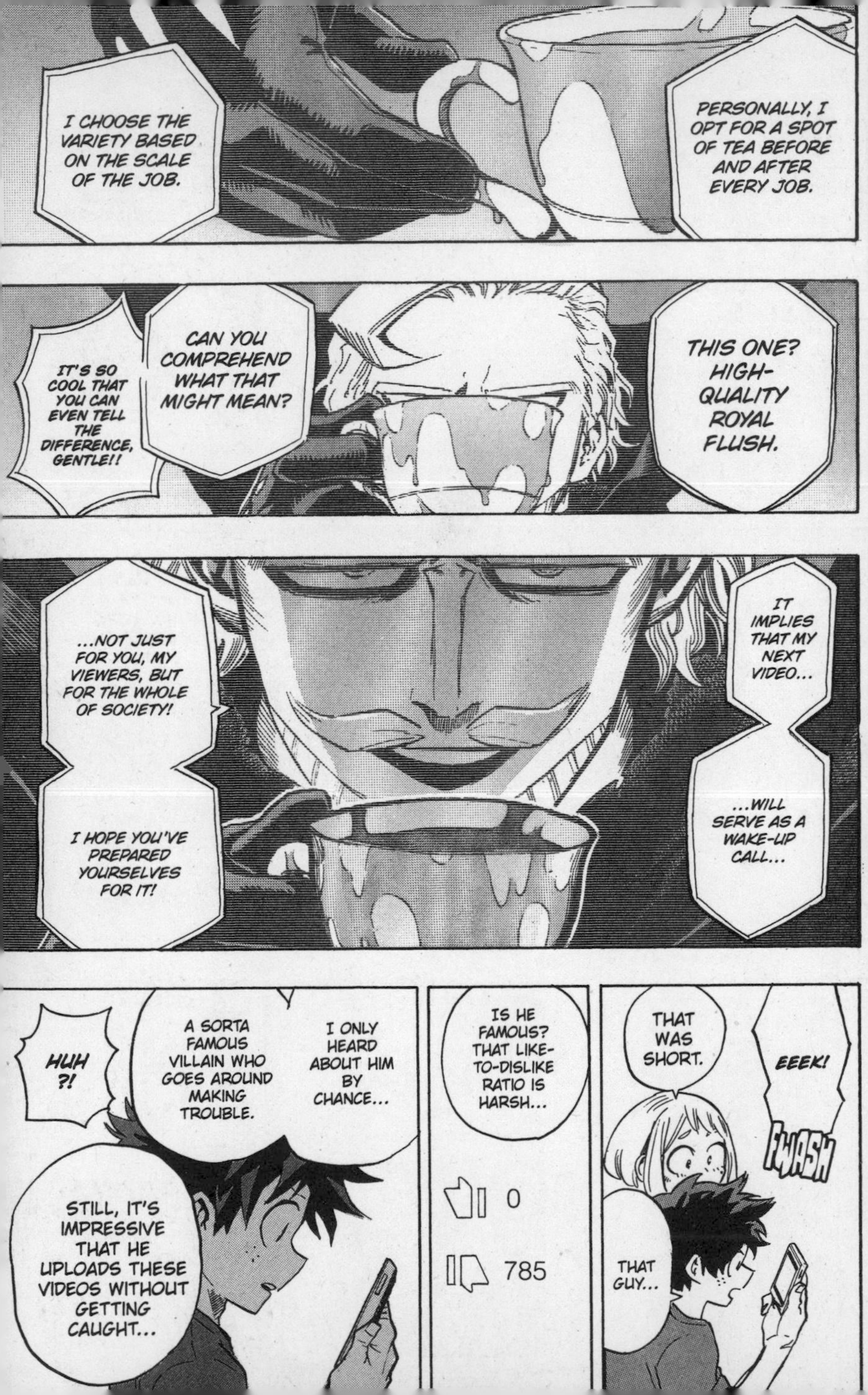
PERSONALLY, I OPT FOR A SPOT OF TEA BEFORE AND AFTER EVERY JOB.
I CHOOSE THE VARIETY BASED ON THE SCALE OF THE JOB.
THIS ONE? HIGH-QUALITY ROYAL FLUSH.
CAN YOU COMPREHEND WHAT THAT MIGHT MEAN?
IT'S SO COOL THAT YOU CAN EVEN TELL THE DIFFERENCE, GENTLE!!
IT IMPLIES THAT MY NEXT VIDEO...
...WILL SERVE AS A WAKE-UP CALL...
...NOT JUST FOR YOU, MY VIEWERS, BUT FOR THE WHOLE OF SOCIETY!
I HOPE YOU'VE PREPARED YOURSELVES FOR IT!
EEEK!
FWASH
THAT WAS SHORT.
THAT GUY...
IS HE FAMOUS? THAT LIKE-TO-DISLIKE RATIO IS HARSH...
0
785
I ONLY HEARD ABOUT HIM BY CHANCE...
A SORTA FAMOUS VILLAIN WHO GOES AROUND MAKING TROUBLE.
HUH ?!
STILL, IT'S IMPRESSIVE THAT HE UPLOADS THESE VIDEOS WITHOUT GETTING CAUGHT...

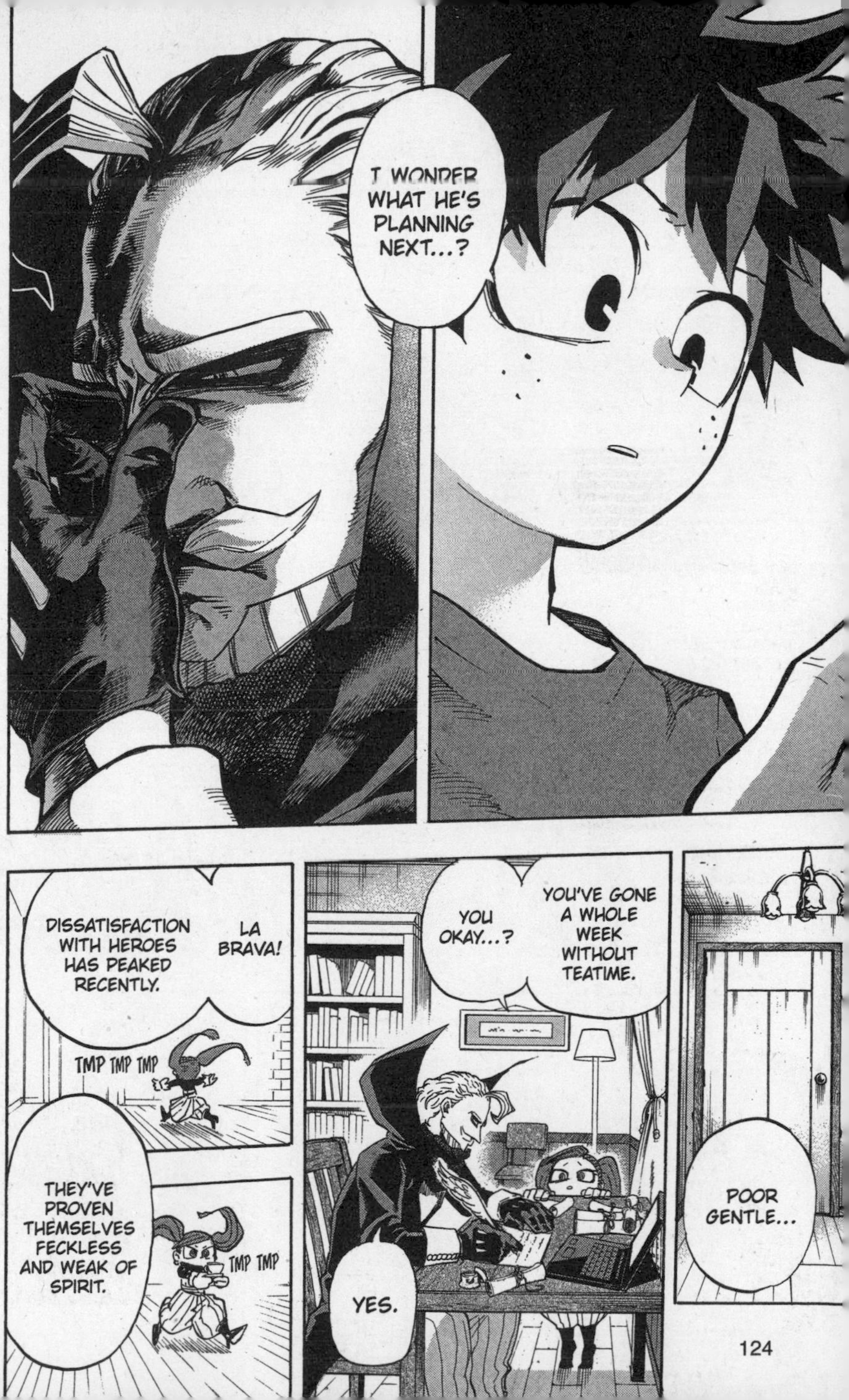
I WONDER WHAT HE'S PLANNING NEXT...?
POOR GENTLE...
YOU'VE GONE A WHOLE WEEK WITHOUT TEATIME.
YOU OKAY...?
YES.
LA BRAVA!
DISSATISFACTION WITH HEROES HAS PEAKED RECENTLY.
TMP TMP TMP
THEY'VE PROVEN THEMSELVES FECKLESS AND WEAK OF SPIRIT.
TMP TMP

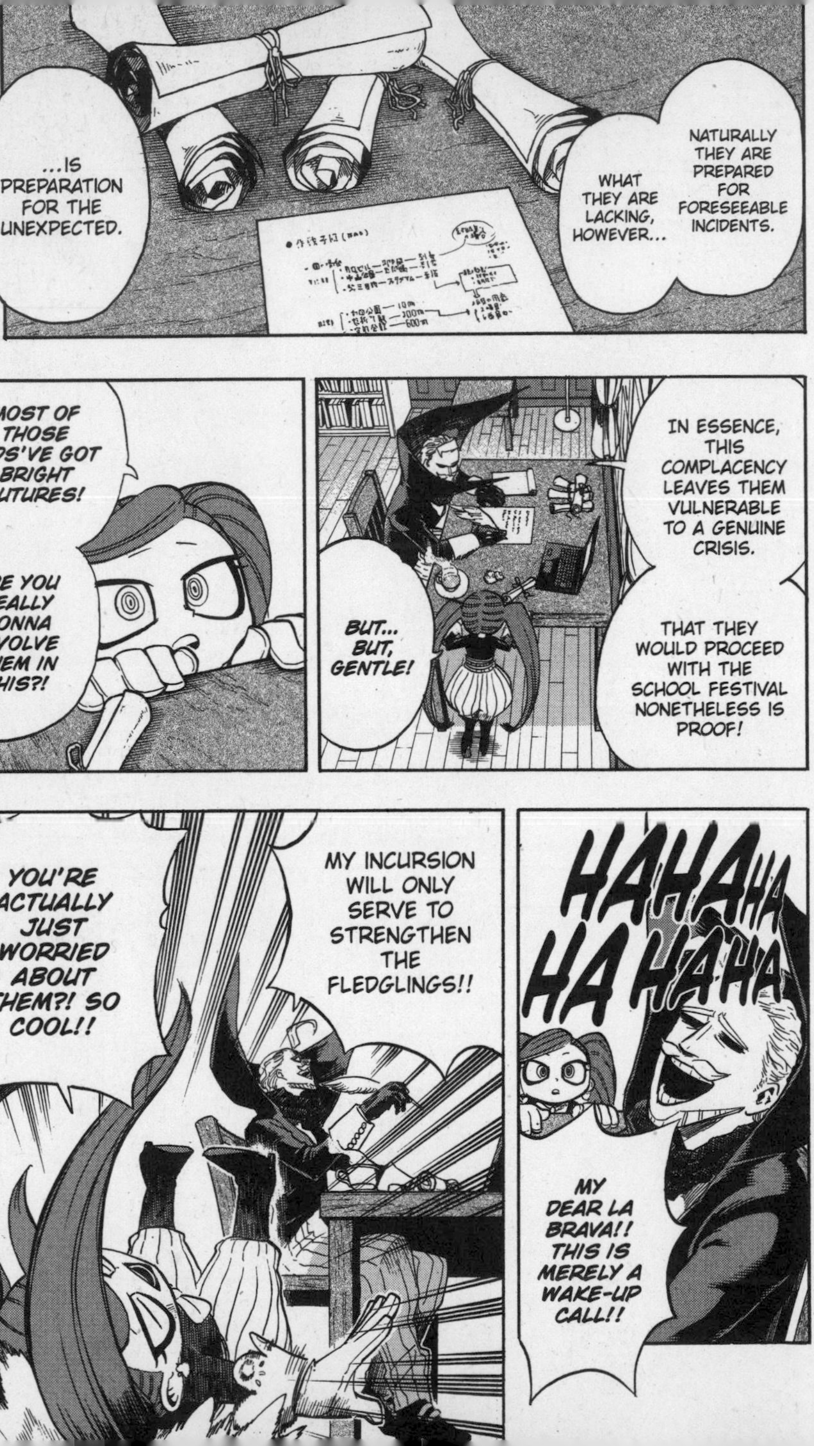
NATURALLY THEY ARE PREPARED FOR FORESEEABLE INCIDENTS.
WHAT THEY ARE LACKING, HOWEVER...
...IS PREPARATION FOR THE UNEXPECTED.
IN ESSENCE, THIS COMPLACENCY LEAVES THEM VULNERABLE TO A GENUINE CRISIS.
THAT THEY WOULD PROCEED WITH THE SCHOOL FESTIVAL NONETHELESS IS PROOF!
BUT... BUT, GENTLE!
MOST OF THOSE KIDS'VE GOT BRIGHT FUTURES!
ARE YOU REALLY GONNA INVOLVE THEM IN THIS?!
HAHAHA HA HAHAHA
MY DEAR LA BRAVA!! THIS IS MERELY A WAKE-UP CALL!!
MY INCURSION WILL ONLY SERVE TO STRENGTHEN THE FLEDGLINGS!!
YOU'RE ACTUALLY JUST WORRIED ABOUT THEM?! SO COOL!!

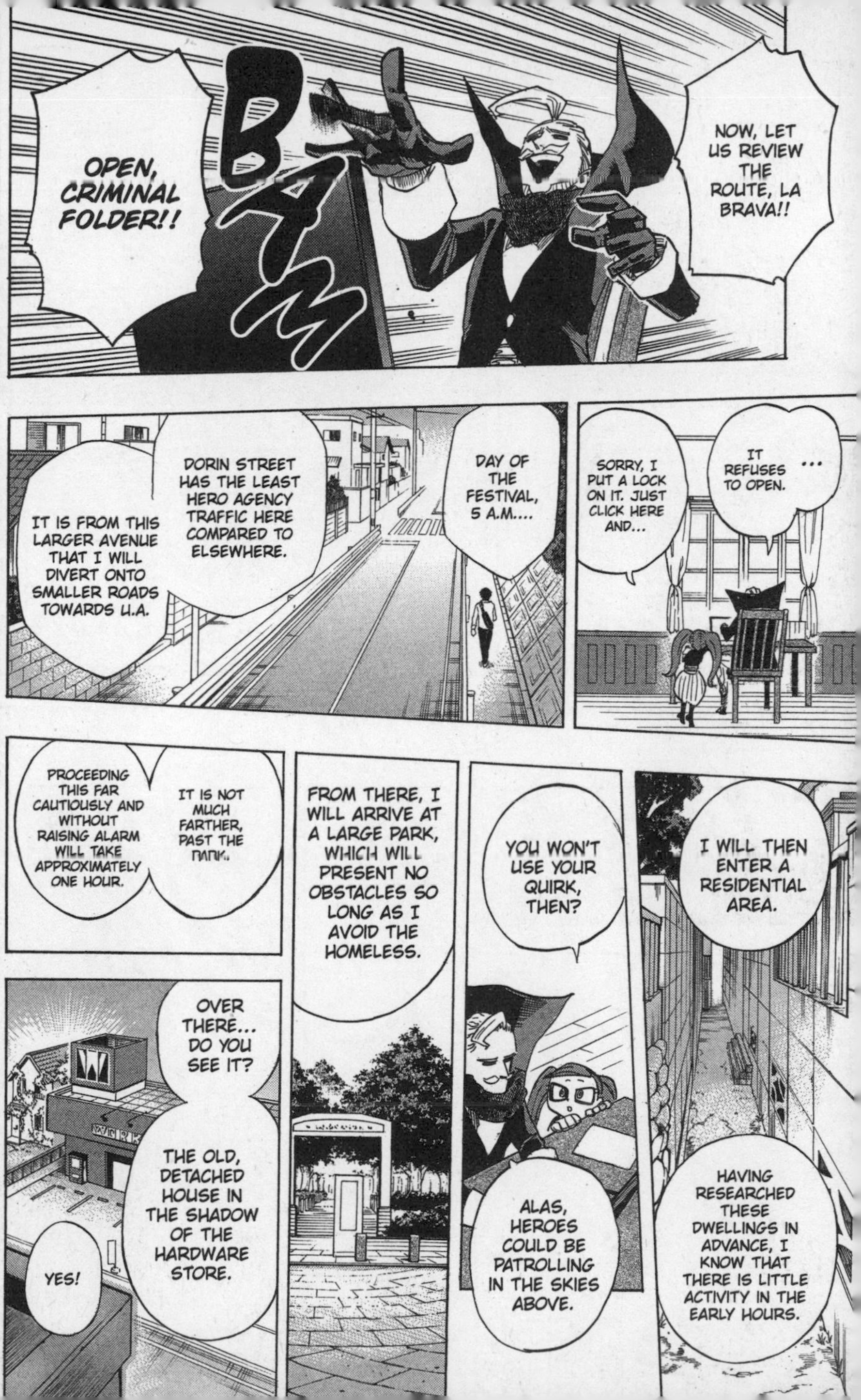
NOW, LET US REVIEW THE ROUTE, LA BRAVA!!
BAM
OPEN, CRIMINAL FOLDER!!
...
IT REFUSES TO OPEN.
SORRY, I PUT A LOCK ON IT. JUST CLICK HERE AND...
DAY OF THE FESTIVAL, 5 A.M....
DORIN STREET HAS THE LEAST HERO AGENCY TRAFFIC HERE COMPARED TO ELSEWHERE.
IT IS FROM THIS LARGER AVENUE THAT I WILL DIVERT ONTO SMALLER ROADS TOWARDS U.A.
I WILL THEN ENTER A RESIDENTIAL AREA.
HAVING RESEARCHED THESE DWELLINGS IN ADVANCE, I KNOW THAT THERE IS LITTLE ACTIVITY IN THE EARLY HOURS.
YOU WON'T USE YOUR QUIRK, THEN?
ALAS, HEROES COULD BE PATROLLING IN THE SKIES ABOVE.
FROM THERE, I WILL ARRIVE AT A LARGE PARK, WHICH WILL PRESENT NO OBSTACLES SO LONG AS I AVOID THE HOMELESS.
IT IS NOT MUCH FARTHER, PAST THE PARK.
PROCEEDING THIS FAR CAUTIOUSLY AND WITHOUT RAISING ALARM WILL TAKE APPROXIMATELY ONE HOUR.
OVER THERE... DO YOU SEE IT?
THE OLD, DETACHED HOUSE IN THE SHADOW OF THE HARDWARE STORE.
YES!

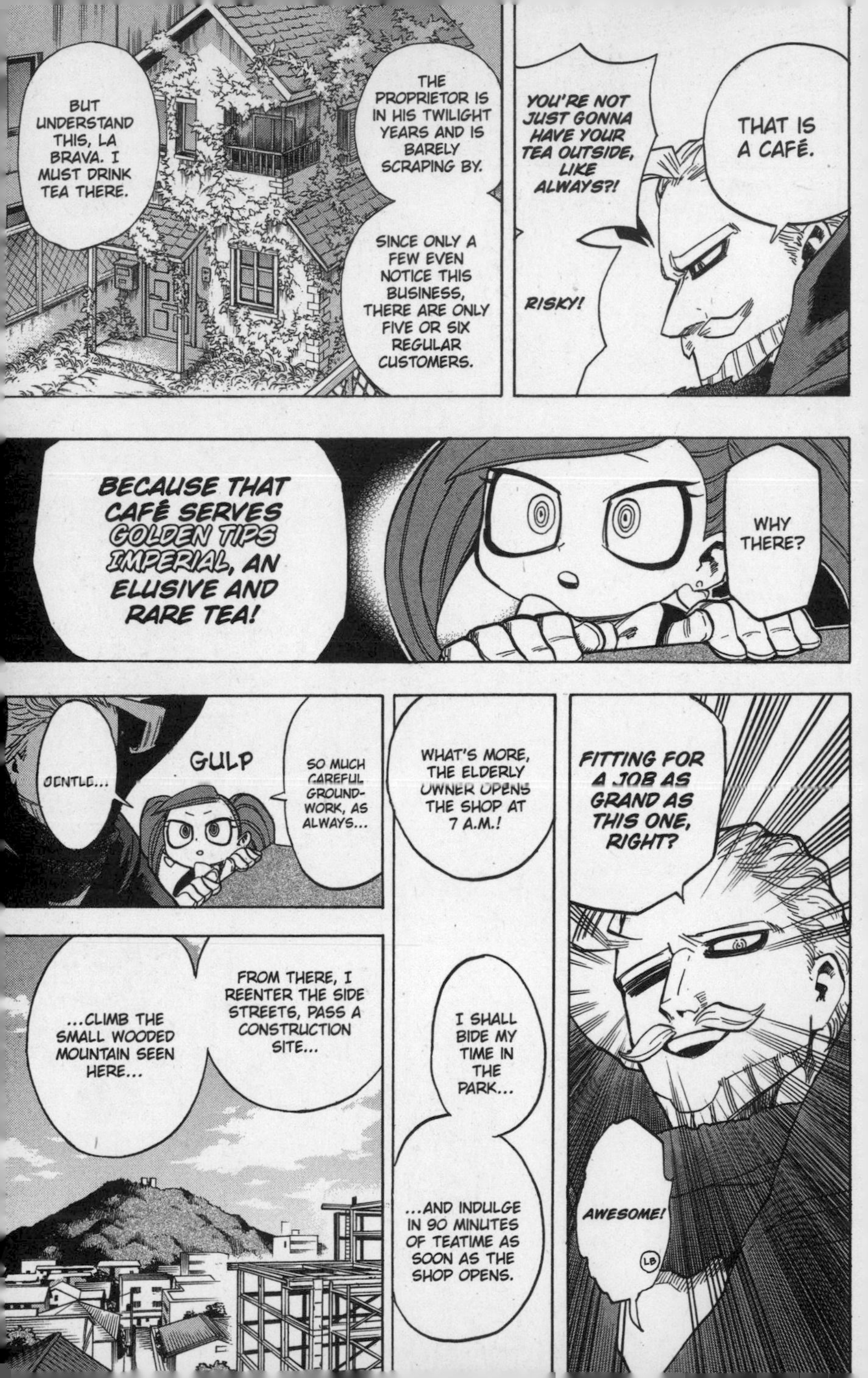
THAT IS A CAFÉ.
YOU'RE NOT JUST GONNA HAVE YOUR TEA OUTSIDE, LIKE ALWAYS?!
RISKY!
THE PROPRIETOR IS IN HIS TWILIGHT YEARS AND IS BARELY SCRAPING BY.
SINCE ONLY A FEW EVEN NOTICE THIS BUSINESS, THERE ARE ONLY FIVE OR SIX REGULAR CUSTOMERS.
BUT UNDERSTAND THIS, LA BRAVA. I MUST DRINK TEA THERE.
WHY THERE?
BECAUSE THAT CAFÉ SERVES GOLDEN TIPS IMPERIAL, AN ELUSIVE AND RARE TEA!
FITTING FOR A JOB AS GRAND AS THIS ONE, RIGHT?
AWESOME!
WHAT'S MORE, THE ELDERLY OWNER OPENS THE SHOP AT 7 A.M.!
I SHALL BIDE MY TIME IN THE PARK...
...AND INDULGE IN 90 MINUTES OF TEATIME AS SOON AS THE SHOP OPENS.
SO MUCH CAREFUL GROUND-WORK, AS ALWAYS...
GULP
GENTLE...
FROM THERE, I REENTER THE SIDE STREETS, PASS A CONSTRUCTION SITE...
...CLIMB THE SMALL WOODED MOUNTAIN SEEN HERE...

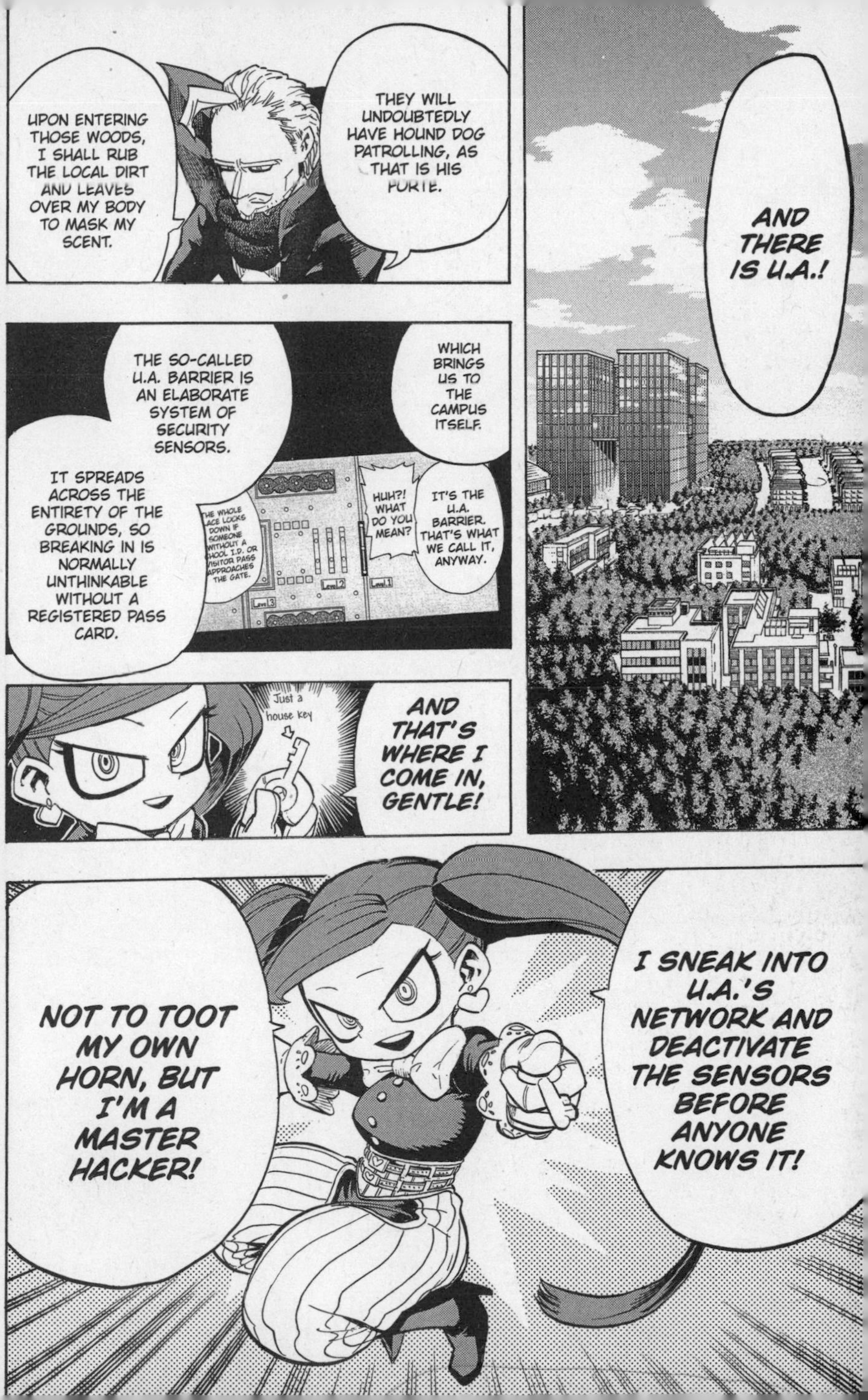
AND THERE IS U.A.!
THEY WILL UNDOUBTEDLY HAVE HOUND DOG PATROLLING, AS THAT IS HIS FORTE.
UPON ENTERING THOSE WOODS, I SHALL RUB THE LOCAL DIRT AND LEAVES OVER MY BODY TO MASK MY SCENT.
WHICH BRINGS US TO THE CAMPUS ITSELF.
THE SO-CALLED U.A. BARRIER IS AN ELABORATE SYSTEM OF SECURITY SENSORS.
IT'S THE U.A. BARRIER. THAT'S WHAT WE CALL IT, ANYWAY.
HUH?! WHAT DO YOU MEAN?
Level 1
Level 2
Level 3
HE WHOLE LACE LOCKS DOWN IF SOMEONE WITHOUT A HOOL I.D. OR VISITOR PASS APPROACHES THE GATE.
IT SPREADS ACROSS THE ENTIRETY OF THE GROUNDS, SO BREAKING IN IS NORMALLY UNTHINKABLE WITHOUT A REGISTERED PASS CARD.
AND THAT'S WHERE I COME IN, GENTLE!
Just a house key
I SNEAK INTO U.A.'S NETWORK AND DEACTIVATE THE SENSORS BEFORE ANYONE KNOWS IT!
NOT TO TOOT MY OWN HORN, BUT I'M A MASTER HACKER!

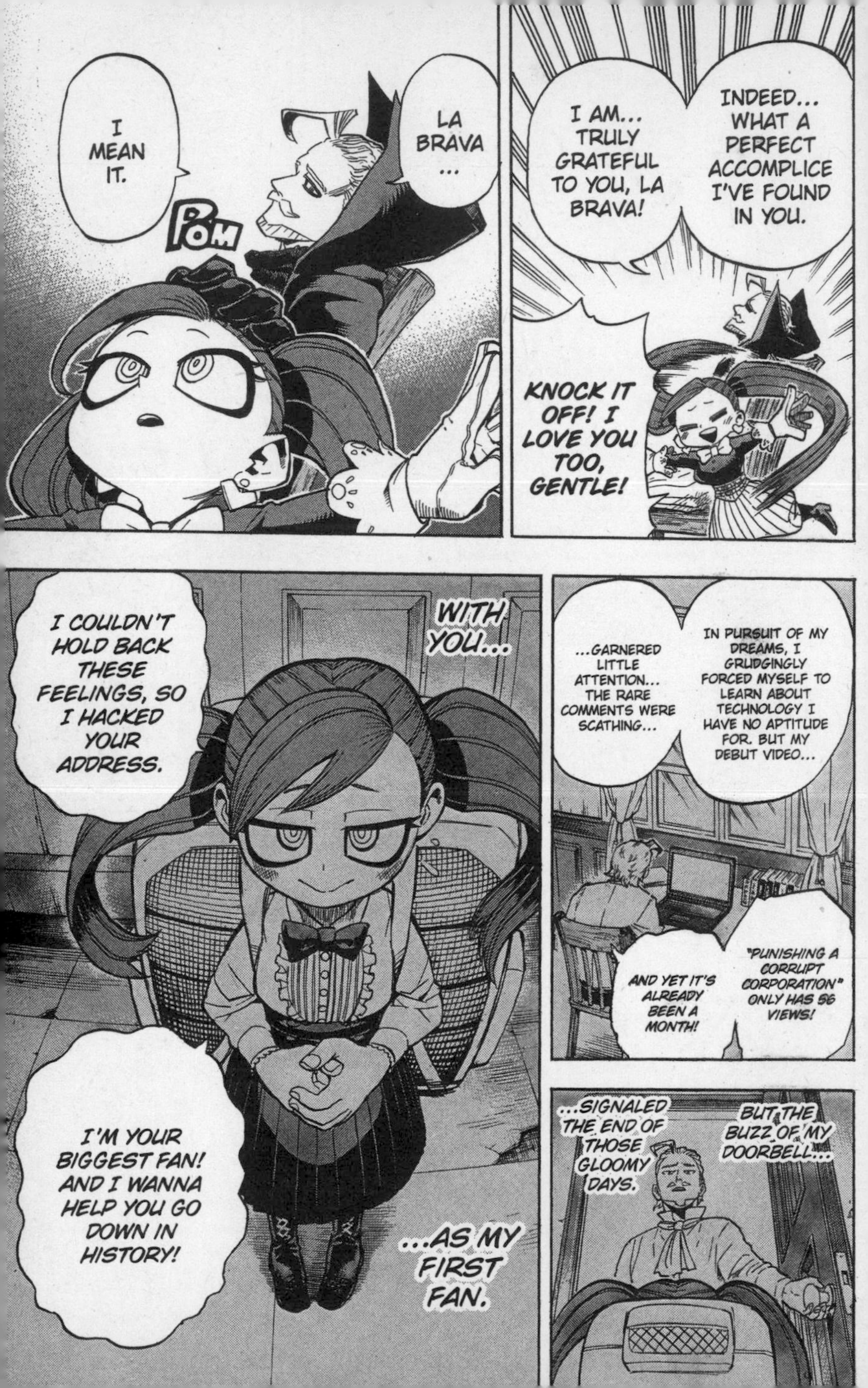
INDEED... WHAT A PERFECT ACCOMPLICE I'VE FOUND IN YOU.
I AM... TRULY GRATEFUL TO YOU, LA BRAVA!
KNOCK IT OFF! I LOVE YOU TOO, GENTLE!
LA BRAVA ...
I MEAN IT.
POM
IN PURSUIT OF MY DREAMS, I GRUDGINGLY FORCED MYSELF TO LEARN ABOUT TECHNOLOGY I HAVE NO APTITUDE FOR. BUT MY DEBUT VIDEO...
...GARNERED LITTLE ATTENTION... THE RARE COMMENTS WERE SCATHING...
"PUNISHING A CORRUPT CORPORATION" ONLY HAS 56 VIEWS!
AND YET IT'S ALREADY BEEN A MONTH!
BUT THE BUZZ OF MY DOORBELL...
...SIGNALED THE END OF THOSE GLOOMY DAYS.
WITH YOU...
I COULDN'T HOLD BACK THESE FEELINGS, SO I HACKED YOUR ADDRESS.
I'M YOUR BIGGEST FAN! AND I WANNA HELP YOU GO DOWN IN HISTORY!
...AS MY FIRST FAN.

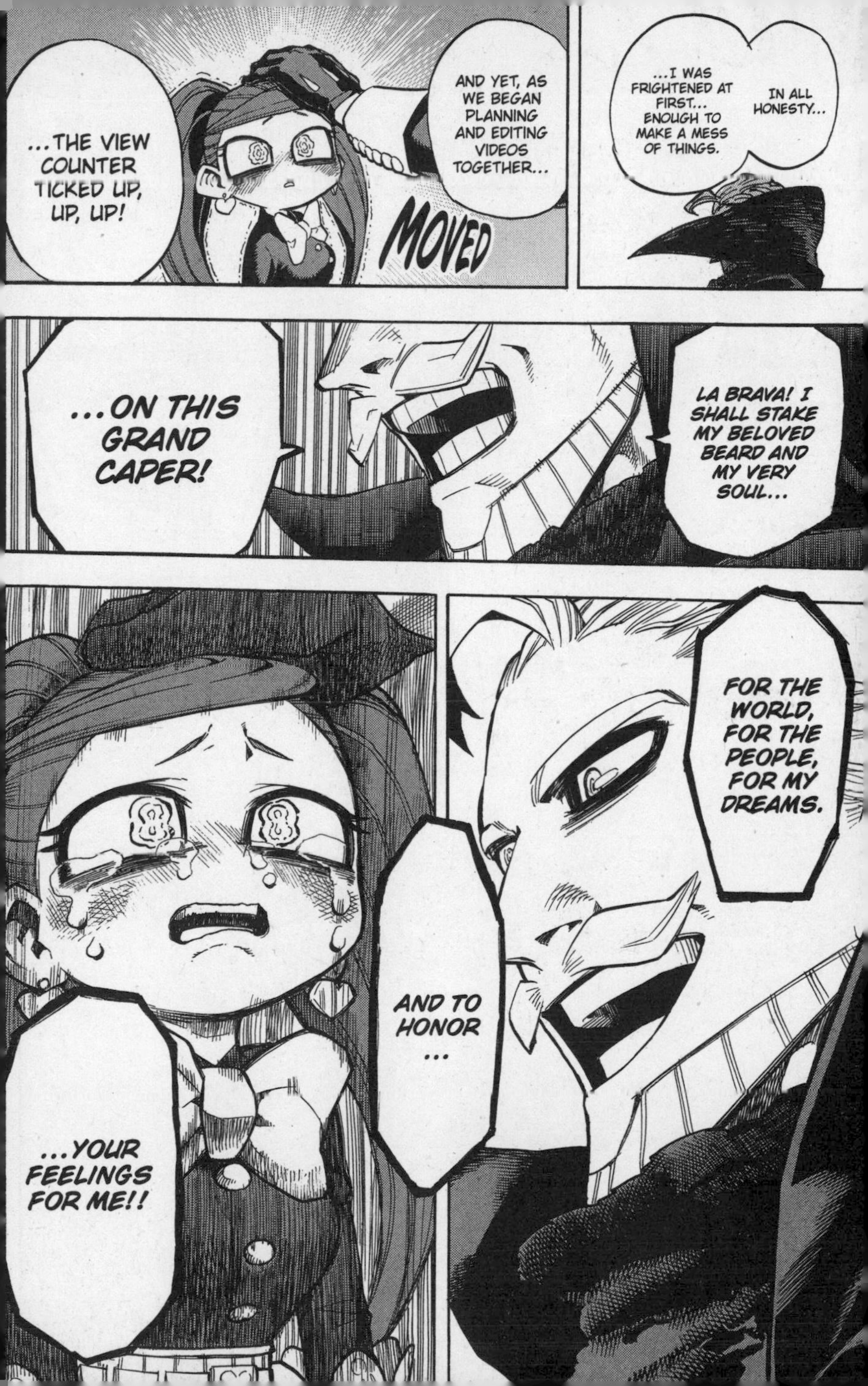
IN ALL HONESTY...
...I WAS FRIGHTENED AT FIRST... ENOUGH TO MAKE A MESS OF THINGS.
AND YET, AS WE BEGAN PLANNING AND EDITING VIDEOS TOGETHER...
MOVED
...THE VIEW COUNTER TICKED UP, UP, UP!
LA BRAVA! I SHALL STAKE MY BELOVED BEARD AND MY VERY SOUL...
...ON THIS GRAND CAPER!
FOR THE WORLD, FOR THE PEOPLE, FOR MY DREAMS.
AND TO HONOR ...
...YOUR FEELINGS FOR ME!!

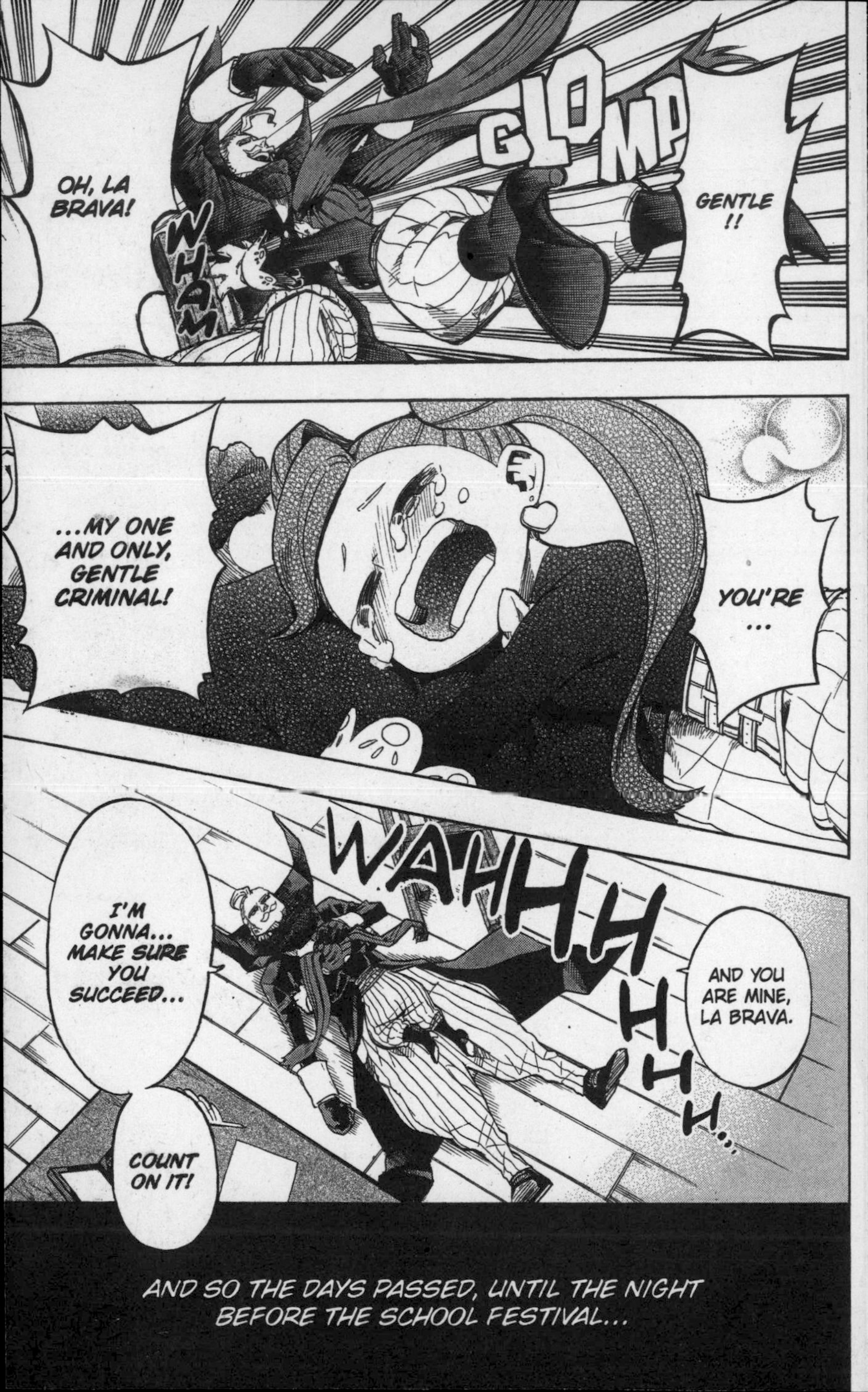
GENTLE !!
GLOMP
OH, LA BRAVA!
WHAM
YOU'RE ...
...MY ONE AND ONLY, GENTLE CRIMINAL!
WAHHHHHHH...
AND YOU ARE MINE, LA BRAVA.
I'M GONNA... MAKE SURE YOU SUCCEED...
COUNT ON IT!
AND SO THE DAYS PASSED, UNTIL THE NIGHT BEFORE THE SCHOOL FESTIVAL...

GENTLEMAN

GENTLE CRIMINAL [32]
[TANJURO TOBITA]

STREET CLOTHES

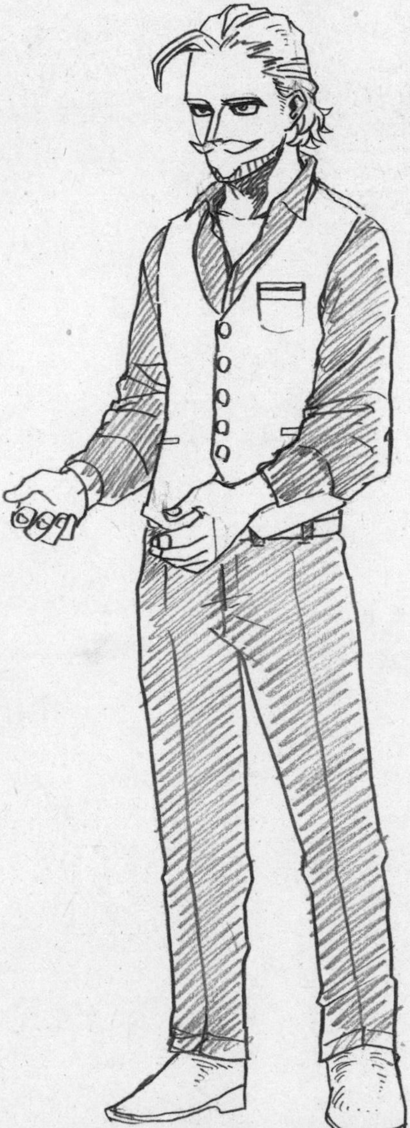

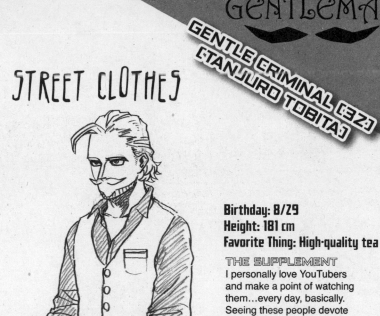

Birthday: 8/29
Height: 181 cm
Favorite Thing: High-quality tea

THE SUPPLEMENT

I personally love YouTubers and make a point of watching them…every day, basically. Seeing these people devote themselves to entertainment is something to behold.

He was underemployed for a while, but after several years of saving up money, he made preparations to start playing the part of “Gentle.”

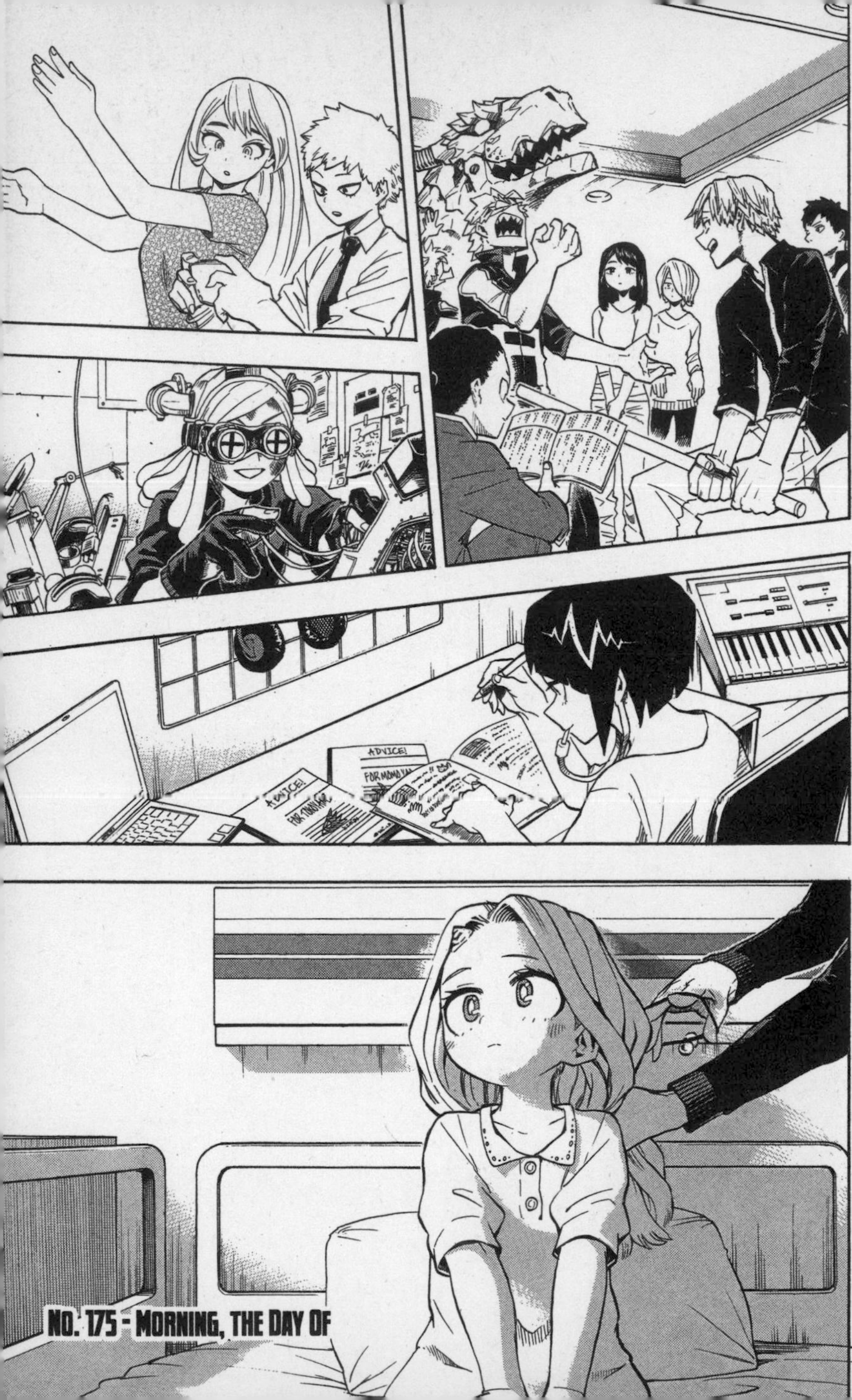

ADVICE!
ADVICE!
No. 175 - Morning, the Day Of

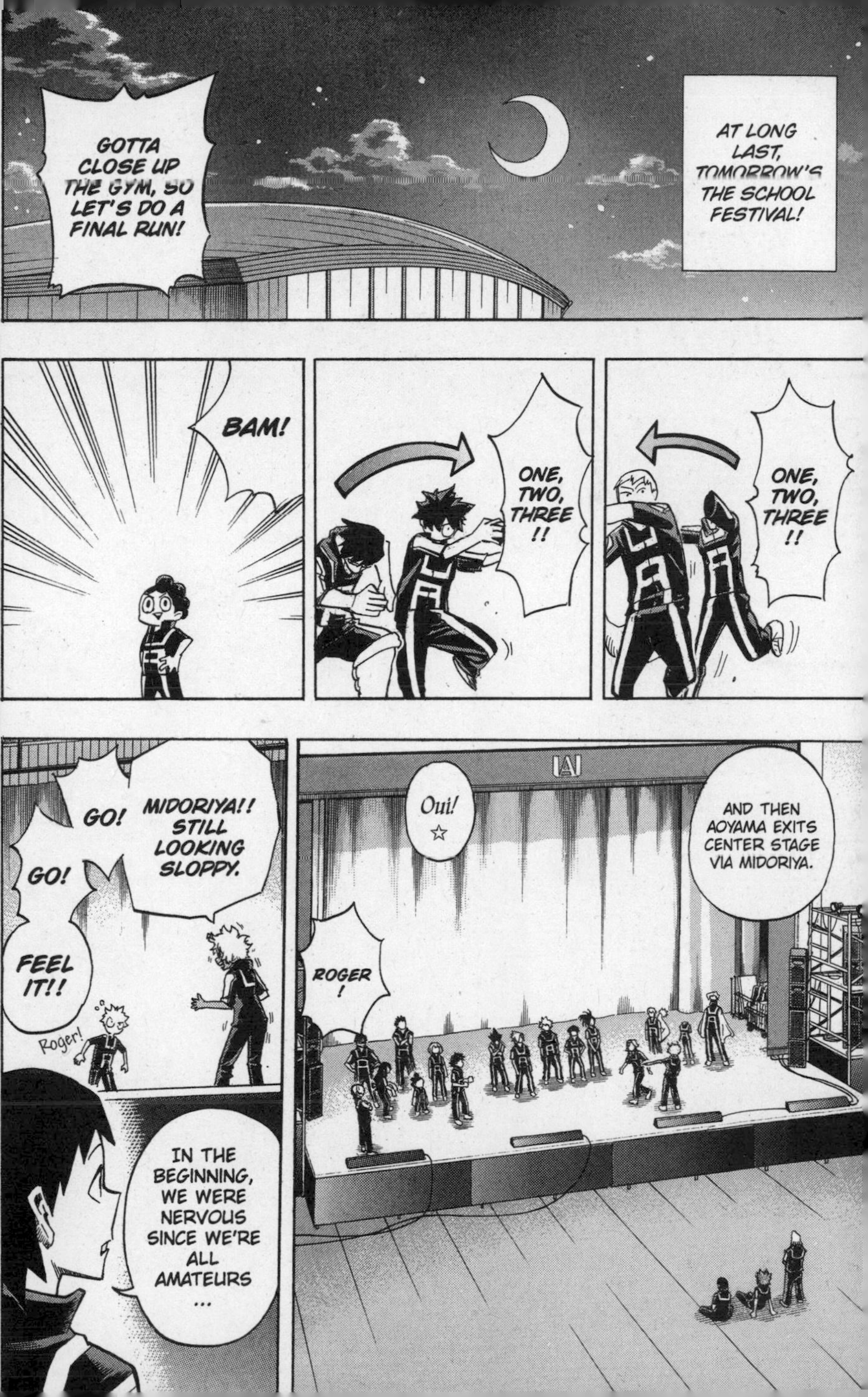
AT LONG LAST, TOMORROW'S THE SCHOOL FESTIVAL!
GOTTA CLOSE UP THE GYM, SO LET'S DO A FINAL RUN!
ONE, TWO, THREE !!
ONE, TWO, THREE !!
BAM!
AND THEN AOYAMA EXITS CENTER STAGE VIA MIDORIYA.
Oui! ☆
ROGER !
MIDORIYA!! STILL LOOKING SLOPPY.
GO!
GO!
FEEL IT!!
Roger!
IN THE BEGINNING, WE WERE NERVOUS SINCE WE'RE ALL AMATEURS ...

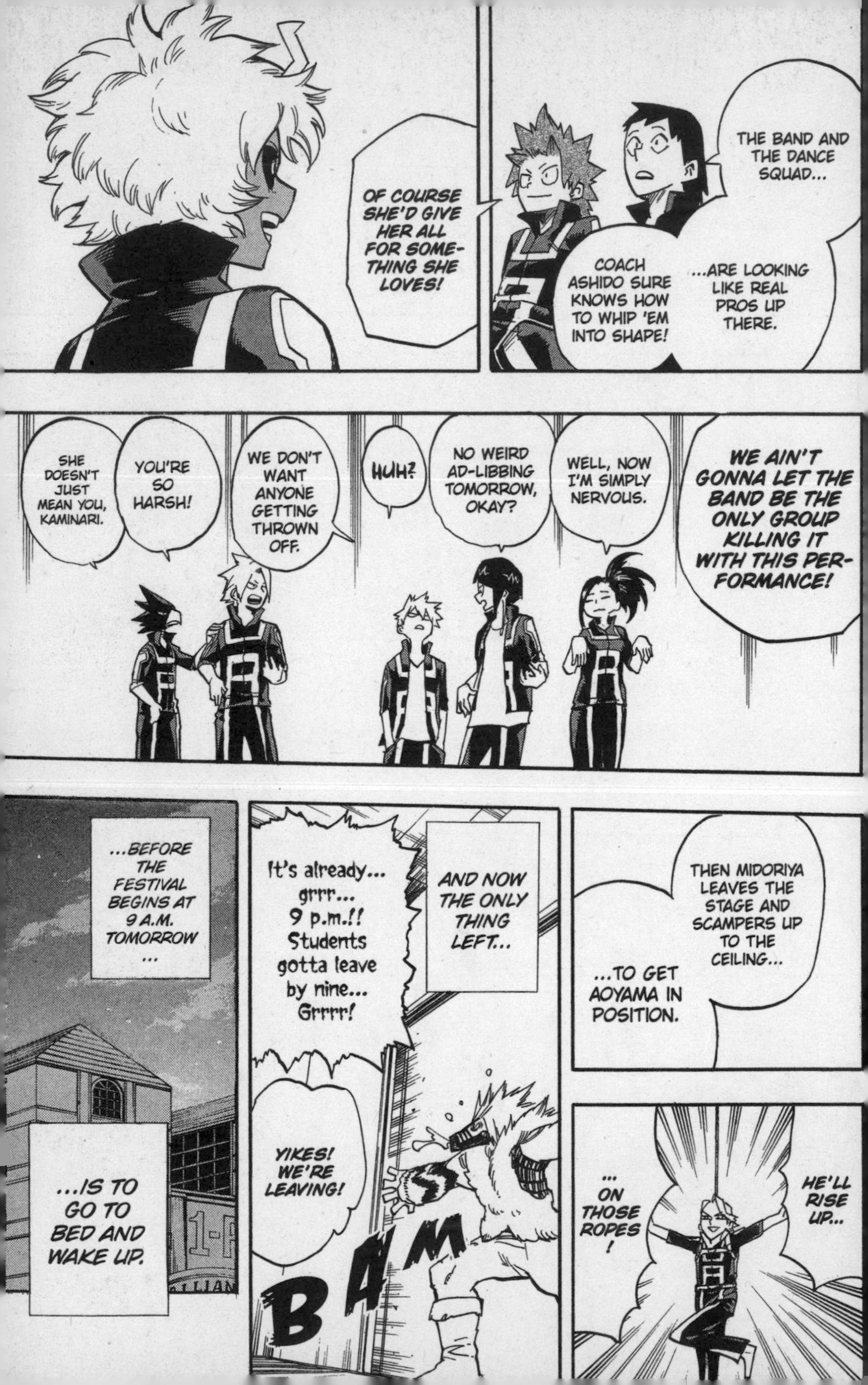
THE BAND AND THE DANCE SQUAD...
...ARE LOOKING LIKE REAL PROS UP THERE.
COACH ASHIDO SURE KNOWS HOW TO WHIP 'EM INTO SHAPE!
OF COURSE SHE'D GIVE HER ALL FOR SOME-THING SHE LOVES!
WE AIN'T GONNA LET THE BAND BE THE ONLY GROUP KILLING IT WITH THIS PER-FORMANCE!
WELL, NOW I'M SIMPLY NERVOUS.
NO WEIRD AD-LIBBING TOMORROW, OKAY?
HUH?
WE DON'T WANT ANYONE GETTING THROWN OFF.
YOU'RE SO HARSH!
SHE DOESN'T JUST MEAN YOU, KAMINARI.
THEN MIDORIYA LEAVES THE STAGE AND SCAMPERS UP TO THE CEILING...
...TO GET AOYAMA IN POSITION.
HE'LL RISE UP...
...ON THOSE ROPES!
AND NOW THE ONLY THING LEFT...
It's already... grrr... 9 p.m.!! Students gotta leave by nine... Grrrr!
YIKES! WE'RE LEAVING!
BAM
...BEFORE THE FESTIVAL BEGINS AT 9 A.M. TOMORROW...
...IS TO GO TO BED AND WAKE UP.

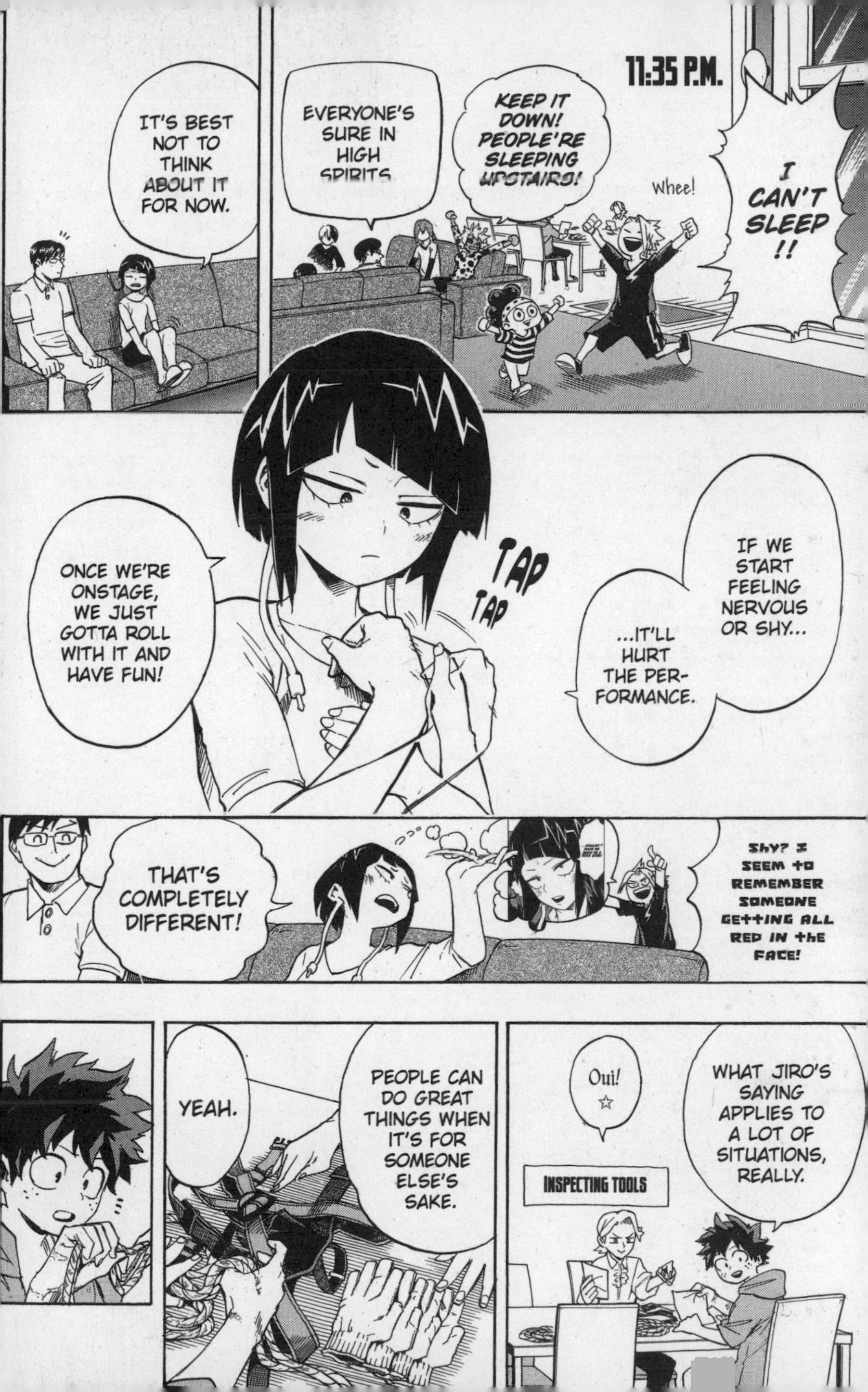
11:35 P.M.
I CAN'T SLEEP!!
Whee!
KEEP IT DOWN! PEOPLE'RE SLEEPING UPSTAIRS!
EVERYONE'S SURE IN HIGH SPIRITS.
IT'S BEST NOT TO THINK ABOUT IT FOR NOW.
IF WE START FEELING NERVOUS OR SHY...
...IT'LL HURT THE PERFORMANCE.
TAP TAP
ONCE WE'RE ONSTAGE, WE JUST GOTTA ROLL WITH IT AND HAVE FUN!
Shy? I seem to remember someone getting all red in the face!
THAT'S COMPLETELY DIFFERENT!
WHAT JIRO'S SAYING APPLIES TO A LOT OF SITUATIONS, REALLY.
Oui! ☆
INSPECTING TOOLS
PEOPLE CAN DO GREAT THINGS WHEN IT'S FOR SOMEONE ELSE'S SAKE.
YEAH.

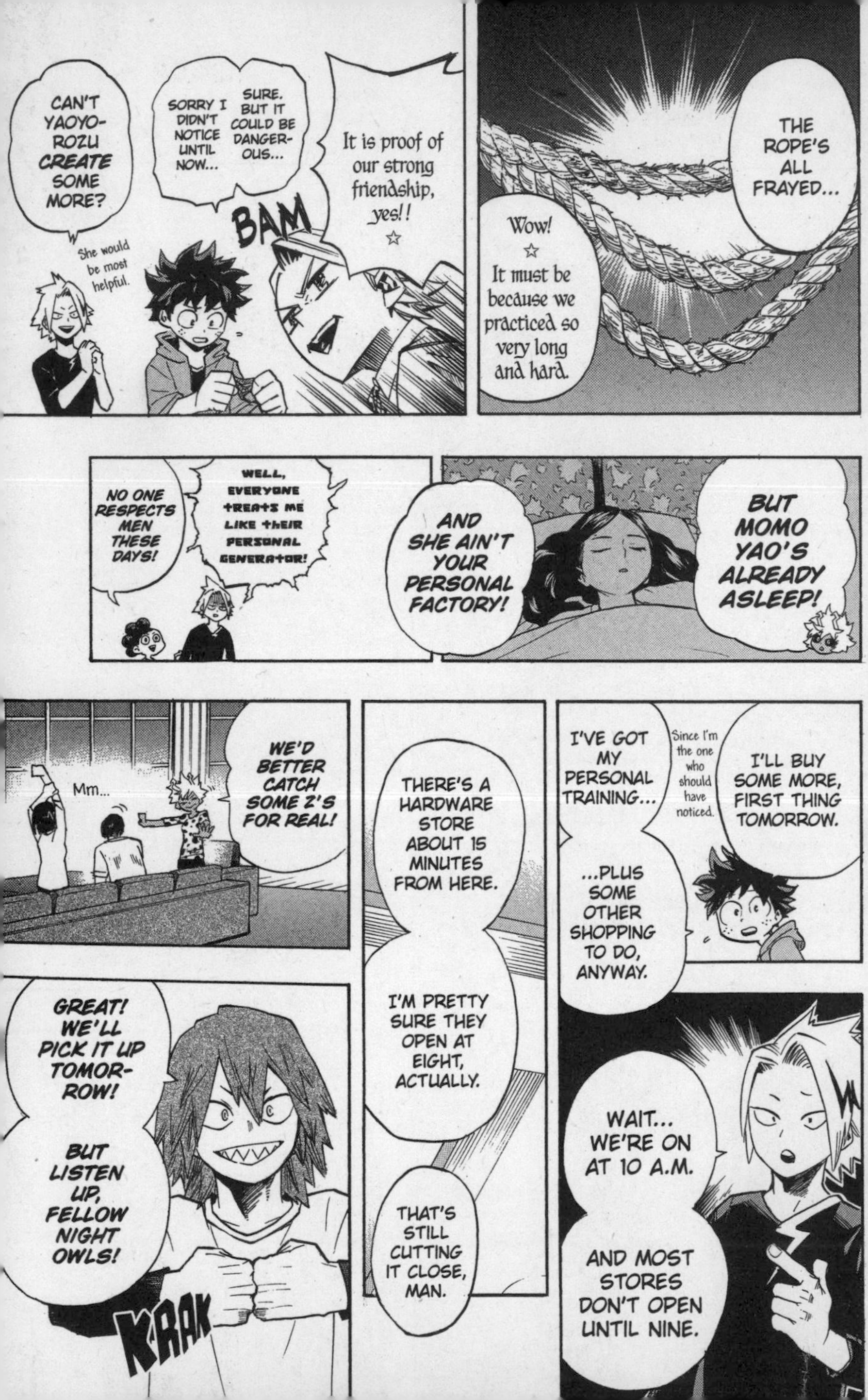
THE ROPE'S ALL FRAYED...
Wow! ☆ It must be because we practiced so very long and hard.
It is proof of our strong friendship, yes!! ☆
BAM
SURE. BUT IT COULD BE DANGEROUS...
SORRY I DIDN'T NOTICE UNTIL NOW...
CAN'T YAOYOROZU CREATE SOME MORE?
She would be most helpful.
BUT MOMO YAO'S ALREADY ASLEEP!
AND SHE AIN'T YOUR PERSONAL FACTORY!
WELL, EVERYONE TREATS ME LIKE THEIR PERSONAL GENERATOR!
NO ONE RESPECTS MEN THESE DAYS!
I'LL BUY SOME MORE, FIRST THING TOMORROW.
Since I'm the one who should have noticed.
I'VE GOT MY PERSONAL TRAINING...
...PLUS SOME OTHER SHOPPING TO DO, ANYWAY.
WAIT... WE'RE ON AT 10 A.M.
AND MOST STORES DON'T OPEN UNTIL NINE.
THERE'S A HARDWARE STORE ABOUT 15 MINUTES FROM HERE.
I'M PRETTY SURE THEY OPEN AT EIGHT, ACTUALLY.
THAT'S STILL CUTTING IT CLOSE, MAN.
WE'D BETTER CATCH SOME Z'S FOR REAL!
Mm...
GREAT! WE'LL PICK IT UP TOMORROW!
BUT LISTEN UP, FELLOW NIGHT OWLS!
KRAK

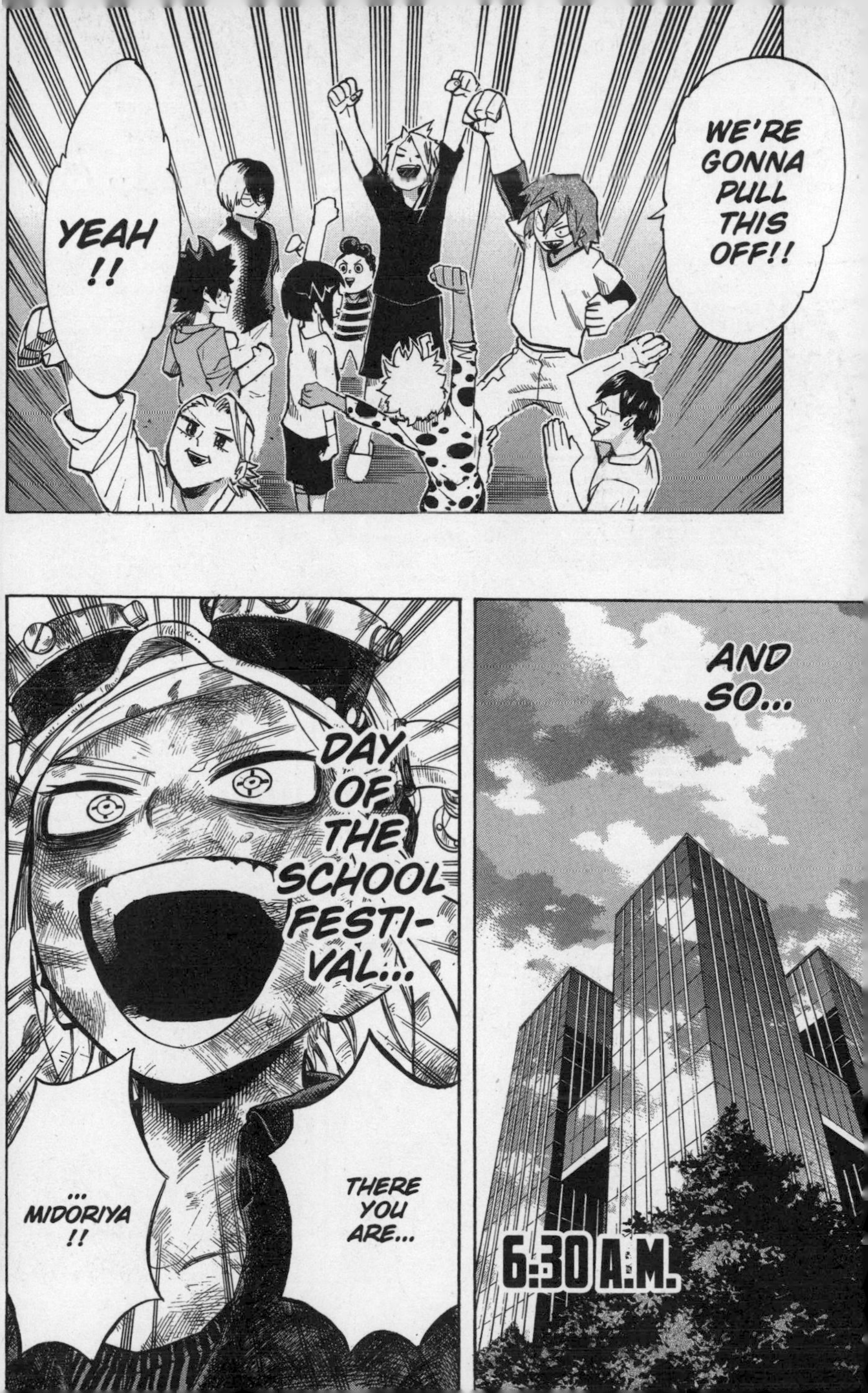
WE'RE GONNA PULL THIS OFF!!
YEAH!!
AND SO...
6:30 A.M.
DAY OF THE SCHOOL FESTI-VAL...
THERE YOU ARE...
...MIDORIYA!!

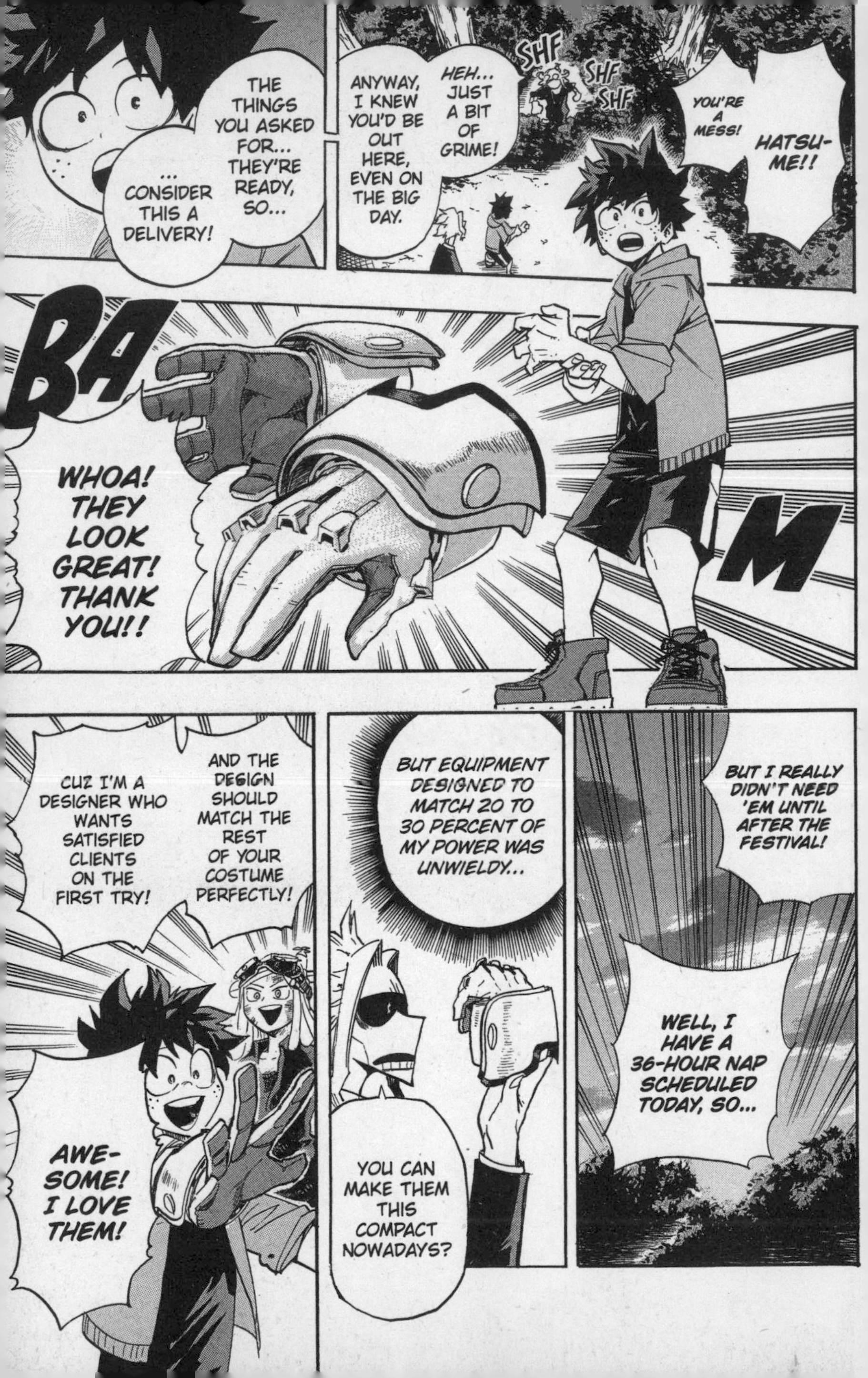
HATSU-ME!!
YOU'RE A MESS!
SHF SHF SHF
HEH... JUST A BIT OF GRIME!
ANYWAY, I KNEW YOU'D BE OUT HERE, EVEN ON THE BIG DAY.
THE THINGS YOU ASKED FOR... THEY'RE READY, SO...
... CONSIDER THIS A DELIVERY!
BAM
WHOA! THEY LOOK GREAT! THANK YOU!!
BUT I REALLY DIDN'T NEED 'EM UNTIL AFTER THE FESTIVAL!
WELL, I HAVE A 36-HOUR NAP SCHEDULED TODAY, SO...
BUT EQUIPMENT DESIGNED TO MATCH 20 TO 30 PERCENT OF MY POWER WAS UNWIELDY...
YOU CAN MAKE THEM THIS COMPACT NOWADAYS?
AND THE DESIGN SHOULD MATCH THE REST OF YOUR COSTUME PERFECTLY!
CUZ I'M A DESIGNER WHO WANTS SATISFIED CLIENTS ON THE FIRST TRY!
AWE-SOME! I LOVE THEM!

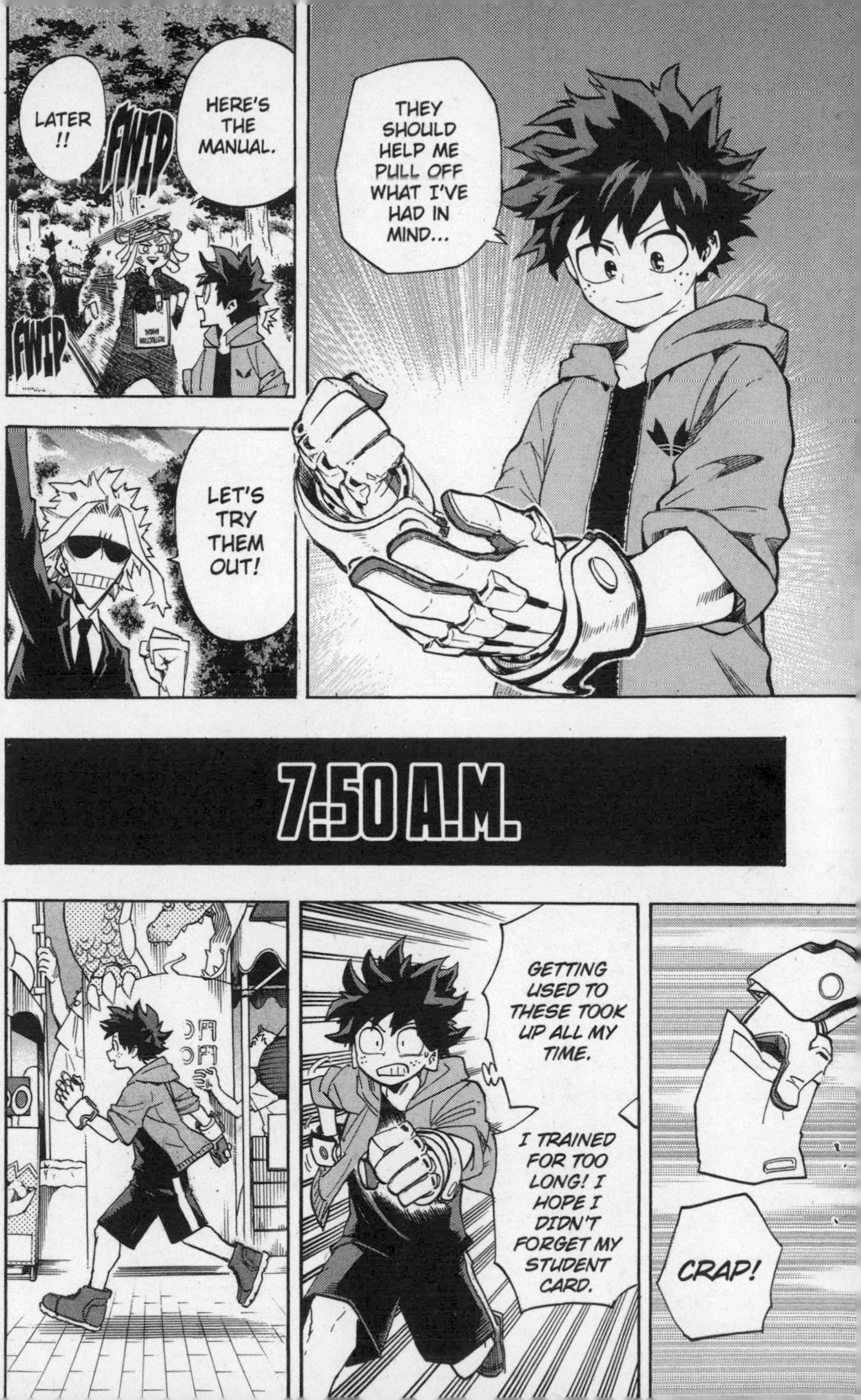
THEY SHOULD HELP ME PULL OFF WHAT I'VE HAD IN MIND...
HERE'S THE MANUAL.
FWIP
LATER!!
FWIP
LET'S TRY THEM OUT!
7:50 A.M.
CRAP!
GETTING USED TO THESE TOOK UP ALL MY TIME.
I TRAINED FOR TOO LONG! I HOPE I DIDN'T FORGET MY STUDENT CARD.

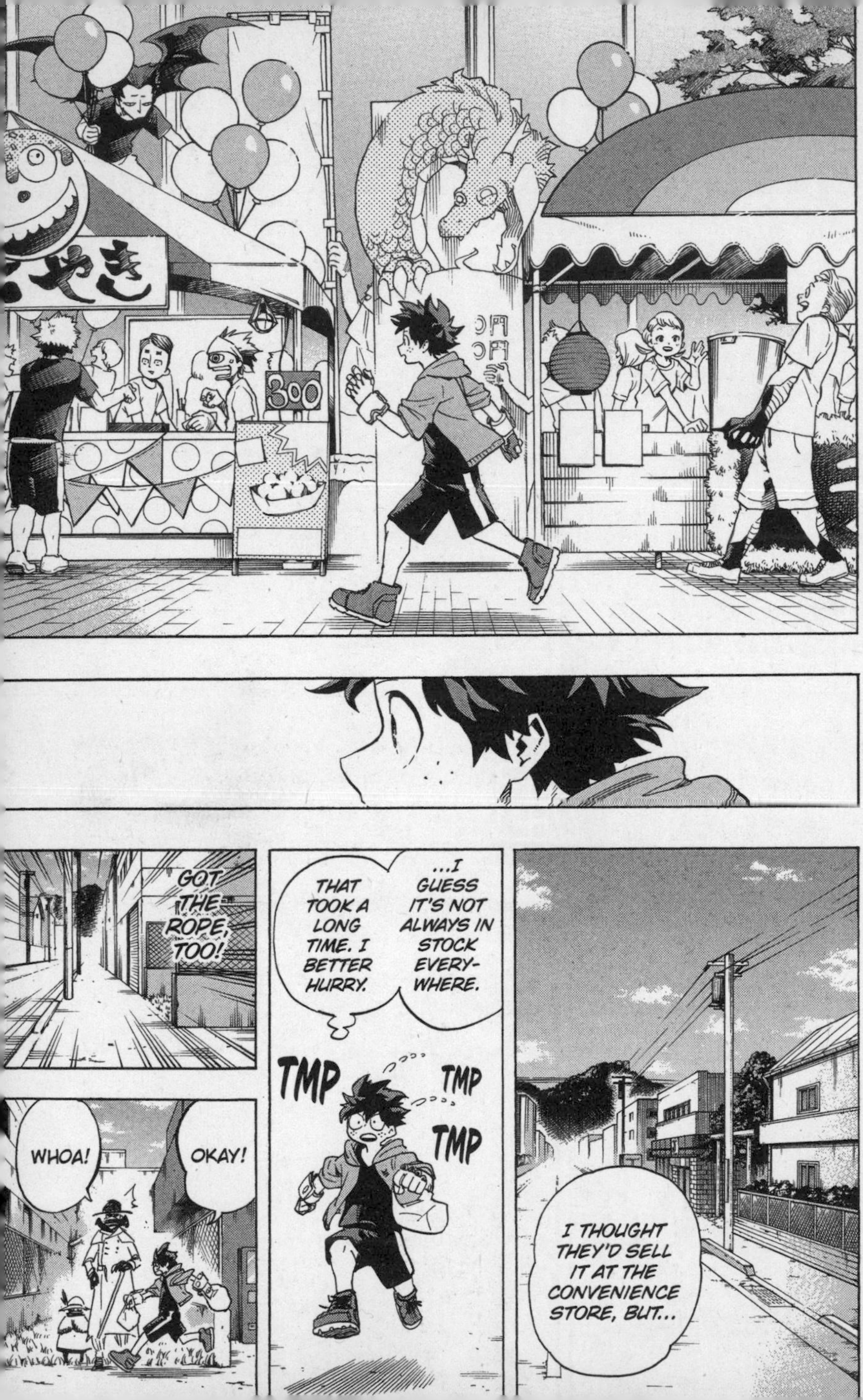
300
I THOUGHT THEY'D SELL IT AT THE CONVENIENCE STORE, BUT...
...I GUESS IT'S NOT ALWAYS IN STOCK EVERY-WHERE.
THAT TOOK A LONG TIME. I BETTER HURRY.
TMP
TMP
TMP
GOT THE ROPE, TOO!
OKAY!
WHOA!

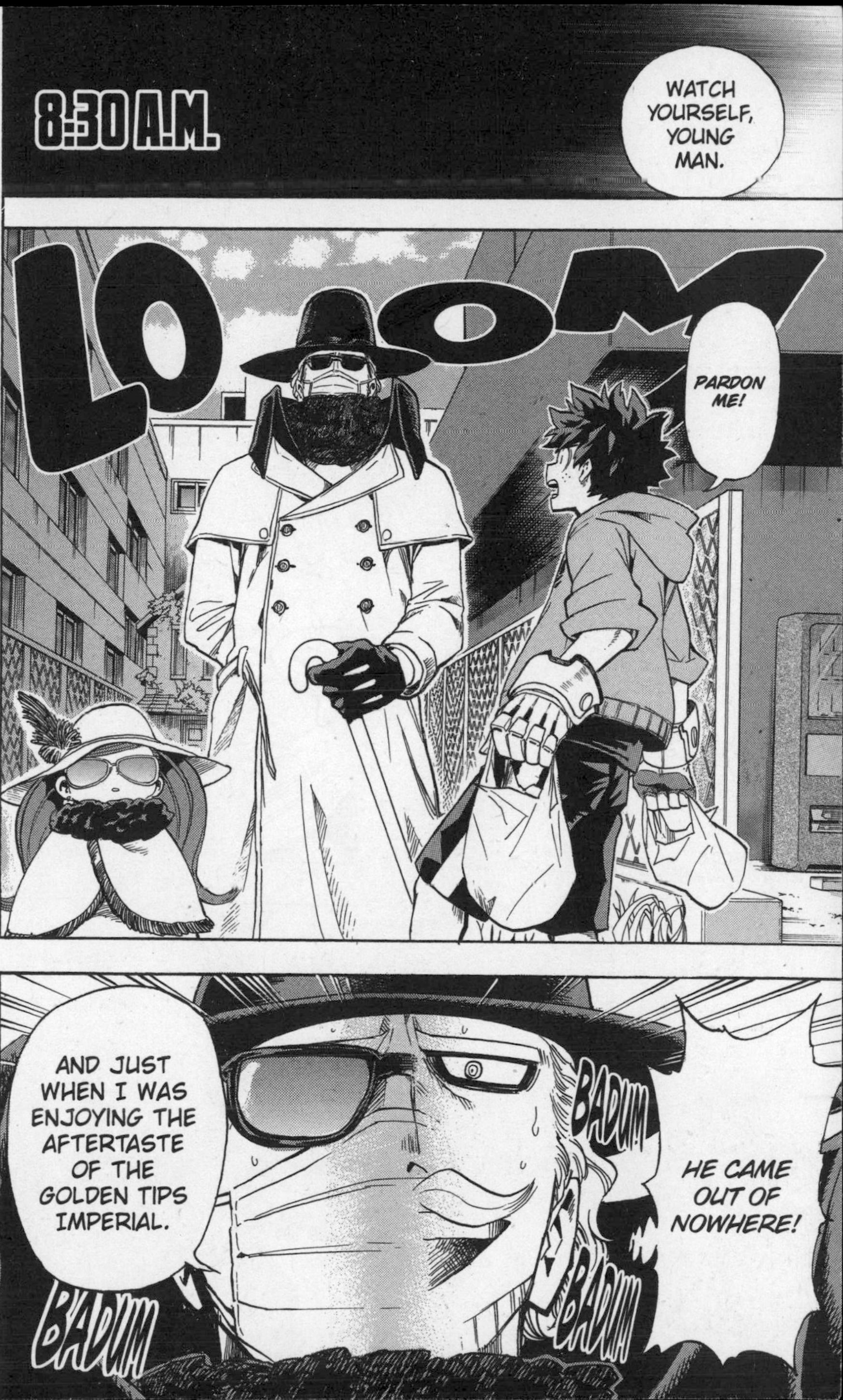
WATCH YOURSELF, YOUNG MAN.
8:30 A.M.
PARDON ME!
LOOOM
BADUM
HE CAME OUT OF NOWHERE!
BADUM
AND JUST WHEN I WAS ENJOYING THE AFTERTASTE OF THE GOLDEN TIPS IMPERIAL.
BADUM

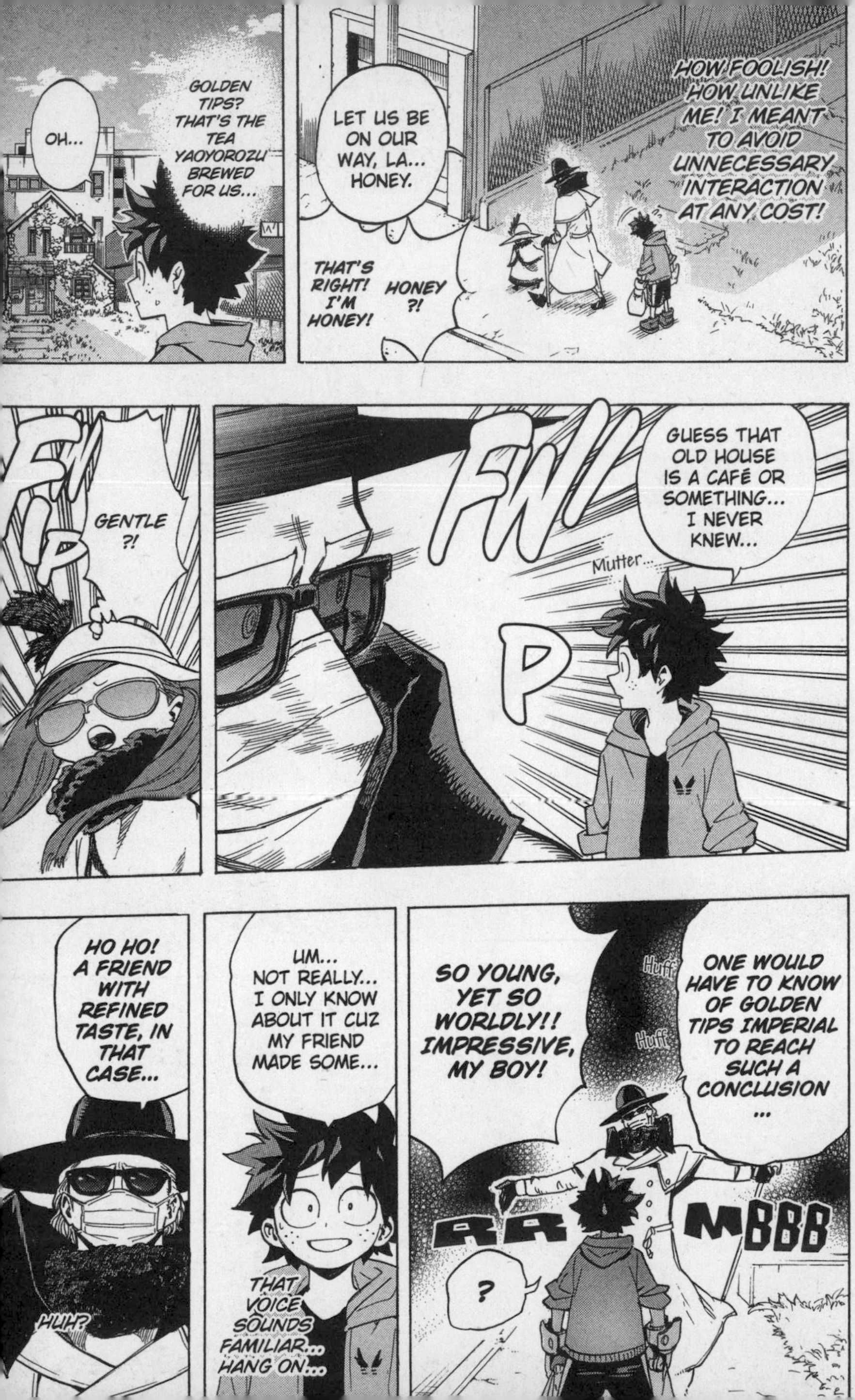
HOW FOOLISH! HOW UNLIKE ME! I MEANT TO AVOID UNNECESSARY INTERACTION AT ANY COST!
LET US BE ON OUR WAY, LA... HONEY.
HONEY ?!
THAT'S RIGHT! I'M HONEY!
GOLDEN TIPS? THAT'S THE TEA YAOYOROZU BREWED FOR US...
OH...
GUESS THAT OLD HOUSE IS A CAFÉ OR SOMETHING... I NEVER KNEW...
Mutter...
FW
P
FW
IP
GENTLE ?!
ONE WOULD HAVE TO KNOW OF GOLDEN TIPS IMPERIAL TO REACH SUCH A CONCLUSION ...
Huff
Huff
SO YOUNG, YET SO WORLDLY!! IMPRESSIVE, MY BOY!
RR
MBBB
?
UM... NOT REALLY... I ONLY KNOW ABOUT IT CUZ MY FRIEND MADE SOME...
THAT VOICE SOUNDS FAMILIAR... HANG ON...
HO HO! A FRIEND WITH REFINED TASTE, IN THAT CASE...
HUH?

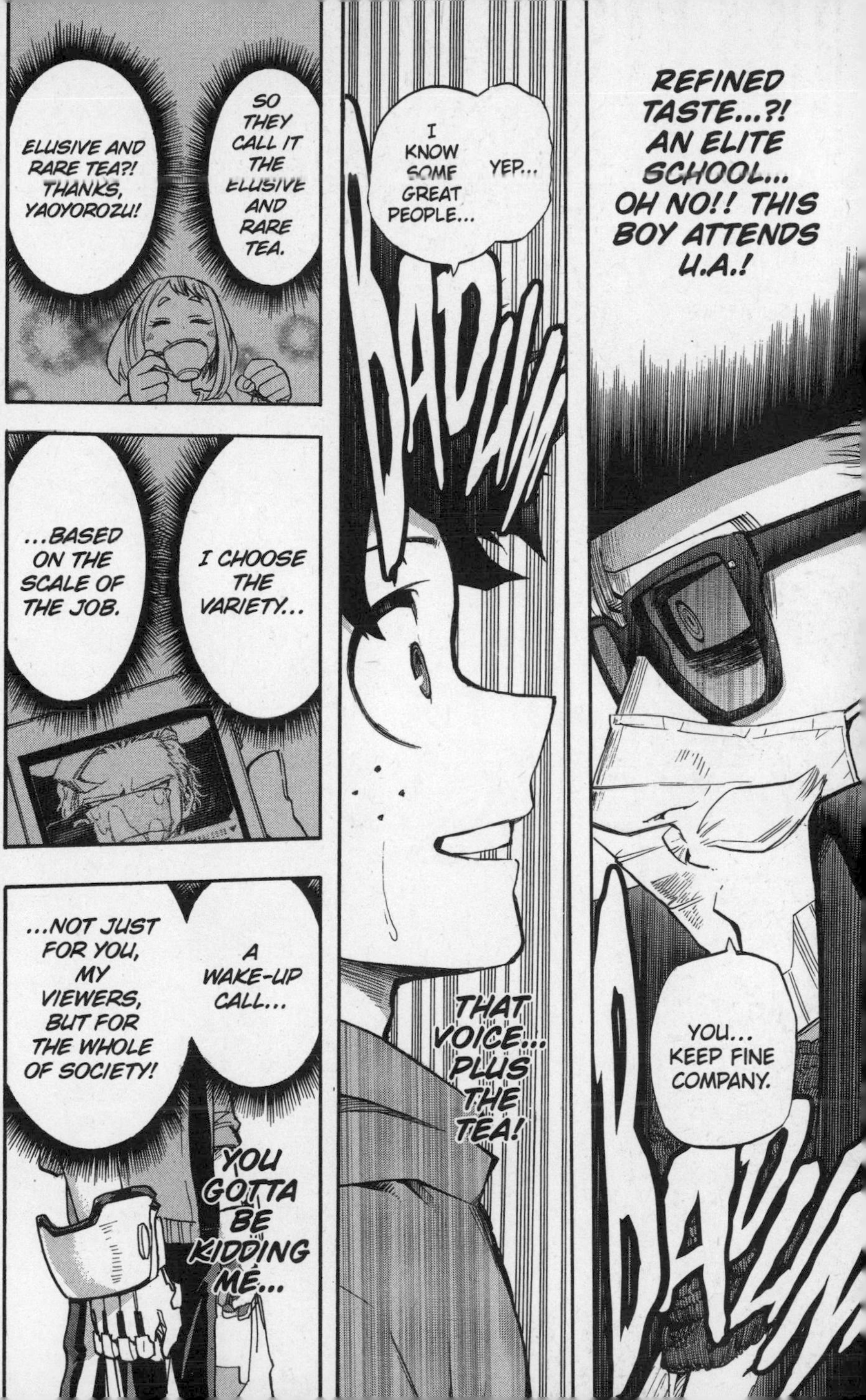
REFINED TASTE...?! AN ELITE SCHOOL... OH NO!! THIS BOY ATTENDS U.A.!
YOU... KEEP FINE COMPANY.
I KNOW SOME GREAT PEOPLE... YEP...
THAT VOICE... PLUS THE TEA!
SO THEY CALL IT THE ELUSIVE AND RARE TEA.
ELUSIVE AND RARE TEA?! THANKS, YAOYOROZU!
I CHOOSE THE VARIETY...
...BASED ON THE SCALE OF THE JOB.
A WAKE-UP CALL...
...NOT JUST FOR YOU, MY VIEWERS, BUT FOR THE WHOLE OF SOCIETY!
YOU GOTTA BE KIDDING ME...

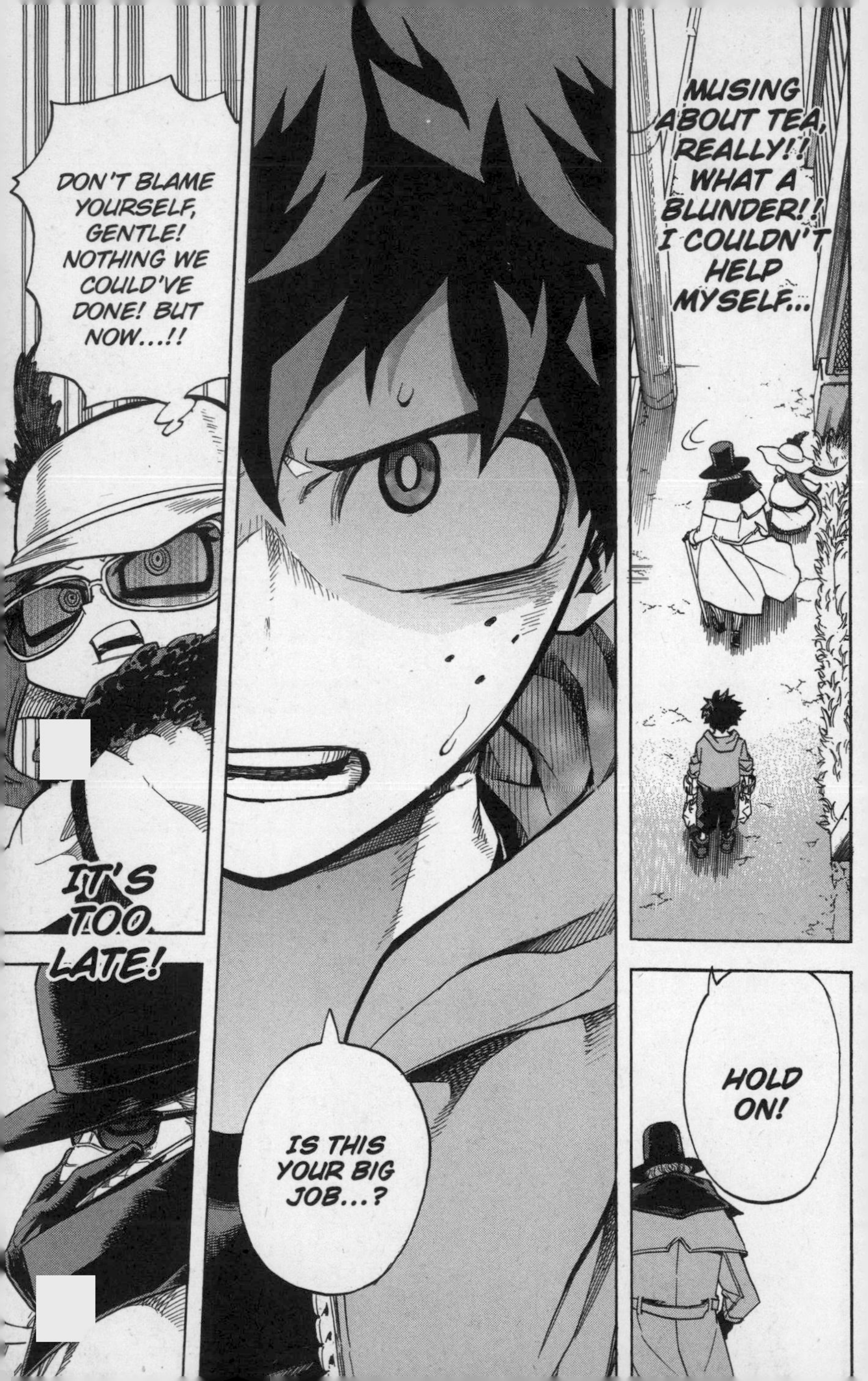
MUSING ABOUT TEA, REALLY!! WHAT A BLUNDER!! I COULDN'T HELP MYSELF...
HOLD ON!
IS THIS YOUR BIG JOB...?
DON'T BLAME YOURSELF, GENTLE! NOTHING WE COULD'VE DONE! BUT NOW...!!
IT'S TOO LATE!

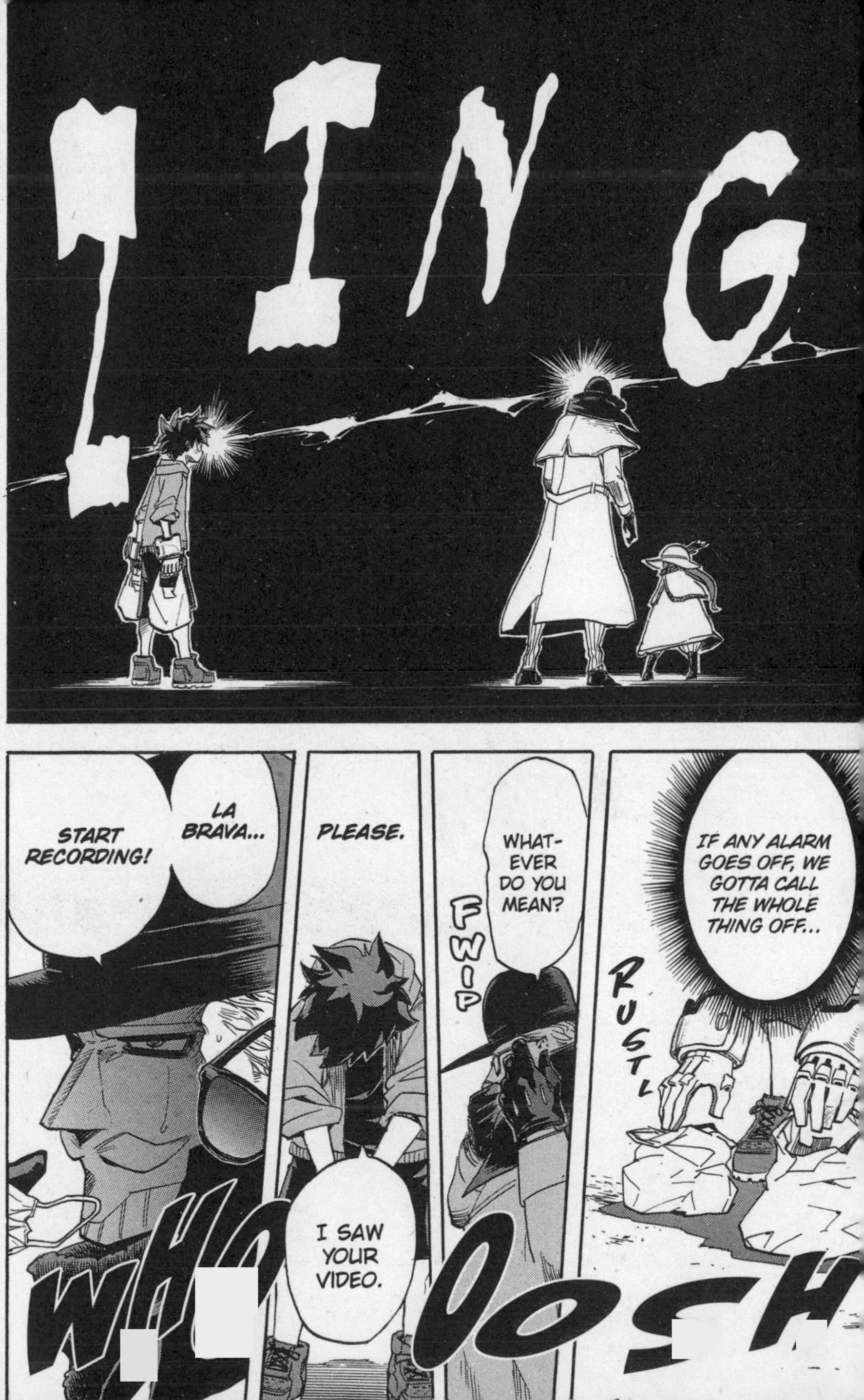
IING
IF ANY ALARM GOES OFF, WE GOTTA CALL THE WHOLE THING OFF...
RUSTL
WHAT-EVER DO YOU MEAN?
FWIP
PLEASE.
I SAW YOUR VIDEO.
LA BRAVA...
START RECORDING!
WHOOOSH

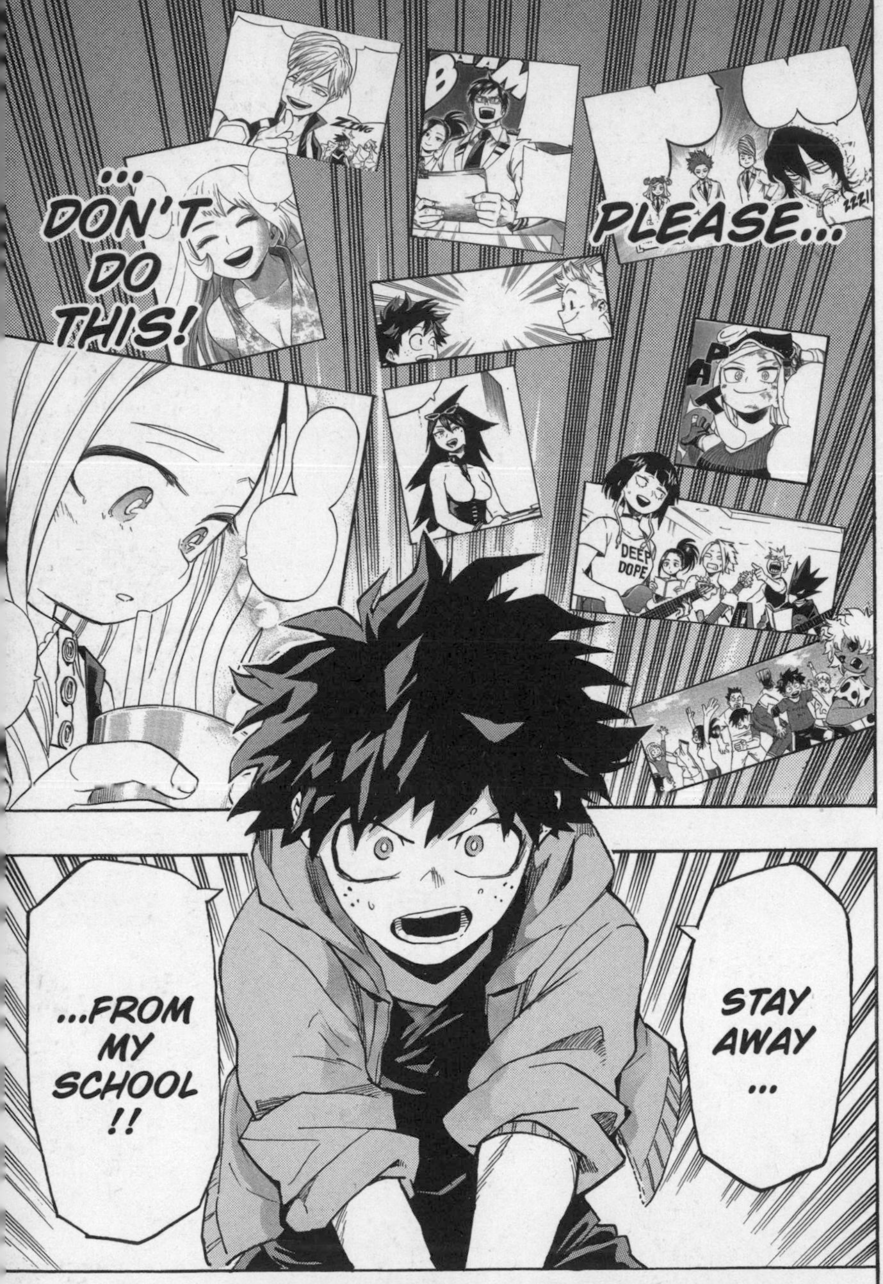
PLEASE...
...DON'T DO THIS!
BAM
ZING
DEEP DOPE
STAY AWAY...
...FROM MY SCHOOL!!

8:32 A.M. 1 HOUR & 28 MINUTES UNTIL CLASS 1-A'S PERFORMANCE...

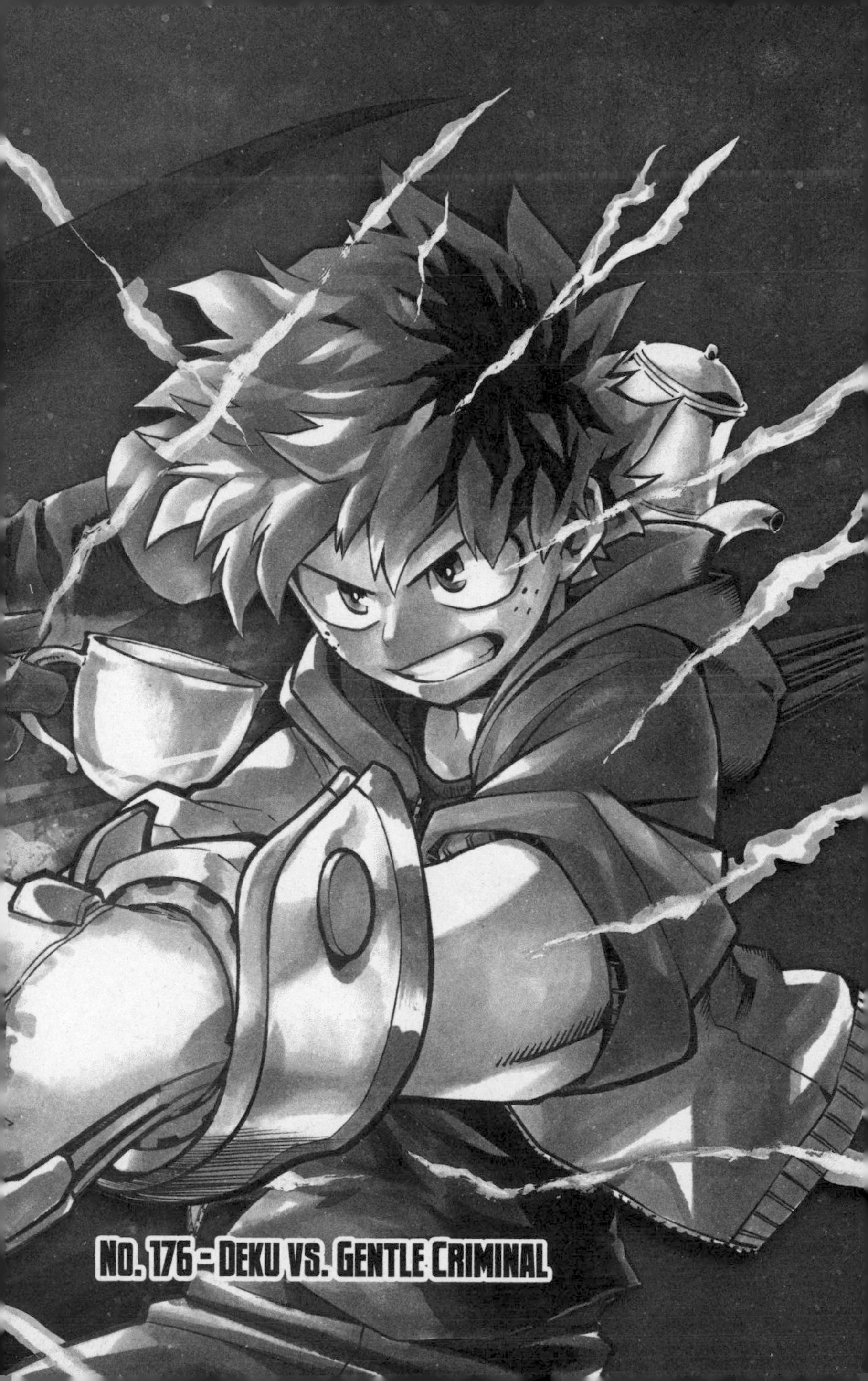
No. 176 - Deku vs. Gentle Criminal

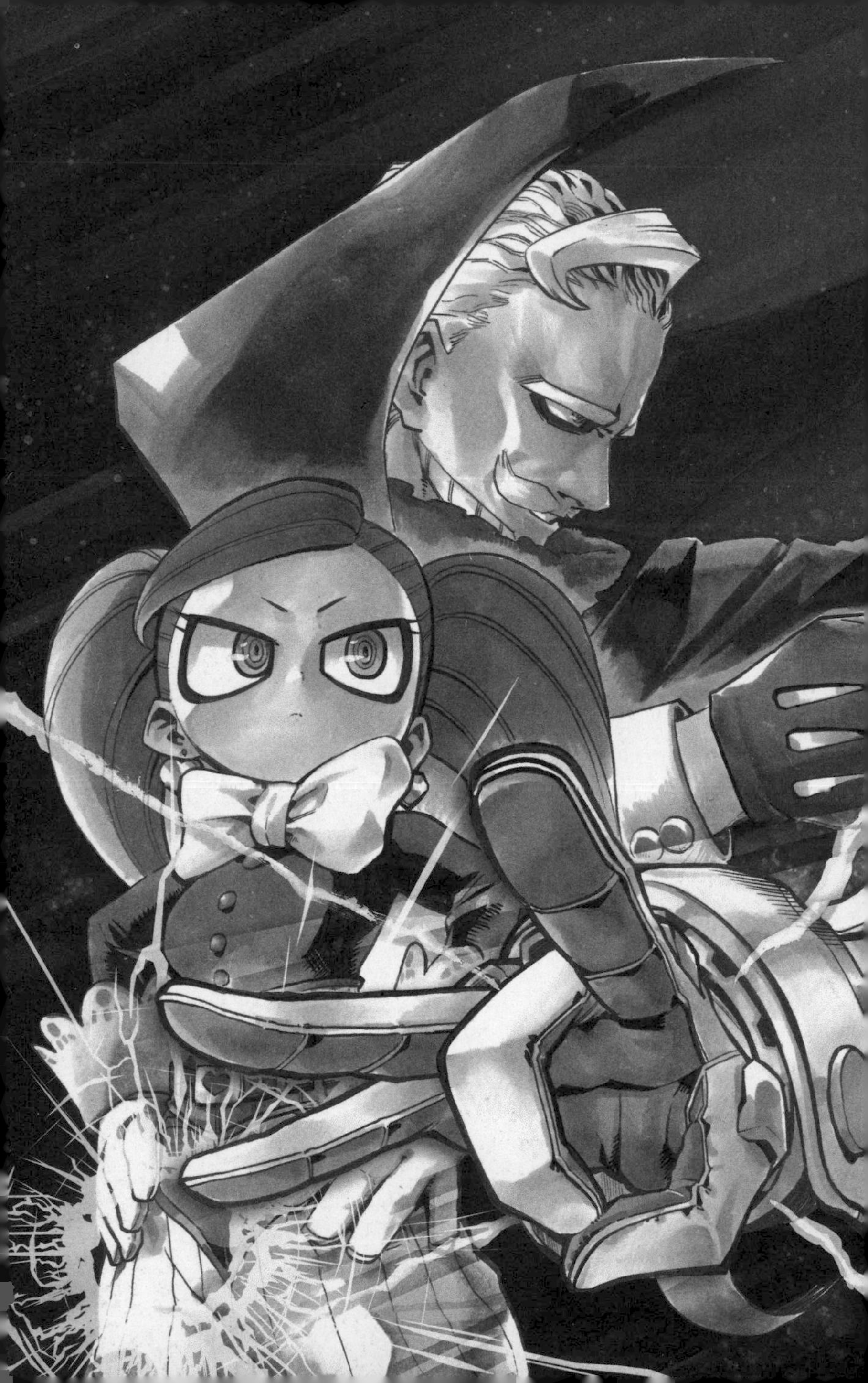

MY HERO ACADEMIA

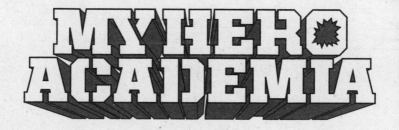

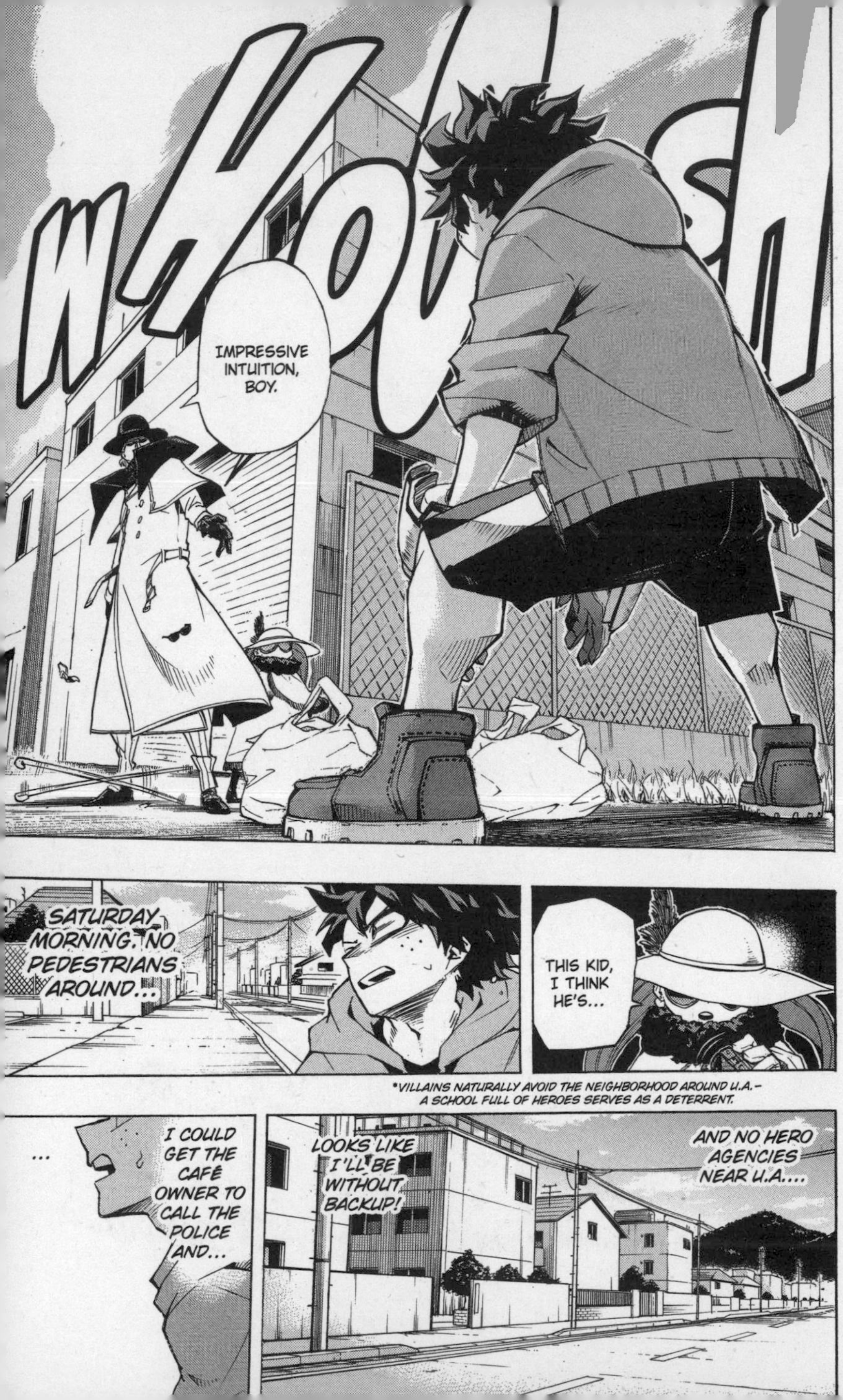
WHOOSH
IMPRESSIVE INTUITION, BOY.
THIS KID, I THINK HE'S...
SATURDAY MORNING. NO PEDESTRIANS AROUND...
*VILLAINS NATURALLY AVOID THE NEIGHBORHOOD AROUND U.A.–
A SCHOOL FULL OF HEROES SERVES AS A DETERRENT.
AND NO HERO AGENCIES NEAR U.A....
LOOKS LIKE I'LL BE WITHOUT BACKUP!
I COULD GET THE CAFÉ OWNER TO CALL THE POLICE AND...
...

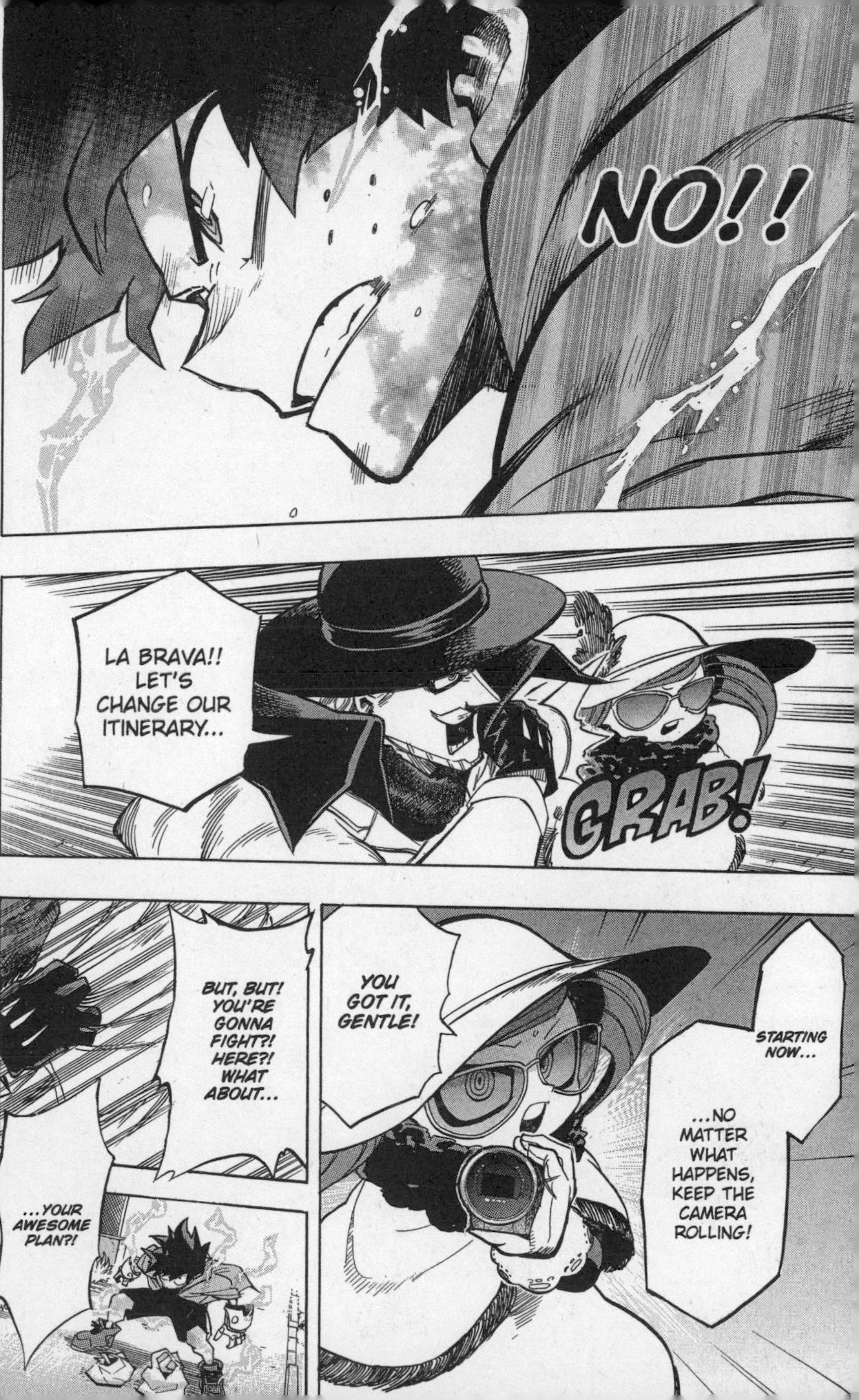
NO!!
LA BRAVA!! LET'S CHANGE OUR ITINERARY...
GRAB!
STARTING NOW...
...NO MATTER WHAT HAPPENS, KEEP THE CAMERA ROLLING!
YOU GOT IT, GENTLE!
BUT, BUT! YOU'RE GONNA FIGHT?! HERE?! WHAT ABOUT...
...YOUR AWESOME PLAN?!

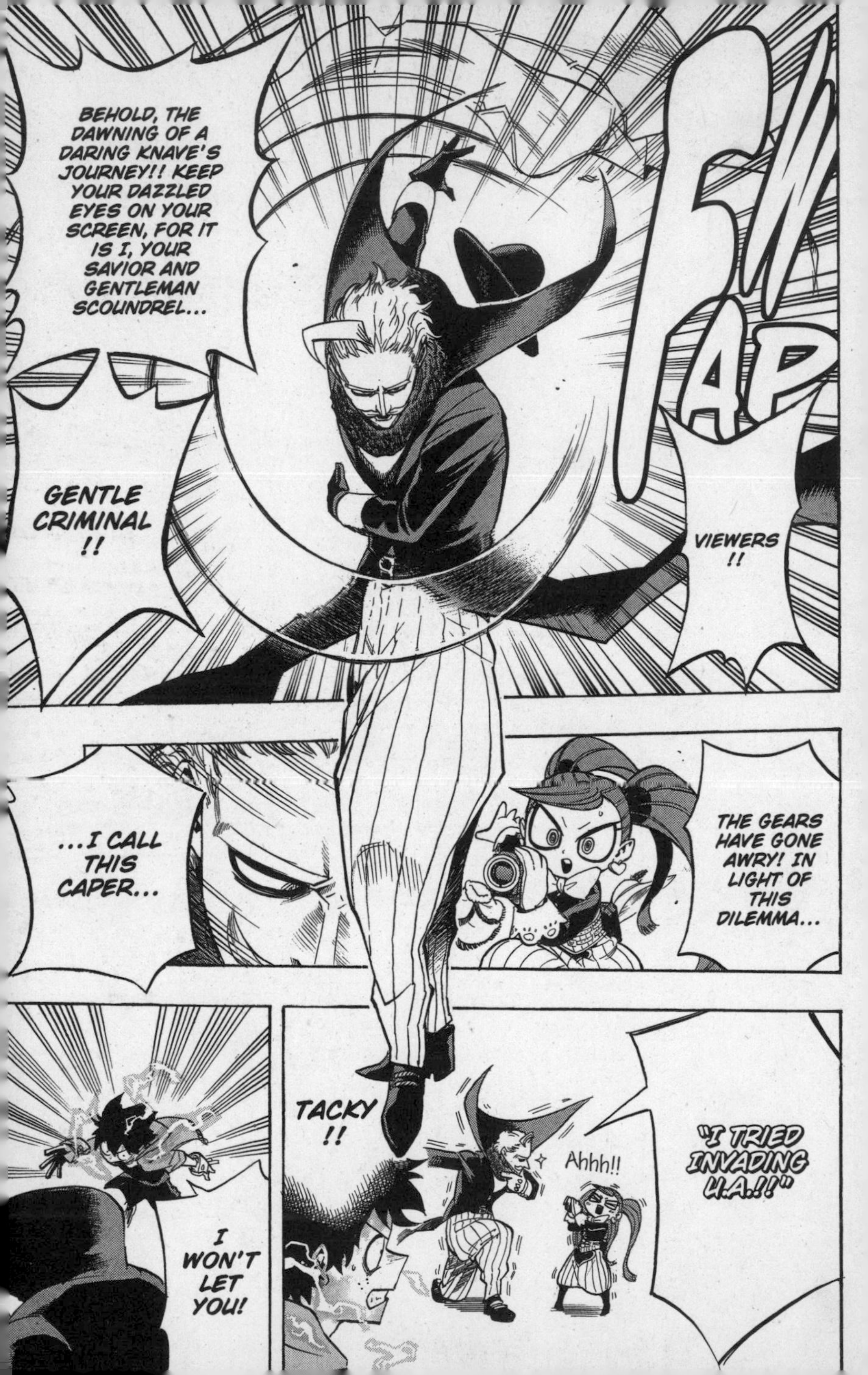
FWAP
VIEWERS!!
BEHOLD, THE DAWNING OF A DARING KNAVE'S JOURNEY!! KEEP YOUR DAZZLED EYES ON YOUR SCREEN, FOR IT IS I, YOUR SAVIOR AND GENTLEMAN SCOUNDREL...
GENTLE CRIMINAL!!
THE GEARS HAVE GONE AWRY! IN LIGHT OF THIS DILEMMA...
...I CALL THIS CAPER...
"I TRIED INVADING U.A.!!"
Ahhh!!
TACKY!!
I WON'T LET YOU!

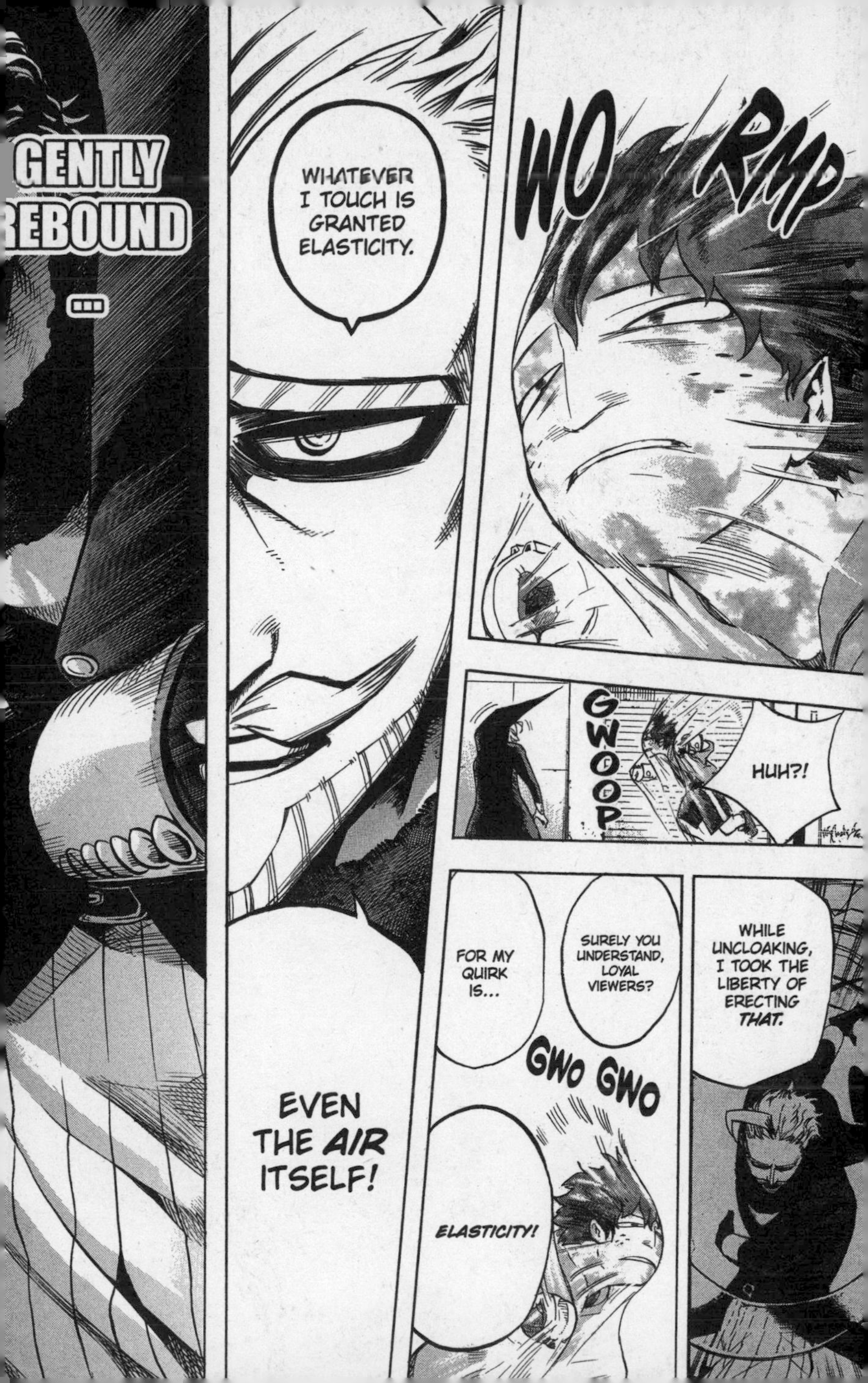
WO RMP
HUH?!
GWOOP
WHILE UNCLOAKING, I TOOK THE LIBERTY OF ERECTING *THAT.*
SURELY YOU UNDERSTAND, LOYAL VIEWERS?
FOR MY QUIRK IS...
GWO GWO
ELASTICITY!
WHATEVER I TOUCH IS GRANTED ELASTICITY.
EVEN THE *AIR* ITSELF!
GENTLY REBOUND
...

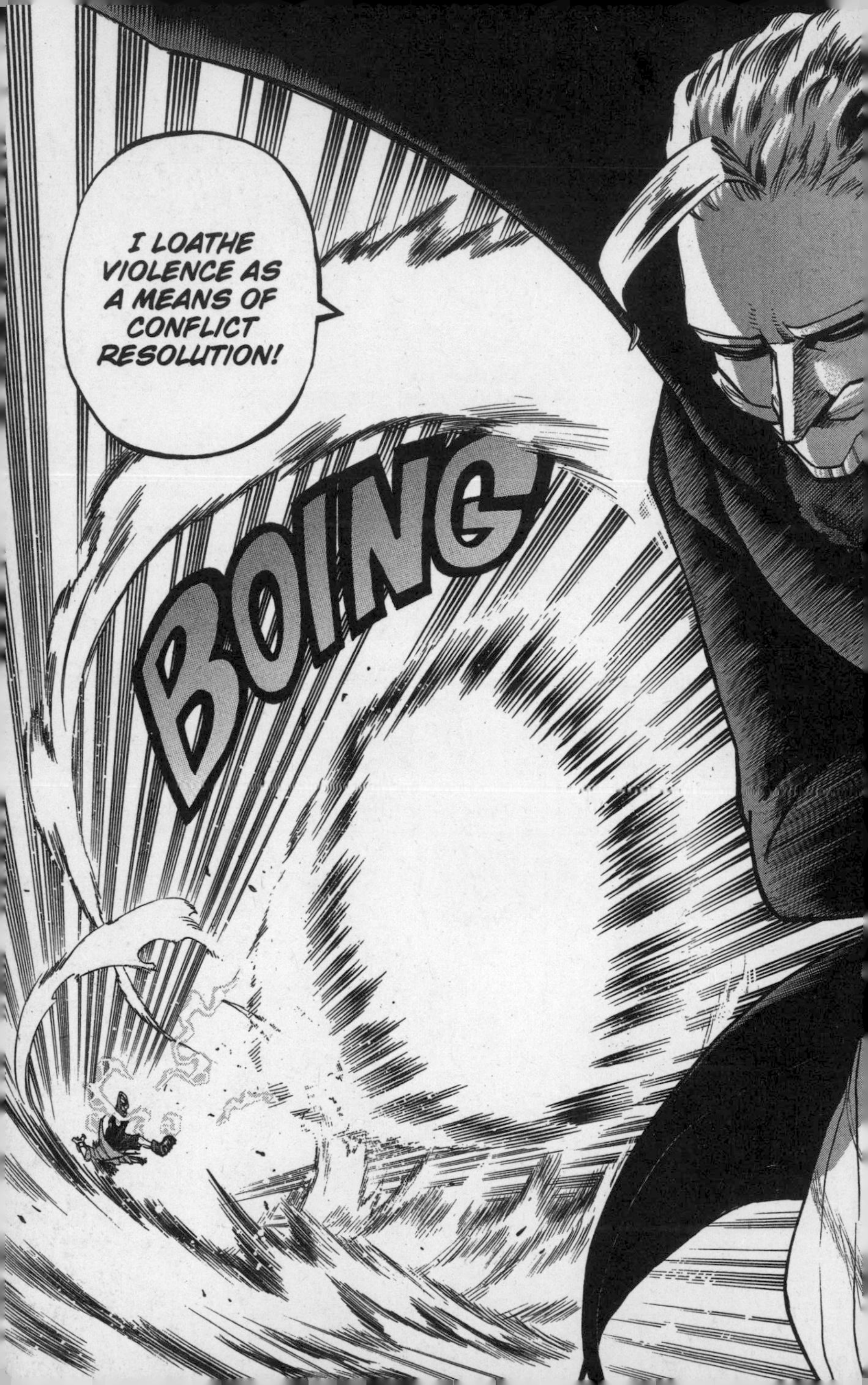
I LOATHE VIOLENCE AS A MEANS OF CONFLICT RESOLUTION!
BOING

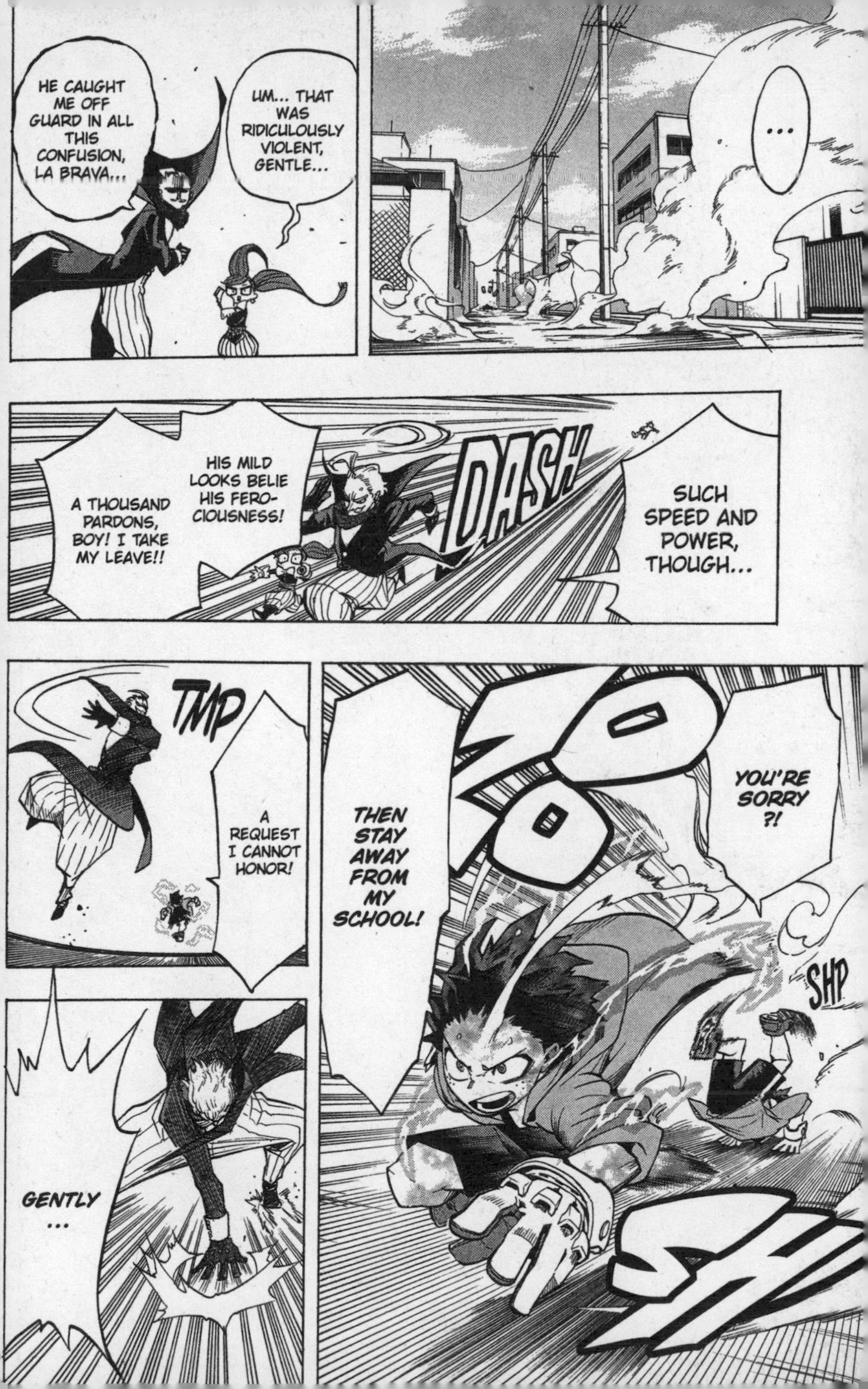
...
UM... THAT WAS RIDICULOUSLY VIOLENT, GENTLE...
HE CAUGHT ME OFF GUARD IN ALL THIS CONFUSION, LA BRAVA...
SUCH SPEED AND POWER, THOUGH...
DASH
HIS MILD LOOKS BELIE HIS FERO-CIOUSNESS!
A THOUSAND PARDONS, BOY! I TAKE MY LEAVE!!
YOU'RE SORRY?!
THEN STAY AWAY FROM MY SCHOOL!
SHP
TMP
A REQUEST I CANNOT HONOR!
GENTLY...

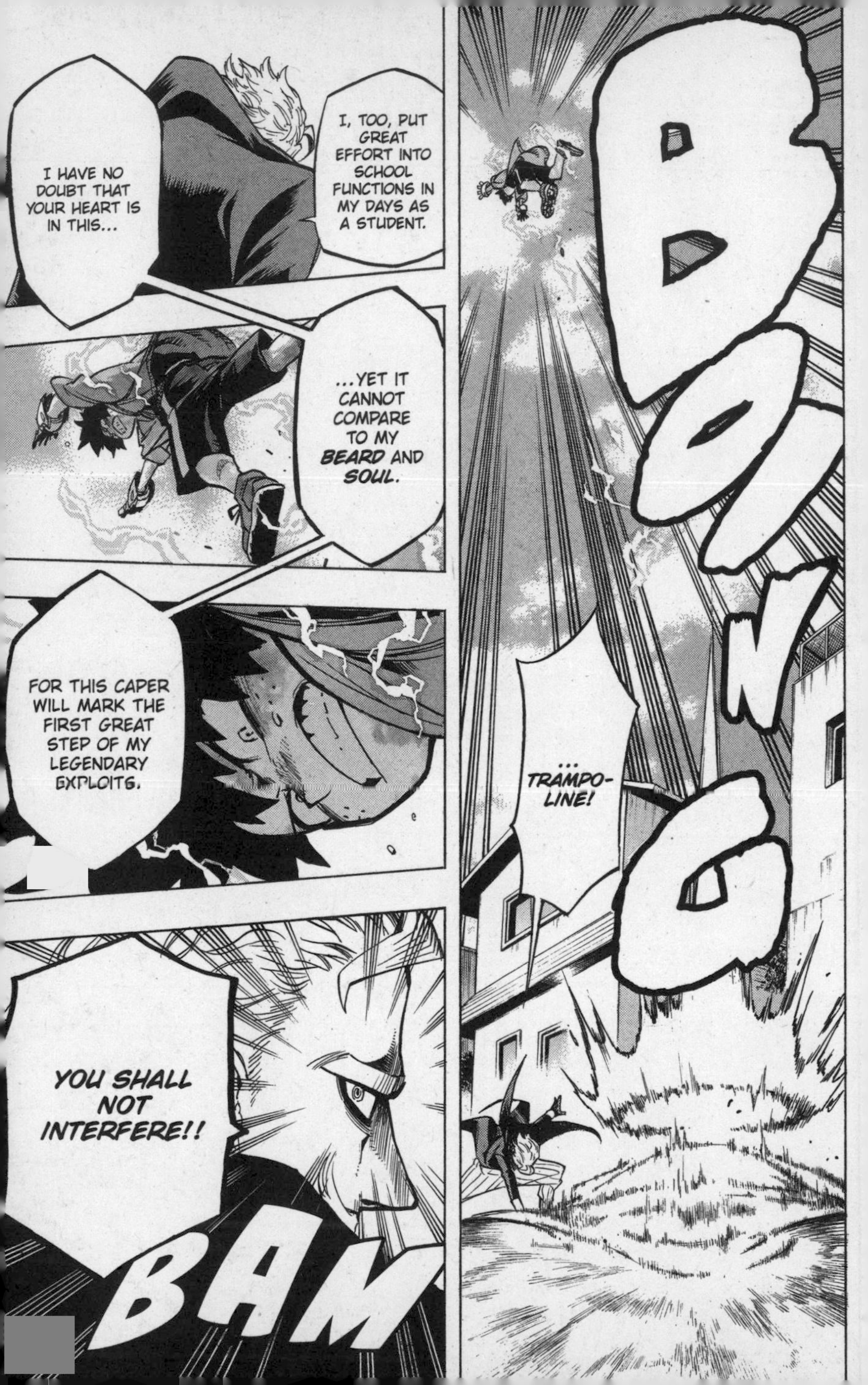
...TRAMPO-LINE!
I HAVE NO DOUBT THAT YOUR HEART IS IN THIS...
I, TOO, PUT GREAT EFFORT INTO SCHOOL FUNCTIONS IN MY DAYS AS A STUDENT.
...YET IT CANNOT COMPARE TO MY *BEARD* AND *SOUL*.
FOR THIS CAPER WILL MARK THE FIRST GREAT STEP OF MY LEGENDARY EXPLOITS.
YOU SHALL NOT INTERFERE!!
BAM

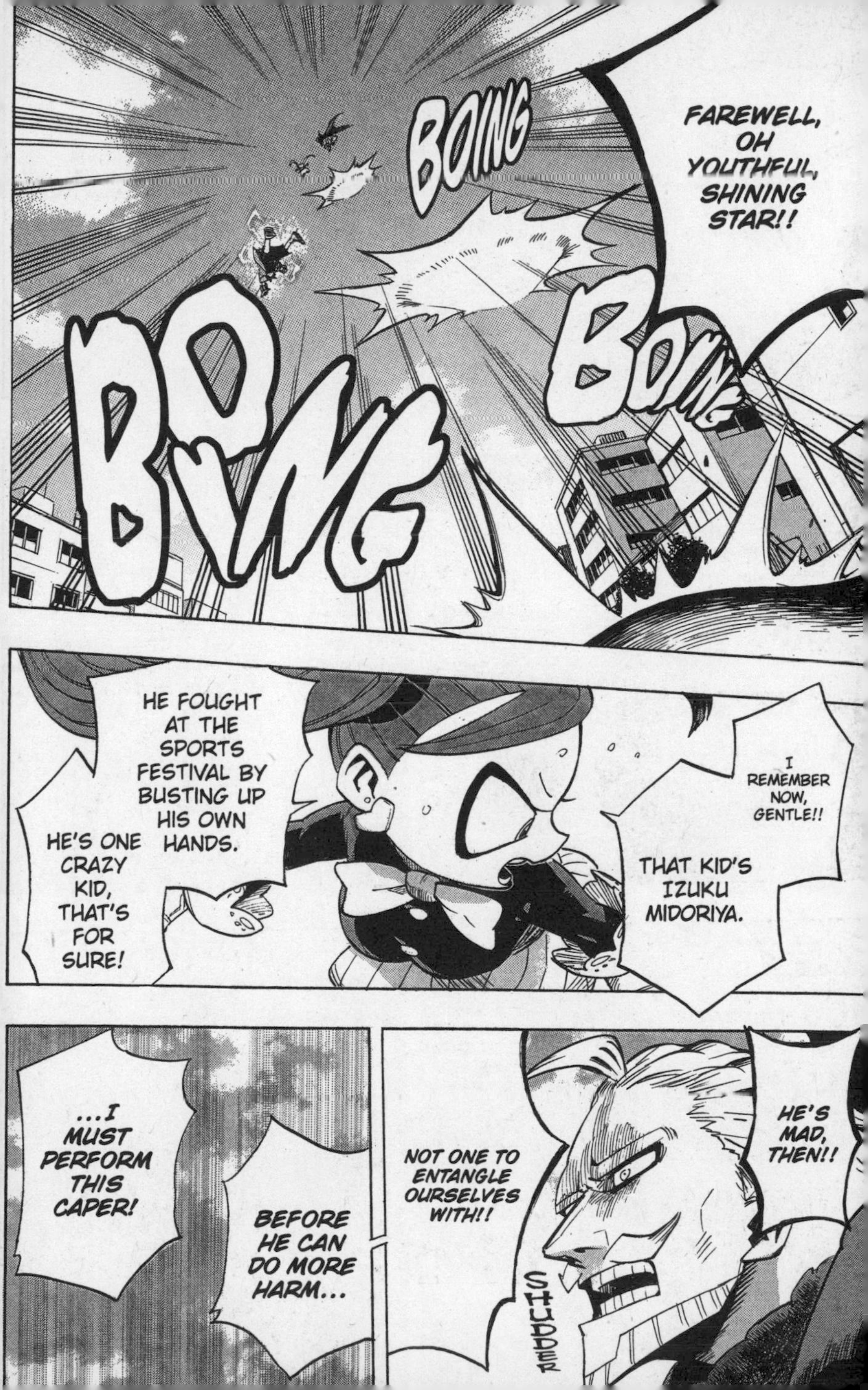
FAREWELL, OH YOUTHFUL, SHINING STAR!!
BOING
BOING
BOING
I REMEMBER NOW, GENTLE!!
THAT KID'S IZUKU MIDORIYA.
HE FOUGHT AT THE SPORTS FESTIVAL BY BUSTING UP HIS OWN HANDS.
HE'S ONE CRAZY KID, THAT'S FOR SURE!
HE'S MAD, THEN!!
SHUDDER
NOT ONE TO ENTANGLE OURSELVES WITH!!
BEFORE HE CAN DO MORE HARM...
...I MUST PERFORM THIS CAPER!

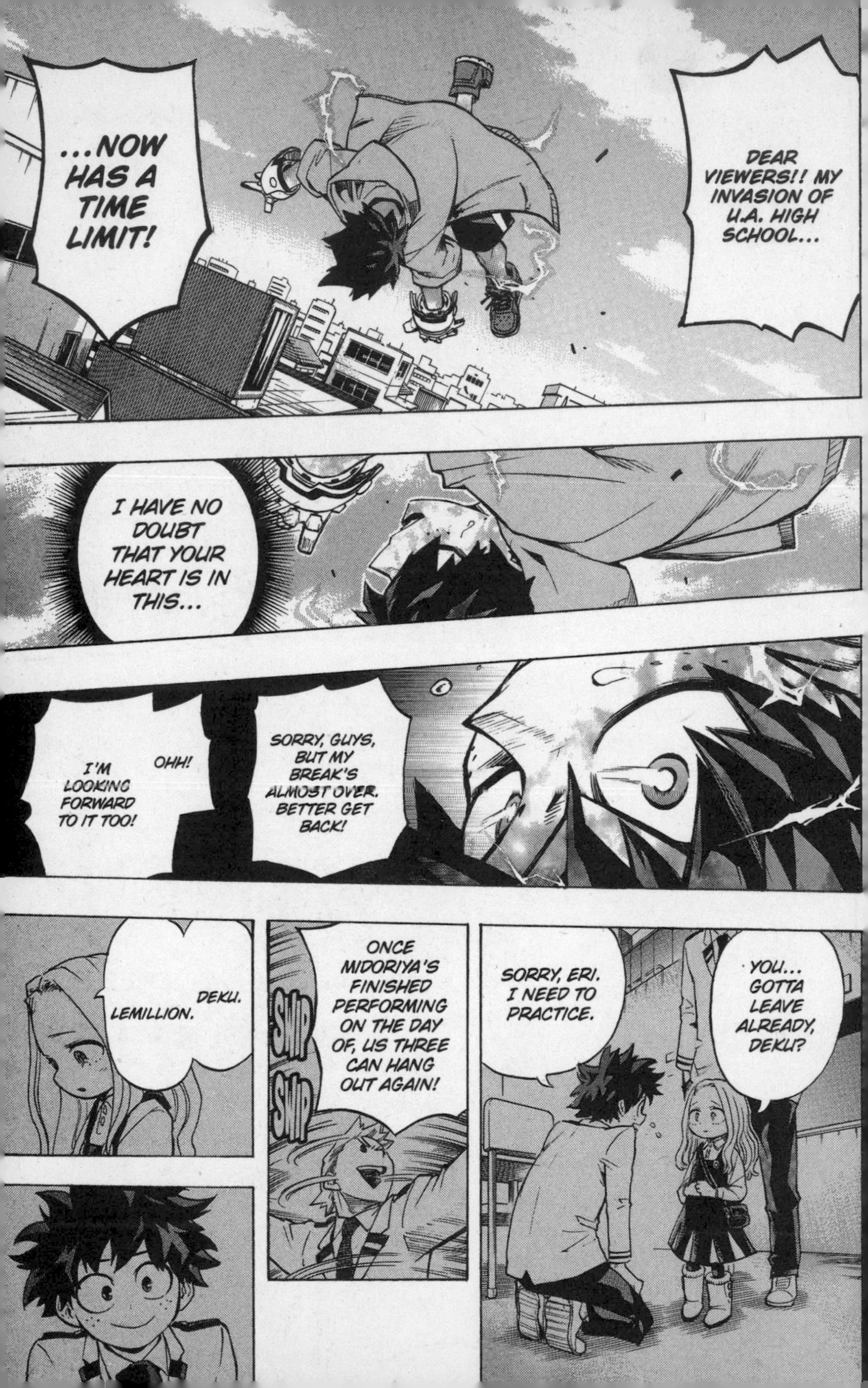
DEAR VIEWERS!! MY INVASION OF U.A. HIGH SCHOOL...
...NOW HAS A TIME LIMIT!
I HAVE NO DOUBT THAT YOUR HEART IS IN THIS...
SORRY, GUYS, BUT MY BREAK'S ALMOST OVER. BETTER GET BACK!
OHH!
I'M LOOKING FORWARD TO IT TOO!
YOU... GOTTA LEAVE ALREADY, DEKU?
SORRY, ERI. I NEED TO PRACTICE.
SHP
SHP
ONCE MIDORIYA'S FINISHED PERFORMING ON THE DAY OF, US THREE CAN HANG OUT AGAIN!
DEKU.
LEMILLION.

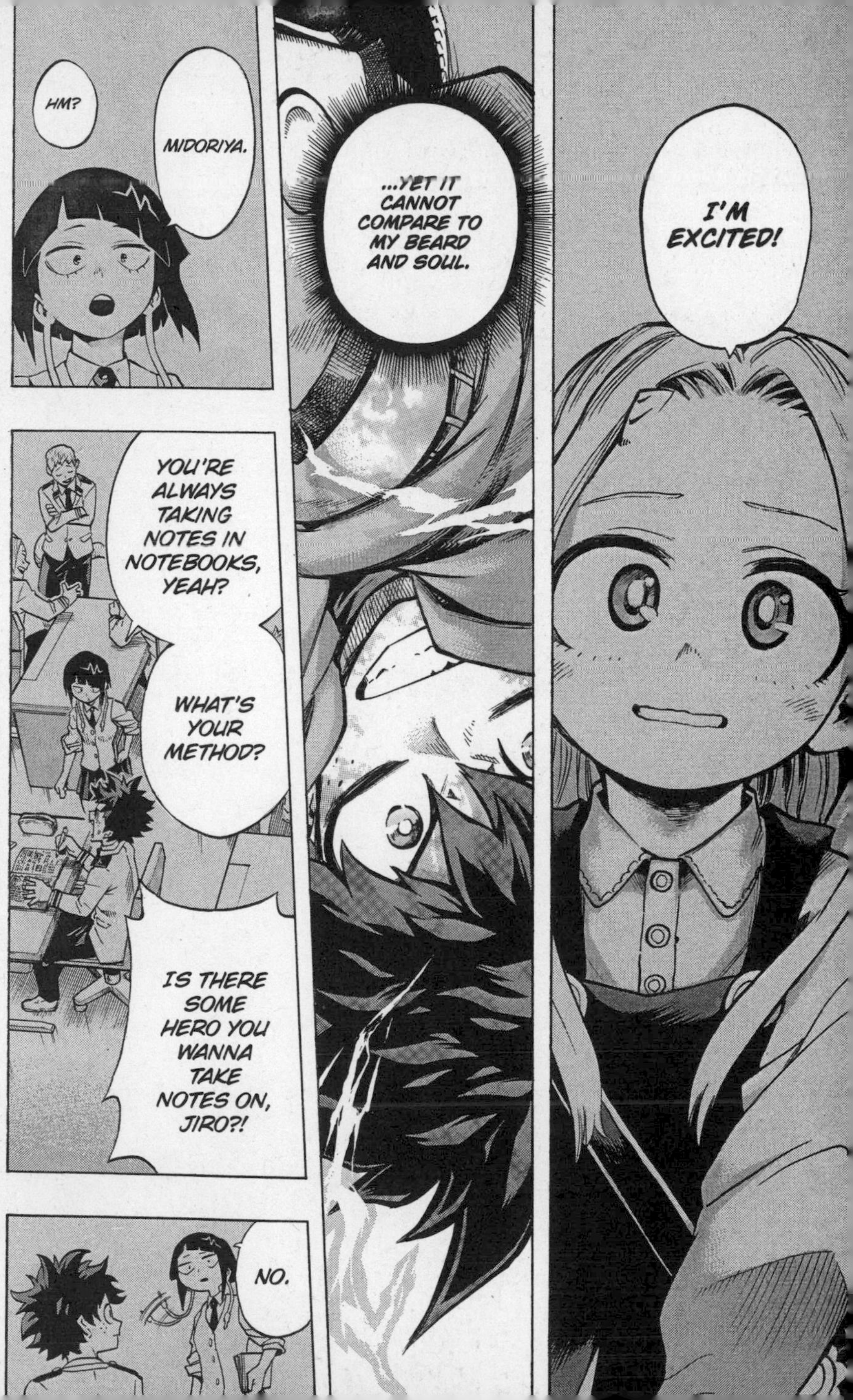
I'M EXCITED!
...YET IT CANNOT COMPARE TO MY BEARD AND SOUL.
MIDORIYA.
HM?
YOU'RE ALWAYS TAKING NOTES IN NOTEBOOKS, YEAH?
WHAT'S YOUR METHOD?
IS THERE SOME HERO YOU WANNA TAKE NOTES ON, JIRO?!
NO.

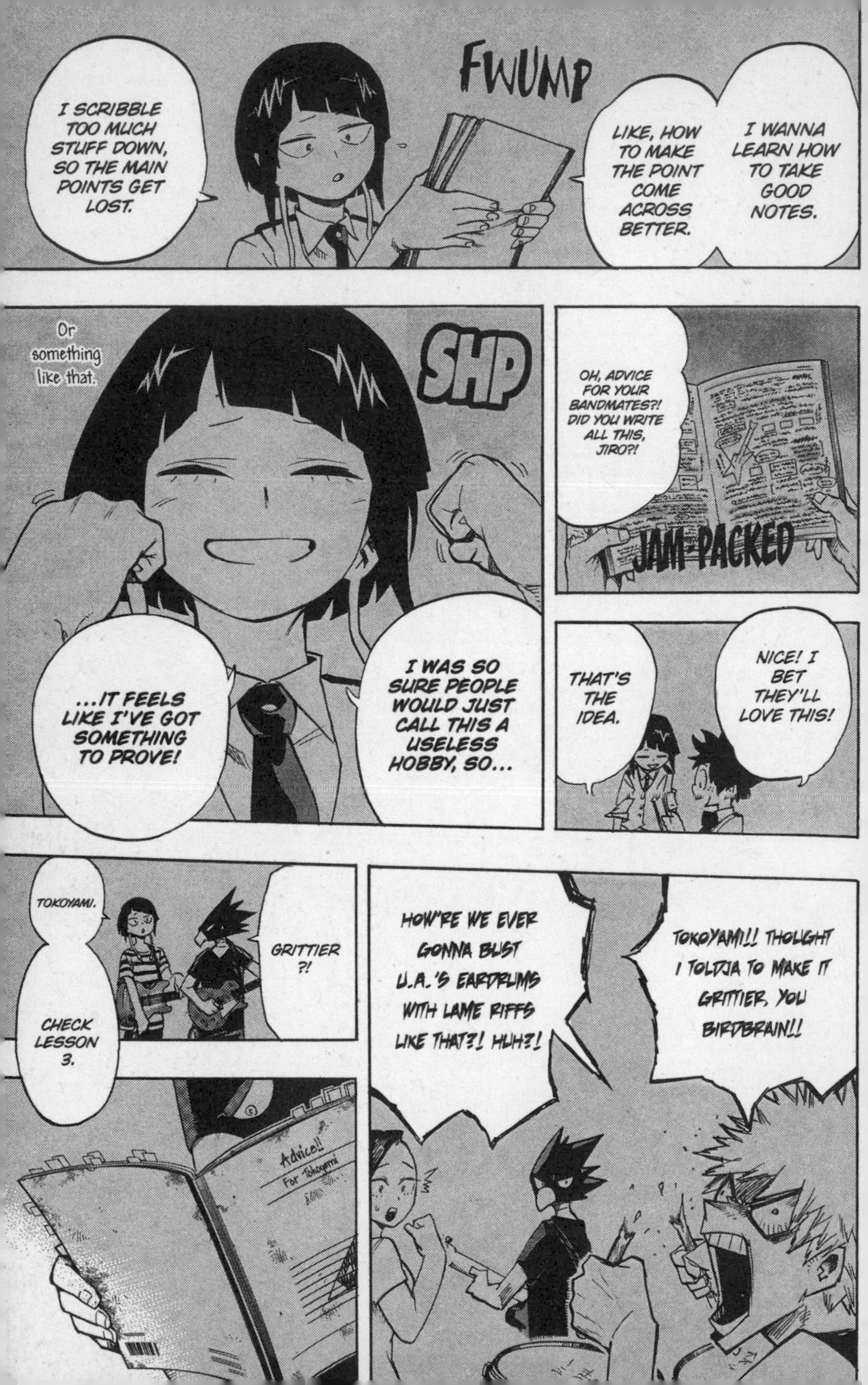
I WANNA LEARN HOW TO TAKE GOOD NOTES.
LIKE, HOW TO MAKE THE POINT COME ACROSS BETTER.
FWUMP
I SCRIBBLE TOO MUCH STUFF DOWN, SO THE MAIN POINTS GET LOST.
OH, ADVICE FOR YOUR BANDMATES?! DID YOU WRITE ALL THIS, JIRO?!
JAM-PACKED
NICE! I BET THEY'LL LOVE THIS!
THAT'S THE IDEA.
SHP
Or something like that.
I WAS SO SURE PEOPLE WOULD JUST CALL THIS A USELESS HOBBY, SO...
...IT FEELS LIKE I'VE GOT SOMETHING TO PROVE!
TOKOYAMI!! THOUGHT I TOLDJA TO MAKE IT GRITTIER, YOU BIRDBRAIN!!
HOW'RE WE EVER GONNA BUST U.A.'S EARDRUMS WITH LAME RIFFS LIKE THAT?! HUH?!
GRITTIER?!
TOKOYAMI.
CHECK LESSON 3.
Advice!!
For Tokoyami

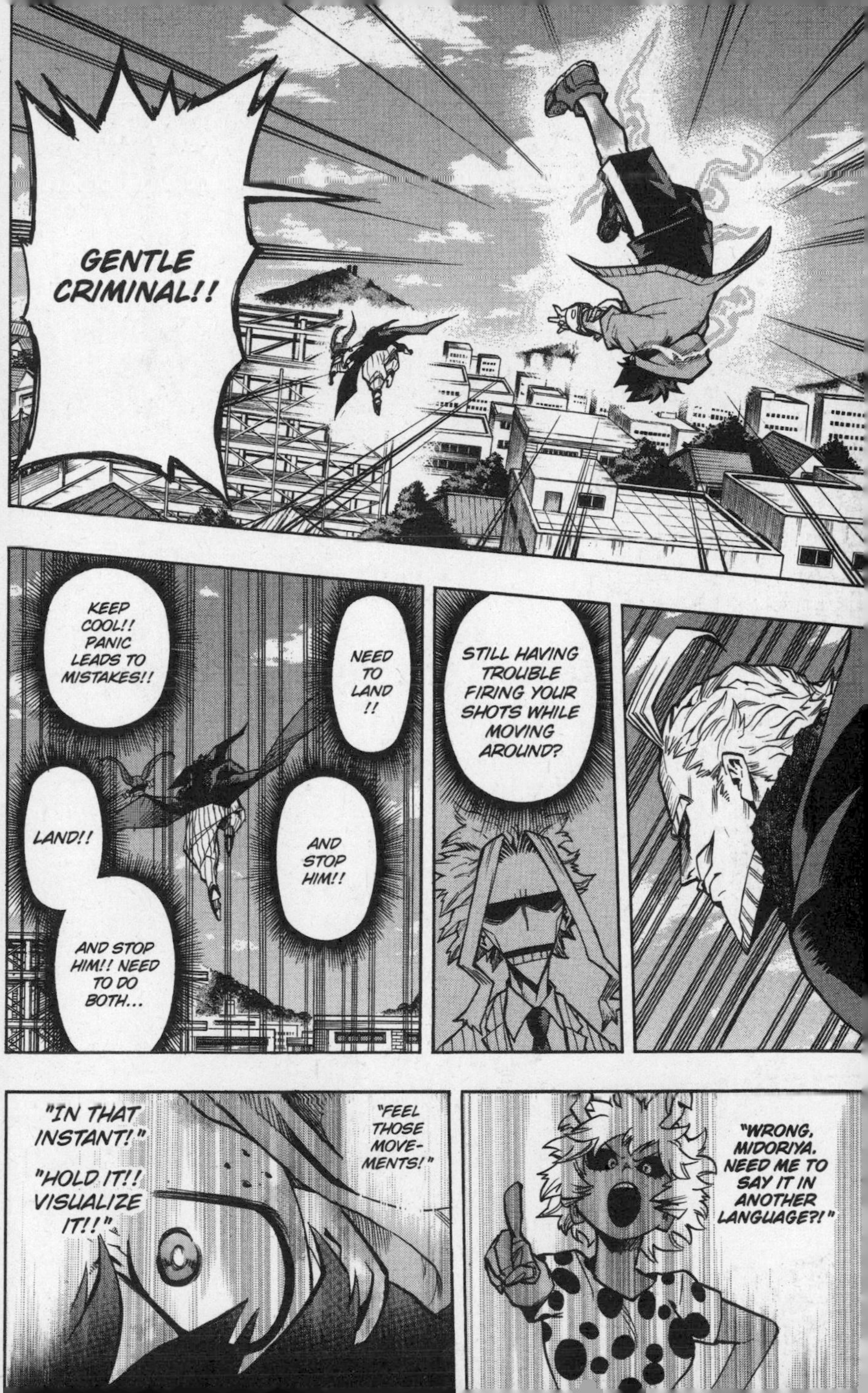
GENTLE CRIMINAL!!
STILL HAVING TROUBLE FIRING YOUR SHOTS WHILE MOVING AROUND?
KEEP COOL!! PANIC LEADS TO MISTAKES!!
NEED TO LAND !!
AND STOP HIM!!
LAND!!
AND STOP HIM!! NEED TO DO BOTH...
"WRONG, MIDORIYA. NEED ME TO SAY IT IN ANOTHER LANGUAGE?!"
"FEEL THOSE MOVE-MENTS!"
"IN THAT INSTANT!"
"HOLD IT!! VISUALIZE IT!!"

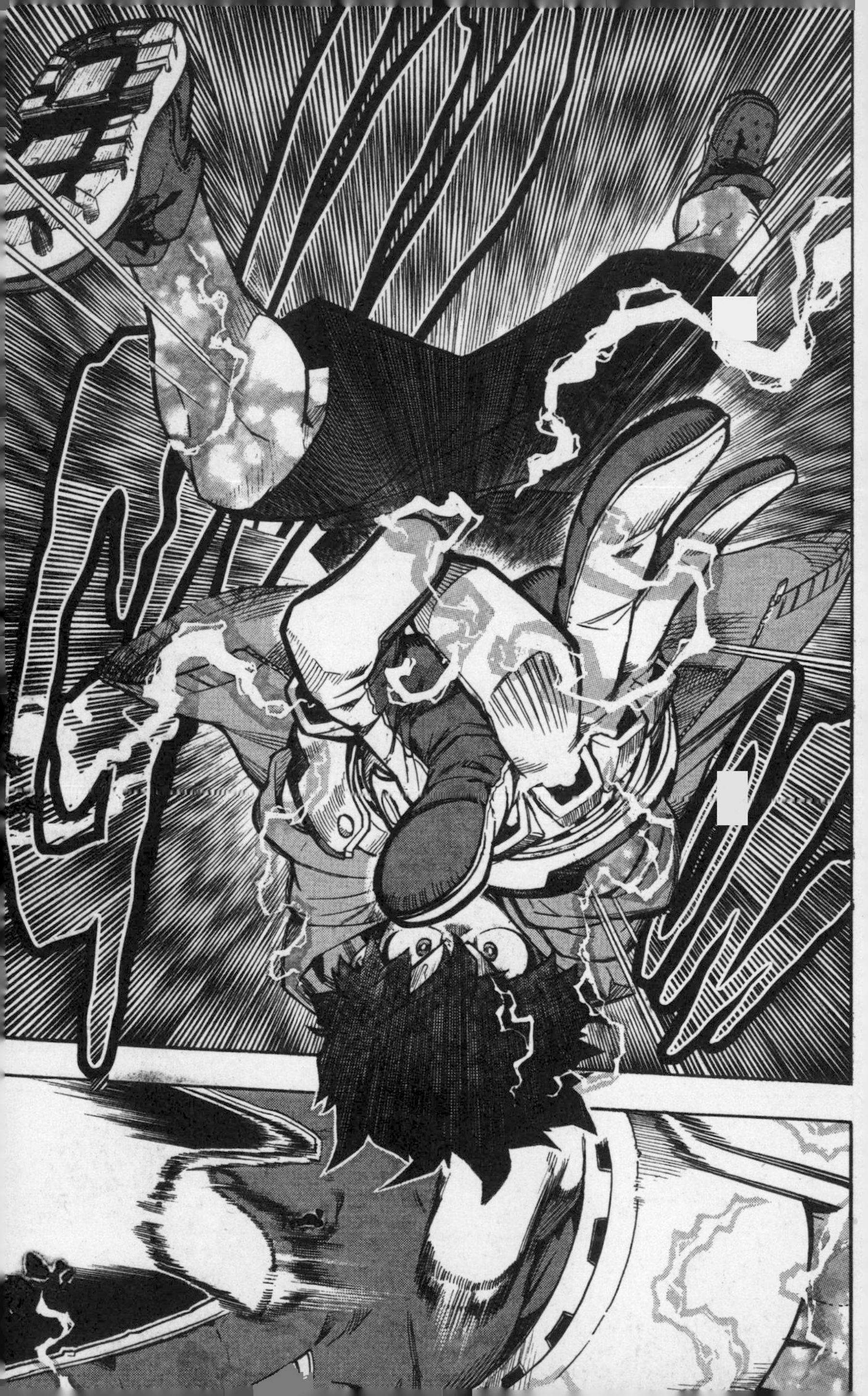

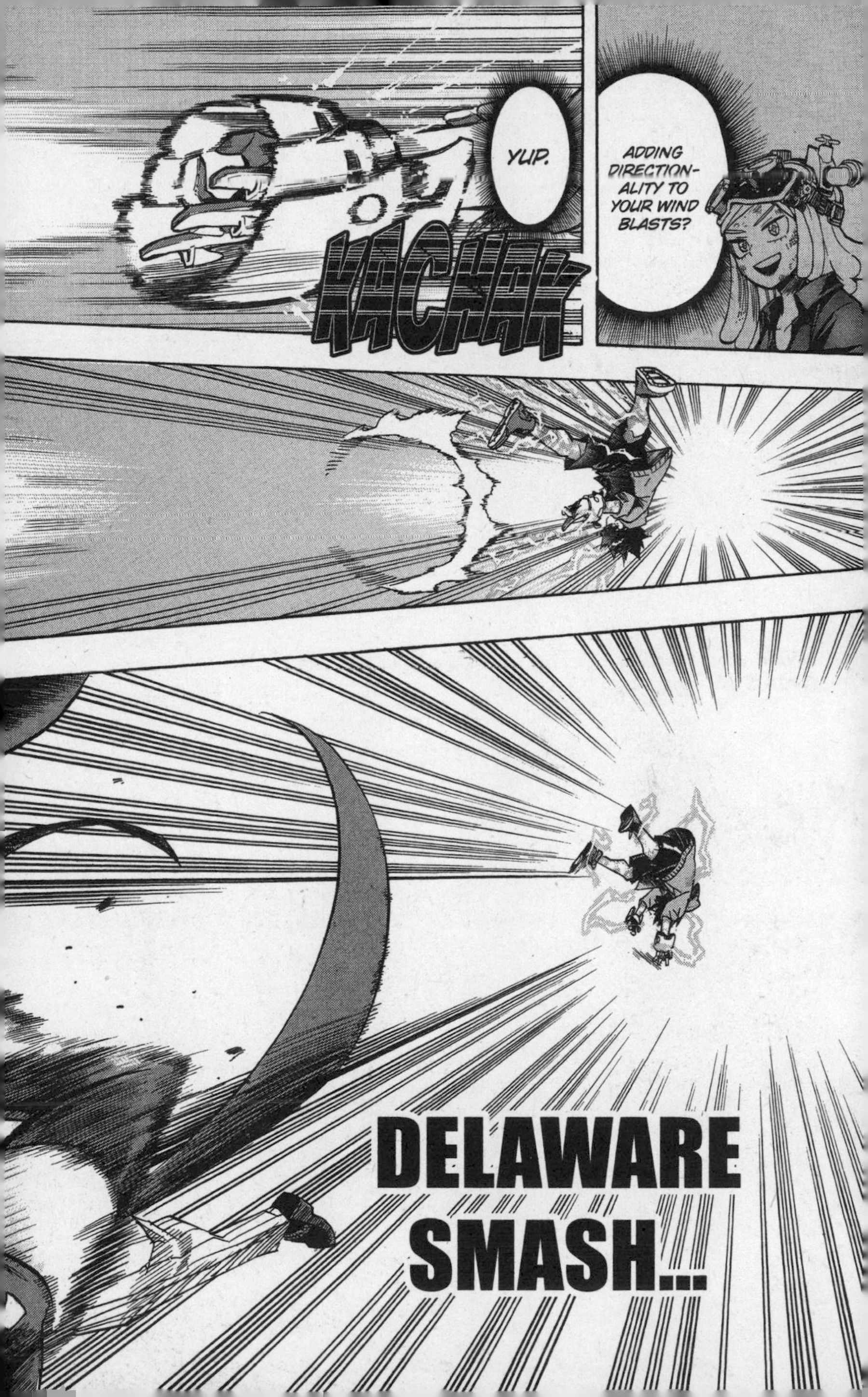
ADDING DIRECTION-ALITY TO YOUR WIND BLASTS?
YUP.
KACHAK
DELAWARE SMASH...

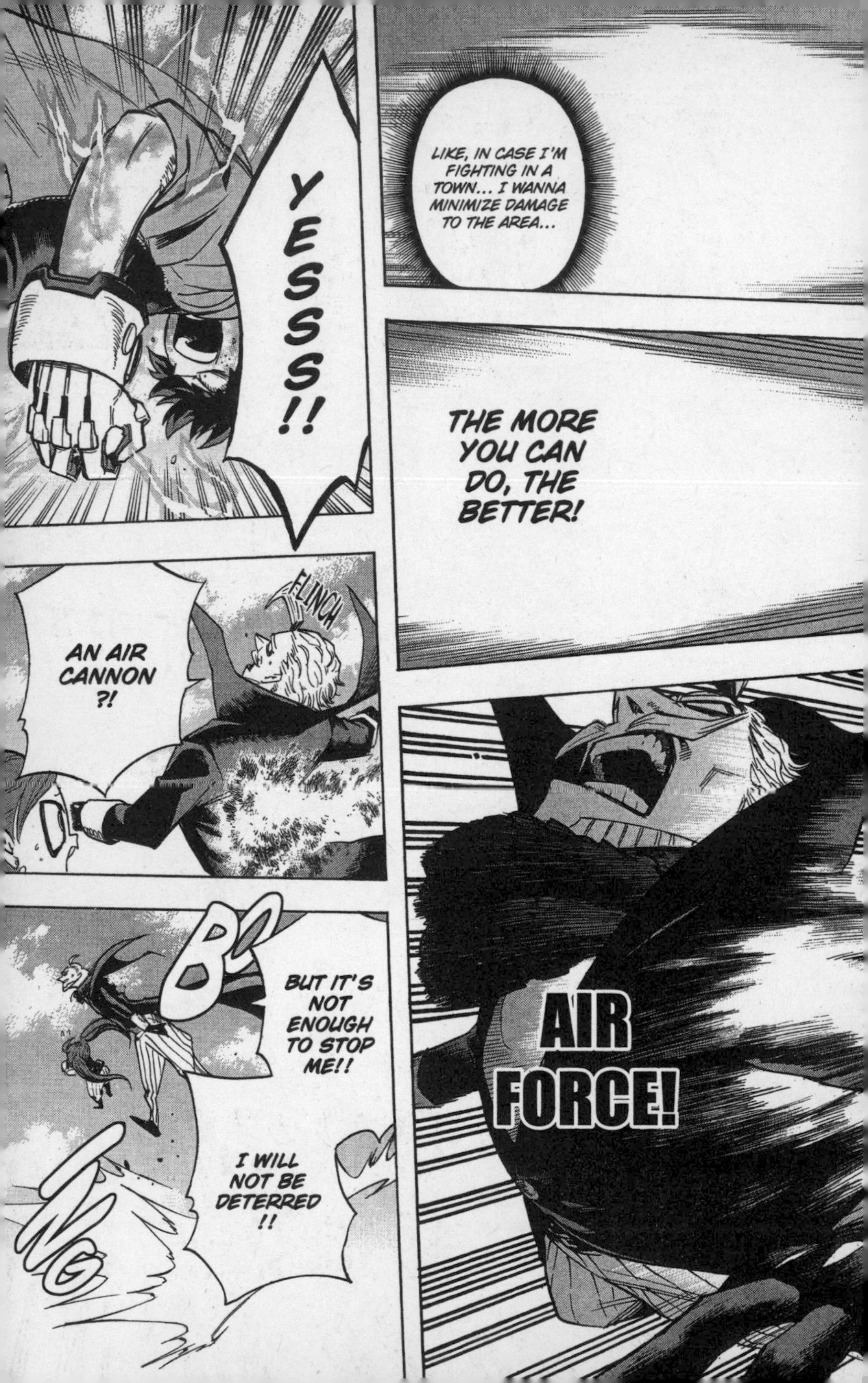
LIKE, IN CASE I'M FIGHTING IN A TOWN... I WANNA MINIMIZE DAMAGE TO THE AREA...
YESSS!!
THE MORE YOU CAN DO, THE BETTER!
FLINCH
AN AIR CANNON ?!
AIR FORCE!
BO
BUT IT'S NOT ENOUGH TO STOP ME!!
I WILL NOT BE DETERRED !!
NG

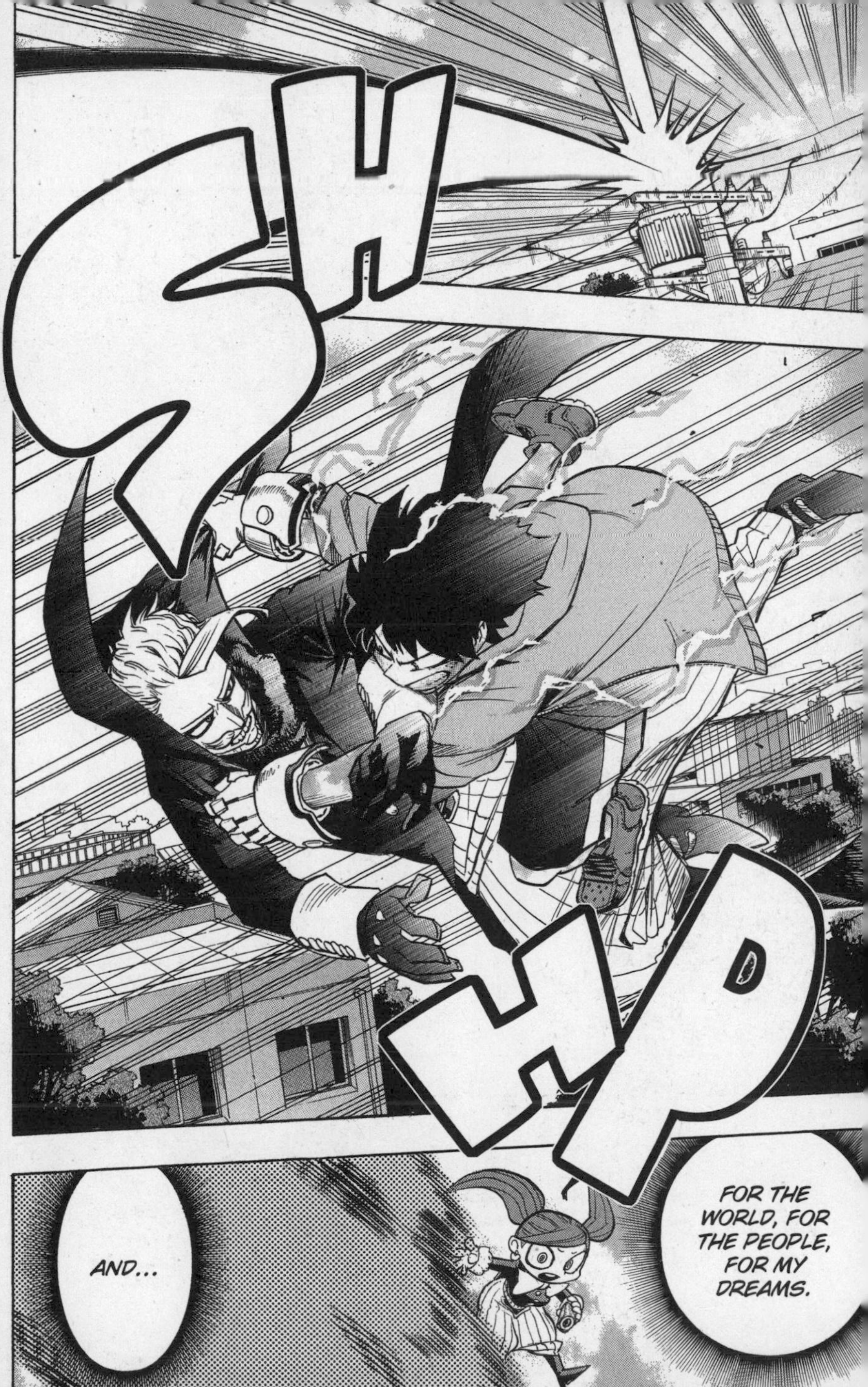
SHIP
FOR THE WORLD, FOR THE PEOPLE, FOR MY DREAMS.
AND...

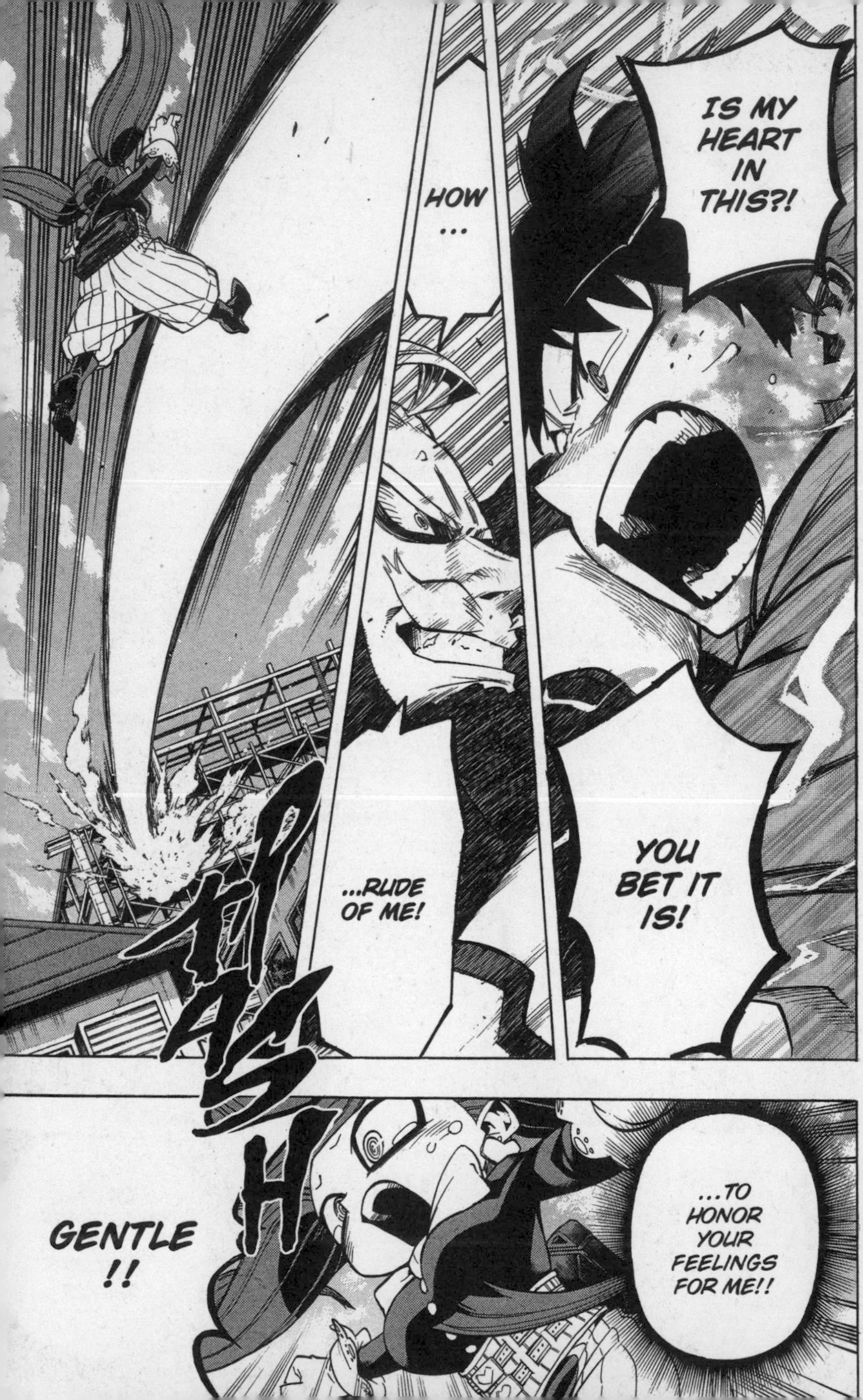
IS MY HEART IN THIS?!
YOU BET IT IS!
HOW ...
...RUDE OF ME!
...TO HONOR YOUR FEELINGS FOR ME!!
GENTLE !!

LOVE

LA BRAVA [Z1] [MANAMI AIBA]

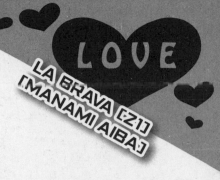

STREET CLOTHES

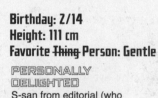

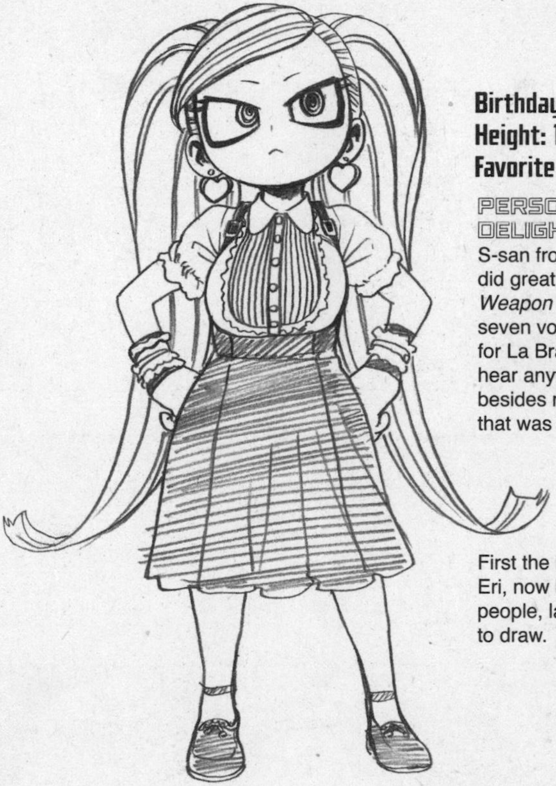

Birthday: 2/14
Height: 111 cm
Favorite ~~Thing~~ Person: Gentle

PERSONALLY DELIGHTED

S-san from editorial (who did great work on *Spring Weapon No. 01*, for all seven volumes!) praised me for La Brava. It's not often I hear anything from anyone besides my own editor, so that was kind of wonderful.

First the Masegaki kids, then Eri, now her… A lot of tiny people, lately. They're fun to draw.

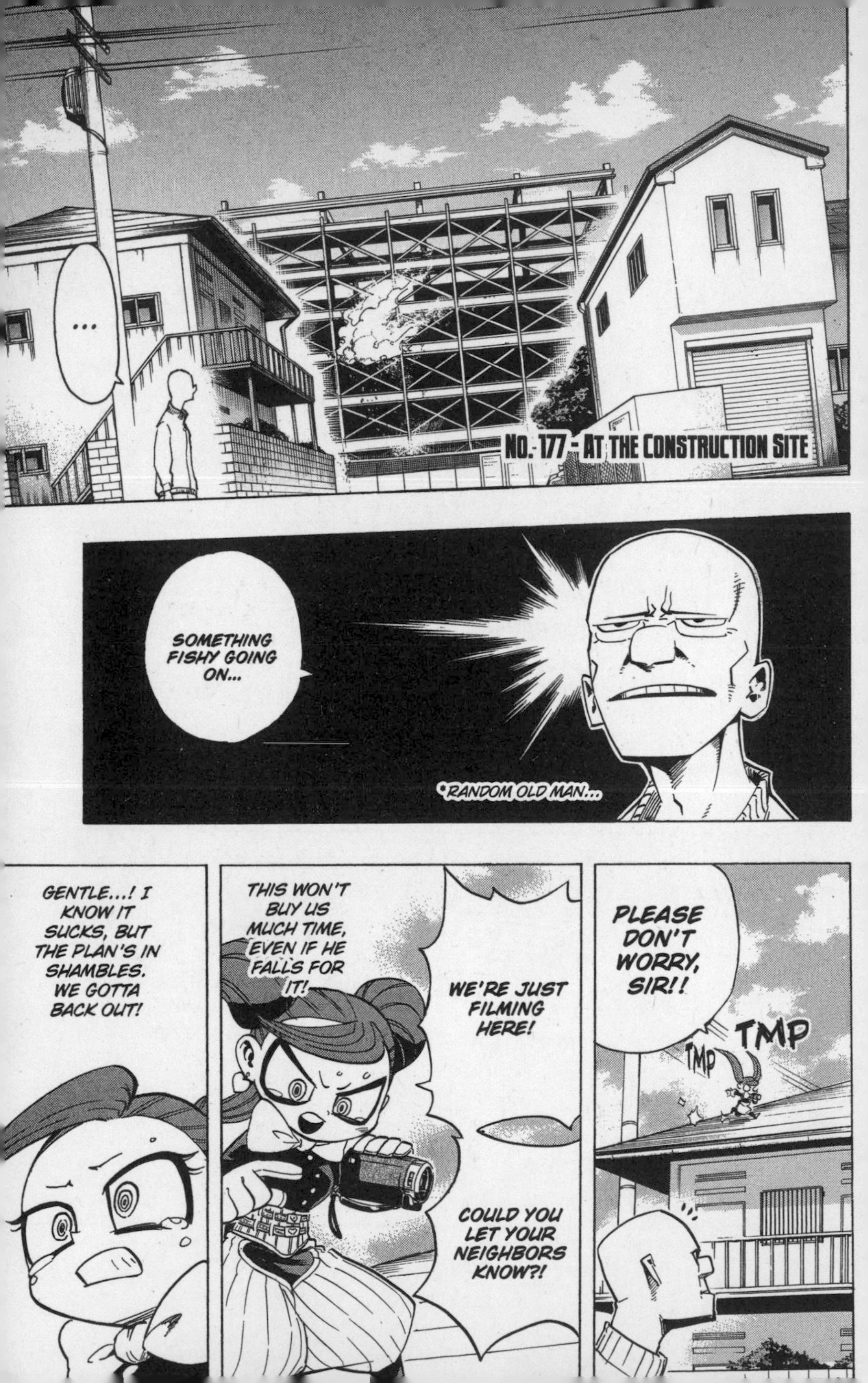
...
No. 177 - At the Construction Site
SOMETHING FISHY GOING ON...
*RANDOM OLD MAN...
PLEASE DON'T WORRY, SIR!!
TMP TMP
WE'RE JUST FILMING HERE!
COULD YOU LET YOUR NEIGHBORS KNOW?!
THIS WON'T BUY US MUCH TIME, EVEN IF HE FALLS FOR IT!
GENTLE...! I KNOW IT SUCKS, BUT THE PLAN'S IN SHAMBLES. WE GOTTA BACK OUT!

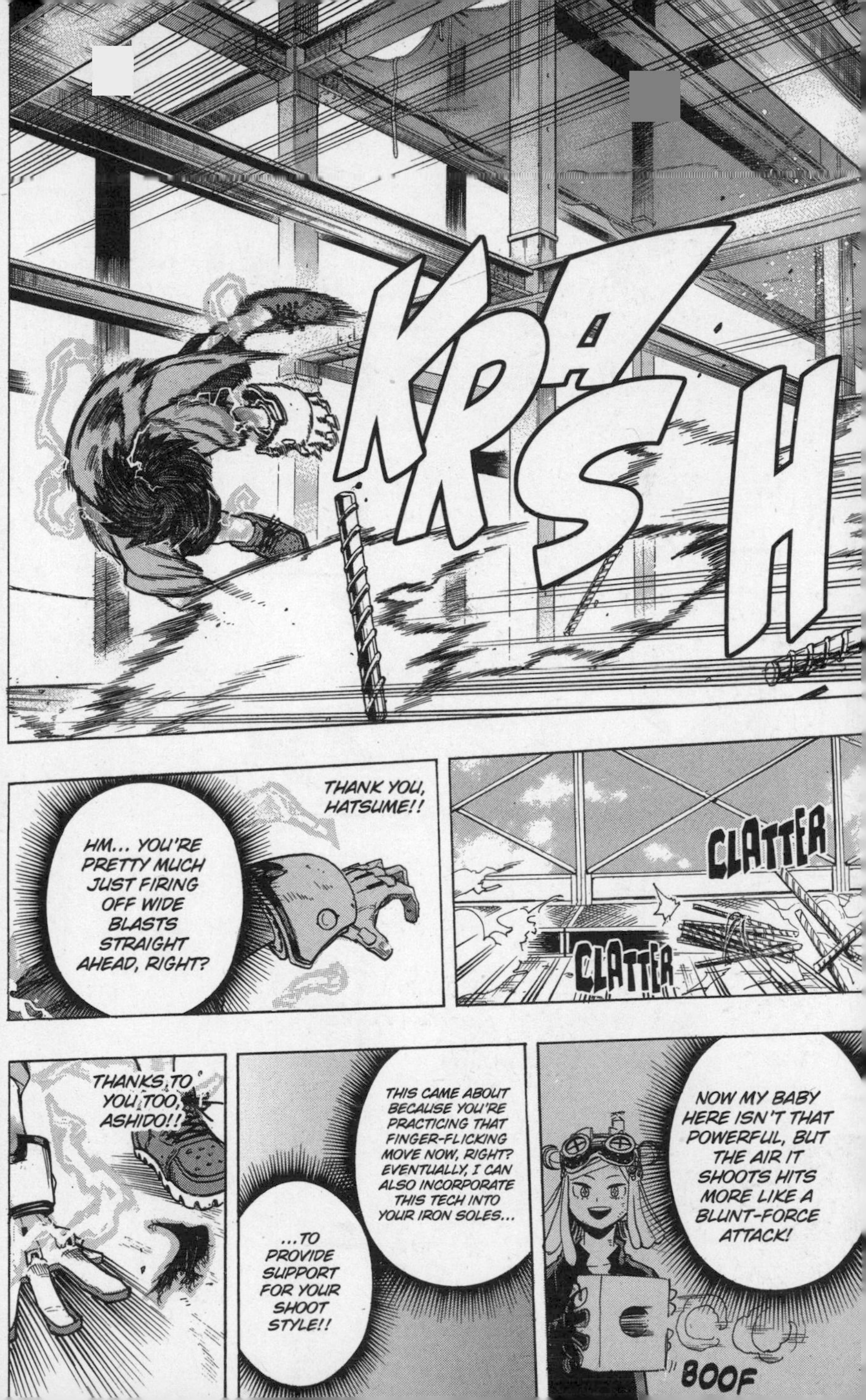
KRASH
CLATTER
CLATTER
THANK YOU, HATSUME!!
HM... YOU'RE PRETTY MUCH JUST FIRING OFF WIDE BLASTS STRAIGHT AHEAD, RIGHT?
NOW MY BABY HERE ISN'T THAT POWERFUL, BUT THE AIR IT SHOOTS HITS MORE LIKE A BLUNT-FORCE ATTACK!
BOOF
THIS CAME ABOUT BECAUSE YOU'RE PRACTICING THAT FINGER-FLICKING MOVE NOW, RIGHT? EVENTUALLY, I CAN ALSO INCORPORATE THIS TECH INTO YOUR IRON SOLES...
...TO PROVIDE SUPPORT FOR YOUR SHOOT STYLE!!
THANKS TO YOU TOO, ASHIDO!!

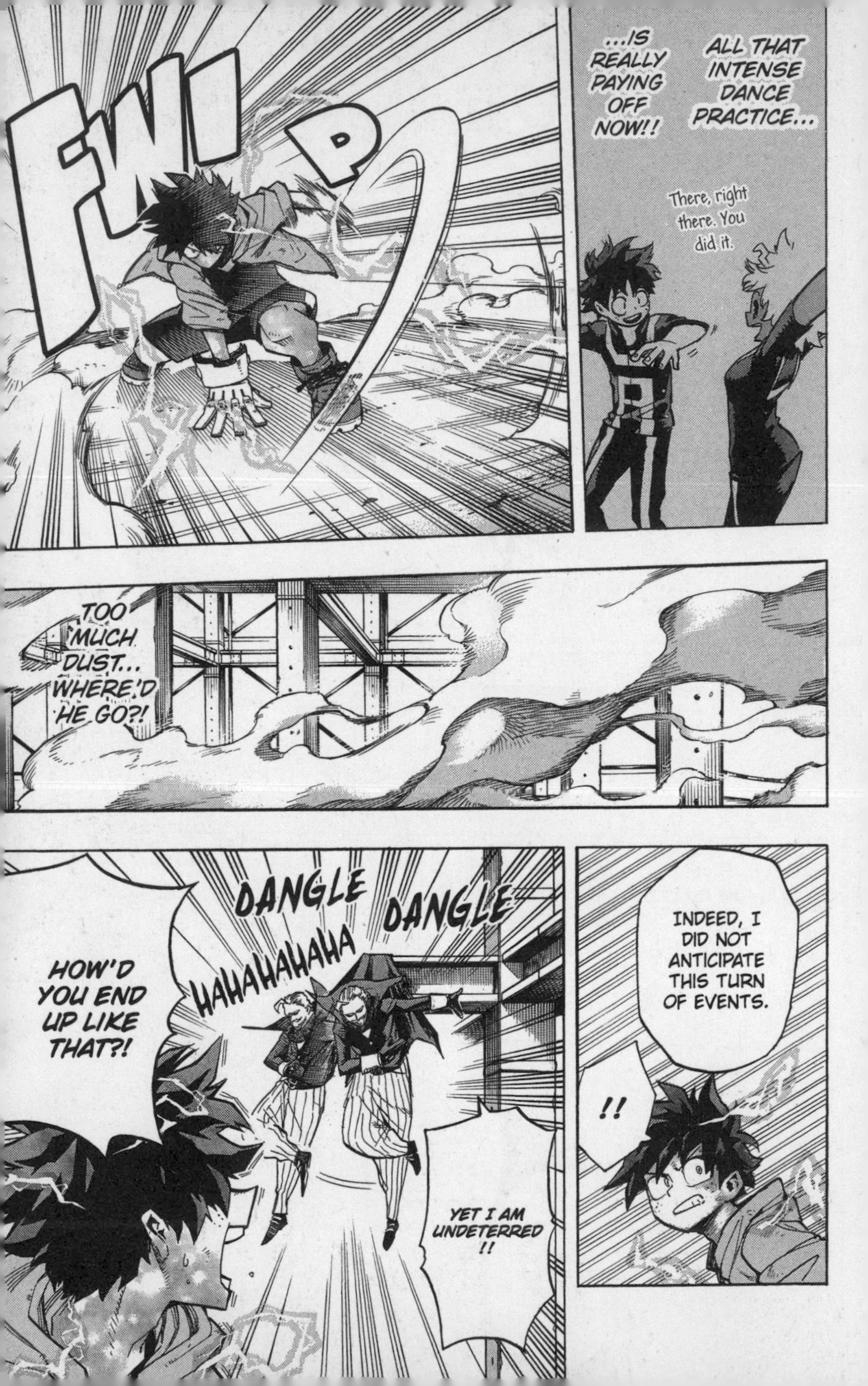
ALL THAT INTENSE DANCE PRACTICE...
...IS REALLY PAYING OFF NOW!!
There, right there. You did it.
FWIP
TOO MUCH DUST... WHERE'D HE GO?!
INDEED, I DID NOT ANTICIPATE THIS TURN OF EVENTS.
!!
DANGLE
DANGLE
HAHAHAHAHA
HOW'D YOU END UP LIKE THAT?!
YET I AM UNDETERRED!!

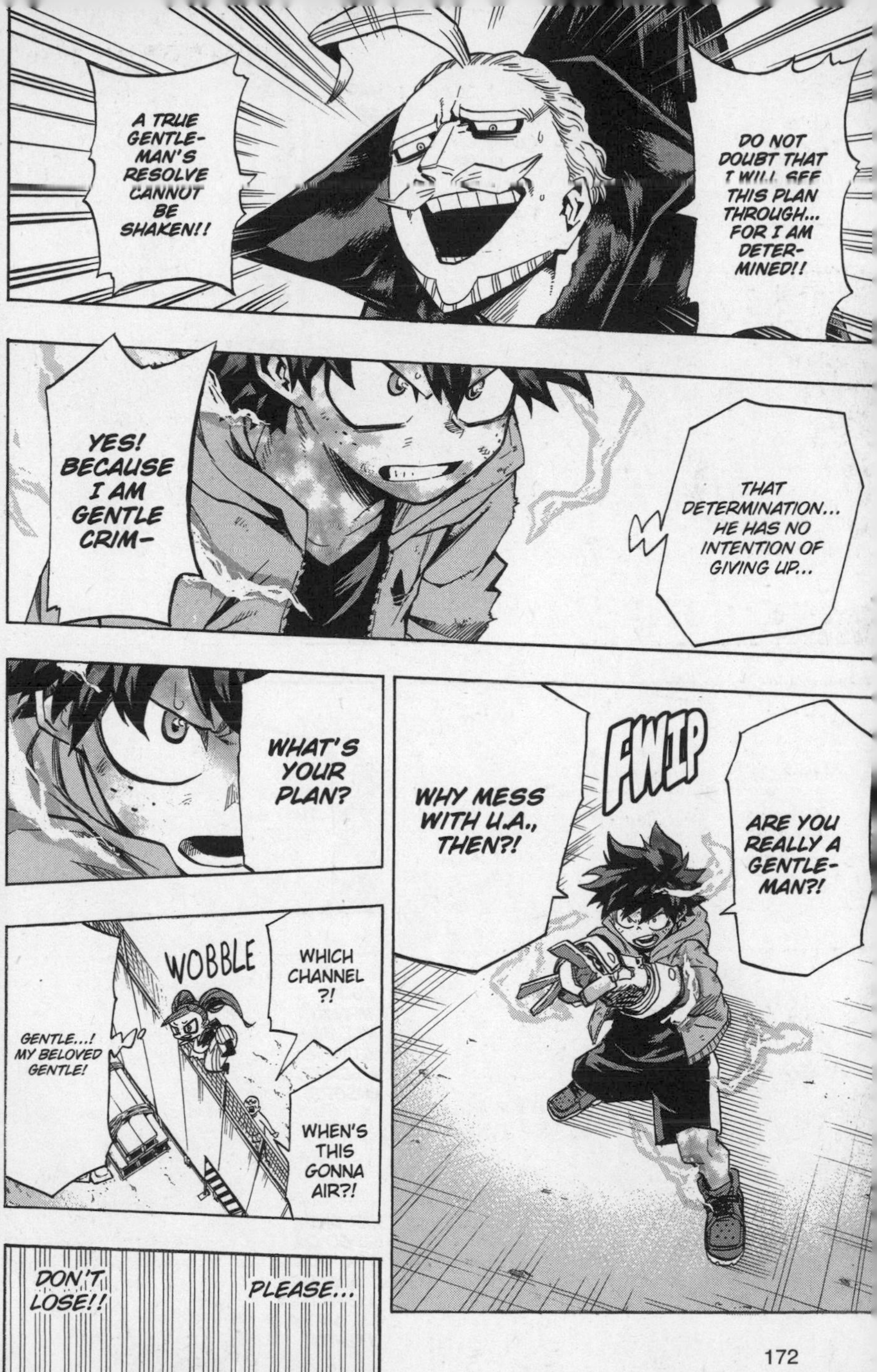
DO NOT DOUBT THAT I WILL SEE THIS PLAN THROUGH... FOR I AM DETERMINED!!
A TRUE GENTLEMAN'S RESOLVE CANNOT BE SHAKEN!!
THAT DETERMINATION... HE HAS NO INTENTION OF GIVING UP...
YES! BECAUSE I AM GENTLE CRIM-
FWIP
ARE YOU REALLY A GENTLEMAN?!
WHY MESS WITH U.A., THEN?!
WHAT'S YOUR PLAN?
WHICH CHANNEL ?!
WHEN'S THIS GONNA AIR?!
WOBBLE
GENTLE...! MY BELOVED GENTLE!
PLEASE...
DON'T LOSE!!

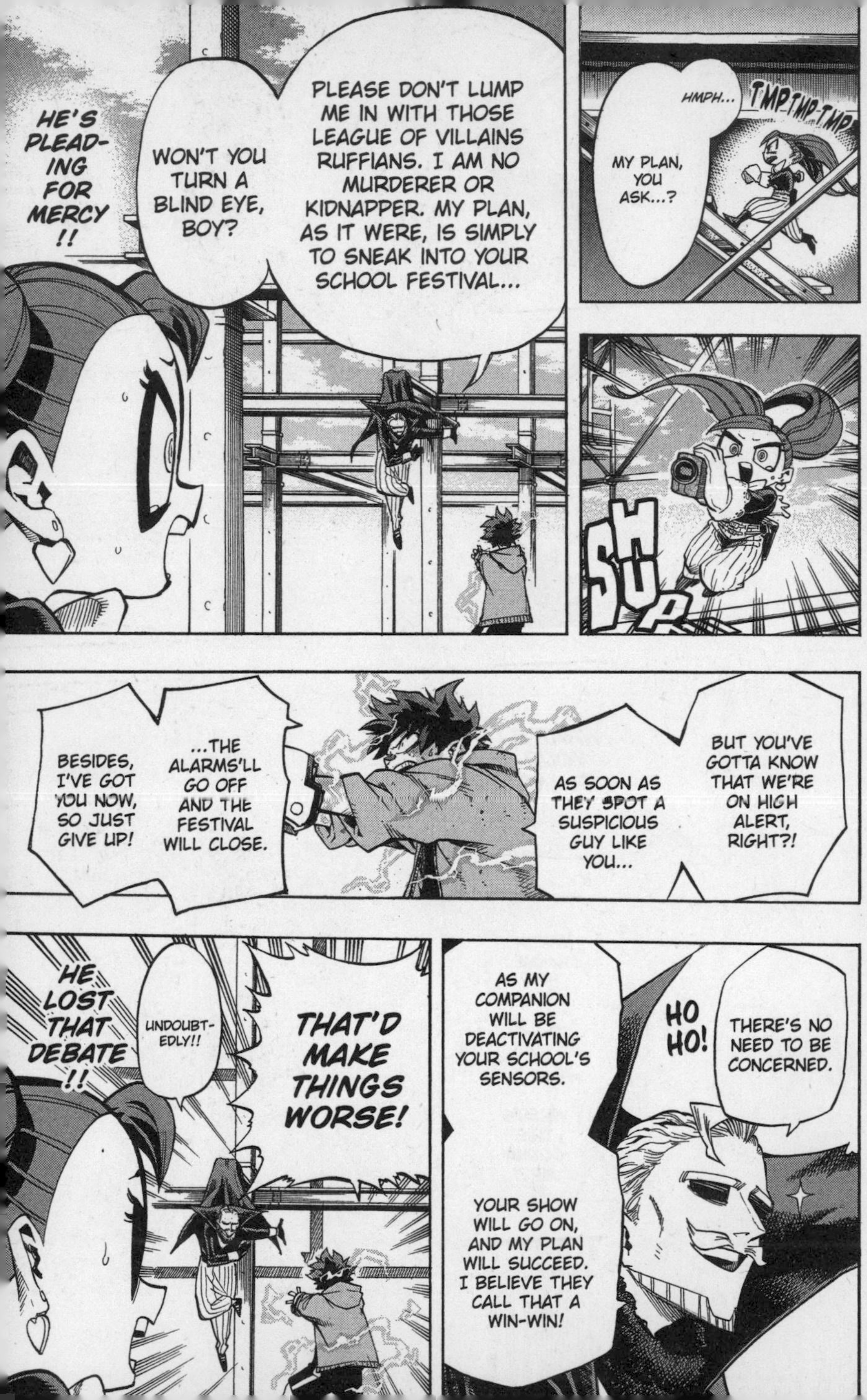
HMPH...
TMP TMP-TMP
MY PLAN, YOU ASK...?
SHUP
PLEASE DON'T LUMP ME IN WITH THOSE LEAGUE OF VILLAINS RUFFIANS. I AM NO MURDERER OR KIDNAPPER. MY PLAN, AS IT WERE, IS SIMPLY TO SNEAK INTO YOUR SCHOOL FESTIVAL...
WON'T YOU TURN A BLIND EYE, BOY?
HE'S PLEADING FOR MERCY!!
BUT YOU'VE GOTTA KNOW THAT WE'RE ON HIGH ALERT, RIGHT?!
AS SOON AS THEY SPOT A SUSPICIOUS GUY LIKE YOU...
...THE ALARMS'LL GO OFF AND THE FESTIVAL WILL CLOSE.
BESIDES, I'VE GOT YOU NOW, SO JUST GIVE UP!
THERE'S NO NEED TO BE CONCERNED.
HO HO!
AS MY COMPANION WILL BE DEACTIVATING YOUR SCHOOL'S SENSORS.
YOUR SHOW WILL GO ON, AND MY PLAN WILL SUCCEED. I BELIEVE THEY CALL THAT A WIN-WIN!
THAT'D MAKE THINGS WORSE!
UNDOUBTEDLY!!
HE LOST THAT DEBATE!!

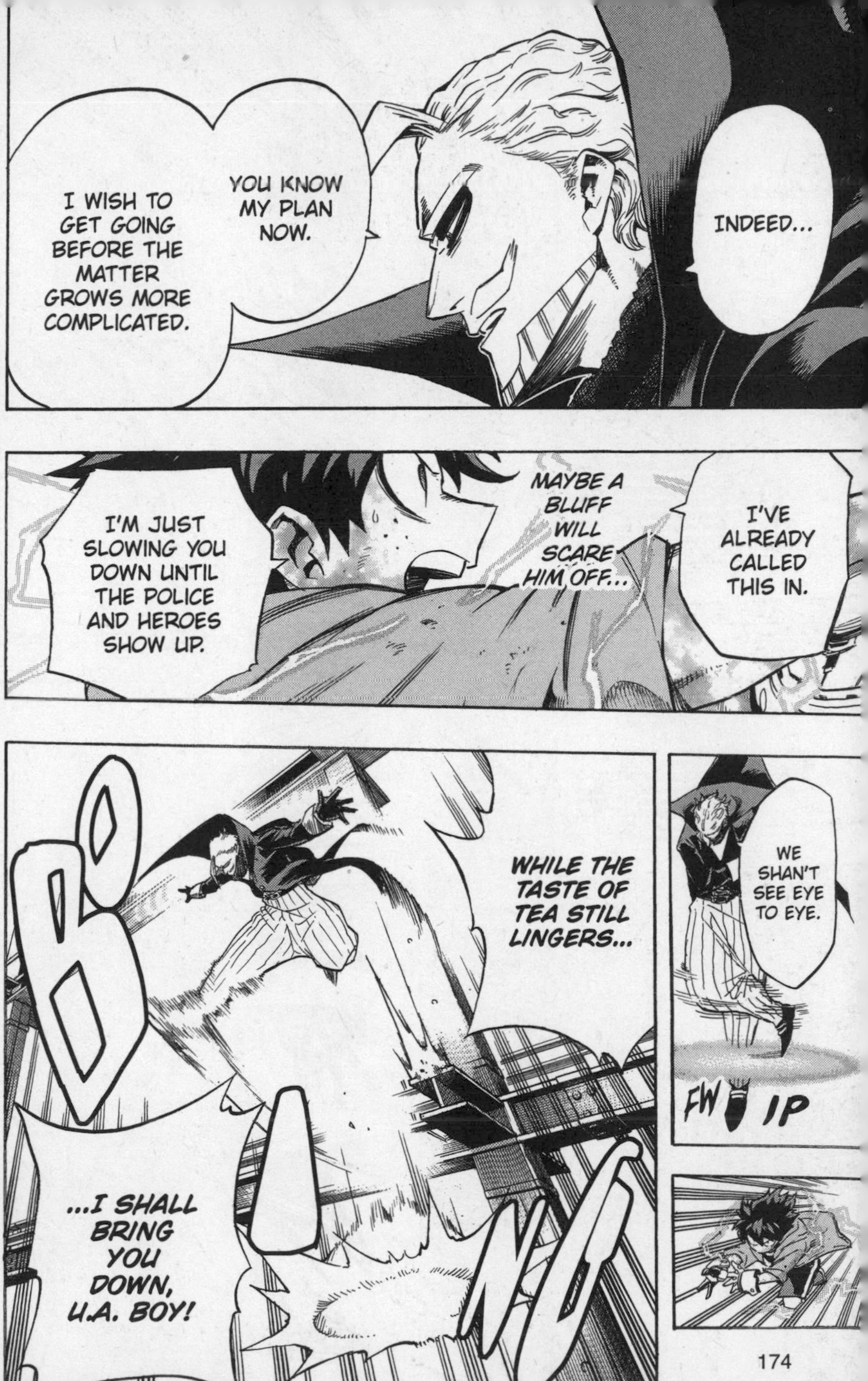
INDEED...
YOU KNOW MY PLAN NOW.
I WISH TO GET GOING BEFORE THE MATTER GROWS MORE COMPLICATED.
I'VE ALREADY CALLED THIS IN.
MAYBE A BLUFF WILL SCARE HIM OFF...
I'M JUST SLOWING YOU DOWN UNTIL THE POLICE AND HEROES SHOW UP.
WE SHAN'T SEE EYE TO EYE.
FWIP
WHILE THE TASTE OF TEA STILL LINGERS...
...I SHALL BRING YOU DOWN, U.A. BOY!

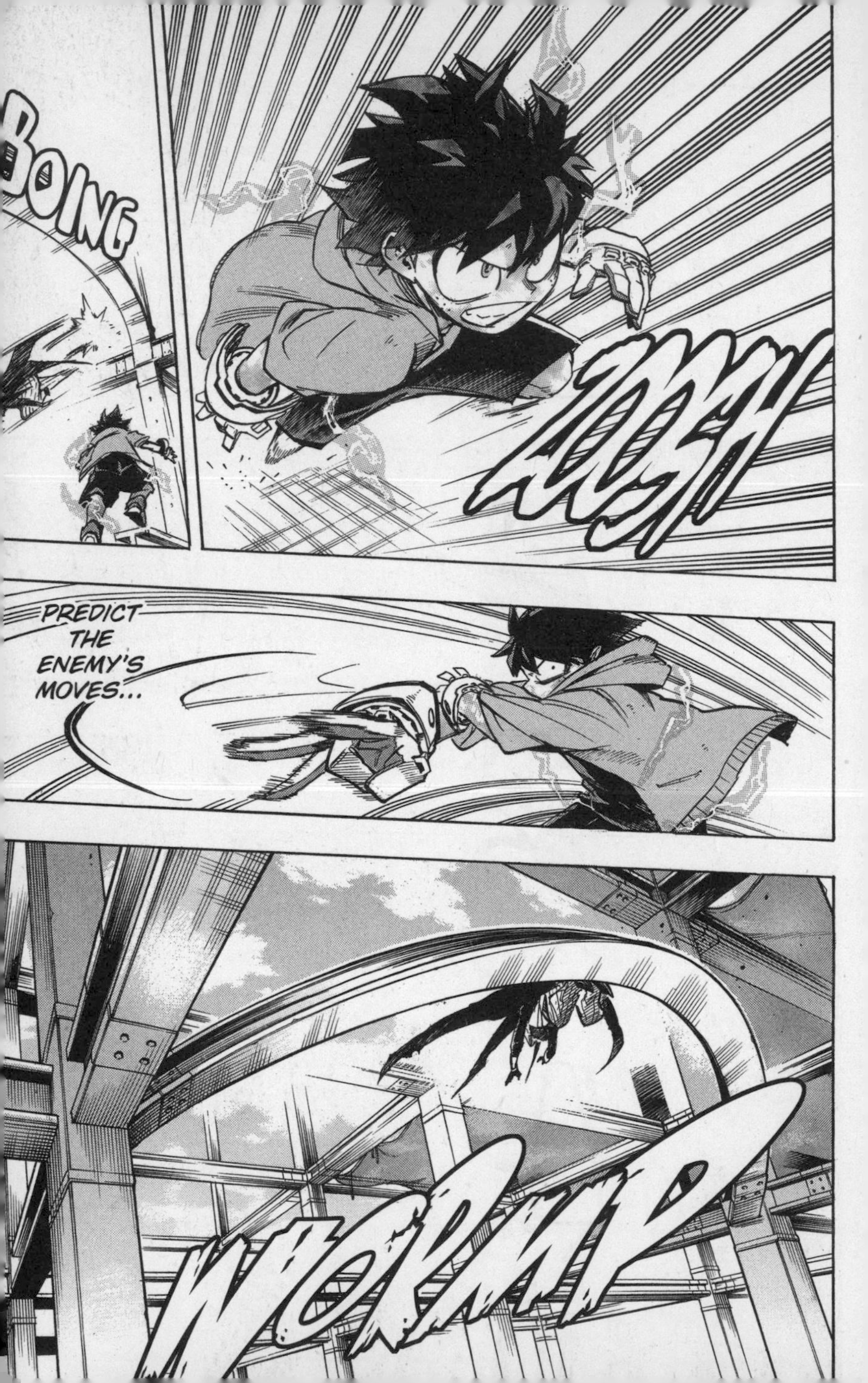
ZOOSH
BOING
PREDICT THE ENEMY'S MOVES...
WOMP

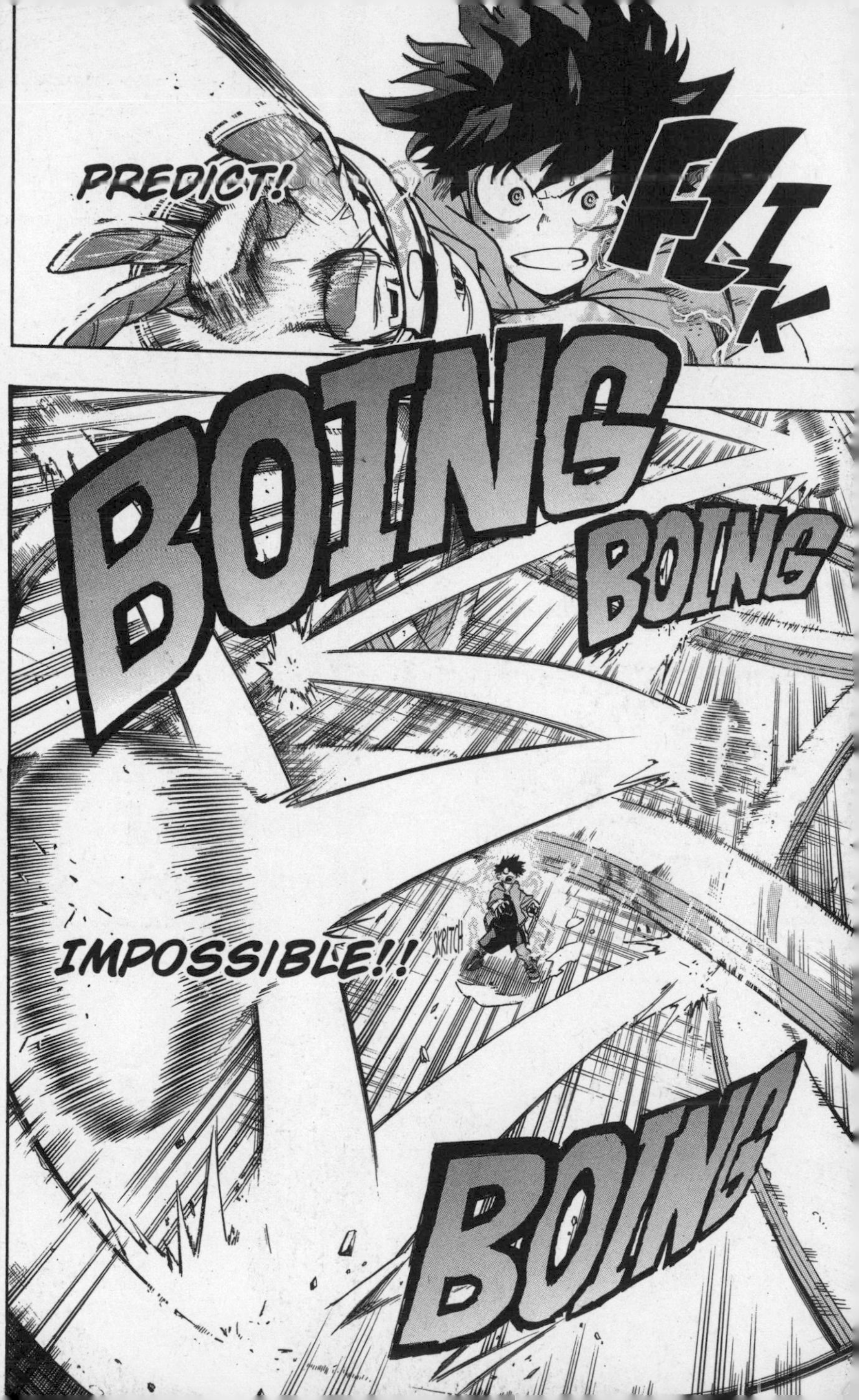
PREDICT!
FLIK
BOING
BOING
IMPOSSIBLE!!
SKRITCH
BOING

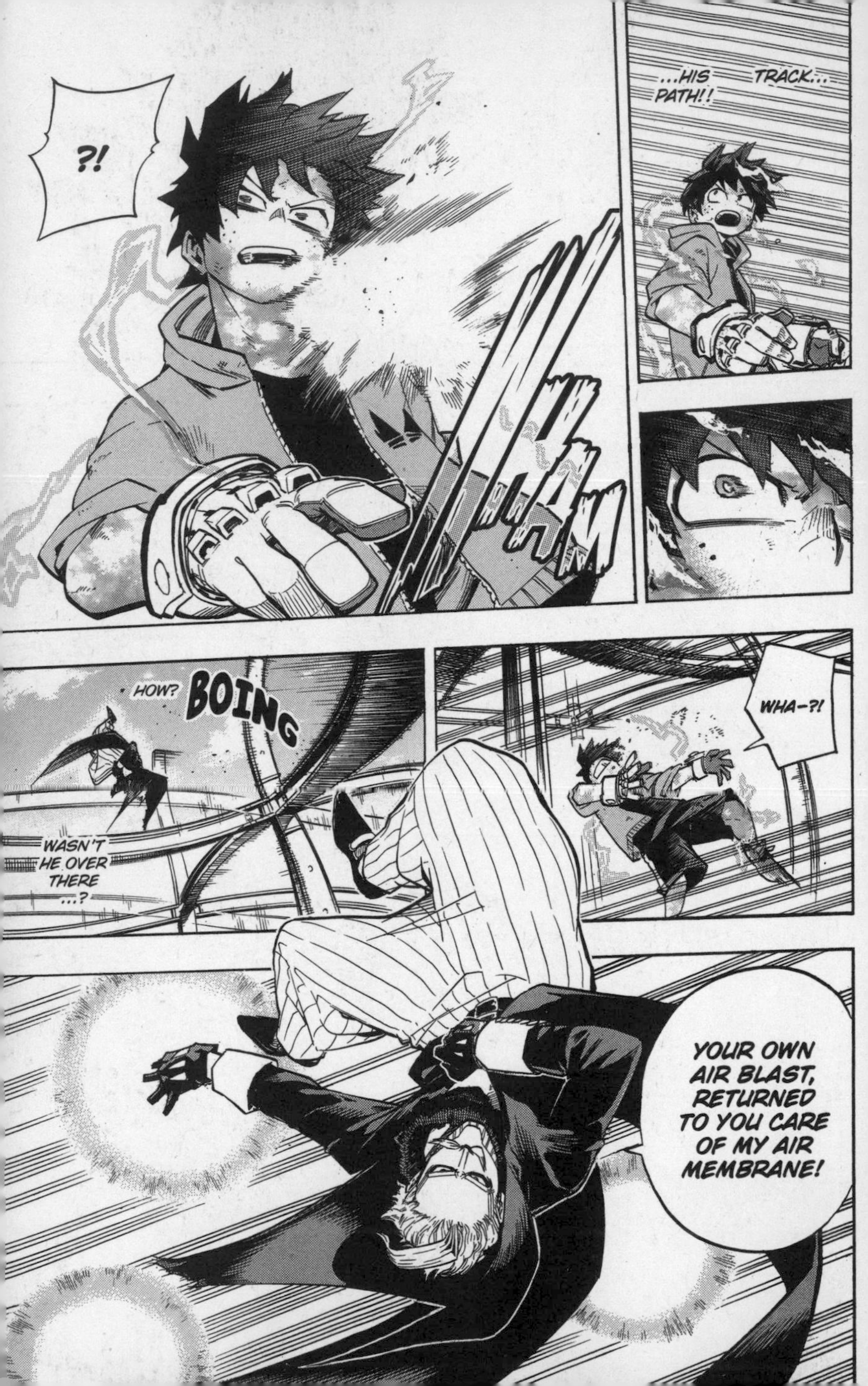
TRACK...
...HIS PATH!!
?!
WHAM
WHA-?!
HOW?
BOING
WASN'T HE OVER THERE ...?
YOUR OWN AIR BLAST, RETURNED TO YOU CARE OF MY AIR MEMBRANE!

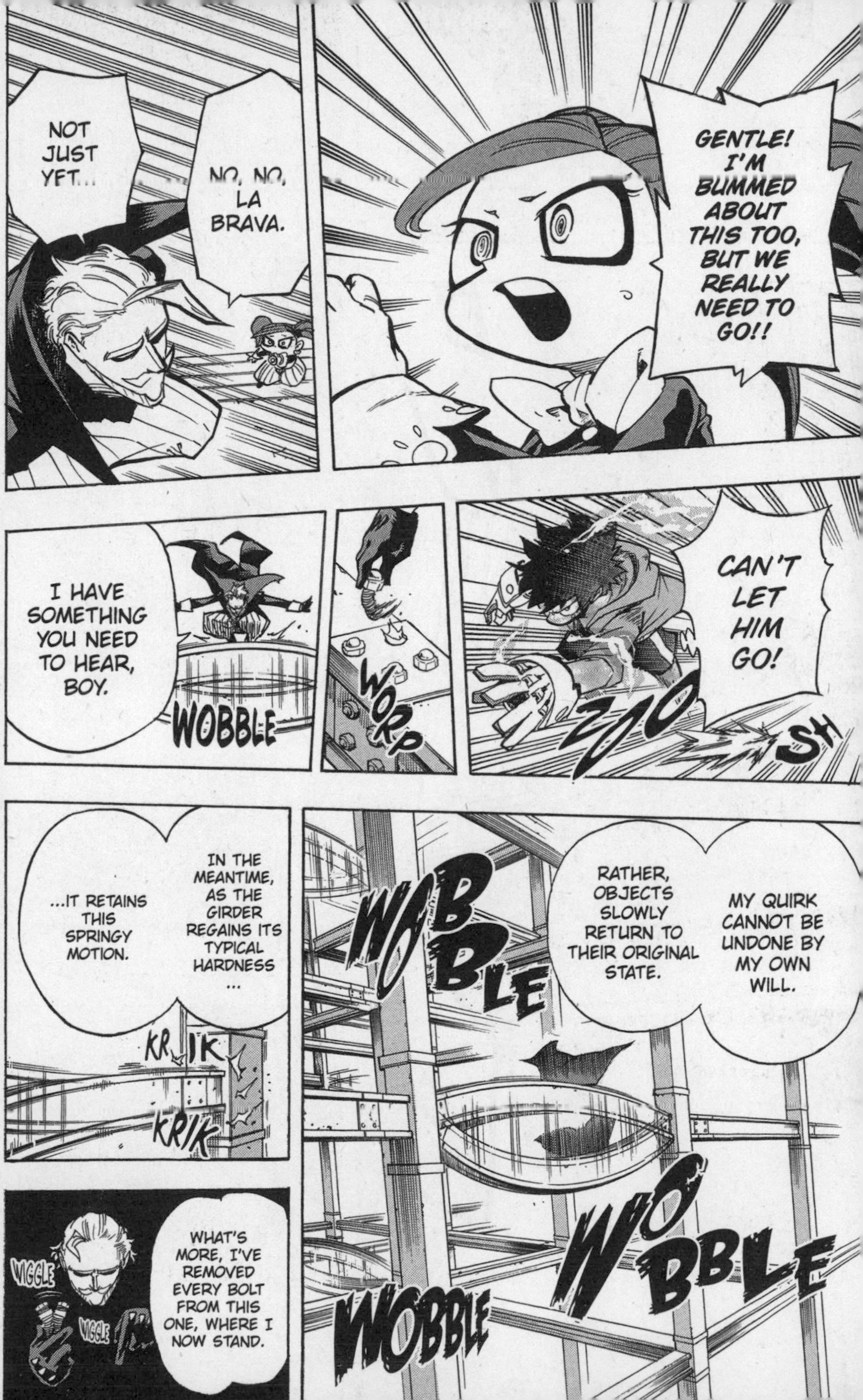
GENTLE! I'M BUMMED ABOUT THIS TOO, BUT WE REALLY NEED TO GO!!
NO, NO, LA BRAVA.
NOT JUST YET...
CAN'T LET HIM GO!
ZOOSH
WORP
I HAVE SOMETHING YOU NEED TO HEAR, BOY.
WOBBLE
MY QUIRK CANNOT BE UNDONE BY MY OWN WILL.
RATHER, OBJECTS SLOWLY RETURN TO THEIR ORIGINAL STATE.
WOBBLE
WOBBLE
WOBBLE
IN THE MEANTIME, AS THE GIRDER REGAINS ITS TYPICAL HARDNESS...
...IT RETAINS THIS SPRINGY MOTION.
KRIK
KRIK
WHAT'S MORE, I'VE REMOVED EVERY BOLT FROM THIS ONE, WHERE I NOW STAND.
WIGGLE
WIGGLE

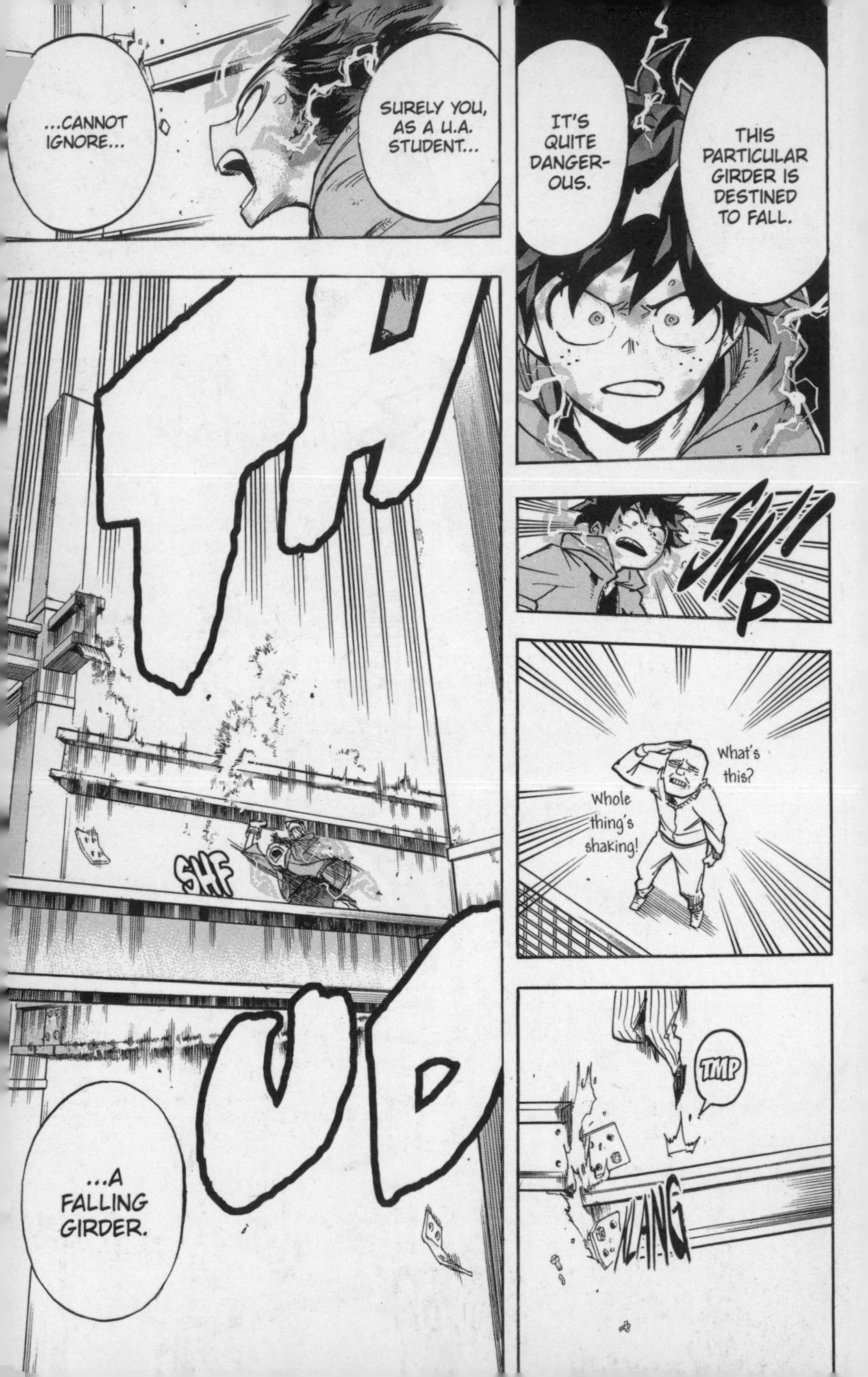
THIS PARTICULAR GIRDER IS DESTINED TO FALL.
IT'S QUITE DANGER-OUS.
SURELY YOU, AS A U.A. STUDENT...
...CANNOT IGNORE...
SHWP
What's this?
Whole thing's shaking!
TMP
KLANG
THUD
SHF
...A FALLING GIRDER.

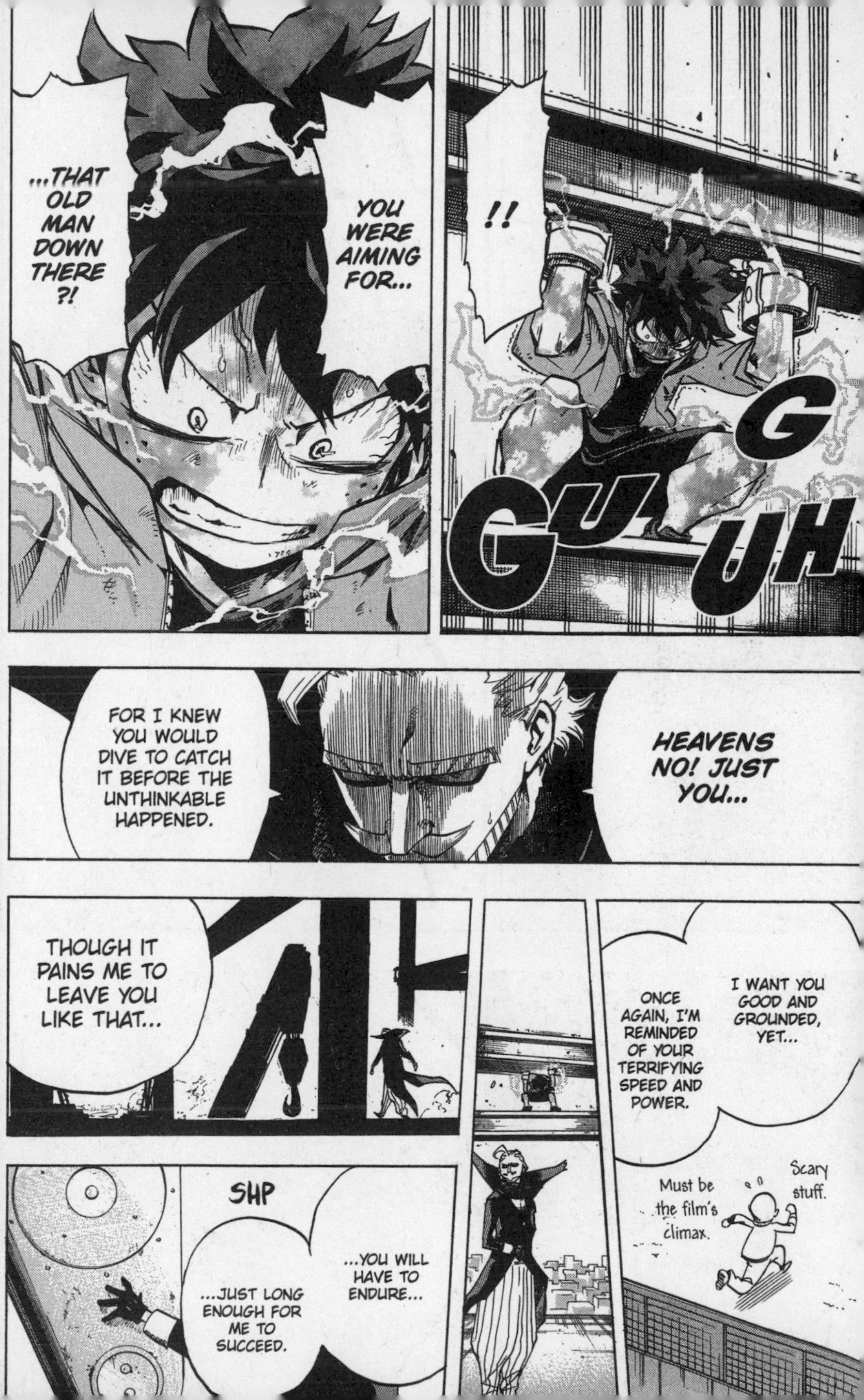
!!
GU G UH
YOU WERE AIMING FOR...
...THAT OLD MAN DOWN THERE?!
HEAVENS NO! JUST YOU...
FOR I KNEW YOU WOULD DIVE TO CATCH IT BEFORE THE UNTHINKABLE HAPPENED.
I WANT YOU GOOD AND GROUNDED, YET...
ONCE AGAIN, I'M REMINDED OF YOUR TERRIFYING SPEED AND POWER.
THOUGH IT PAINS ME TO LEAVE YOU LIKE THAT...
Scary stuff.
Must be the film's climax.
SHP
...YOU WILL HAVE TO ENDURE...
...JUST LONG ENOUGH FOR ME TO SUCCEED.

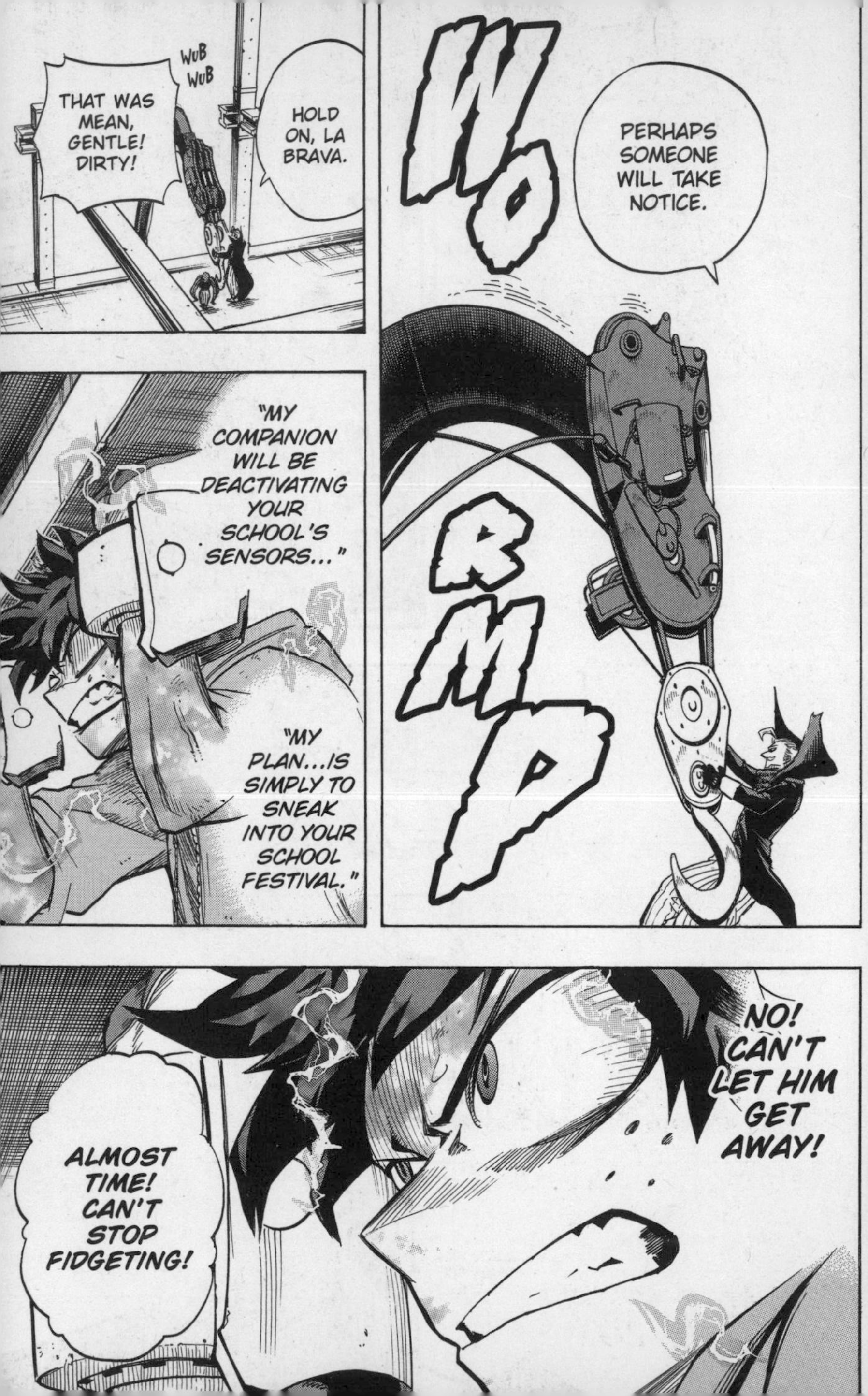
WORMP
PERHAPS SOMEONE WILL TAKE NOTICE.
WUB WUB
HOLD ON, LA BRAVA.
THAT WAS MEAN, GENTLE! DIRTY!
"MY COMPANION WILL BE DEACTIVATING YOUR SCHOOL'S SENSORS..."
"MY PLAN...IS SIMPLY TO SNEAK INTO YOUR SCHOOL FESTIVAL."
NO! CAN'T LET HIM GET AWAY!
ALMOST TIME! CAN'T STOP FIDGETING!

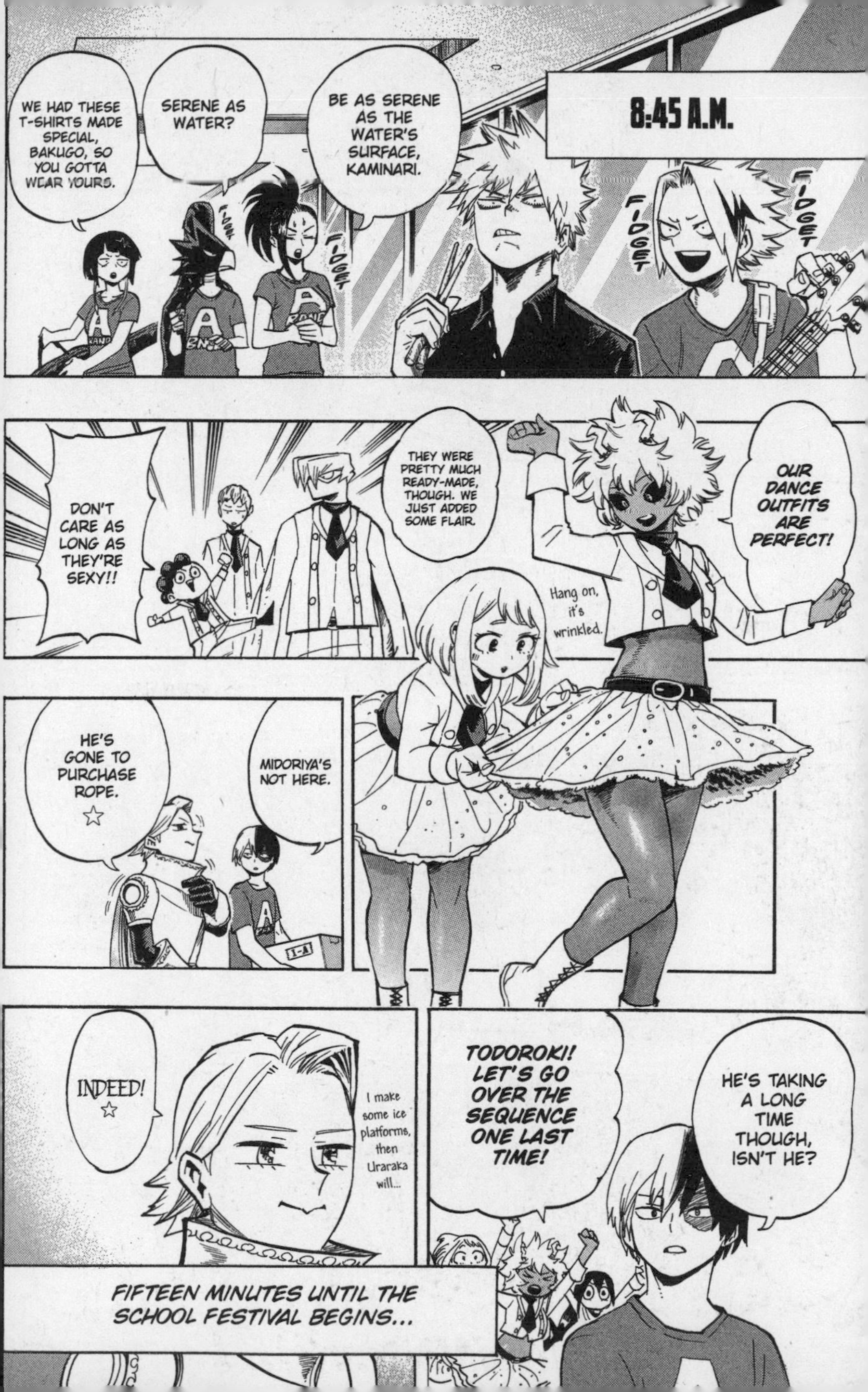
8:45 A.M.
FIDGET FIDGET
BE AS SERENE AS THE WATER'S SURFACE, KAMINARI.
SERENE AS WATER?
FIDGET
FIDGET
WE HAD THESE T-SHIRTS MADE SPECIAL, BAKUGO, SO YOU GOTTA WEAR YOURS.
OUR DANCE OUTFITS ARE PERFECT!
THEY WERE PRETTY MUCH READY-MADE, THOUGH. WE JUST ADDED SOME FLAIR.
DON'T CARE AS LONG AS THEY'RE SEXY!!
Hang on, it's wrinkled.
MIDORIYA'S NOT HERE.
HE'S GONE TO PURCHASE ROPE. ☆
1-A
HE'S TAKING A LONG TIME THOUGH, ISN'T HE?
TODOROKI! LET'S GO OVER THE SEQUENCE ONE LAST TIME!
I make some ice platforms, then Uraraka will...
INDEED! ☆
FIFTEEN MINUTES UNTIL THE SCHOOL FESTIVAL BEGINS...

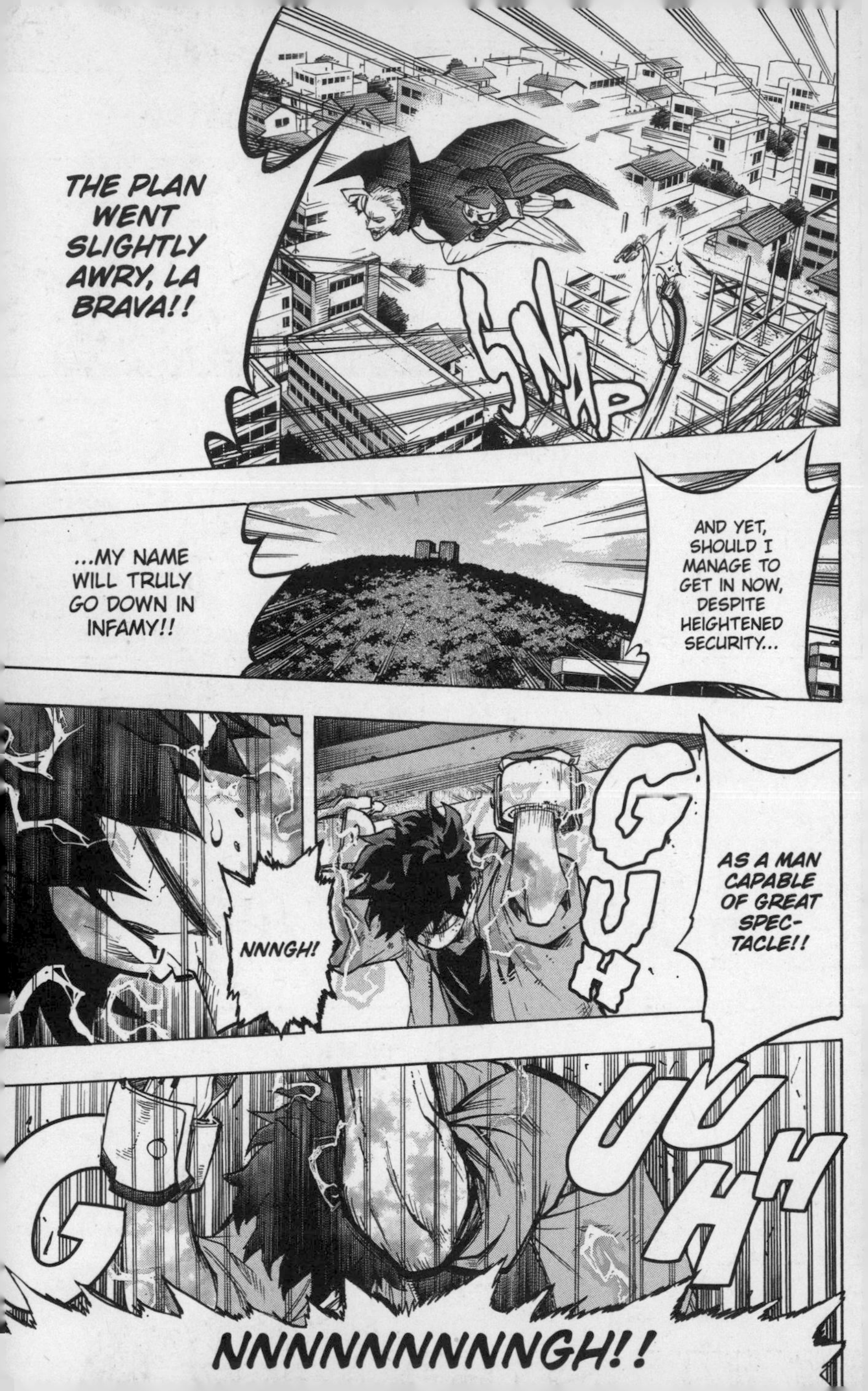
THE PLAN WENT SLIGHTLY AWRY, LA BRAVA!!
SNAP
AND YET, SHOULD I MANAGE TO GET IN NOW, DESPITE HEIGHTENED SECURITY...
...MY NAME WILL TRULY GO DOWN IN INFAMY!!
AS A MAN CAPABLE OF GREAT SPEC-TACLE!!
GUH
NNNGH!
GUUHHH
NNNNNNNNNNGH!!

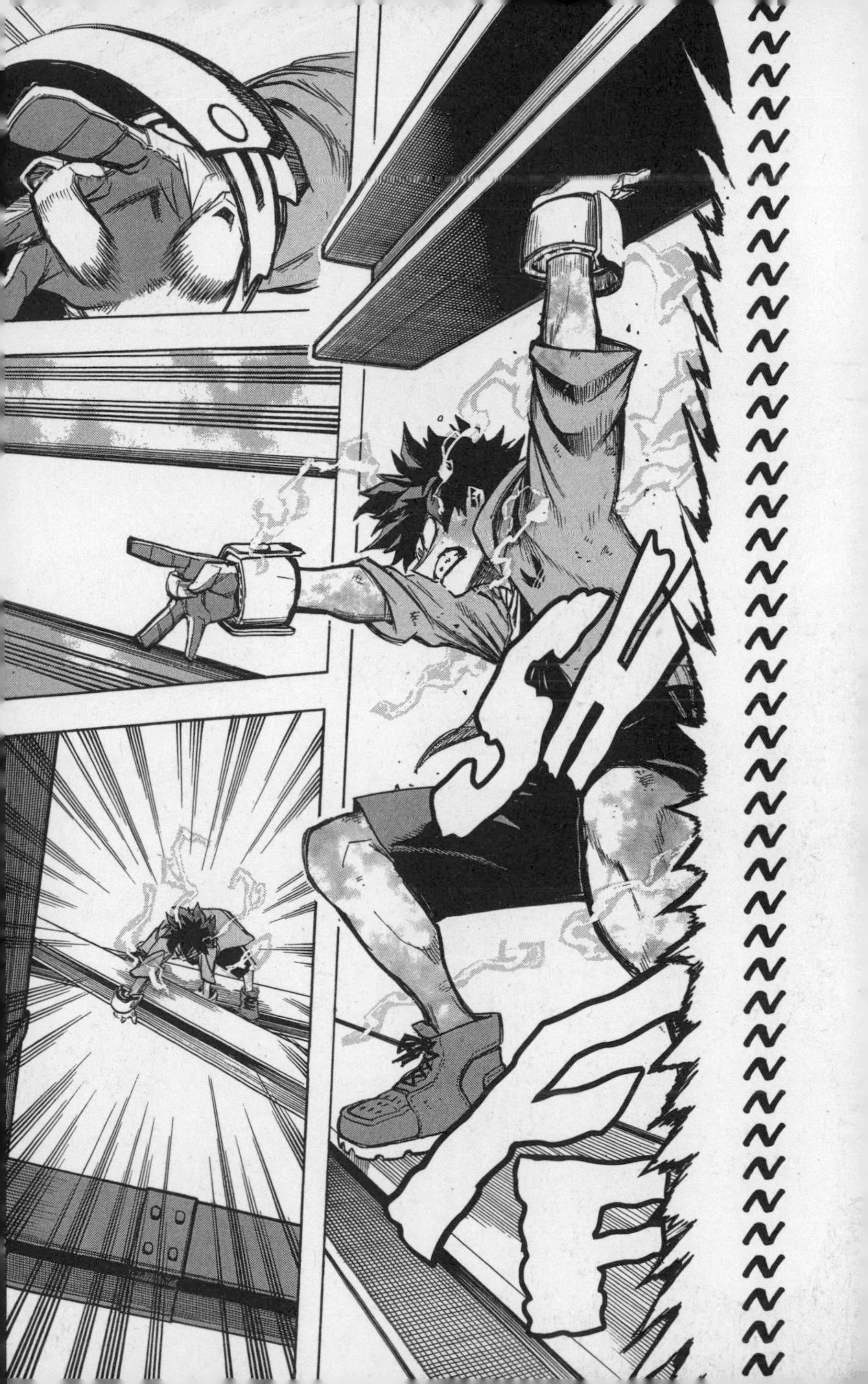

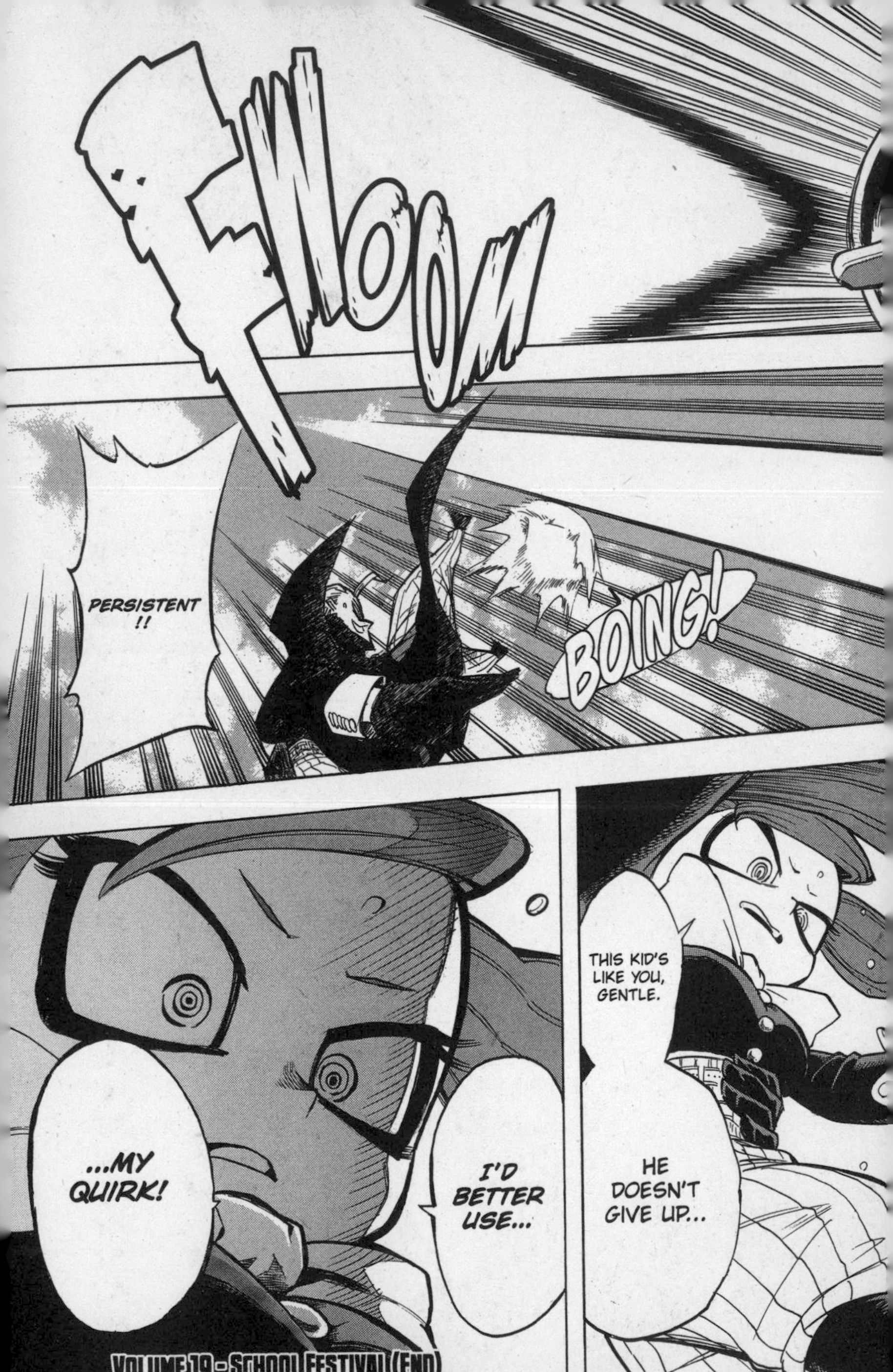
WHOOM
BOING!
PERSISTENT !!
THIS KID'S LIKE YOU, GENTLE.
HE DOESN'T GIVE UP...
I'D BETTER USE...
...MY QUIRK!

VOLUME 19 - SCHOOL FESTIVAL (END)

BIBIMI KENRANZAKI [17]

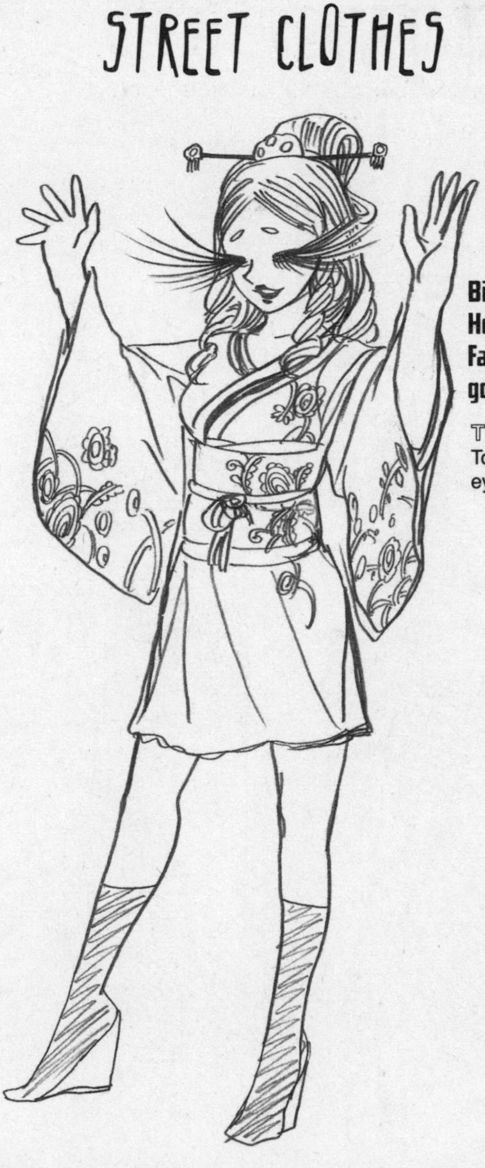
STREET CLOTHES

Birthday: 3/5
Height: 160 cm
Favorite Things: Gorgeous people, gorgeous things

THE BEAUTIFUL
Too beautiful. Drawing those eyelashes is so fun.

THE SCRAPPED COSTUMES

Why scrapped? Too cool. Not playful enough.

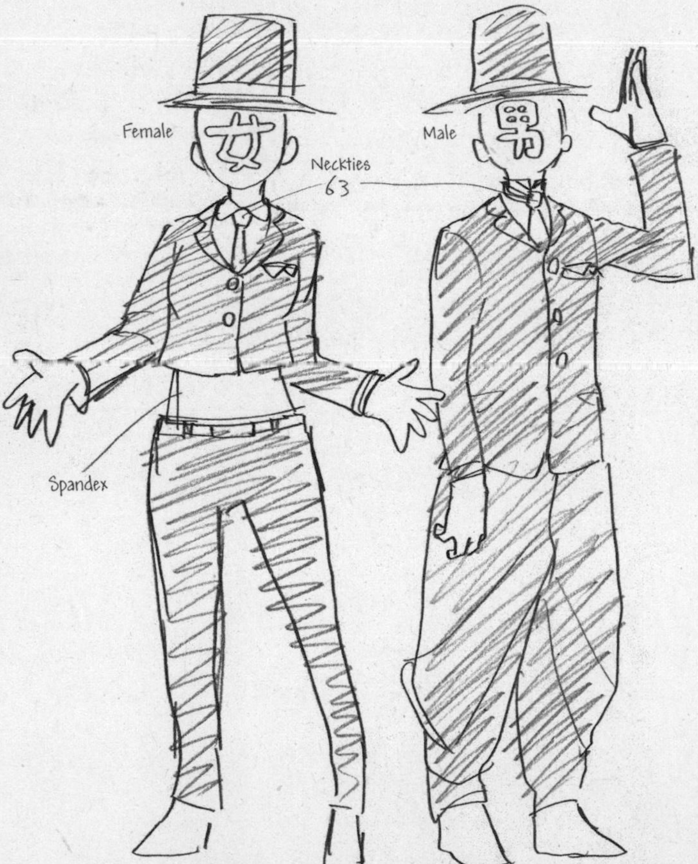

Female
女
Male
男
Neckties
63
Spandex

AFTERWORD

Feels like just yesterday we were celebrating getting into double digits with the volumes, and now we're already at volume 19. About to hit the twenties.

I originally envisioned that, assuming the serialization went swimmingly, the series would end at about this length, but it just keeps stretching out. Funny how that happens…!

It was either last year or the year before, in an interview with some foreign media outlet, that I said, "We might be seeing more from Shinso." But that still hasn't happened.

Anyhow, the story's really stretching out. Or you might say expanding? I'm working on the next volume at full throttle, so thanks for reading!!

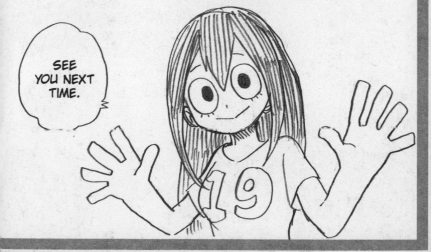

SEE YOU NEXT TIME.

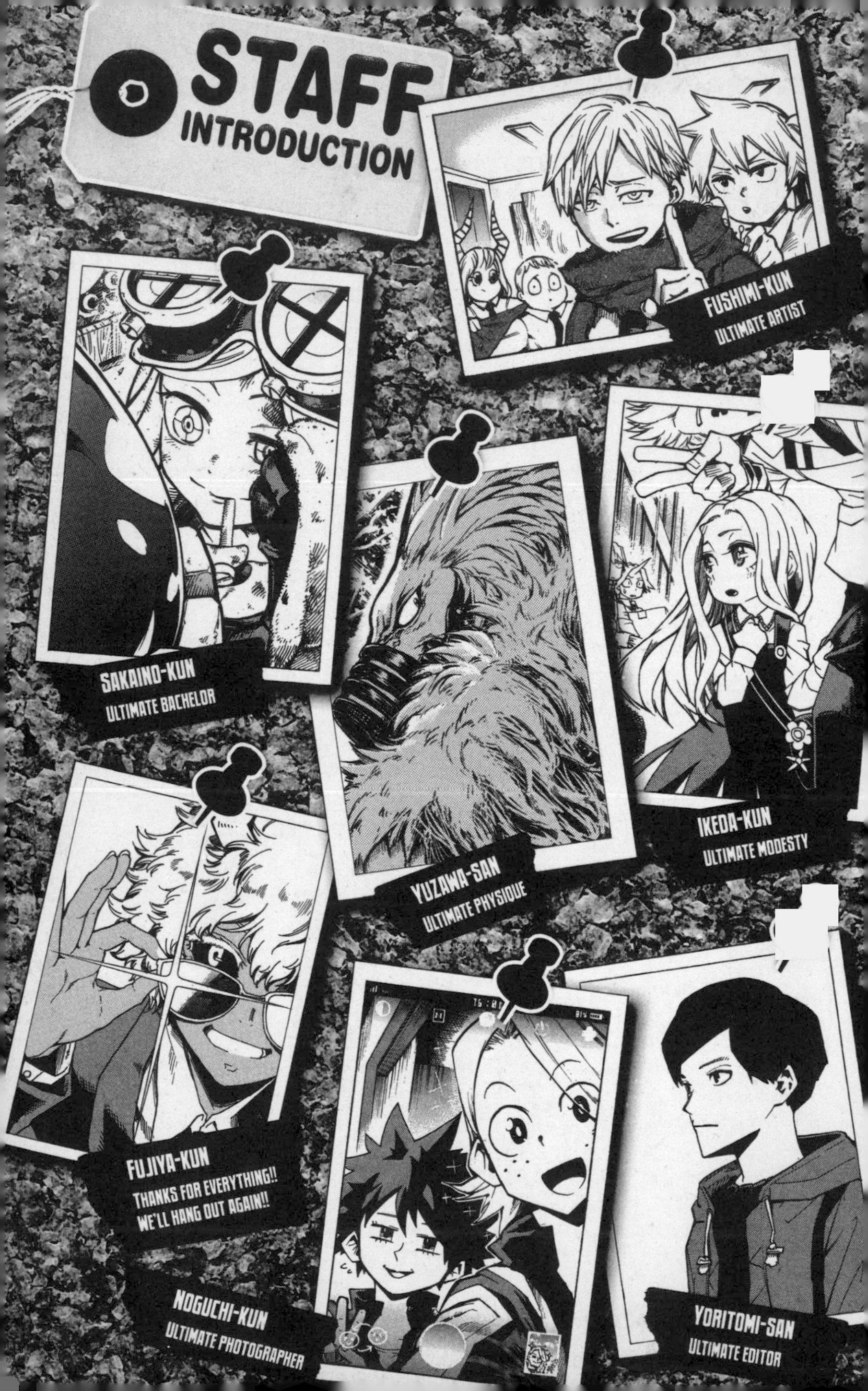
STAFF INTRODUCTION
FUSHIMI-KUN
ULTIMATE ARTIST
IKEDA-KUN
ULTIMATE MODESTY
YUZAWA-SAN
ULTIMATE PHYSIQUE
SAKAINO-KUN
ULTIMATE BACHELOR
YORITOMI-SAN
ULTIMATE EDITOR
NOGUCHI-KUN
ULTIMATE PHOTOGRAPHER
FUJIYA-KUN
THANKS FOR EVERYTHING!! WE'LL HANG OUT AGAIN!!

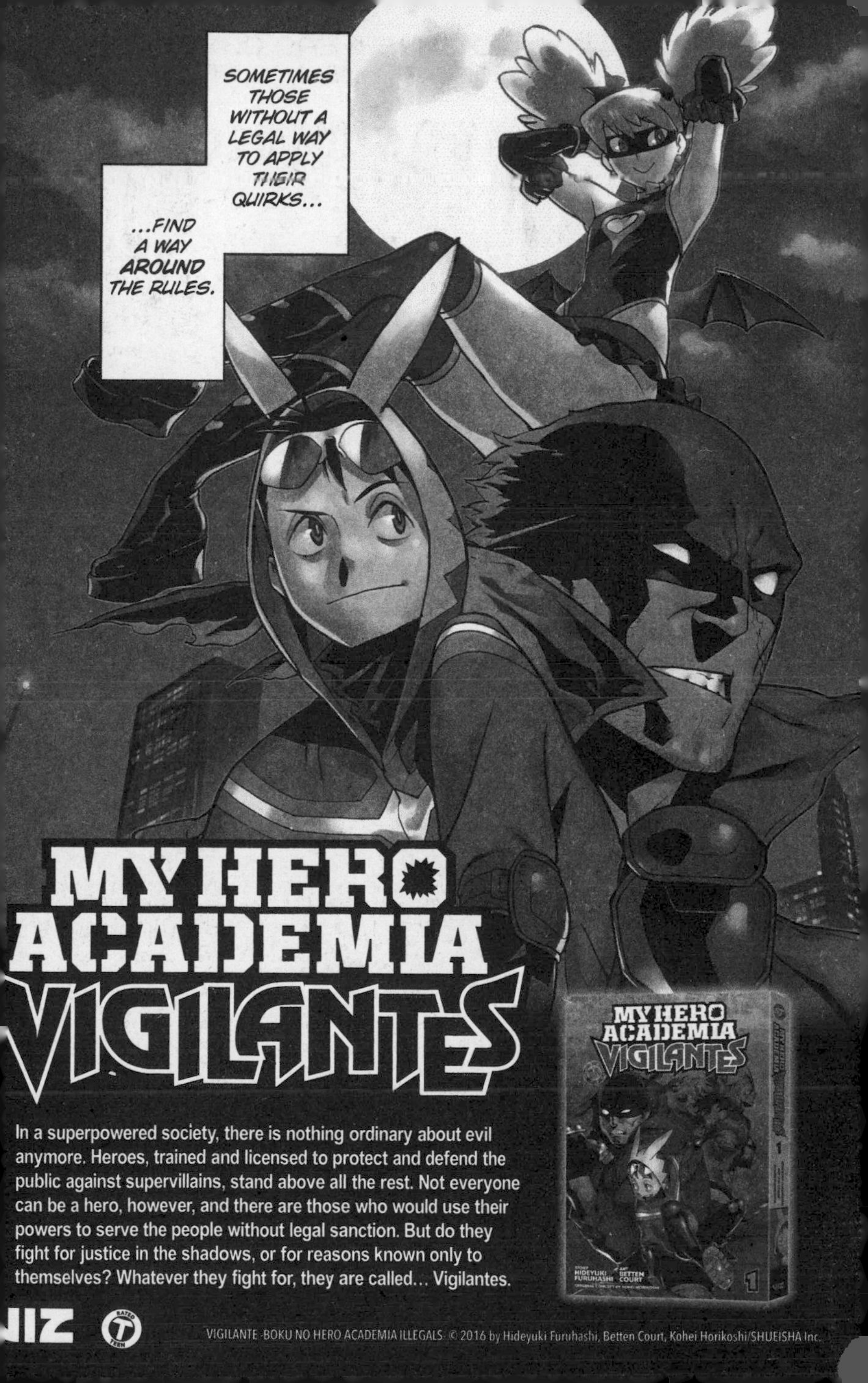
SOMETIMES THOSE WITHOUT A LEGAL WAY TO APPLY THEIR QUIRKS...
...FIND A WAY AROUND THE RULES.
MY HERO ACADEMIA VIGILANTES
MY HERO ACADEMIA VIGILANTES
HIDEYUKI FURUHASHI
BETTEN COURT
1
In a superpowered society, there is nothing ordinary about evil anymore. Heroes, trained and licensed to protect and defend the public against supervillains, stand above all the rest. Not everyone can be a hero, however, and there are those who would use their powers to serve the people without legal sanction. But do they fight for justice in the shadows, or for reasons known only to themselves? Whatever they fight for, they are called… Vigilantes.
VIZ
RATED T TEEN
VIGILANTE -BOKU NO HERO ACADEMIA ILLEGALS- © 2016 by Hideyuki Furuhashi, Betten Court, Kohei Horikoshi/SHUEISHA Inc.

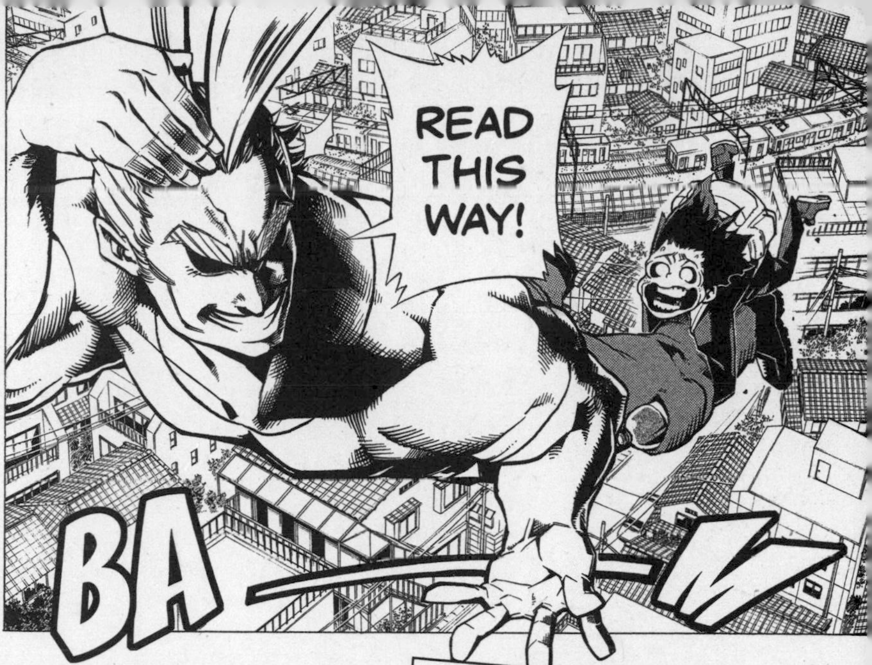
READ THIS WAY!
BAM

MY HERO ACADEMIA

reads from right to left, starting in the upper-right corner. Japanese is read from right to left, meaning that action, sound effects and word-balloon order are completely reversed from English order.

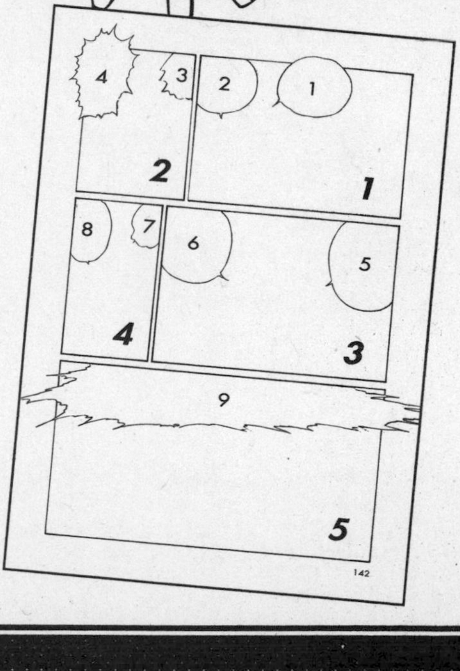
1
2
3
4
1
2
5
6
7
8
3
4
9
5
142

BRAIN-BODY SCRAMBLE QUIZ!!

FINAL BOSS
Eyyy!
STRONGEST

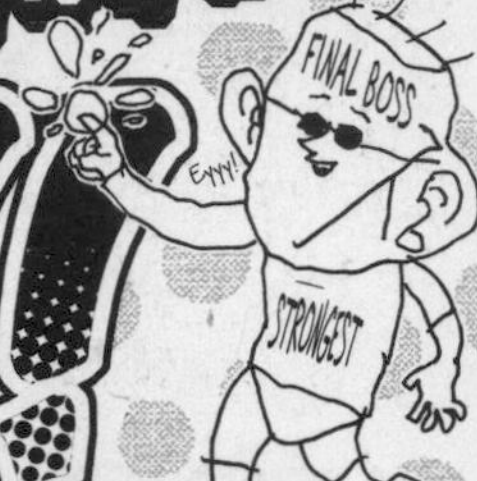

THE MEDDLER

Big trouble!! There's a new villain named the Meddler, and he's shuffled everyone's brains and bodies around!! In order to switch everyone back, you have to figure out who's who! Only you can save them!! But if this kind of thing isn't your speed, worry not—the answers are at the bottom of the page!!

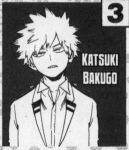

1
IZUKU MIDORIYA
2
ALL MIGHT
3
KATSUKI BAKUGO
4
OCHACO URARAKA
5
SHOTA AIZAWA
6
TENYA IDA

ANSWERS: (1) IDA, (2) KAMINARI, (3) AIZAWA, (4) BAKUGO, (5) ALL MIGHT, (6) URARAKA, (7) JIRO, (8) ASHIDO, (9) TOKOYAMI.

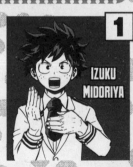

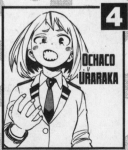

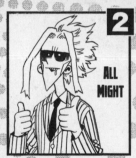

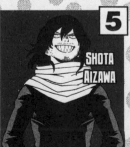

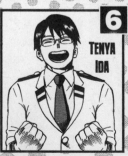

My Hero Academia vol.19

School Festival

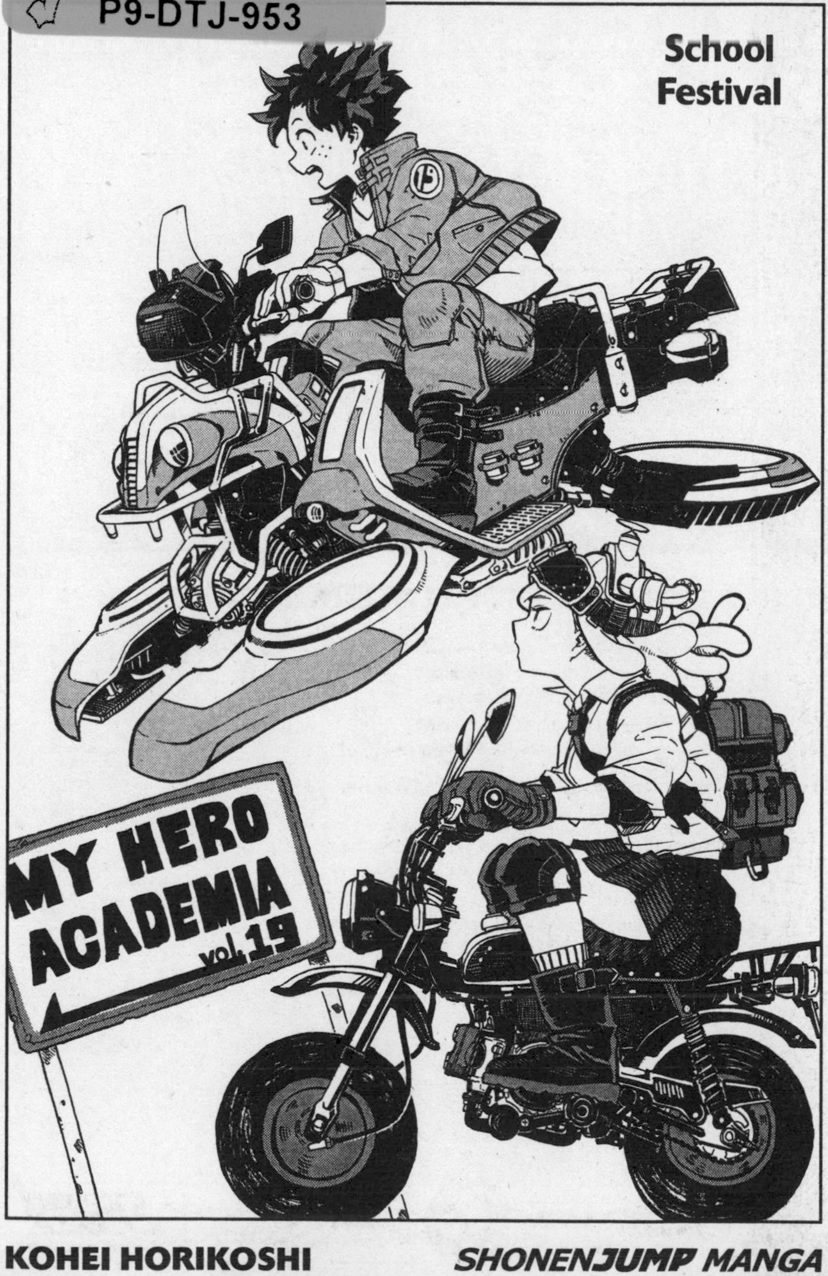
MY HERO
ACADEMIA
vol.19

KOHEI HORIKOSHI

SHONENJUMP MANGA